TO MAKE A NATION
The Rediscovery of
American Federalism

SAMUEL H. BEER

THE BELKNAP PRESS OF
HARVARD UNIVERSITY PRESS
Cambridge, Massachusetts
London, England

First Harvard University Press paperback edition, 1994

Library of Congress Cataloging-in-Publication Data

Beer, Samuel Hutchison, 1911–
To Make a Nation: The Rediscovery of American Federalism / Samuel H. Beer.
p. cm.
Includes index.
ISBN 0-674-89317-4 (cloth)
ISBN 0-674-89318-2 (pbk.)
1. Federal government—United States—History. 2. Political science—United
States—History. 3. Political science—History.
I. Title.
JK325.B38 1993
321.02'0973—dc20   92-12077
                                              CIP

To J. K. B.

Preface

I HAVE NEVER ENJOYED writing as much as while working on this book. Working is not the right word. It was more like carrying on a series of conversations with a number of brilliant colleagues. To call these eminent thinkers colleagues may seem impertinent. I use that term because I found myself questioning and cross-questioning each of them much as I would another student of politics today, seeking not simply to reconstruct his thought, but rather to see how he would react to an idea of mine. I framed the initial questions and they spoke to me through what they had written at various times in the past. I was not content with mere summaries. I pressed each reply for explanation when it was vague or ambiguous or suggestive of further meaning related to my inquiry. If, for instance, my respondent said that the people were sovereign, I wanted to know how he dealt with the implication that such a power must in some manner speak with one voice.

My inquiry started from a certain view of federalism, a rough approximation of what I have called the national theory, and it turned to the history of ideas in order to test, to clarify, to amplify, and to put into a larger theoretical context this rudimentary conception. I could not resist the true historian's temptation to become interested in the past for its own sake. The beauty of the Thomistic universe, for instance, must excite the admiration, indeed the envy, of the modern mind. Nor was I indifferent to the historian's concern with the influence of one thinker upon another. In my account the ideas which inspired the American Revolution and which informed the Constitution descend largely from the failed democratic revolution of the English seventeenth century, the Commonwealth. As with most political scientists, however, my primary interests have been contemporary and theoretical. I have used the history of ideas to state as fully and accurately as possible that element of American political culture which I have called the national theory of federalism. Hence, the book begins with the confrontation of the "new federalism" of Ronald Reagan with the "new federalism" of Lyndon Johnson.

In the quest for a usable past, I believe I have been faithful to that past as it actually was. No one, however, will mistake this book for "value-free political science." My commitment to the national idea is passionate and personal and goes back to my earliest years. I can still hear my parents tell the story of how, as we crossed the state border on our return from a trip to New England by motor car in 1915, I proclaimed loudly from the back seat, "Thank God for Ohio!" In those years my pride in my home state was focused on the belief, fostered by family and friends, that Ohio had mustered more troops in defense of the Union than any other state. I am not surprised to find that my conception of the role of the states in the nation as set forth in this book is congruent with those sentiments.

In short, I did not escape the immense formative influence of the Civil War upon the American political mind. That influence took a very specific shape in the persons of my grandfathers. Since my paternal grandmother, having been widowed, married again, there were three, all of whom had served in the Northern armies. In my memory a certain military aura surrounded her second husband, who continued to be addressed as "Colonel" long after his service. The connection had operational effects: my maternal grandfather, for instance, would not permit my father to court his daughter until he had been assured that my father's father had done his military service, and on the right side. In my Ohio hometown what that generation had done to preserve the Union was richly commemorated on Memorial Day and the Fourth of July. The authority of their achievement was greater still because it was not explained, let alone denied or disputed. The reader will, therefore, understand my amazement when I learned, while finishing high school in Virginia at Staunton Military Academy, that, in the opinion of teachers whom I greatly respected as men and citizens, there was another view of the War between the States. My confusion was given an opportunity for expression by an essay contest on "Patriotism" sponsored by the Colonial Dames of Virginia. In response I attempted what I took to be a comparative study of the internecine wars of the ancient Greek republics with the unification of England under its medieval parliament. I had been reading John Richard Green's *History of the English People* and was sufficiently taken in by its Radical slant to suppose that I was examining the fate of popular government under two different constitutions. The essay, while not explicitly about federalism, was emphatic in its evaluation of Union and the sentiments necessary for its survival.

In themselves these events cannot be of much interest to anyone but myself. Their recall reveals for me the ultimate source of the pleasure I have taken in writing this book and the seriousness with which I have applied myself to it. The reader also deserves a glimpse of this motivation. In that perspective, the book is an act of piety. I want to state as honestly, clearly, and amply as I can the case for what my grandfathers did in the War. And by so stating it to honor them.

So much for the influence of that highly personalized past on this book. When many years later I took up political science as a professional study, my interests were in political theory and comparative government, especially the government and politics of Great Britain. Any interest in federalism was slight, only to be aroused unexpectedly in the early 1960s. Two events combined to bring this about. One was an encounter with a student in a course on American government that I was teaching in a summer school program at Harvard. This program brought together from other countries a number of young men of post-college age who were already making careers in politics, journalism, and other professions. As a survey, my course was obliged to give some attention to federalism, which, frankly, I treated as a boring and unimportant topic. A vigorous and intelligent member of the class from Yugoslavia took quite the opposite view. He was dismayed by what Americans made of federalism in contrast with its role in his own country. Summarizing his objections, he said in effect, "In federal America you try to make everyone alike. By contrast in Yugoslavia our federal scheme heightens the diversity of its separate peoples, encouraging the cultivation of their different languages, religions, and cultures."

At about the same time, the Republican candidate for President, Barry Goldwater, was attacking the centralization of government under the Great Society, one of his main arguments being the old Southern heresy that the Union was nothing more than a compact among the separate states. Goldwater, who incidentally had been a classmate of mine at Staunton, was the first Republican candidate for President to call himself explicitly a "conservative." While I had admired and liked him as a fellow cadet, his ideological position fired up the liberalism I had acquired when working in Washington in the early days of the New Deal.

This double stimulus, scholarly and partisan, caused me to take federalism seriously, asking what was the American doctrine and whether it had any relevance to contemporary problems. For some time I wrote mainly about present-day intergovernmental relations, but the historical questions that kept coming up finally led to this book. To prompt my thinking I had turned to Herbert Croly's *Promise of American Life,* first published in 1909, which in my opinion is the best single work on American political thought and which, moreover, is the one book with the greatest influence on this present volume. For Croly, the two governing ideas of American politics have been "the principle of nationality" and "the principle of democracy," given expression at the time of the founding by Alexander Hamilton and Thomas Jefferson, respectively. From that time, according to Croly, the two wings of the American party system have usually been distinguished by their emphasis on one or the other of these principles. At our best, the two were combined, supremely by Abraham Lincoln, as Croly hoped they would again be by Theodore Roosevelt. This did not mean merely, as some have thought, that the Hamiltonian means of a strong federal government would be used to promote the Jeffersonian ends of self-government and equal rights. Croly's emphasis was on the Hamiltonian purpose of nation-building as a goal different from, but complementary to, Jeffersonian democracy. Following this line of thought, he conceived the Constitution as made not only by but also for the democratic nation. Its authority came not from a compact among the states but from being ordained by the sovereign people. Its purpose accordingly was to promote their excellence both as individuals and as a nation.

I recall the difficulty I had convincing a colleague who, although agreeing with my general line of argument, doubted that one can identify a distinct Hamiltonian end. Yet surely our experience in recent years shows that simply to protect and to extend "rights" is not enough. For one thing, the political consequence is to fragment and divide the electorate among the various claimant groups. The public interest also requires that these guarantees be directed toward bringing their beneficiaries into the common life of the nation. A policy of integration aims not only at the equalization of rights but also at the civic inclusion of persons.

Croly's insights have been pretty well confirmed by my reading of how the leading minds among the framers conceived the Constitution in general and its federal arrangements in particular. I do not anticipate universal agreement with what I say. Some students of these subjects will surely take issue with my conclusion that you can find a single coherent viewpoint which makes sense of the federal arrangements of the Constitution. The best comparable work on this question is a series of brilliant essays by the late Martin Diamond. He and I agree on much, but are seriously divided by his conclusion that the federalism of the framers, far from having a coherent rationale, combined two incompatible forms, one state-centered, the other nation-centered. In his opinion, this was not just a compromise but rather the choice of a people who could not decide whether they were one community or many. *A fortiori,* I differ not only with Diamond on federalism but also with the common opinion that the Constitution as a whole was the outcome of compromises so great as to prevent it from having any overall rationale.

Those are not unreasonable views. For a time, while trying to square my Crolyesque presumptions with the record, I shared them. But as I dug into the background of the thinking of the advocates of the Constitution during its framing and ratification, I was more and more struck by the powerful logic of their federal design and the extent to which, despite much compromise, they were able to embody it in our fundamental law. The state-centered view expressed in the compact theory put forward by the opponents of the Constitution survived their defeat. The national theory, however, went on to exercise the dominating influence on intergovernmental relations. We can therefore recapture its meaning for today from its formulation in that distant yesterday.

Scholarly specialists will be interested in the question of the coherence or incoherence of the original principles of the Constitution and its federal system. But this book should attract a wider audience because of its participation in that old and serious controversy in American politics and American scholarship between the national and the compact approaches. In the Introduction I have sketched the history of that controversy, which has divided public opinion from the anti-Federalist attack on the Constitution to the Reaganite championship of states' rights and which today threatens to resurface in the acrimonious debate over multiculturalism. On the scholarly plane, federalism, which as a matter of law centers on the division of authority between the federal and the state governments, may seem to be a humdrum question of public administration. The conflicting premises from which the different views are derived and their implications for institutions and policies, however, embody sharply different views of liberty, democracy, community, the economy, and political development.

This connection with the great issues of politics is illustrated by the big switch in the attitudes of the political parties toward federalism, marked especially by the opposing positions they adopted during the New Deal. The conservatives, who under the names of Federalist, Whig, and Republican, had been partisans of the national position, took up the cause of the old Democrats, who from the days of Jefferson had espoused states' rights. Similarly, the opposition to the national view today will be found among the neoconservatives. I trust I am not merely displaying my political bias if I express my irritation at these Republican partisans when I see them not only exhibiting their usual elitism but also deserting the most admirable of their traditions. It is too much to burden the Democrats with the task of standing for both the democratic and the national ideals, although to be sure Franklin Roosevelt did it.

In their antinational stance, the neoconservatives have much in common with the militant multiculturalists, from whom in most other respects they greatly differ. The former are strongly against, the latter strongly for, action by the federal government. And needless to say, on questions of redistribution of wealth and power the two sides are sharply opposed. Yet neither has much sympathy for, or grasp of, that prime object of the republic which George Washington termed "the consolidation of the union." For the nationalists that meant that government generally, and the federal government especially, had the obligation to use their best powers to make the nation freer, wealthier, more powerful, and more virtuous; in short, to make it more of a nation.

For neoconservatives like Ronald Reagan, on the other hand, whether or not there is a national community, the responsibility for perfecting any such union does not reside with government. In his memorable phrase, "Government is not the solution to our problem; government is the problem," he therefore sought to shed the responsibilities of the federal government, not because he thought that the states would assume them but because he felt sure the states would not. The premise of this antigovernmental imperative is individualism. It is, however, a brand of individualism which, as F. H. Bradley said of certain nineteenth-century philosophers, conceived each member of society as being as morally self-contained and self-sufficient as if he were enclosed in "an impervious globe."

For the nationalists, diversity among the people is to be welcomed and promoted. In the most obvious example, the diversity consisting in the division of labor increases the productivity of the economy as a whole. Similarly, in the political process the mutual enlightenment resulting from the confrontation of different ideas and interests fosters decisions closer to the needs of the people and to the circumstances in which they live. The same holds for moral and social relations. A diversity of ethnic identities, for instance, can be a source of cultural enrichment. All such happy instances of *e pluribus unum*, however, depend in no small measure upon the context of law and policy maintained by government. Multiculturalism, therefore, as the recognition of this potential of ethnic diversity is basic to the national outlook.

The advocacy of cultural diversity, however, can take a contrary turn. The ethnic group may be so committed to its identity that it rejects anything more than a narrow and external relation to the rest of society. Economic relations instrumental to the material well-being of the group will be accepted, as well as provisions for the physical security afforded by a legal system and a force for external defense. But social relationships that affect the moral and cultural outlook of members of the group are excluded. The ideal is not the melting pot in which group identities are complementary to one another in a larger national identity but the mosaic society in which the rationale is not integration but self-imposed segregation. As vigorously as the neoconservative, the militant multiculturalist rejects government that is national in scope or purpose. Although armed with radically opposed political values, the two camps assail national federalism from left and right.

The controversy, scholarly and partisan, which this book joins goes back to the founding of the republic. My historical treatment has a much further reach. The start from Aquinas may seem odd. But I found myself driven to go back that far if I was going to get a firm grasp on the premises and implications of national federalism. Federalism in this form was shaped by the Western world's rejection of and escape from the Middle Ages. The conclusion of Chapter 1 develops the connection. It is indirect but important. Considering the ideal and material strength of the ancient hierarchic and corporatist philosophy, it is something of a miracle that we ever escaped. At any rate, to put the matter briefly, this prolonged and hard-fought revolution, springing from a new and radical individualism, was directed by the republican thrust for government by the many against government by the few and, inseparably, by the assertion of the nation as the unit of authority and the focus of purpose.* Government by the few can do with few rules. Government by the many requires a

---

*A word on the use of certain terms. Usually I have referred to the doctrine of government by the many as "republican" rather than "democratic." In the 1780s the two terms were often treated as synonymous, although there was some preference, as in Madison's usage, for "republican," in order to distinguish representative from direct democracy. Today the term democracy has come to be associated with standards of participation and rights so much wider than those prevailing then that it makes for clarity to use the less demanding term republican. Nor do I mean to give that term the special meaning which identifies the republican cause of those days with the idea of "civic humanism." In recent years this concept has been used to distinguish "republicanism" from "liberalism," the latter term being taken to mean conduct governed by self-interest, while the former, presumably echoing classical thought, refers to a higher standard which leads the citizenry to reject self-interest in favor of the common interest. The framers of the Constitution did value altruism, but they took a more relaxed and realistic view of the motivation necessary for the success of popular government.

system of institutions, preferably made explicit in a written constitution, which will protect it against self-destructive chaos and which will elicit its intrinsic excellence. Along with such institutions as representation, separation of powers, and bicameralism, national federalism took its place in the advance toward orderly and effective self-government.

When it comes to identifying the source of this break from the Western tradition of many centuries, I find it not in the Renaissance but in the Reformation. That was the Americans' view of the origin of their political ideas and attitudes from John Adams's *Dissertation on the Canon and Feudal Law* (1765) to George Bancroft's *History of the United States* (1882–1886). I make Milton the foremost spokesman of the central process of popular government, "rational deliberation" as philosophers call it today, or "government by discussion" to use Walter Bagehot's term. If I were to claim any originality in matters of historical scholarship, I would cite my depiction of James Harrington as the advocate of not only the constitutional republic but also national federalism. Many historians of the idea of federalism see it as emerging only in the compact model. From that historical perspective national federalism must appear as an invention of the Americans. Recognizing its earlier formulation by Harrington does not detract from the ingenuity and vision of our founders. It does, however, strengthen our perception of the relation of federalism and democracy. Along with other elements of constitutionalism, federal arrangements are often regarded as essentially a means of checking the democratic process and setting limits on the sphere of government action. In Harrington's writing we see national federalism in its earliest incarnation as part of a scheme of "rational deliberation" designed not to restrain popular government but to elicit its superior capacities. In the later American view, on which Harrington had a good deal of influence, constitutionalism also appears not as a barrier to but an instrument of self-government.

I cannot put my account of this earlier history and theory in context without paying tribute to another influence, hardly less in the long run than that of Croly. I am thinking of Alexander Dunlop Lindsay, my tutor in political theory at Balliol College, at that time also the master of the college. Lindsay was the last of the Oxford idealists, more a Kantian than a Hegelian and more a Calvinist than a Kantian. What I learned from him came from what he said rather than from what he wrote, although his little gem of a book, *The Modern Democratic State,* has served to prompt my recollections in later years. It was from him that I first learned to think seriously about "government by discussion" as a method of democratic decision making. I had some notion of other models, such as majority rule in class politics and the brokering of interests in distributive politics. Lindsay sought to show how the mutual enlightenment of different points of view could lead toward conclusions worthy of general assent. In the American manner, he traced this model of the democratic process back to the liberal wing of the Reformation, specifically in England the congregational practice of the Puritan sects.

A second contribution was his notion of the purpose of the state as being "to make the community more of a community." In this conception, which he owed more to his idealism than to his Calvinism, he was arguing in the idealist manner that the relations of individuals can be not only, as in economic exchange, instrumental but also, as in an integrated society, constitutive of the minds and characters of its members. What Lindsay's teaching led me to read in idealist sociology and philosophy gave me a larger framework into which I could fit the institutional and historical analysis to which Croly had directed me. I have adapted one of Lindsay's more important terms when I refer to the Hamiltonian purpose as being "to make the nation more of a nation." By that I do not intend to attribute the idealist meaning to the American founder. Later on American thought did move in this direction in the writing of our great Romantics, Emerson, Thoreau, and Whitman. Without diminishing his radical individualism, Thoreau succinctly expressed the idea of social communion when, referring to a conversation with his neighbor, Hosmer, he concluded: "And then we parted, each of us taking something of the other with him." To elaborate that topic would take me well beyond the limits of this book. Such a mode of thought, however, is strongly suggested by James Wilson's discussion of "social union," with which I conclude the third and last part.

Samuel H. Beer
Greensboro, Vermont
July 28, 1992

Acknowledgments

IN THE WRITING of this book I have had a good deal of help from others. Not the least has come from the clash of opinion with positions radically different from my own. For the most part, I have found these helpful contrasts in the published work of other scholars, living and dead. Where the elaboration of such disagreements entails reference to specific works, I have tried to confine my discussion to the Notes. All such antagonists, whether or not specifically mentioned, I hereby thank.

The Notes and References also include contributions from sources in general agreement with my argument. The References are not a bibliography of all works I have consulted but only a list of the citations which have been given in shorter and less cumbersome form in the Notes. Indeed, I have been so parsimonious as to omit most of my own previous writings on federalism.

In a more personal way I am indebted to a number of scholars and friends who have put their learning and good sense at my service by criticizing what I have said in many earnest conversations and what I have written in hardly fewer letters and drafts. For such help I wish to thank Timothy Conlan, Stephen Conrad, Martha Derthick, Ernest Fortin, Robert Faulkner, Peter Hall, Hugh Heclo, Harvey Mansfield, Jr., Richard Nathan, Melvin Richter, and Michael Walzer. I owe a special debt of gratitude to Shannon Stimson and Stephen Holmes, who helped bring this book to completion, thanks to their superb professional criticism and their unfailing friendship and encouragement.

Among those who helped with research, I especially appreciate the work of Alan Houston, Russell Muirhead, and Mark Henrie. I am also grateful for the financial assistance I have received from the Center for American Political Studies at Harvard and from Project 87, sponsored by the American Historical Association and the American Political Science Association.

Contents

Introduction: The National Idea in American Politics   1
The Promise of Nationhood   4
The Trial of Sectionalism   8
The Impact of Industrialism   15
The Challenge of Racism   18
Federalism and Political Theory   20

PART ONE
From Hierarchy to Republicanism   27

1. The Rule of the Wise and the Holy: Thomas Aquinas   31
The Ontology of Inequality   32
Value, Utility, and Authority   35
Hierarchies of Virtue and Grace   39
Federalism from the Top Down   45
The Enchanted World   50
Deference to the Divine Likeness   53
Old Tory Politics   56

2. The Idea of the National Republic: John Milton   66
The Masterless Man   68
Government by Discussion   74
Elite and People   77
Nation and Purpose   81

3. A Constitution for the National Republic: James Harrington 84
    The Dilemma of Scale: Machiavelli 86
    Constitutionalism and the Public Interest 92
    Representation from the Bottom Up 101
    The Machinery of Rational Deliberation 108
    Federalism for Utility or for Liberty? 119
    A Commonwealth for Increase 128

                            PART TWO
            The National and Republican Revolution   133

4. The Conflict of Ideas   139
    Edmund Burke and the Old Whig Constitution 140
    Blackstone and Sovereignty 146
    Benjamin Franklin and National Purpose 153

5. The Decade of Agitation   163
    Actual vs. Virtual Representation 164
    The Parliamentary Option 168
    The Federal Option 177
    Imperial Federalism 185
    Liberty vs. Union 190

6. The Discovery of the Nation   195
    How the Congress Was Chosen 196
    How the Congress Governed 199
    How the States Were Created 200
    Tom Paine's National and Federal Republic 206

                           PART THREE
            The National and Republican Constitution   215

7. Montesquieu's Confederate Republic   219
    The Structure 220
    The Mechanics 224
    The Confederate Republic in America 231
    The Anti-Federalist Case 237

8. Madison's Compound Republic   244
    Critique of Compact Federalism 245
    The New Legitimacy 249
    Critique of the Small Republic Theory 255
    Justice and the Public Interest 261
    Government by Discussion: Hume 264
    Government by Discussion: Madison 270
    Toward Power and Justice 275

9. Auxiliary Precautions   279
    Representation 280
    Separation of Powers 283
    Why Have States? 289
    The People as Common Superior 295
    The Control of Faction 301

10. Sovereignty and Ratification   308
    How the Constitution Was Ordained 309
    Madison's Gap 313
    The National Solution 317
    Joseph Story's Classic Exposition 325
    Critique of Article VII 330
    Sovereignty, the Constitution, and Democracy 336

11. James Wilson's Social Union   341
    Purpose, Medieval and Modern 343
    The Four Great Objects 349
    The Fragility of Reason 357
    Participation and Public Affection 360
    The Social Passion 365
    Public Affection and Federalism 372

Conclusion: Liberty and Union   379
    Strong Democracy 380
    Constitutionalism for Self-Government 383
    Federalism and Liberty 386
    Radicalism and Prudence 389

Notes   395
References   443
Index   459

Introduction:
The National Idea
in American Politics

THE NATIONAL IDEA is a way of looking at American government and American society. It embraces a view of where the authority of government comes from and a view of what it should be used for. As a concept of authority, it identifies the whole people of the nation as the source of the legitimate powers of any and all governments. As a concept of purpose, it tells us that we are one people and guides us toward what we should make of ourselves as a people. The national idea envisions one people, at once sovereign and subject, source of authority and substance of history, affirming, through conflict and in diversity, our unity of being and becoming.

Because the national idea is also a democratic idea, these concepts of authority and purpose are interdependent. Self-government is reflexive. The people who govern are also the object of government. A government of the people, therefore, gets its legitimacy both from being a government by the people and from being a government for the people. Its citizens judge it by both standards, attaching value to the manner in which their government is carried on and to the policies which it pursues.

This theory of legitimacy is national and democratic. It is also federal. In the national perspective, although we are one people who enjoy a common life as one nation, we have set up not a unitary but a dual system of government. In establishing this system, the American people authorized and empowered two sets of governments: a general government for the whole, and state governments for the parts. The constitutional authority for the two sets of government is therefore coordinate. Neither created the other, and both are subject

1

to the same ultimate legitimating power, the sovereign people. And periodically the people in this constituent capacity amend these institutions, by which in their governing capacity they direct the day-to-day affairs of the nation.

From our revolutionary beginnings the national idea has been widely accepted as a description of historical fact and a theory of legitimacy of American federalism. The American political tradition, however, has also sustained another view. In this opposing view, one of these levels of government, the federal government, was brought into existence not by the act of a sovereign people but by a compact among sovereign states. From this compact theory inferences follow that radically contradict the conclusions of the national theory. While the national theory has, on balance, had much the greater influence on thought and action, the compact theory has survived and continues even today to show itself in the feelings of citizens, the rhetoric of politicians, and the actions of governments.

When President Reagan took office in 1981, for instance, he proclaimed a "new federalism." Its central thrust was to cut back on the activities of the federal government by reducing or eliminating a vast number of programs, the principal cuts falling on federal aid to state and local governments. The President wished to do this because he judged these activities to be inefficient, unnecessary, and sometimes positively harmful. He also claimed that they were improper under the Constitution—not so much in the strict sense that they violated specific provisions of our fundamental law as in the larger philosophical and historical sense that they offended against the true meaning of the document.

In his first inaugural address on January 20, 1981, accordingly, President Reagan promised to "restore the balance between levels of government." And while he did not elaborate his political philosophy, he made clear in a phrase or two his reliance upon the compact theory of the Constitution to justify his new federalism. "The Federal government," he declared at one point in his address, "did not create the states; the states created the Federal government."

This allegation did not pass without comment. In response to President Reagan's use of the compact theory, eminent academic critics counterattacked in terms of the national theory. Richard P.

Morris of Columbia University called the President's view of the historical facts "a hoary myth about the origins of the Union" and went on to summarize the evidence showing that "the United States was created by the people in collectivity, not by the individual states." No less bluntly, Henry Steele Commager of Amherst College said President Reagan did not understand the Constitution, which in its own words asserts that it was ordained by "We, the People of the United States," not by the states severally. An ardent liberal, he went on to argue that this view of the origin of the Constitution abundantly justified and even mandated the new purposes served by federal power in recent times.[1]

The argument between the President and the professors was not simply about history. Nor was it mainly about the constitutional authority of the federal and the state governments. Their primary disagreement was over public policy, specifically, the use of federal authority in recent years to expand the social and economic programs of the welfare state, especially those dating from the "new federalism" of Lyndon Johnson. President Reagan had taken office as the champion of conservative attitudes that had been gathering force around the country for a generation. He articulated these attitudes in a distinctive vision of American society at home and abroad and in a set of strategies for realizing that vision. Expressing in a new public philosophy the old and familiar values of rugged individualism, he sought to cut back the welfare state and to restore the free market—or in the language of political economy, to shift social choice from public choice toward market choice. Declaring in his first inaugural address that the excessive growth of the public sector in recent years meant that "government is not the solution to our problem; government is the problem," he proposed to "reverse" that growth. Intrinsic to this goal was his promise of another "new federalism" which would "restore the balance between levels of government." The reduction of federal grant programs would at once help restore the federal–state balance and promote the free market.

Some critics called him insincere, claiming that when he said he wanted to restore the federal–state balance, what he really wanted to do was to cut federal spending on social and economic programs.

No doubt he was mainly interested in the impact of his policies on American society. But that is no reason for saying that he was not also interested in reducing what he thought was excessive centralization of power in the federal system. In American politics, thinking about federalism has usually had those two aspects: a concern with both the pattern of authority and the pattern of purpose, with the balance of power between levels of government and with the policies for which that power is used. When President Reagan called in the compact theory to lend support to his views on public policy, he was doing what its adherents before him had often done. In their way the nationalists had done the same, right from the days when Alexander Hamilton, as Secretary of the Treasury, set the course of the first administration of George Washington.

The Promise of Nationhood

Like the other founders, Hamilton sought to establish a regime of republican liberty, that is, a system of government which would protect the individual rights of person and property and which would be founded upon the consent of the governed. He was by no means satisfied with the legal framework produced by the Philadelphia Convention. Fearing the states, he would have preferred a much stronger central authority, and, distrusting the common people, he would have set a greater distance between them and the exercise of power. He was less concerned, however, with the legal framework than with the use that would be made of it.[2] He saw in the Constitution not only a regime of liberty, but also and especially the promise of nationhood.

He understood, moreover, that this promise of nationhood would have to be fulfilled if the regime of liberty itself was to endure. The scale of the country almost daunted him. At the Philadelphia Convention, as its chief diarist reported, Hamilton "confessed he was much discouraged by the amazing extent of Country in expecting the desired blessings from any general sovereignty that could be substituted."[3] This fear echoed a common opinion of the time. The great Montesquieu had warned that popular government was not suitable for a large and diverse country. If attempted, he predicted, its counsels would be distracted by "a thousand private views" and its extent would provide cover for ambitious men seeking despotic power.[4]

One reply to Montesquieu turned this argument on its head by declaring that such pluralism would be a source of stability. In his famous *Federalist* 10 James Madison argued that the more extensive republic, precisely because of its diversity, would protect popular government by making oppressive combinations less likely. As elaborated by Madison, Hamilton, and other champions of the new regime, their hopes for a more extensive republic rested on more than its promise of a mechanical balance of groups. Hamilton summarized these views in the farewell address that he drafted for Washington in 1796. Its theme was the importance of union if the regime of liberty was to survive. This union would not consist merely in a balance of groups or a consensus of values, and certainly not merely in a strong central government or a common framework of constitutional law. It would be rather a condition of the American people, uniting them by sympathy as well as interest in what Washington termed "an indissoluble community of interest as *one nation.*"[5]

Hamilton's nationalism was expressed not only in his belief that Americans were "one people" rather than thirteen separate peoples but even more emphatically in his commitment to governmental activism. This concern that the American people must make vigorous use of their central government for the tasks of nation-building separated him sharply from Thomas Jefferson, Washington's Secretary of State, who leaned toward the compact theory. The classic expression of this difference of opinion between the two members of the cabinet—the champion of federal power and the champion of states' rights—was their conflict over the proposed Bank of the United States. Jefferson feared that the bank would corrupt his cherished agrarian order and discovered no authority for it in the Constitution. Hamilton, believing that a central bank was necessary to sustain public credit, to promote economic development, and—in his graphic phrase—"to cement more closely the union of the states," found in a broad construction of the "necessary and proper" clause ample constitutional authorization.[6]

Should the words "necessary and proper" be construed narrowly, as Jefferson said, or broadly, as Hamilton advised? A generation later the question came before the Supreme Court in *McCulloch v. Maryland* (1819).[7] Speaking for the Jeffersonian reply, appellants advanced the theory that the Constitution was a compact of sovereign states and therefore should be strictly construed, in order to safeguard state power against the federal government. In the Court's decision, however, John Marshall argued from the national theory that the Constitution was "ordained and established" directly by the people of the United States and concluded in almost the same words used by Hamilton that the crucial phrase "necessary and proper" should be broadly construed to mean not "indispensable" but "appropriate."[8] Looking back today and recognizing that the words of the disputed clause could bear either construction, but that American government could never have adapted to the needs of a complex modern society in the absence of the doctrine of implied powers, the reader must feel relieved that at this critical moment in the development of our juristic federalism the national idea prevailed.

Hamilton was not only a nationalist and centralizer, he was also an elitist. Along with the bank, his first steps to revive and sustain the public credit were the full funding of the federal debt and the federal assumption of debts incurred by the states during the war of independence. These measures had their fiscal and economic purposes. Their social impact, moreover, favored the fortunes of those members of the propertied classes who had come to hold the federal and state obligations. This result, while fully understood, was incidental to Hamilton's ultimate purpose, which was political. As with the bank, that purpose was to strengthen the newly empowered central government by attaching to it the interests of these influential members of society. Hamilton promoted capitalism, not because he was a lackey to the capitalist class—indeed, as he once wrote to a close friend, "I hate moneying men"[9]—but just the opposite: his elitism was subservient to his nationalism.[10]

In the same cause he was not only an elitist but also an integrationist. I use that term expressly because of its current overtones, wishing to suggest Hamilton's perception of how diversity need not be divisive but may lead to mutual dependence and union. Here again he broke from Jefferson, who valued homogeneity. Hamilton, on the other hand, planned for active federal intervention to diversify the economy by the development of commerce and industry. His great report on manufactures is at once visionary and far-seeing— "the embryo of modern America," a recent writer termed it.[11]

The economy he foresaw would be free, individualist, and competitive. The federal government, however, would take action to make it more likely that entrepreneurs invested their money in ways most advantageous to the national welfare. Bounties, premiums, and other aids, in addition to a moderately protective tariff, would be employed to develop industry, along with a federal commission to allocate funds. There would be federal inspection of manufactured goods to protect the consumer and to enhance the reputation of American goods in foreign markets.[12] The purpose was to make the country rich and powerful. At the same time, the interdependence of agriculture and industry and especially of South and North would enhance the union. The outcome, writes a biographer, would be to make the United States "one nation indivisible, bound together by common wants, common interests and common prosperity."[13]

Hamilton is renowned for his statecraft—for his methods of using the powers of government for economic, political, and social ends. But that emphasis obscures his originality, which consisted in his conceptualization of those ends. His methods were derivative, being taken from the theory and practice of state-builders of the seventeenth and eighteenth centuries from Colbert to Pitt. Hamilton used this familiar technology, however, to forward the unprecedented attempt to establish republican government on a continental scale.[14] In his scheme, the unities of nationhood would sustain the authority of such a regime. By contrast, those earlier craftsmen of the modern state in Bourbon France or Hohenzollern Prussia or Whig Britain could take for granted the established authority of a monarchic and aristocratic regime. They too had their techniques for enhancing the attachment of the people to the prince. But in America the people *were* the prince. To enhance their attachment to the ultimate governing power, therefore, meant fortifying the bonds that united them as a people. If the authority of this first nation–state was to suffice for its governance, the purpose of the state would have to become the development of the nation. This was the essential Hamiltonian end: to make the nation more of a nation.

The Trial of Sectionalism

The national idea, so launched by statesmen of the federalist persuasion, confronted three great trials: the trial of sectionalism, culminating in the Civil War; the trial of industrialism, culminating in the great depression and the New Deal; and the trial of racism, which continues to rack our country today.

In the course of the struggle with sectionalism, John C. Calhoun defined the issue and threw down the challenge to nationalism when he said: "the very idea of an *American People,* as constituting a single community, is a mere chimera. Such a community never for a single moment existed—neither before nor since the Declaration of Independence." This was a logical deduction from the compact theory, which in Calhoun's system made of each state a "separate sovereign community."[15]

His leading opponent, Daniel Webster, has been called the first great champion of the national theory of the union.[16] If we are thinking of speech rather than action, that was true, since Hamilton's contribution, while earlier, was more in the realm of deeds than words. Webster never won the high executive power that he sought, and the cause of union for which he spent himself frequently suffered defeat during his lifetime. But the impact on history of words such as his is not to be underestimated. "When finally, after his death, civil war did eventuate," concludes a biographer, "it was Webster's doctrine, from the lips of Abraham Lincoln, which animated the North and made its victory inevitable."[17] Webster gave us not only doctrine but also imagery and myth. He was not the narrow legalist and materialistic whig of some critical portraits. And if his oratory is too florid for our taste today, its effect on his audiences was overpowering. "I was never so excited by public speaking before in my life," exclaimed George Ticknor, an otherwise cool Bostonian, after one address. "Three or four times I thought my temples would burst with the gush of blood." Those who heard him, it has been said, "experienced the same delight which they might have received from a performance of *Hamlet* or Beethoven's Fifth Symphony."[18] Poets have been called the "unacknowledged legislators of the world." This legislator was the unacknowledged poet of the republic.

To say this is to emphasize his style. What was the substance of his achievement? Historians of political thought usually and correctly look first to his memorable debate with Senator Robert Hayne of South Carolina in January 1830.[19] Echoing Calhoun's deductions from the compact theory, Hayne had stated the doctrine of nullification. This doctrine would deny to the federal judiciary the right to draw the line between federal and state authority, leaving such questions of constitutionality to be decided—subject to various qualifications—by each state itself.

In reply, Webster set forth with new boldness the national theory of authority. Asking what was the origin of "this general government," he concluded that the Constitution is not a compact between the states. It was not established by the governments of the several states, or by the people of the several states, but by "the people of the United States in the aggregate." In Lincolnian phrases he called it "the people's Constitution, the people's government, made for the people, made by the people and answerable to the people," and clinched his argument for the dependence of popular government on nationhood with the memorable and sonorous coda, "Liberty and union, one and inseparable, now and forever."

These later passages of his argument have almost monopolized the attention of historians of political thought. Yet it is in an earlier and longer part that he developed the Hamiltonian thrust, looking not to the origins but to the purpose of government. These initial passages of the debate had not yet focused on the problems of authority and nullification. The question was rather what to do with a great national resource—the public domain, already consisting of hundreds of millions of acres located in the states and territories and owned by the federal government. Large tracts had been used to finance internal improvements—such as roads, canals, and schools—as envisioned by Hamilton and ardently espoused by the previous President, John Quincy Adams.[20]

When Webster defended such uses, citing the long-standing agreement that the public domain was for "the common benefit of all the States," Hayne made a revealing reply. If that was the rule, said he, how could one justify "voting away immense bodies of these lands— for canals in Indiana and Illinois, to the Louisville and Portland Canal, to Kenyon College in Ohio, to Schools for the Deaf and Dumb." "If grants of this character," he continued, "can fairly be considered as made for the common benefit of all the states, it can only be because all the states are interested in the welfare of each—a principle, which, carried to the full extent, destroys all distinction between local and national subjects."[21]

Webster seized the objection and set out to answer it. His task was to show when a resource belonging to the whole country could legitimately be used to support works on "particular roads, particular canals, particular rivers, and particular institutions of education in the West." Calling this question "the real and wide difference in political opinion between the honorable gentleman and myself," he asserted that there was a "common good" distinguishable from "local goods," yet embracing such particular projects. Senator Hayne, he said, "may well ask what interest has South Carolina in a canal in Ohio. On his system, it is true, she has no interest. On that system, Ohio and Carolina are different governments and different countries . . . On that system, Carolina has no more interest in a canal in Ohio than in Mexico." For Webster, reasoning from the national theory, on the contrary, "Carolina and Ohio are parts of the same country, states, united under the same general government, having interests, common, associated, intermingled."[22]

In these passages the rhetoric is suggestive, but one would like a more specific answer: what is the difference between a local and a general good? Suddenly Webster's discourse becomes quite concrete. His approach is to show what the federal government must do by demonstrating what the states cannot do. Using the development of transportation after the peace of 1815 for illustration, he shows why a particular project within a state, which also has substantial benefits for other states, will for that very reason probably not be undertaken by the state within which it is located.

"Take the instance of the Delaware breakwater," he said. (This was a large artificial harbor then under federal construction near the mouth of Delaware Bay.)[23] "It will cost several millions of money. Would Pennsylvania ever have constructed it? Certainly never, . . . because it is not for her sole benefit. Would Pennsylvania, New Jersey and Delaware have united to accomplish it at their joint expense? Certainly not, for the same reason. It could not be done, therefore, but by the general government."[24]

The example illustrates a standard argument of political economy for centralization. Where the effects of government activity within one jurisdiction spill over into other jurisdictions, there is a case for central intervention to promote this activity, if it is beneficial, or to restrain it, if it is harmful. This spillover argument is one criterion of the "common good," and, as Webster pointed out, its logic calls for action in such cases by the government representing the whole country.

Hayne was right to shrink from the logic of this argument. For its logic does mean that in a rapidly developing economy such as that of America in the nineteenth century, increasing interdependence would bring more and more matters legitimately within the province of the federal government. But logic was not the only aspect of Webster's argument that Hayne was resisting. In the spirit of Hamilton, Webster did perceive the prospect of increasing interdependence and recognized that it could fully realize its promise of wealth and power only with the assistance of the federal government. Moreover, he looked beyond the merely material benefits that such intervention would bring to individuals, classes, and regions toward his grand objective, "the consolidation of the union."[25] This further criterion of the common good could under no circumstances be reconciled with Hayne's "system."

Like Hamilton, Webster sought to make the nation more of a nation. As he conceived this objective, however, turning his imagination toward the vistas of social possibility being opened by the rising romantic movement of his day, he portrayed far more perceptively than the Federalists the power of sympathy as well as interests to unite the nation. By "consolidation" Webster did not mean only attachment to the union arising from economic benefits. Indeed, he blamed Hayne for regarding the union "as a mere question of present and temporary expedience; nothing more than a mere matter of profit and loss . . . to be preserved, while it suits local and temporary purposes to preserve it; and to be sundered whenever it shall be found to thwart such purposes."[26]

The language brings to mind the imagery of another romantic nationalist, Edmund Burke, when in his famous assault upon the dry rationalism of the eighteenth century he proclaimed that "the state ought not to be considered as nothing better than a partnership agreement in a trade of pepper and coffee, calico or tobacco, or some other such low concern, to be taken up for a little temporary interest, and to be dissolved at the fancy of the parties," but rather as "a partnership in all science; a partnership in all art; a partnership in every virtue, and in all perfection."[27]

Setting forth his conception of the nation in a later formulation, Webster echoed Burke's words and phrasing even more exactly: "The Union," he said, "is not a temporary partnership of states. It is an association of people, under a constitution of government, uniting their power, joining together their highest interests, cementing their present enjoyments, and blending into one indivisible mass, all their hopes for the future."[28] For Webster as for Burke, the nation was held together not only by calculations of self-interest, but also by sentiments of "public affection."

Webster articulated this conception most vividly not in Congress or before the Supreme Court but at public gatherings on patriotic occasions. There the constraints of a professional and adversarial audience upon his imagination were relaxed and his powers as a myth-maker released. Consider what some call the finest of his occasional addresses,[29] his speech at the laying of the cornerstone of the Bunker Hill Monument on June 17, 1825. As in his advocacy and in his debates, his theme was the union. What he did, however, was not to make an argument for the union but to tell a story about it—a story about its past with a lesson for its future.[30]

The plot was simple: how American union foiled the British oppressors in 1775. They had thought to divide and conquer, anticipating that the other colonies would be cowed by the severity of the punishment visited on Massachusetts and that the other seaports would be seduced by the prospect of gain from trade diverted from Boston. "How miserably such reasoners deceived themselves!" exclaimed the orator. "Everywhere the unworthy boon was rejected with scorn. The fortunate occasion was seized, everywhere, to show to the whole world that the Colonies were swayed by no local interest, no partial interest, no selfish interest." In the imagery of Webster, the battle of Bunker Hill was a metaphor of that united people. As Warren, Prescott, Putnam, and Stark had fought side by side; as the four colonies of New England had on that day stood together with "one cause, one country, one heart"; so also "the feeling of resistance . . . possessed the whole American people." So much for Calhoun and his "system"!

From this myth of war Webster drew a lesson for peace. "In a day of peace, let us advance the arts of peace and the works of peace . . . Let us develop the resources of our land, call forth its powers, build up its institutions, and see whether we also, in our day and generation, may not perform something worthy to be remembered."

With his own matchless sensibility Abraham Lincoln deployed the doctrine and imagery of Webster to animate the North during the Civil War. In his message to Congress of July 4, 1861, Lincoln justified his use of the "war power" of the federal government to put down the rebellion in a lucid and uncompromising version of the nationalist view of the origins of the Republic:

> Originally some dependent colonies made the Union, and, in turn, the Union threw off their old dependence for them, and made them States . . . The Union, and not themselves separately, produced their independence and liberty. By conquest or purchase the Union gave to each of them whatever independence or liberty it has. The Union is older than any of the States, and, in fact, it created them as States.[31]

From this it followed that "the States have their status in the Union, and they have no other legal status. If they break from this, they can only do so against the law and by revolution." There could therefore be no constitutional right of secession, nullification, interposition, or, indeed, of what was called not many years ago "massive resistance" by any one or more states. Short of revolution, as he had said in his first inaugural address, states, like individuals, must rely on the democratic process under the Constitution for the protection of their rights. "A majority held in restraint by constitutional checks and limitations, and always changing easily with deliberate changes of popular opinions and sentiments," he concluded in a memorable formulation, "is the only true sovereign of a free people." That people, in short, was not only the sovereign authority which gave both states and nation a frame of government in the Constitution, it was also the authority which went on to govern them under that framework.[32]

No less for Lincoln than for his nationalist predecessors the national idea was also a perspective on public policy. In the same message of July 4, 1861, to Congress he further justified his use of the war power in this statement of purpose:

> This is essentially a people's contest. On the side of the Union it is a struggle for maintaining in the world that form and substance of government whose leading object is to elevate the condition of man— to lift artificial weights from all shoulders; to clear paths of laudable pursuit for all; to afford all an unfettered start, and a fair chance in the race of life.[33]

If this purpose were to be realized for "all" the nation, it was not enough simply to defeat secession. Positive steps had to be taken for "a new birth of freedom." During the very war years Lincoln not only gave slavery the death blow; as the heir of the Hamiltonian vision of commercial and industrial development, he also presided over the enactment of federal intervention in the fields of banking and currency, transportation, the tariff, land grants to homesteaders, and aid to higher education.[34]

In seeking to legitimize secession, Jefferson Davis replied with a forceful statement of compact theory. Like Lincoln, he identified the source of the Constitution's authority by a view of its origins. The federal government, he said, was not established directly by the people of the United States but by a compact among the several states. Under the Constitution, which sets forth the terms of this compact, as under the "close alliance" and "Confederation" among the rebellious colonies, "each state," he argued, "was, in the last resort, the sole judge as well of its wrongs as of the mode and measure of redress." For these reasons the nature of the Constitution itself justified the southern states, when, provoked by the northern states' "persistent abuse of the powers . . . delegated to Congress," they resumed "all their rights as sovereign and independent States and dissolved their connection with the other States of the Union."[35]

President Davis did not contend that no power to impose customs duties on imports had been vested in Congress by the Constitution. Relying on the compact theory, he charged that the Congress had abused its constitutional authority. The power to impose custom duties, he claimed, could properly be used only for revenue, not for protection. The northern states, however, exploiting their preponderance in Congress, had put through a protective tariff, which enriched their commercial and manufacturing classes at the expense of the agricultural South. By "the tyranny of an unbridled majority," they had invaded the "constitutional liberties" which the fundamental law, if properly construed, would protect. Finally, they had attacked interests of "transcendent magnitude" by "impairing the security of property in African slaves," whose labor had become "absolutely necessary for the wants of civilized man."

In the eyes of the South, the stakes were not only self-government, feasible only in a decentralized system, but also individual liberty, economic well-being, and civilization itself. For Jefferson Davis as for Abraham Lincoln, these wider perspectives gave meaning to the law of American federalism, lending it legitimacy, resolving its ambiguities, defining its purpose, and arousing passions that raised armies and sustained them at great sacrifice by soldiers and civilians through four years of war.

The Impact of Industrialism

The Lincolnian program set the course of national development for the next several generations. An enormous expansion of the economy propelled America into the age of industrialism, which in due course engendered its typical problems of deprivation, inequality, and class conflict.

A Republican, Theodore Roosevelt, first attempted to cope with these problems in terms of the national idea. Throughout his public career, an associate has written, Roosevelt "kept one steady purpose, the solidarity, the essential unity of our country . . . All the details of his action, the specific policies he stated, arise from his underlying purpose for the Union." Like other progressives, Roosevelt was disturbed by the rising conflicts between groups and classes and sought to offset them by timely reform. In this sense integration was TR's guiding aim, and he rightly christened his cause "The New Nationalism." Effective advocacy of this cause, however, fell to another Roosevelt a generation later, when the failings of industrialism were raising far greater dangers to the union.

None of the main points in Franklin Roosevelt's famous inaugural address of March 4, 1933, can be summarized without reference to the nation. The emergency is national because of the "interdependence of the various elements in, and parts of, the United States." Our purpose must be, first, "the establishment of a sound national economy" and beyond that "the assurance of a rounded and permanent national life." The mode of action must be national, conducted by the federal government and carried out "on a national scale," helped "by national planning." No other thematic term faintly rivals the term "nation" as noun or adjective in emphasis. Democracy is mentioned only once; liberty, equality, or the individual not at all.[36]

Franklin Roosevelt's nationalism was threefold. First it was a doctrine of federal centralization, and in his administration, in peace as well as war, the balance of power in the federal system swung sharply toward Washington. Second, Roosevelt called not only for a centralization of government but also for a nationalization of politics. In these years a new kind of mass politics arose. The old rustic and sectional politics gave way to a new urban and class politics dividing electoral forces on a nationwide basis.[37]

The third aspect of Roosevelt's nationalism was expressed in his policies. Those policies do not make a neat package and include many false starts and failures and ad hoc expedients. Yet in their overall impact one can detect the old purpose of "consolidation of the union."

During the very first phase of the New Deal, based on the National Industrial Recovery Act, this goal was explicit. In its declaration of policy, the act, having declared a "national emergency," called for "cooperative action among trade groups" and "united action of labor and management" under "adequate government sanctions and supervision."[38] Engulfed in red, white, and blue propaganda, the NRA, after a first brief success, failed to achieve that coordinated effort and had virtually collapsed by the time it was declared unconstitutional in 1935. The second New Deal which followed, however, brought about fundamental and lasting changes in the structure of the American government and economy.

The paradox of the second New Deal is that although at the time it was intensely divisive, in the end it enhanced national solidarity. The divisiveness will be readily granted by anyone who remembers the campaign of 1936. The tone was set by Roosevelt's speech accepting the Democratic nomination. In swollen and abrasive hyperbole he promised that, just as 1776 had wiped out "political tyranny," so 1936 would bring "economic tyranny" to an end. The "economic royalist" metaphor that was launched into the political battle by this speech expressed the emerging purpose of the New Deal to create a new balance of power in the economy by means of a series of basic structural reforms.[39] The Wagner Act was the most important and characteristic. Utilizing its protections of the right to organize and to bargain collectively, trade unions swept through industry in a massive organizing effort. Despite bitter and sometimes bloody resistance in what can only be called class war, over the years not only practices but also attitudes were altered. The life of the working stiff was never again the same.

The Rooseveltian reforms expressed a "politics of civic inclusion."[40] In their material aspect they brought about a distribution of benefits and a redistribution of power in favor of certain groups. No less important was their symbolic significance as recognition of the full participation of these groups in the common life of the nation. Industrial labor and recent immigrants won a degree of acceptance in the national consciousness and in everyday social intercourse that they had not previously enjoyed. In Roosevelt's appointments to the judiciary, Catholics and Jews were recognized as never before. He named the first Italo-American and the first blacks ever appointed to the federal bench. As Joseph Alsop has observed, "the essence of his achievement" was that he "included the excluded."[41] "Remember, remember always," he reminded the DAR, "that all of us . . . are descended from immigrants and revolutionists."

By this time, a great switch in the attitude of the political parties toward federalism had taken place. The conservatives, who under the names of Federalist, Whig, and Republican had been partisans of national activism, took up the cause of the old Democrats, who from the days of Jefferson had espoused states' rights.

The Challenge of Racism

None of these conflicts in nation-building is ever wholly terminated. Sectionalism still flares up from time to time, as between frostbelt and sunbelt. So also does class struggle. Similarly today, the cleavages between ethnic groups that boiled up with a new bitterness in the 1960s are far from being resolved. In this nation of immigrants, "ethnicity" has been an old and fundamental feature of our politics. In the sixties the new word came into use to signify new facts as ethnic identity gained as a ground of claims and denials. "From the mid-sixties," one writer has reported, ". . . the ethnic identity began to gain on the general American identity. Indeed the very term 'American' became depreciated in the late 1960's."[42] Once again the question whether we were one nation and one people was put in doubt.

The issue is not just ethnicity but race. To be sure, ethnic pluralism is a fact—there are said to be ninety-two ethnic groups in the New York area alone—but this broad focus obscures the burning issue, which is the coexistence of blacks and whites in large numbers on both sides. That question of numbers is crucial. In other times and places one can find instances of a small number of one race living in relative peace in a society composed overwhelmingly of the other race. "Tokenism" is viable. But the facts rule out that solution for the United States. So also does the national idea. What we are attempting under its imperatives has never been attempted by any country at any time. It is to create within a liberal, democratic framework a society in which a vast number of both black and white people live in free and equal intercourse, political, economic, and social. It is a unique, a stupendous demand, but the national idea asks nothing less.

For John F. Kennedy and Lyndon Johnson, the question was, first of all, civil rights. This meant securing for blacks the legal and political rights that had been won for whites in other generations. But the problem of civil rights, which was mainly a problem of the South, merged with the problem of black deprivation, which was especially a problem of northern cities. Johnson's "poverty program" typified the main thrust of the Great Society measures which he built on the initiatives of Kennedy. To think of these measures as concerned simply with "the poor" is to miss the point. The actual incidence of poverty meant that their main concern would be with the living conditions and opportunities of blacks, and especially those who populated the decaying areas of the great urban centers swollen by migration from the South to the North during and after World War II.[43]

These programs were based on the recognition that membership in one ethnic group rather than another can make a great difference to your life chances. In trying to make the opportunities somewhat less unequal, they sought to bring the individuals belonging to disadvantaged groups—as was often said—"into the mainstream of American life." The rhetoric of one of Johnson's most impassioned speeches echoes this purpose. Only a few days after a civil rights march led by Martin Luther King had been broken up by state troopers in full view of national television, he introduced the Voting Rights Act of 1965 into Congress. Calling upon the myths of former wars, like other nationalist orators before him, he harked back to Lexington and Concord and to Appomattox Court House in his summons to national effort.

"What happened in Selma," he continued, "is part of a larger movement which reaches into every section and state of America. It is the effort of American Negroes to secure for themselves the full blessings of American life." Then, declaring that "their cause must be our cause too," he closed with a solemn echo of the song of the marchers: "*And . . . we . . . shall . . . overcome.*"[44]

From the defeat of "massive resistance" mounted by the advocates of states' rights to the many victories for civil rights on the legal front, the effort of this new federalism to consolidate the union has made substantial progress. Still, no one would say that our statecraft—poverty programs, affirmative action, busing—has been adequate to the objective. Indeed, the very basis of that statecraft in our political culture has come under attack. In the name of "multi-culturalism," activists claiming to speak for black and other ethnic groups have revived the ideal of segregation in a new form. In their rhetoric the metaphor of the "melting pot," in which the various ethnic identities are assimilated into an American identity, is rejected in favor of a "mosaic society" in which old identities are preserved and made central to the social, economic, and political life of those sharing them. "Instead of a nation composed of individuals making their own free choices," writes Arthur Schlesinger, Jr., "America increasingly sees itself as composed of groups more or less indelible in their ethnic character. The national ideal had once been *e pluribus unum*. Are we now to belittle *unum* and glorify *pluribus*? Will the center hold? Or will the melting pot yield to the Tower of Babel?"[45]

Federalism and Political Theory

So much for a brief sketch of the fortunes of the national idea in American political history. What is the connection of this idea with our federal arrangements?

Intrinsic to this way of looking at democratic nationalism in America is a theory of federalism. This theory is about the division of authority between the federal and the state governments and about the purposes which this distribution of power is expected to serve. It is a theory in the sense that it is a coherent body of thought describing and justifying the federal system in the light of certain fundamental principles. These are the principles of democracy and nationality on which the Constitution as a whole is based. The thrust of my argument is that this curious arrangement of a constitutionally protected vertical division of power is an intentional and functional institution—not an historical accident or the upshot of mere compromise—of the self-governing American people as they seek over time to make and remake themselves as a nation.

The significance of this theory as a choice among possible regimes is brought out by the contrast with compact theory. From the viewpoint of compact theory, federalism and nationalism, the states and the nation, are opposed. This is opposition in a quite fundamental sense: not merely a conflict between state government and federal government but between state and nation as political communities. For, if the center of political life is in each of the separate states of the nation, it cannot be in the nation as a whole. Or, to put the matter even more bluntly, in so far as the compact model is a correct description, the true nation in America is not the United States but the separate states of which it is composed. We are not one people but several.

Radically different conclusions follow from the opposing view of the location of our nationality, the source of our democracy, and the function of the federal–state division of authority. In contrast with compact theory, national theory takes a far more generous view of the powers and responsibilities of the federal government. Throughout our history, it has informed and supported the broad against the narrow construction of the constitutional power of the federal government. National theory, however, is not merely a doctrine of centralization. As its advocates at the time of the founding continually emphasized, the national point of view not only tolerates but indeed requires a federal arrangement.

In this conception the American republic is one nation served by two levels of government, the object of both being to protect and advance the well-being of the nation. The states are not rival communities carved out of the greater jurisdiction which, although they are incapable of real material or moral independence, seek to act on an exclusive and inward-looking concern for their distinct interests. Like the federal government, state governments also express the national will. The nation can use both levels or either level of government to make itself more of a nation: that is, to make the United States a freer, wealthier, more powerful, and indeed more virtuous human community.

Federalism is not a humdrum matter of public administration but a serious question of political philosophy. The conflict of ideas on federalism between the conservative President and liberal professors illustrates the point. It also calls for further inquiry. The task of this book, accordingly, is to clarify and amplify the national theory of American federalism. Its approach is through the history of ideas. That means looking at intellectual origins, primarily how the leading minds at the time of the founding of the American republic explained what they were trying to do, with particular attention to the topic of federalism. The thought of these advocates of popular government itself descended from a long and controversial past. If we are to get at the meaning of what they said and the significance of their choice, we will need to look at that past.

The book has three parts. First, we shall look at the authoritarian and corporatist themes which dominated Western political thought in the centuries before the rise of modern republicanism. Nowadays the American founders are sometimes criticized for failing fully to appreciate and to institutionalize the values of contemporary liberal democracy. It should put these criticisms in context and reveal the radicalism and audacity of the founders when we see the profound depth of their departure from the old hierarchic tradition which, although greatly weakened, still informed British rule at home and in the colonies. The chapter on Aquinas should convey something of the imaginative scope and intellectual power of that tradition against which republican thought rebelled and in contrast with which it defined itself.

For access to the thought of the precursors of the American uprising against the hierarchic tradition and to the republican mind which had originally broken with that mentality, we shall turn to the spokesmen of the failed republican revolution of the English seventeenth century, the Commonwealth. In these writers, and especially James Harrington, we shall find not only the individualistic, democratic, and national premises of republican thought but also the embodiment of these values in institutions of constitutional, representative, and federal government strikingly like those championed by the American leaders of 1787.

In the second part of the book, we pass from these contrasts and comparisons to the reassertion of many of the essentials of Commonwealth republicanism by the colonists in their criticism of British rule and their proposals for reform. The purpose of this comparison of similars is not mainly to show influence. It is rather to explore the implications of the premises of republican thought as they were ever more forcefully asserted in the demands of the American dissidents. These developing ideas reached a logical conclusion in 1776 when Tom Paine drew up his ultimatum demanding an independent, national, and distinctly federal republic.

Part three presents the conception of the national and federal republic which won its substantial victory with the framing and ratification of the Constitution. This formulation of national theory is found chiefly in what was said and written by Madison and Hamilton, strengthened by James Wilson's elaboration. Again the national view is clarified by the contrast with compact theory which, as expounded by Montesquieu, was advanced by the opponents of the Constitution.

One may well ask why it is necessary to go to all this trouble of looking into history in search of theory when we already have at hand the authoritative document which ordains the federal–state allocation of power. The reason is that the Constitution, for all its splendid eighteenth-century lucidity, displays much blank space. Whether one is trying to say what is the law of American federalism or what is the proper use to be made of that law, one can hardly arrive at an unambiguous conclusion without explicitly or implicitly supplementing the argument by drawing on a framework of theory.

American federalism is at once a system of law and a structure of power. It has both a juristic and a behavioral aspect. As a system of law, it is a government in which the allocation of authority between levels is secured by some exceptional legal protection.[46] That last point is the crux. Federalism is not mere decentralization, even where decentralization is substantial and persistent. Any polity except the very smallest will have territorial subdivisions. In a unitary system the bodies governing these subdivisions will receive their authority from the ordinary statutory law of the central government. The distinctive thing about a federal system is that the authority of these bodies is assured by a law which is superior to the statutory law of the center and which indeed is also the source of authority of that law. Decentralization is constitutional, not merely statutory. That is, as in the United States, the division of authority between the two levels of government is set out in a legal document which can be amended only by a process of consent wider than and different from the process required for the ordinary statutory law of the central government.

By themselves, the words of this legal source, the Constitution, do not tell us what the law is. Our verbal federalism does not unambiguously determine our juristic federalism. A classic example is that fundamental controversy over the meaning of the "necessary and proper" clause. As we have seen, the Hamiltonian reading won out only with the aid of the national theory of authority and purpose.

But even when the words have been given a clear legal meaning, the result, our juristic federalism, still leaves open the question of how governments will actually use these constitutionally legal powers. As a structure of power, American federalism is this actual pattern of use of constitutional authority by the governments of different levels. The law of the Constitution, even when clearly determined, however, does not say whether or how far that authority should be exercised. Our juristic federalism does not unambiguously determine our behavioral federalism. With regard to the federal–state allocation of authority, people may agree on the same "juridical map," to use Harry Scheiber's graphic phrase, yet strongly differ on the actual extent of power that may be legitimately exercised under its authorization. Jefferson Davis, as we observed, did not deny the power of Congress to levy custom duties. Construing those powers, however, in the light of the compact theory, he found the protective tariff so illegitimate and obnoxious as to support the case for secession.

A government may or may not use its duly authorized powers. They may lie dormant for years, only to be revived with transforming effect. For instance, the power conferred on Congress by the Constitution to spend for "the general welfare" was recognized by Alexander Hamilton and other worthies of the early republic.[47] It was not greatly used, however, until the twentieth century when, thanks especially to programs inaugurated by the Great Society, federal grants in aid to state and local governments brought about a rapid and marked centralization of power. Without a significant change in our juristic federalism, a "new federalism" in the behavioral sense came into existence.[48]

A generation later, President Reagan proclaimed another "new federalism," although in a sense opposite to the "new federalism" of the Johnson years. By a reduction of intergovernmental aid, he achieved a significant shift in the federal–state balance of power.[49] Accepting much the same juristic federalism but calling upon two opposing strands of theory, the two Presidents found the rhetoric to legitimate two different patterns of power and policy.

Whether one tries to think about federalism or to do something about it, one cannot avoid acting on theory. It would seem reasonable, therefore, to try to state that theory as clearly and fully as possible. The excursion into history of ideas attempted in this book is intended to be a help in this task. This reconstruction of nationalist thought presents, I believe, a past which is usable today, while remaining faithful to that past as it actually was.

PART ONE

FROM HIERARCHY
TO REPUBLICANISM

I N 1765 as the agitation against the Stamp Act launched the American colonies on a decade of rebellion, the young John Adams published a series of newspaper articles that came to be known as *A Dissertation on the Canon and Feudal Law*. In them he defined the issue, as he saw it, between the British government and the American dissidents. This was no lawyer's brief, citing old laws and charters and wrangling over practice and precedent. While the Stamp Act was the immediate occasion for his fiery polemic, Adams did not mention it until his last pages. The framework in which he set that incident was breathtaking in scope: nothing less than a history of government since the birth of Christ, informed by a theory of how freedom is won or lost by mankind, and culminating in the conflict between Britain and the colonies.

The merits of Adams's account was that it portrayed the underlying conflict of systems that motivated that transforming decade. Behind the British claims Adams discerned the pretensions of the medieval ideal, "the two greatest tyrannies . . . the canon and the feudal law." Arrayed against them was the plan of government formed by the first settlers who had been brought to America by "a love of universal liberty," religious and civil, and who had "an utter contempt of all that dark ribaldry of hereditary, indefeasible right—the Lord's anointed—and the divine, miraculous original of government with which priesthood had enveloped the feudal monarch in clouds and mysteries."[1]

In Adams's political science, as ignorance and superstition promote tyranny, so also enlightenment and education evoke and sustain liberty. Inaugurated by the Reformation, "the struggle between the people and the confederacy" broke out in the conflict with "the execrable race of Stuarts" and led to the settlement of America by the Puritans. The Americans founded their liberties on "knowledge diffused generally through the whole body of the people." While, needless to say, Adams was sensitive to the rights of property, he found that "the preservation of the means of knowledge among the lowest ranks is of more importance to the public than all the property of all the rich men in the country." Accordingly, in the current crisis, he admonished his countrymen: "let every sluice of knowledge be opened and aflowing . . . Let us dare to read, think, speak and write."

In light of this view of history and theory, Adams saw the Stamp Act not simply as the taking of property without the consent of the governed but as something much more serious: an attack upon the whole system of free communication and free discussion that was the chief mechanism of self-government in the colonies. He saw in the act "a design . . . to strip us in great measure of the means of knowledge by loading the press, the colleges and even an almanack and a newspaper with restraints and duties." It was entirely logical, therefore, that he should link the Stamp Act with what his close friend the Reverend Johnathan Mayhew saw as the first covert steps being taken by the Church of England to carry out its long-held "formal design to root out Presbyterianism, etc., and to establishing episcopacy and bishops" in the colonies. Inspiring this twofold effort, according to Adams, was the intention to bring about "an entire subversion of the whole system of our fathers by the introduction of the canon and the feudal law into America."[2]

Taken literally, that charge was a gross exaggeration, as Adams acknowledged by immediately adding that in Britain the old system was "greatly mutilated." Yet he had gone to the heart of the conflict between Britain and America. He was right to see that the conflict was between the idea that the many must look to the few for instruction in and direction toward the common good and the idea that the many can themselves determine the common good and direct the polity toward its realization. He was right, therefore, to clarify the emerging republican aspiration of his day by setting it out in stark contrast with the hierarchic tradition from which the Commonwealthmen of the seventeenth century had broken. It will similarly help us grasp what republicanism meant to those early English rebels and their American successors if we first take a look at the ancient political orthodoxy against which they took up arms.

CHAPTER 1

The Rule of the Wise
and the Holy:
Thomas Aquinas

FORMULATED AND REFORMULATED by many writers, the hierarchic tradition could not be a single, logically consistent system of
thought. It persistently displayed, however, certain leading themes,
whose fortunes Arthur Lovejoy has traced over a period of more
than two thousand years under the title of his masterly study, *The
Great Chain of Being.*[1] The germinal thought came from Plato. It
had been developed by Aristotle and the Neo-Platonists, Christian-
ized by theologians of the early Church, and passed on to the middle
ages, especially by Augustine and the Pseudo-Dionysius. In the thirteenth century, after the recovery of Aristotle, Thomas Aquinas fused
classical and Christian elements into a culminating synthesis. We
may look at the Thomistic system for a clear and robust view of the
principles of the hierarchic tradition in political thought against
which the Commonwealth republicans revolted and to which they
sought to provide an alternative conception of politics and government. What follows is not meant to be a comprehensive account of
medieval political thought, even less a history of medieval political
institutions. Its purpose is to use Aquinas's classic exposition of the
hierarchic idea as a magnifying glass to bring fully into view the
deeper lineaments of that idea.[2]

According to the medieval synthesis of classical and Christian
thought, the hierarchy that prevailed in human affairs was included
in and justified by a greater hierarchy that prevailed in the cosmos.
The cosmos had been created and was governed by God, the Perfect
Being. It consisted of an immense number of orders of lesser beings—
angels, men, animals, vegetable life, and inanimate things, down to

31

"the last dregs of being" which were hardly anything at all. Although enormously diverse, it was not a mere aggregate or miscellany but a cosmos, because these orders were distinguished from one another by degrees of being, of value, of utility, and of authority, which at the same time joined them together as complementary parts of a harmonious whole. Hierarchic, corporatist, and organic, this cosmos was natural, but above all divine, unified by God's love for and providence over His created world and by His created world's love for and obedience to Him. In contrast with republican principles, its principles were authoritarian and deferential.[3]

The Ontology of Inequality

The ethics and politics of the hierarchic outlook depended on its metaphysics. For its adherents, inequality pervaded human society and, indeed, the whole cosmos. The way they thought about inequality, however, differed vastly from the way we do today. Above all, their ontology gave them—or, rather, imposed upon them—a justification and an explanation of inequality which are available to few, if any, modern minds, but which for those who accepted the premises had compelling moral and intellectual force.

The difference is not that people today deny the fact of inequalities of ability or the need for inequalities of power. Among supporters of popular government, whether of the Left or the Right, it would be generally agreed that some situations justify one or a few having exceptional power over many. Thanks to his expertise, the surgeon in the hospital or the engineer in the space program properly has wide authority in the common enterprise. Other reasons may be organizational, such as the need for a CEO with a final coordinative role. These justifications depend upon what we like to believe are sound empirical findings. Our explanations of inequality likewise run along empirical and scientific lines. Psychologists study why some children are more gifted than others, sociologists how persons with certain talents—such as Pareto's lions and foxes—rise to power in the state. Broadly, the method of explanation is to get at the causes of change, to identify the antecedent conditions which uniformly produce such consequences, and to use the theory so derived to explain particular cases.

Occasionally Aquinas also offers practical, empirical reasons for hierarchy, and his observations can be quite shrewd. When we follow his system to its premises, however, we are transported into quite another realm of the spirit. We may identify these premises as his essentialism and his monism.

Essentialism, that great Platonic gift, is fundamental to Aquinas's outlook. To his way of thinking, for a thing to be, it must be something. If it exists, there must be an answer to the question, "*What* is it?" This "whatness" is its "essence" *(essentia)*. In Aquinas's medieval Latin, *quidditas* (literally "whatness") is a synonym for *essentia*.[4] According to the essentialist outlook, the essence, by thus giving a character to the particular thing, makes its existence possible. Yet the essence itself is not something one can see or feel or hear or touch: to the senses it is imperceptible. Yet it is intelligible: it can be grasped by the mind.[5] So, for instance, an observer sees some dots on a piece of paper and is able, thanks to their circular form, to perceive them as a whole and say, "Oh, yes, a circle." He does not "see" the circle, which is the form in which the dots are arranged. Yet the form is there and he can grasp it intellectually in a definition as framed by Euclid: "a plane figure contained by one line such that all the straight lines falling upon it from one point among those lying within the figure are equal to one another." This same imperceptible form, the ideal circle, can be found in many particulars.

Similarly, one hears some notes of music, but it is their harmony that makes them not just a series of noises but a musical composition. To perceive the notes as a harmonious whole, however, takes some musical understanding, which may well be beyond some listeners. In this sense the harmony is inaudible. It is, however, intelligible. Thus, a harmonic combination results when two notes are an octave apart; that is, they have vibrations in the ratio of 2:1. Accordingly, writes Aquinas, "the formula of the essence" of "the octave interval is 2:1."[6] In the same way, the essence of "man" is "rational animality," and the fact that his soul is characterized by this essence is what makes any particular man human. That essence cannot be seen, but rational creatures can grasp the definition and, thanks to it, perceive and distinguish members of the human order amongst the rest of creation.

Some philosophers—the nominalists—say that these forms are purely conventional, imposed by the human mind upon the unorganized data of the senses. The essentialist, while agreeing that the essence of a thing is not always immediately and rightly perceived by all observers, would say that the essences are really there, determining the kinds of things that can exist. Essence makes existence possible.

Conceivably, a world of particulars so derived from a realm of essence could be ordered on a principle of equality. Such was not the inclination of the adherents of the hierarchic tradition. To the question, "Why, when God made all things he did not make them equal," Augustine echoes the reply of this school: *"non essent omnia, si essent aequalia"*—if all things were equal, they would not exist.[7] For Thomas Aquinas, as for the others, "order" *(ordo)* can mean only the ranking of things on a scale of inequality.[8]

This scale is constituted in a very special way, one order including the kind of being, the essence, of another order and also the kind of being distinctive to itself. The germ of this notion of a hierarchy of ever more inclusive being can be found in Plato. In *The Republic,* for instance, the virtue of the philosopher guardians includes both the virtues of the warrior and those of the working classes—both courage and temperance—and also the philosopher's own special virtue, wisdom. According to Lovejoy, however, it was Aristotle who elaborated the notion, especially in his *De Anima.* In this treatise, writes Lovejoy, Aristotle suggested a "hierarchical arrangement of all organisms" which was based on "the 'powers of the soul' possessed by them, from the nutritive, to which plants are limited, to the rational, characteristic of man 'and possibly another kind superior to him', each higher order possessing all the powers of those below it in the scale, and an additional differentiating one of its own."[9]

While essentialism does not logically imply this idea, it is a necessary premise of it. Because it is immaterial, an essence can be present in the many members of one order of particular beings; for the same reason it can also, as essence, be embraced by the more inclusive nature of another order. Thus, man's essence, his soul, includes the nutritive and sensitive forms of the souls of plants and brute animals as well as his own characteristic "rational animality."

Lovejoy calls the basic Aristotelian idea "the principle of unilinear gradation"[10] and identifies it as one of the fundamental assumptions of the notion of "the great chain of being." Its significance for political theory is more forcefully brought out if we think of it as the principle of "inclusive hierarchy." For it is by this notion of radical inequality that the hierarchic tradition solves the fundamental political problem of unity in diversity: the many are made one by being included essentially in another that is one.

Was this idea of inclusive hierarchy merely an arbitrary preference on the part of its advocates, or did it have some close logical connection with the premises of their thought? Essentialism, as we have just observed, was a necessary assumption. One can conceive of a world, however, in which some entities share the natures of others but in which some sets of related beings are not related to other sets. Such a pluralistic universe, of course, would not be perfect since it would lack those forms of being which would presumably arise from the relating of its unrelated parts. It might be in the course of perfecting itself, displaying what the modern era calls progress. Or, as some moderns have concluded, it might be in decline and decay. In either case, it would not be static; it would have a history, or histories.

If, on the other hand, one starts from monism—that is, from the premise of a perfect world which includes all forms of being—such discontinuities would have to be tidied up by a series of ever more inclusive beings. For if those more inclusive beings did not exist, the world would lack something and not be perfect. In short, the assumption of a perfect world implies that its parts will be ordered hierarchically. To use Lovejoy's terms, in such a static cosmos, the principle of plenitude implies the principle of unilinear gradation. *Non essent omnia, si essent aequalia.* Inequality is the law of being.

Value, Utility, and Authority

In its fully developed form, as in the Thomistic system, the hierarchic idea portrays the cosmos as a ladder of qualitative decrease—the German term *Stufenkosmos* is apt—leading downward from the perfect and all-inclusive being, God, through orders with ever less inclusive being toward nothingness, nonbeing. This hierarchy of less inclusive being is also a hierarchy of descending value. "That which first falls in the intellect," writes Aquinas, "is *being,* and therefore everything that we apprehend we consider as being, and consequently as *one,* and as *good,* which are convertible with *being.*" Hence we say that "*essence is being* and *one* and *good.*"[11] Being in any degree implies value, since all things participate, more or less, in God's being. All being is good, as affirmed when the first chapter of Genesis concludes its account of the six days of creation: "And God saw all the things that He had made, and they were very good (Gen. 1:31)."[12] Evil exists, but only as privation of being. That relative privation itself is necessary for the perfection of the created world, which consists in its comprehension of every order of being from the greatest to the least.

Aquinas summarizes the idea of inclusive hierarchy in a paraphrase of Aristotle: "Now, formal distinction always requires inequality, because as the Philosopher says, the forms of things are like numbers in which species vary by the addition or subtraction of unity. Hence, in natural things species seem to be arranged in a hierarchy: as the mixed things are more perfect than the elements, and plants than minerals, and animals than plants, and men than other animals; and in each of these one species is more perfect than others."[13]

These orders of being and value are complementary to one another in a teleological sense. Each has an end or purpose which it has a "natural aptitude" to fulfill and which is useful to other higher beings and through them to the whole. "All the parts are directed to the perfection of the whole," wrote Aquinas, "in so far as one part serves another."[14] In this scheme, whether we think of the cosmos or of human society, there is a division of labor; in this sense, the whole constitutes an economy.

Aquinas recognized that this division of labor enables men in society to provide for needs they could not have provided for in isolation.[15] No more than classical writers, however, did he recognize that over time increasing specialization could add to the material abundance of a society. From his concept of a static society in a static cosmos, any notion of economic development is absent. In Aquinas's view the diversification of capacities embodied in the division of labor does not result from intelligent adaptation to circumstances. It proceeds rather from the fact that "different men are born with aptitudes and tendencies for the different functions and the various ways of living."[16] In this unchanging economy, therefore, each member and each order has one and only one function. It is a violation of nature and a grave source of disorder if any member attempts to move out of his station in life and to perform a function for which he is not naturally fitted.[17] In order to guide the members toward and maintain them in this natural order, there is "a governing power" which "impels toward the common good *(bonum commune)* of the many, over and above that which impels toward the particular good *(bonum proprium)* of each individual."[18] The connection of service and use in this economy is not the result of free exchange. It is a relationship of superordination and subordination, a sector of that scheme of government by which divine providence rules universally. In this providential economy there is no private sector.

Exemplifying this relationship, vegetative life serves the consumption needs of animal life. "Brute animals," wrote Aquinas, "though bereft of intellect, yet, since they have some kind of knowledge, are placed by order of the divine providence above plants and other things devoid of knowledge.[19] As a rational animal, man has powers of the soul that put him above the lesser creatures. Different men, moreover, have reason in different degrees with the result that the higher use and command the lower while the lower serve and defer to the higher. The distinction, as Aquinas draws it out in the *Summa contra Gentiles,* is between "intellectual" and "operative" power *(virtus intellectiva, virtus operativa).* The intellectual power "by its very nature is a directive and governing power," while "the operative power follows the rule of the intellectual power" *(virtus operativa sequitur regimen virtutis intellectivae).* Aquinas supports this proposition with two arguments by analogy: (1) the organic analogy: "In man," he writes, "the members of the body move at the will's command"; and (2) the political analogy: "The same may also be seen," he continues, "if they [the intellectual and operative powers] be in different subjects; since those men who excel in the operative power need to be directed by those who excel in the intellectual

power." "Therefore," he concludes, "the nature of the divine providence requires that other creatures be ruled by intellectual creatures."[20]

In this political analogy, the relationship of ruler and ruled is one
of authority and deference. The grounds of the ruler's authority is
his "intellectual power" [*virtus intellectiva*]. And in conformity with
the hierarchic principle, that intellectual power includes the lesser
operative power as well as the distinctive power of governing.
"While providence," wrote Aquinas, "requires both the disposition
of order, which is effected by a cognitive power, and execution,
which is the work of the operative power, rational creatures share in
both powers, while other creatures have only the latter."[21] The distinction between rulers and ruled is not absolute. The inferiors who
"excel in operative power" are still rational beings with their share,
although a lesser one, of the directive power. In turn, their superiors
who "excel in intellectual power" are subject to "the higher intellectual creatures" with "more universal forms" and "more universal
powers." Among men as among the angels and between men and
angels and between angels and God, "the lower intellectual natures
must be governed by the higher."[22]

In human society, accordingly, this possession of a more inclusive
form of being confers authority on the rulers and elicits deference
from the ruled. Each needs the other in this teleological cosmos, but
in different ways. The ruler needs the ruled to perform tasks serving
the ruler. The ruled needs the ruler to guide him in his service to the
ruler. The ruler will know what this subordinate task is in the
profound sense that he has the very same power of the soul to
perform that service, although he does not directly exercise it. In the
teleological scheme, this service is the good of the ruled. To understand this subordinate service, as the ruler does, is both to know
what is good for the ruled and to understand that good as a harmonious part of the common good.

How the good of the ruler is identical with the common good is
illustrated by this passage where Aquinas is discussing how God
governs all things by his providence:

> For whenever certain things are ordered to a certain end, they are all
> subject to the disposal of the one to whom chiefly that end belongs.

This may be seen in an army, since all the parts of the army, and their actions, are directed to the good of the general, namely, victory, as their ultimate end; for which reason the government of the whole army belongs to the general.[23]

Needless to say, knowledge of this kind, arising from the ontological status of the ruler, cannot be reduced to modern notions of greater intelligence, more good will, or greater expertise. To try to do so would gravely distort the vision and sadly diminish its grandeur. A classical or medieval aristocrat is not the same as a talented eighteenth-century gentleman or an altruistic twentieth-century engineer. Exemplifying the law of the cosmos, the higher order differs from the lower order among men not merely because its members are more intelligent or more expert or more altruistic but because they embrace a higher order of being, a more comprehensive range of the stuff of ultimate reality.

One is reminded of those paintings of the medieval parliament in England. The king dominates the scene. A huge figure, lavishly adorned with symbols of transcendent authority, he is flanked by the lords spiritual and temporal, smaller and less richly bedizened, while the commons, soberly attired, their backs to the viewer, huddle together anonymously at the very bottom.[24] These contrasts in scale among the figures reflected not only courtly sycophancy but also contemporary perceptions of differentiated being.

Hierarchies of Virtue and Grace

In his discussion of virtue in the *Summa Theologica,* Aquinas examines more closely the powers of the soul and their relation to the hierarchy of value and authority in human affairs. Virtue *(virtus)* is the perfection of the powers of the soul. The soul has a twofold end. One consists in the perfection of man's natural powers, the speculative and moral virtues. The other, a vision of God in eternal life, can be achieved only by the infusion of the theological virtues of faith, hope, and charity by the grace of the Holy Spirit.[25] The cultivation of man's natural powers is the main concern of secular government. The pursuit of his supernatural end is the main concern of ecclesiastical government. In this Christian view, however, the former activity depends on the latter: man cannot perfect his natural virtues without supernatural assistance.

Following Aristotle, Aquinas identifies the speculative virtues as wisdom, science, and understanding. His list of moral virtues, however, is the Platonic four (from which Aristotle developed his list of ten): prudence (practical wisdom), fortitude, temperance, and justice. The virtues are themselves related in an inclusive hierarchy. Among the speculative virtues wisdom obtains "the highest place," "for it contains beneath itself both understanding and science, as judging both of the conclusions of sciences and of the principles on which they are based." Among the moral virtues, prudence, which is wisdom in its practical aspect, is the "directing principle" of the other moral virtues. Moreover, "since man is a political animal," the four moral virtues are called "political virtues; since it is by reason of them that man deports himself well in the conduct of human affairs." For the ruler, prudence, "the virtue which commands," is the primary virtue.[26]

By nature men have no virtue in perfection but only the ability to acquire that perfection. While all persons need training to fulfill their potential, they are, however, not born equal in this regard. A disposition to virtue is common to human nature, according to Aquinas. "But," he continues, "since such a disposition has a certain latitude, it happens that different degrees of this disposition are becoming to different men in respect of the individual nature."[27] From this difference it follows that some have greater need of training and direction than others, and that some will be better suited to give that training and direction. For Aquinas, as for Aristotle, this inequality in disposition is by nature. It would obtain, even in a state of innocence. For, since he is "a social being," man "in the state of innocence would have a social life." But since the "many, as such, seek many things," they must have "the governance of one," if they are to have a social life. Fortunately, moreover, they are unequal, some surpassing others in "knowledge and justice"; hence, there are by nature persons with superior powers who can govern for the "common good."[28] The problem of pluralism is solved by the hierarchy of virtue.

Government, in short, is necessary regardless of the Fall. This subjection is not a "servile" subjection by which a superior makes use of a subject for his own private good but a kind of subjection "whereby the superior makes use of his subjects for their own benefit and good; and this kind of subjection existed even before sin. For the good of order would have been wanting in the human family if some were not governed by others wiser than themselves." Echoing Aristotle, Aquinas gives this example: "So by such a kind of subjection woman is naturally subject to man because in man the discernment of reason predominates."[29] So for Aquinas as for Aristotle, authority and deference are natural. Simple finitude—the less inclusive being of some members of the human species—provides a ground for government.

And so far as the order of nature prevails, this natural hierarchy works harmoniously.[30] God governs the universe by the eternal law. As a rational being, man participates in the eternal law by "the light of natural reason whereby we discern what is good and what is evil, which is the function of the natural law." From "the precepts of the natural law," the rulers of men proceed to "particular determinations, devised by human reason," which are called "human laws."[31] By such human laws, the wise lead the less wise toward the perfection of the virtue of which they are capable. Developing Aristotle's dictum that the "intention of every lawgiver is to make men good," Aquinas says that "the proper effect of law is to lead its subjects to their proper virtue."[32]

The fall of man, however, has introduced a certain disharmony into this scheme, which leads to a further function for the secular ruler. Now, because of human perversity, there is need not only for guidance but also for coercion. The law, accordingly, has two functions: it is "a rule of human acts," but also "it has coercive powers." In consequence, "the righteous and virtuous" are subject to the law only in the first sense, since "the will of the good is in harmony with law."[33] For "in the good," writes Aquinas, "besides the natural knowledge of what is good, there is the added knowledge of faith and wisdom; and, again, besides the natural inclination to what is good, there is the added interior motive of grace and virtue."[34] In the case of "the wicked," however, "the natural inclination to virtue is corrupted by vicious habits, and moreover, the knowledge of what is good is darkened in them by passions and habits of sin."[35] To restrain "by force and fear" those who are "dissolute and prone to vice," the secular ruler wields the material sword of physical coercion. He does so for two reasons: so that they will "leave others in peace" and so that they may become habituated "to do willingly what hitherto they did from fear, and thus become virtuous." The preservation of "domestic tranquility" by coercion is not the only purpose of human law. For those who would be vicious, as for those who would be virtuous, the law of secular authority has an educative value.

In the Thomistic system, the natural law alone cannot account for or sustain an ordered society. For fallen man cannot follow its dictates without the further illumination and motivation of the Christian faith. Outside the Christian community, not even the limited ends of natural man, the perfection of the moral and speculative virtues, can be achieved. Man's last end, moreover, is not the perfection of these natural virtues but rather a vision of God by which men become "partakers of the divine nature."[36] This ultimate purpose is the foundation of the authority of ecclesiastical government. It also further amplifies and elevates the functions of secular government.

No man by his own effort can heal his corrupted nature and so perfectly conform his will to the law of sacrificial love as to merit eternal happiness.[37] If and when this transformation of his nature takes place, it is by the free and unmerited grace of God effected through the Holy Spirit. "Man by his will does works meritorious of eternal life," wrote Aquinas, but only if "prepared with the grace of God."[38] By this gift of sanctifying grace (*gratia gratum faciens*; literally, "grace that makes pleasing"), Aquinas says, "man himself is united with God," being thereby "justified" and "made worthy to be pleasing to God."[39] By grace men become "partakers of the divine nature." Thanks to this increase in being, they acquire new powers, the infused virtues of faith, hope, and charity, which direct them to their "supernatural happiness."[40]

Most versions of Christian doctrine accept the notion that salvation can be achieved only through free grace. They often differ, however, over how that grace is bestowed. For medieval Christianity sanctifying grace was dispensed solely through the sacerdotal priesthood, that authority being derived from Christ's commission to his disciples when, after the resurrection, as reported in John 20:12, he breathed upon them and said: "Receive ye the Holy Ghost: whosoever sins ye remit, they are remitted unto them; and whose soever sins ye retain, they are retained." From the early centuries of the Christian era, it was believed that sinful man could be redeemed by Christ only through the mediation of the priesthood (sacerdotium). Only by submission to its teaching and discipline and by partaking of the sacraments, above all Communion, under its administration could the believer hope for the possibility—he could not have the certainty—of redemption.[41]

In the system of ecclesiastical government erected on the basis of these beliefs, as in secular government, hierarchy prevailed, and authority and deference defined the relation of the various orders. As between the clergy (ordo clericalis) and the laity (ordo laicalis), the line between ruler and ruled was even sharper than in the secular realm. The clergy were self-perpetuating, priests being properly ordained only by bishops who themselves had been consecrated by other bishops in the direct line of apostolic succession. By the rite of ordination, sacramental grace (gratia sacramentalis) was conferred on the priest. This rite imprinted an indelible character (character indelibilis) on his soul, adding to it the powers to consecrate, offer, and administer the body and blood of Christ and to prepare the faithful for its reception by the other sacraments and by instruction and guidance in matters of faith and morals.

Knowledge of the faith, which, surpassing natural reason, must reach man through divine revelation, descends to man hierarchically. For, says Aquinas,

> divine revelation reaches those of lower degree through those who are over them, in a certain order; to men, for instance, through the angels, and to the lower angels through the higher, as Dionysius explains. In like manner, therefore, the unfolding of faith must needs reach men of lower degree through those of higher degree. Consequently, just as the higher angels, who illumine those who are below them, have a fuller knowledge of divine things than the lower angels, as Dionysius states, so too, men of higher degree, whose business it is to teach others, are under obligation to have a fuller knowledge of matters of faith, and to believe them more explicitly.[42]

Priests who are placed over others with care of souls must "know what the people have to believe and fulfill in the law" and the higher priests, or bishops, most know "even those points of law which may offer some difficulty, and to know them more perfectly according as they are in a higher position."[43] "Private individuals," wrote Aquinas, " . . . have no business to decide matters of faith."[44]

From the Thomistic viewpoint, ecclesiastical rulers, like secular rulers, knew what was good for the ruled. The priest's knowledge of divine law enabled him to instruct believers in what the faith required them to believe.[45] By their own unaided efforts they could not discover the divine truth, nor recognize it if it were presented to them. Once inducted into the congregation of the faithful, however, they would, thanks to their faith, recognize the authority of the priest and accept the truth of what he taught. Sometimes, they refused their deference. In that case, the priesthood had the right and the duty to judge them and to administer discipline, including denial of access to the sacraments.

These punishments, although only spiritual, may seem sufficiently coercive for believers. Some transgressions, however, required the intervention of the material sword of the secular ruler. Heresy was such a transgression. Aquinas echoed the received opinion when he pronounced this logical but severe judgment:

> Heresy is a sin which merits not only excommunication but also death, for it is worse to corrupt the Faith which is the life of the soul than to issue counterfeit coins which minister to the secular life. Since counterfeiters are justly killed by princes as enemies to the common good, so heretics also deserve the same punishment.[46]

The medieval ruler based his claim to authority not only on the secular law of his realm but also on the grace of God, as signified by sacred unction at the time of his coronation. His duties were, accordingly, to wield the material sword in order to maintain "domestic tranquility" and promote virtue among his subjects, but also and above all to defend the faith. Liberty of conscience, which for republican theory was the sphere most protected against government intervention, was in terms of the medieval ideal the sphere where orthodoxy was most fully articulated and most severely enforced by spiritual and secular authority. The contrast appears vividly in Milton's exclamation: "Give me the liberty to know, to utter, and to argue freely according to conscience, above all liberties."[47]

Federalism from the Top Down

In his *Summa Theologica,* as in most of his other writings, Aquinas is concerned with "sacred science," not political science. Yet Aquinas's conception of God and His Creation and their interrelations is pervaded by a concern with government. Having created the world, God, according to Aquinas, continues to sustain and govern it by his divine providence. Indeed, "government," he says, "is providence itself."[48]

In the treatise on divine government, Aquinas first takes up "The Government of Things in General."[49] There he sets forth the principles by which God governs the world and which *a fortiori* are also the principles by which man, as a rational creature made in God's image, also does and ought to govern. Asking "whether the world is governed by one," he states the case for monarchy as the best form of government. Unity, he affirms, is necessary for being, since without it a thing could not exist; therefore, "a ruler over a multitude" will aim at "unity, or peace." The question then is whether the rule of one or of several would better accomplish this end. Since "what is one in itself is a more apt and better cause of unity than several things united," concludes Aquinas in an empirical vein, "a multitude is better governed by one than by several."[50] The ontological aspiration to perfection lends further support to the monarchic ideal. Asking whether God governs immediately or through others, Aquinas concludes that "He governs some things by means of others."[51] In consequence the existence of such governors adds a certain perfection to the cosmos, since "it is a greater perfection for a thing to be good in itself and also the cause of goodness in others." In this light the governing function is seen not only as a necessary condition for the being of the many but also as the ground of an increase of being in the governors themselves. Thus, the rule of one at various levels of the cosmos contributes to that realization of all possible being which perfects the created world.

At various places Aquinas repeats and amplifies his general argument in favor of monarchy. As we have seen, in the *Summa Theologica* he finds that even in a state of innocence "a social life cannot exist among a number of people unless under the governance of one to look after the common good; for many, as such, seek many things, whereas one attends only to one."[52] Again, in the preliminary observations to his treatise on kingship, Aquinas lays out the necessity for the rule of one, if "the common good of the many" is to be achieved. He illustrates and substantiates his argument by the organic analogy, observing that "in the individual man, the soul rules the body; and among the parts of the soul, the irascible and concuscipible parts are ruled by reason. Likewise, among the members of a body, one, such as the heart or the head, is the principal and moves all the others." And, emphasizing that "every natural governance is the governance of one," he cites the age-old analogy of the beehive where "there is one king [sic] bee," as "in the whole universe there is one God, Maker and Ruler of all things."[53]

When Aquinas talks general principles, his monarchism is unqualified. In his occasional discussion of institutions, he may sometimes seem to stray from the cosmic model. The main question is whether he favored constitutional government in the sense of a mixed regime with a balance of powers.

Certainly Aquinas was a constitutionalist in his consistent advocacy of the rule of law. Even God Himself was subject to the eternal law in that it was impossible for him to deviate from that law, which was his essential being. The governors of mankind, temporal or spiritual, were similarly bound by the natural and divine law. In consequence, according to Aquinas, if a king makes a human law which "in any point . . . departs from the law of nature, it is no longer a law but a perversion of law." Does then a human law bind the king who made it? In one sense, yes; in another, no. Such law, says Aquinas, has two aspects. To its "directive force" *(vis directiva)* as a "rule of human acts," the king is subject in that he should obey the law voluntarily. From its "coercive force" *(vis coactiva)*, however, the king is exempt, since "no man is coerced by himself, and the law has no coercive power save from the authority of the sovereign." In that sense, the king is *legibus solutus:* "none is competent to pass sentence on him."[54]

What remedy, if any, do subjects have when their ruler deviates from the precepts of the natural or the divine law? If the king has ruled against "human good," passive resistance may be an option, since such laws "do not bind in conscience"; if they are contrary to divine law they "must in no way be observed."[55] In the treatise on kingship, Aquinas—if we may conclude that he is the author[56]—goes even farther toward a right of revolution. In some circumstances the community may depose their ruler, now no king but a tyrant, and "raise up" another, acting, however, not as private persons but "by public authority"—which Aquinas leaves undefined.[57] This right of deposition depends upon there being a "covenant" between the king and his subjects which the king has broken. Otherwise, the oppressed subjects can only appeal to a higher authority on earth (if there be one), or in heaven.

Such qualifications do not affect the monarchic principle but merely legitimate occasions when a new monarch may be put in place of an old one who has gone bad. Aquinas takes no generous view of these occasions. In the treatise on kingship his preference for the rule of one is so pronounced, even as compared with aristocracy, that although he grants that monarchy may degenerate into tyranny, he finds the rule of the corrupt tyrant preferable to the rule of corrupt aristocrats.[58]

To defend the rule of law by legitimizing passive resistance or occasional uprisings against intolerable tyranny does not take us very far toward a theory of constitutional balance of powers, let alone self-government. In the treatise on law, Aquinas does grant that popular government is possible. Law-making, he says, may belong to "the whole people" as well as to "a public personnage who has care of the whole People." At a later point he also considers the case of a people who are "free, and able to make their own laws" and who can, accordingly, abolish the law made by their sovereign "who has not the power to frame laws, except as representing the people." But Aquinas does not evaluate the republican alternative. Indeed in his famous definitions of law (*lex*) he omits it entirely, declaring law to be "a dictate of practical reason emanating from the ruler who (*in principe qui*) governs a perfect community" or "an ordinance of reason for the common good promulgated by him who (*ab eo qui*) has the care of the community."[59]

In a classification of the forms of government by which laws may be made, however, he abruptly lays down a proposition that contradicts head-on the hierarchical norm. Claiming to follow Aristotle, he mentions monarchy, aristocracy, oligarchy, democracy, and tyranny and then concludes without further explanation: "There is another type of regime blended of the others *(regimen ex istis commixtum),* and this is the best, and provides law as Isidore understands it, namely that *which men of birth together with the common people have sanctioned*" *(quam majores natu simul cum plebibus sanxerunt).*[60] That evaluation strikingly departs from his usual preferences. One might well imagine that Aquinas is turning away from Platonic and Aristotelian and toward Stoic and Ciceronian doctrine.

Aquinas does not, however, give a connected account of what he means by the mixed regime until at a later point in the treatise on law he sets out his favorable appraisal of the government of Israel under the Old Law.[61] The passages in Exodus, Numbers, and Deuteronomy dealing with the Mosaic regime are among the few places in Scripture where institutions of government get much attention. The references are scattered and often ambiguous. Aquinas further confirms his hierarchical preference by avoiding the more democratic reading.

He does begin with the startling assertion that "all should take some part in government" and goes on to find in the Mosaic regime a government with elements of monarchy, aristocracy, and democracy. We soon learn that a share in law-making for the people or a coercive check on the monarch is not what he had in mind. The best form of government," he writes, "is in a state or kingdom, where one is given the power to preside over all, while under him are others having governing powers." In this system, "the chief ruler," who "rules over all," was chosen not by the people (as in the treatise on kingship), nor indeed by any human agency, but directly by God Himself. "The Lord," says Aquinas, "did not leave even the choice of a king to the people, but reserved this to Himself."

The aristocratic element—those with "governing powers" under the king—were the "seventy-two . . . elders in virtue." (Actually the figure given in Numbers 11:24 is seventy.) According to Aquinas, the scheme was "partly democratic" in that these subordinate rulers were chosen "from all the people" and "by the people."[62] Yet as he also notes, it was Moses who "appointed them rulers." Moreover, by divine law, they were to be "wise men such as fear God . . . who may judge the people at all times."[63] Revealingly, Aquinas reads this divine command as support for the hierarchical principle that "those who excel in intellect are naturally rulers" and that "the fool shall serve the wise."[64] In so far as the people had a voice in choosing their rulers, their function was not to govern themselves but to recognize those whose wisdom and virtue qualified them to govern.

More revealing still is that in giving the number of subordinate rulers, Aquinas prefers the very small figure in Numbers rather than the many thousands indicated by the passage in Exodus on which he otherwise largely depends. The larger number, coming to some eighty thousand, would have greatly extended the social range and extent of participation—for which reason, incidentally, it was emphasized by political radicals during the Puritan revolution.[65]

Whatever their number, these subordinate rulers of the Mosaic regime had against the divinely appointed chief ruler no independent authority of a veto, such as the refusal to "sanction" the laws he proposed. On the contrary, they received their authority from him. Yet Aquinas indicates that their presence limits the "full power" of "kingly authority."[66] Aquinas does not expand on his meaning, but a moment's reflection on the principles of the system suggests how subordinates such as the judges in the Mosaic regime might have a degree of autonomy against higher authority. That would follow from the fact that, as we have seen, the exercise of their distinctive virtue is a necessary condition of cosmic plenitude. In the Thomistic system such a requirement is a normative, though not a coercive, limit upon interference from above. The chief ruler gives the law to his subordinate rulers, but the rulers must be allowed to fulfill their office. There is a kind of federalism from the top. This imposes some limits on direct rule by the chief ruler and creates a sphere of autonomy for the subordinate and for the community that he rules. He does not have a veto over acts of his superior, or a share in the office of his superior, or a power to "sanction"—that is, to approve or disapprove—the law entrusted to him for application by his superior. The limit on the superior is imposed on him from on high. It is not a popular restraint enforced from below. There is no balance of powers in regard to law-making. In this "best form of government," the cosmic norms of authority and deference are faithfully respected.

The Enchanted World

In the Thomistic system, the rule of one was as right in spiritual as in temporal affairs. In addition to the power of order *(potestas ordinis)*, the organization of the body of believers *(congregatio fidelium)* also depended upon another source of authority, the supreme jurisdictional power of the pope. This *potestas jurisdictionis* was also said to have a scriptural foundation, originating in Christ's words conferring the "power of the keys" upon the first bishop of Rome, as recorded in Matthew 16:18, 19. Some contended that this power of binding and loosing was given not solely to Peter, but to all the apostles and that therefore "all bishops are equal."[67] Aquinas rejected this view not only by authority of Scripture but also by philosophical argument. Citing Aristotle, he argued that "wherever there are several authorities directed to one purpose there must needs be one universal authority over the particular authorities," and he concluded magnificently:

> Now the common good is more Godlike than the particular good. Wherefore above the governing power which aims at a particular good there must be a universal governing power in respect of the common good, otherwise there would be no cohesion toward the one object. Hence since the whole Church is one body, it behoves, if this oneness is to be preserved, that there be a governing power in respect of the whole Church, above the episcopal power whereby each particular Church is governed, and this is the power of the Pope.[68]

That resounding inference is a nice summary of Aquinas's cosmology and methodology and suggests how the methodology is derived from the cosmology. That methodology includes reasoning by analogy. If we look into the way Aquinas uses analogy, we will see how deference arises in his system and its contrast with consent in republican theory.

In the passage quoted Aquinas sets forth an empirical argument that would appeal to common sense in any age. Since there are many bishops, says Aquinas, there must be one governing authority in order to maintain the cohesion of the church. Who but the most radical anarchist would disagree? Aquinas, however, does not consider the possibility that the bishops might by some institutional means constitute the supreme governing authority. He rules out self-government. The ultimate governing authority must be one person who is "above" the bishops.

The ground for that conclusion is an argument by correspondence. The common good, we learn, is upheld against the particular goods by a "Godlike" power. Since God is One, the analogy implies that therefore governance on other planes of being should also be one. Argument by correspondence was a common mode of rational demonstration in medieval thought. It is a kind of reasoning by analogy. Thus, in the "angelic analogy," medieval political theorists argued that because the angels were ordered by degree, therefore government in state and church should also be hierarchical.

To argue by analogy is to reason from particular to particular. It has two phases. Its initial phase is the perception of similarity between two things, for example, that the pope is Godlike. In this respect reasoning by analogy is like poetry. For a nominalist, such a figure of speech would exemplify not rational demonstration but literary adornment. When, for instance, Hobbes said that factions in the body politic are like worms in the entrails of the natural man, he meant this not as a similitude but as a simile to make more vivid his statement of what he thought was a general law of political behavior. For Aquinas, however, to perceive such an identity in difference is to grasp an important fact. To see that the pope is Godlike is to grasp a truth about the relation between the pope and the deity. The perception is poetic. It is a metaphor, not a concept. But for the essentialist, poetry is truth because the structure of reality is metaphorical. The essence that makes the two things similar is really present in both, making possible their existence.

Moreover, as the mind moves by analogy from one plane of being to another, its grasp of essence is enlarged and made more universal. To move intellectually by perceptions of similarity *(similitudines)* is to rise in knowledge of the scale of being toward knowledge of the

Perfect Being. By study of God's created world we can come to know Him and can move closer to Him.

According to this outlook, if we want to explain something—to know why something is what it is—we will try to comprehend its place in the scale of being. The pope is what he is because he is Godlike, in a degree created and sustained in God's image by divine providence. Other kinds of information, for example, how some pope came to be elected, or how the institution of the papacy developed, do not answer the important questions. Similarly, the peasant may know how to make hay for his cattle. But the knowledge that counts is the knowledge that enables the philosophical mind to understand how the provision of such herbage fits into the divine plan of cosmic interdependence.[69] In such an explanation the mind grasps the poetic similitudes by which all being is ordered.

The use of analogy is common in modern scientific inquiry. Often a puzzle in one field is lit up by perception of similarities in another field. The resulting hypothesis can then be checked out for confirmation or disconfirmation in the latter context and in further contexts. Thus, the modern political scientist could look at the general conclusion Aquinas draws from his discussion of intellectual and operative powers as such an hypothesis—a very broad one, to be sure—for further testing. He would be interested in the analogy only because it suggested the hypothesis of a universal law. In itself the analogy would have no value for him.

Aquinas's concern would be just the opposite. For him the universal law would be of value principally as a means to something more important. There is an empirically scientific aspect to Aquinas's thought. In contrast with modern science, however, it is limited and secondary. It is limited in that Aquinas's overwhelming concern is the pursuit of an aesthetic and consummatory grasp of the providential ordering of the world. It is secondary in that the acquisition of such conceptual empirical knowledge is only a means to further advance in that primary inquiry, in which the philosophic mind by its perception of similitudes moves up the ladder of being from particular to particular toward a fuller appreciation of divinity. Since the nature of reality is metaphorical, the poetic knowledge of the similitudes is the kind of knowledge that counts. Such knowledge is the truth— quite literally, the truth that saves.

It was an enchanted world. A thing was never only what it seemed to be but was also an emblem of higher things. Language, therefore, could not be univocal but was inherently ambiguous, its symbolic meanings, indeed, being more important than its literal meanings. The enchantment, however, lay not just in this poetic interpenetration of orders but also and especially in the power of the ambiguity of appearances, like the sorcerer's spell, to transport the human spirit into other realms of being. Upon the rise of science and capitalism inevitably followed, in Schiller's haunting phrase, "the disenchantment of this world."[70]

Deference to the Divine Likeness

By similitude also the inferior is moved to appreciate the elevation and therefore to accept the authority of the superior mind.

In the Thomistic system, the individual of lesser degree can be brought by the proper training and discipline to understand and to accept the good pertaining to his station *(bonum proprium)* and to the practice of virtue appropriate to its performance. He cannot achieve the wisdom necessary for rulership nor, *a fortiori,* grasp the idea of the common good *(bonum commune)* into which his particular good fits. Therefore, as Aquinas repeatedly asserts, in human society there must be a separate power which fits the particular goods of the parts into the common good of the whole. The ruled need their rulers.

But how do the members of the lower orders know this? How do they arrive at that truth? In the Thomistic polity, the evil submit out of fear of punishment. The good, however, consent voluntarily to the rule of the wise and the holy. We must look more closely at this process because republican theory introduced a radically different idea of consent.

One possibility is that all members of the community have access by virtue or grace to the truth about the common good and that, therefore, the ruled consent because they already agree with what their rulers require of them. If this were the case, all members of the community could contribute to the determination of the common good and all would accordingly be entitled to take part in government. This is the republican, indeed the democratic, option. It violates the universal law of hierarchy and is obviously not what Aquinas had in mind.

For Aquinas, the ruled consent to the dictates of prince or priest not because they grasp the substance of those dictates. They consent rather because they recognize the legitimacy of the source of those dictates. Recognizing that their ruler, natural or supernatural, has access to a realm of truth and goodness that is quite beyond them, the ruled defer to his determination of fact and value, secular or sacred. How this comes about is best seen in Aquinas's account of ecclesiastical government. According to that account, the faithful are brought to accept the authority of the priest not by the substance of the divine message he brings but by his proof of his authority to deliver it. There are two ways in which the priest may win such deferential consent: by personal charisma and by charisma of office—in Aquinas's terms, by gratuitous grace or by sacramental grace.[71]

The gift of gratuitous grace (*gratia gratis data;* literally, "grace freely bestowed") is "bestowed on a man, beyond the capability of nature, and beyond the merit of the person . . . not to justify him, but rather that he may cooperate in the justification of another."[72] Thanks to this gift, the priest, while he cannot actually "cause another to be united to God," can cause "certain dispositions toward it." In order to do this he must have "the fullness of knowledge of divine things." If, however, he is to persuade others to accept this truth, he must "be able to confirm or prove what he says, or otherwise his words would have no weight." Such confirmation cannot be by argumentation, as in matters that are "within reason." Rather since the knowledge he wishes to impart is "above reason," its confirmation must rest on "what is proper to divine power." Aquinas then lists the gratuitous graces which enable the priest to offer such proofs. They are those same "varieties of gifts" (*charismata*) set forth by Paul in his first letter to the Corinthians: the working of miracles, prophecy, the discerning of spirits, speaking in tongues, and the interpretation of speeches.[73]

By the exercise of such a gift, "the teacher of sacred doctrine does what God alone can do," or "manifests what God alone can know" and thereby establishes his authority as guide and teacher and wins over his listeners to the faith. A classic illustration is Saint Paul's blinding of the sorcerer during his mission to Cyprus, as recounted in the Acts of the Apostles 13:6–12. Personal charisma of this kind, however, is exceptional. Ordinarily the ceremonies of divine worship are the means by which ecclesiastical authority is established and acceptance of its precepts won. The priest receives the capability to perform these ceremonies by the sacramental grace *(gratia sacramentalis)* conferred on him by ordination. Such a power is a gift of grace, but it is a gift attached not to his person but to his office.

Like the behavioral proofs of personal charisma, the ceremonies which only the priest can perform also "reveal the things of God" and turn the soul of the beholder toward Him. Indeed, Aquinas, following Dionysius, says that "the things of God cannot be manifested to man except by means of sensible likenesses." Moreover, "these likenesses move the soul more when they are not only expressed in words . . . as in the case of metaphorical expressions [parables?] . . . but also offered to the senses . . . [and] set before the eyes," as in the ceremonies of divine worship.[74]

Simply to teach the divine law that vests the priesthood with its authority does not in itself win acceptance of that authority. As Aquinas says, "the Gospel does not always cause men to believe in it."[75] It is the ritual of divine worship which leads the beholder to accept that authority, to whose teaching and administration of the law he then willingly defers. These ceremonies have that effect, moreover, because they are likenesses of the divine truth. They acquire their power to move the soul not by arbitrary dictate or mere association. They must be properly designed so that they may act as "rays of divine light," illuminating the soul of the beholder and drawing him toward God.[76]

There is what one might call a science of symbolism, which Aquinas discusses at great length and which explains why certain material things or acts have the properties that enable them to convey the right spiritual sense—as, for instance, the ceremonial uses of water, oil, and wine are similitudes of Christ's spiritual cleansing, healing, and enlivening.[77] Therefore, according to Aquinas, because they signify higher things, the ceremonies of both the Old and the New Law have "a reasonable cause in their relation to something else."[78] These things, as divine truth, are "above reason"; yet the similitudes of divine worship can move the human mind toward them. To behold these ceremonies and to be moved by them is a kind of reasoning by analogy which persuades the beholder to accept the authority of the priest and the truth of his message. As Saint Augustine said, "For my part I should not believe the Gospel, except as moved by the authority of the Catholic Church."[79]

Deference to the authority of secular rulers is similarly won. In general "man's tendency is to reverence less those things which are common" in contrast with "those things which are distinct from others in some point of excellence." By including "a special abode, special vessels and special ministers," the external worship of God inclines men to reverence for God. Similarly, "it is customary among men for kings and princes, who ought to be reverenced by their subjects, to be clothed in more precious garments, and to possess vaster and more beautiful abodes."[80]

In the Thomistic system, in sum, the governed consent to government, not because they understand the truth and goodness of the law, but because they recognize the authority of the law-giver. They recognize that authority because of the personal charisma or charisma of office demonstrated by the ruler. Their consent is the passive consent of deference, not the active consent of self-government.

Old Tory Politics

Our concern is with the influence not of Aquinas but of the idea of hierarchy that his thought so richly exemplifies. Carried forward by many forces, ideal and material, that idea continued to display its power in succeeding generations. A few examples will illustrate the dominating influence against which modern republican thought had to contend and in contrast with which it defined itself.[81]

Toward the middle of the fifteenth century Nicholas of Cusa wrote what has been called the "most nearly complete exposition" of the theories of the conciliar movement.[82] Some modern historians have so read his work as to place him among the "champions of popular sovereignty" and the "ancestors . . . of Sidney and Locke."[83] Making use of ideas descending from Roman and ultimately Stoic sources,

Cusanus could indeed make such bold declarations as: "every ruler-ship . . . can come only from the agreement and consent of the subjects."[84] Not many pages later, however, he shows how much consent fits with and legitimizes authoritarianism: "by a certain natural instinct *(naturali quodam instinctu)* the rule of the wise and the subjection of the ignorant are brought into harmony by common laws of which the wise are the authors, protectors, and executors with the agreement of all the others, concurring to this in voluntary subjection."[85] "The rulers," comments Sigmund, "are chosen because of a natural or supernatural authority which has been recognized by and accepted by their subjects." Illustrating "the dominant tendency in ancient and medieval thought . . . to justify rulership on the basis of Platonic rationalism," he concludes, Cusanus's theory gives "consent . . . only a very secondary role." Accordingly Cusanus was able to switch from being a leader of the conciliar cause to support of papal supremacy with "no substantial alteration of his theory of the church."[86]

Early in the next century Sir Thomas Elyot, a royal official under Henry VIII, brought the political thought of Renaissance humanism to England in an immensely popular work, *The Book Named the Governor* (1531). What he wrote confirms Christopher Morris's conclusion that the Renaissance generally accepted without question from the Middle Ages the idea of the great chain of being.[87] The right political order reflects the cosmic hierarchy. As "God [has] set degrees and estates in all His glorious works," wrote Elyot, "so has He also given not to every man like gifts of grace or nature, but to some more, to some less." So derived, virtue, cultivated by a humanistic education, justifies authority in the state. Aristocracy and democracy are to be avoided. "As there is one God, one sun, one moon, and [yes!] one principal Bee among a hive," so correspondingly in human affairs "the best and most sure governance is by one king and prince." Excelling in virtue, this one sovereign governor, assisted by men of lesser virtue whom he appoints as inferior governors rules "only for the weal of his people."[88] Parliament is not mentioned.

A generation later, in spite of growing attacks from many quarters, the hierarchic tradition powerfully shaped what has been called "the Elizabethan world picture."[89] In *Troilus and Cressida* Shakespeare put into the mouth of Ulysses one of the most quoted renditions of the old outlook with its familiar blending of cosmic, moral, and political principles. "Degree" and "order" are its main themes. First, we learn, the cosmos itself is ordered by "degree":

> The heavens themselves, the planets, and this centre,
> Observe degree, priority, and place . . .

This same premise explains order and disorder in the social and political, as in the natural world:

> O, when degree is shak'd,
> Which is the ladder to all high designs,
> The enterprise is sick!

Thus, for both the order of nature and the order of man:

> Take but degree away, untune that string,
> And hark, what discord follows!   (I, iii, 85–110)

These ancient commonplaces were not accepted without question. In *Lear*, for instance, after Gloucester blames the heavens for his misfortunes, the cynical Edmund ridicules his father for sharing "the excellent foppery of the world" that makes "guilty of our disasters the sun, the moon, and the stars." Still, even here it is implied that these beliefs are widely held. And generally in the plays the analogical and causal connections of the various planes of the great chain of being provide grounds for both plot and poetry. Because "there is a divinity that doth hedge a king," his fall will be less likely and more tragic. A royal murder, as in *Macbeth,* disturbs both the heavens and the earth.

Since our concern is with the ideal barriers to republicanism, we may conclude this sampling from the later history of the hierarchic idea by looking at two official apologies for the old regime, one from an ecclesiastical, the other from a secular, source. Although commissioned by the bishops of a Protestant church, Richard Hooker's *Laws of the Ecclesiastical Polity* (1593 and later) reminds one of Aquinas on many points and was, indeed, warmly welcomed in Rome.[90] The ontology echoes the same old themes. God has created a perfect cosmos, which displays His "most glorious and most abundant virtue," and which has its beginning, its continuance, and its end in Him. In this "rank or chain of things voluntarily derived from the positive will of God," the principle of inclusive hierarchy orders all things from lesser to greater—stones, plants, beasts, men, and angels. "Natural agents," created things animate and inanimate, are "in degree of nature beneath man" and were "made for the use of man." Man has a special perfection. "By proceeding in the knowledge of truth, and by growing in the exercise of virtue, man amongst the creatures of this inferior world aspireth to the greatest conformity with God." And among men this perfection is realized in different degrees. As both Scripture and Plato agree, writes Hooker, by the love of wisdom, "wise men are thereby exalted above men."[91]

As for Aquinas, a fourfold law directs each order and each member of an order toward its perfection and the service of the perfect whole. As for Aquinas, Hooker's constitutionalism, his commitment to the rule of law, derives from his philosophy of being. Similarly again, one fundamental norm is hierarchy, without which there can be no order. "God keeps and requires this law," writes Hooker: "wheresoever there is a coagmentation of many, the lowest be knit to the highest by that which being interjacent may cause each to cleave unto other and so all to continue one . . . This order of things or persons in public societies is the work of polity." In the government of men, therefore: "If persons are ordered, they are distinguished by degree."[92]

Hooker finds an ontological foundation for aristocracy but, departing sharply from Aquinas, not for monarchy. He leaves the authority of the Tudor regime no less secure. In accounting for the origin of governments, like Aquinas, he makes use of a form of contract theory. He was far more explicit in stating the need for "common consent" and far more permissive in leaving the type of regime to the "arbitrary" choice of the society. By interpolating another step in the argument, however, he again showed the easy adaptability of contract theory to all manner of regime. Since "corporations are immortal," he reasons, once a "public society" has given its consent to a form of government, the commands of that government embody consent even if the original "composition and agreement" was made "five hundred years sithence." For Hooker the origin of government in consent implied no right of rebellion, as spokesmen among both Calvinists and Catholics were more and more vociferously asserting in his time. There is irony, not to say mockery, in his logic when he concedes its implication that the original consent may indeed be withdrawn—by "the like universal agreement."[93]

Having judiciously disarmed his opponents by granting their premise but avoiding their conclusion, he moves on with his vindication of the rule of the wise and the holy. The ontology of hierarchy is reconciled with the myth of consent by the necessity of deference. Far from denying the proposition, which he attributes to Aristotle, that "a kind of natural right [inheres] in the noble, wise, and virtuous, to govern them which are of servile disposition," Hooker argues that because "peaceable contentment" is "necessary" the assent of the governed should be given for "the manifestation of this their right." As ever, virtue justifies authority. For Hooker as for Aquinas, "laws do not only teach what is good, but they enjoin it; they have in them a certain constraining force." "Most requisite therefore it is that to devise laws which all men shall be forced to obey none but wise men be admitted." "Men of common capacity but ordinary judgment" should have no part in law-making."[94]

Needless to say, Hooker cannot follow Aquinas on the power of the pope. He must defend the rule of one as embodied in the royal supremacy over the national church. He does so, however, on pragmatic grounds—the need for a final judge—and, in accord with his aristocratic preferences, makes both Convocation and Parliament indispensable to law-making in church and state. "The parliament of England together with the convocation thereunto annexed," he declared, "is that whereupon the very essence of all government in this kingdom doth depend." Since for Hooker, as Faulkner observes, "laws should be devised by the wise," he concludes that "unto the care of ecclesiastical persons the care of devising ecclesiastical laws should be committed as the care of civil unto them which are in those affairs most skilful."[95] In Hooker's world, grace and virtue would still endow the few with authority over the many.

The first of the "execrable race of Stuarts" to rule Britain also found a transcendent ground for hierarchic authority in human affairs. Like Hooker, James I recognized that the "Body" of his kingdom, of which he was the "Head," was composed of "distinct ranks," of "all sorts of people," whom he addressed as "my faithful and loving subjects of all degrees."[96] Unlike Hooker, he emphasized the supreme legitimacy of the rule of one. Repeatedly in his speeches to parliament, echoing his formal writing on political theory, he defended his claim and his actions by the ancient similitudes. As conflict intensified, his rhetoric became more ideological. Proroguing the parliament in 1609, he lectured Lords and Commons in these words:

> The state of monarchy is the supremest thing on earth; for kings are not only God's lieutenants on earth and sit upon God's throne, but even by God himself, they are called Gods. There be three principal similitudes that illustrate the state of monarchy . . . In the scriptures kings are called Gods and so their power after a certain relation compared to the divine power. Kings are also compared to fathers of families . . . and lastly, kings are compared to the head of this microcosm of the body of man.[97]

In the early seventeenth century this pedantic but genuinely learned man could still think it persuasive to defend his claims on power by cosmic analogies and could consider it a kind of reasoning to infer that *because* God rules over the universe and the father over the family and the mind over the body, *therefore,* the king does and should rule over his people. As in past versions of the hierarchic tradition, the likeness consisted not only in legitimate power but also in its ground, a superiority in virtue. The king, wrote James in an early treatise, is "a lamp of godliness and vertue." "Above all vertues," he advised his fellow monarchs, "study to know well your own crafte, which is to rule your people." This royal craft, moreover, meant "know[ing] all crafts, for except ye know every one, how can ye control everyone, which is your proper office." For James, as for Aquinas and Aristotle, the hierarchy of virtue is inclusive.[98] In the light of this conception of his virtue and his office, we can better understand the force he put into his words when he warned this same troublesome parliament, which had challenged him on religion, taxation, and the proregative, "that you do not meddle with the maine points of Government; that is my craft . . . I must not be taught my office."[99]

It is sometimes said that James introduced novel claims to "absolute" power. Actually his claims do not differ a great deal from medieval theory and Tudor practice. If by absolutism we mean authority to rule according to the personal will of the prince, then James was no absolutist. "God," he declared, "placed him as his lieutenant over [the people] upon peril of his soul to procure the weal of both souls and bodies." He fully recognized that he was bound by the law of God. Indeed, his superiority in "vertue" embraced a deeper knowledge of that law. He did claim that, although a king was bound to obey the law of God, there was no earthly power that could punish or coerce him, if he did not obey it. In that sense he was *legibus solutus*. But, as we have seen, Aquinas said the same thing. As for a compact between people and king, James said different things at different times. He was consistent in denying any right of revolution, even against a tyrant.[100]

James was Protestant enough to call the pope Anti-Christ. But he was no follower of John Knox in matters of church organization. "Presbytery," he told the Puritan ministers at the Hampton Court conference in 1604, "agrees with a monarchy as well as God and the Devil."[101] And in his famous exclamation on that occasion, "No bishop, No king," he linked the fortunes of episcopacy and monarchy. In his theory of politics, as we have seen, however, it is monarchy, not episcopacy, let alone papacy, that is "the supremest thing on earth." He held it his first responsibility as king to care for the "weal of both souls and bodies" of his subjects. In discharging his higher duties, he continued to issue the writ *de haeretico comburendo,* although he was the last English monarch to do so. Combatting claims of papal spokesmen, he recalled in long and learned tracts how in times past emperors had deposed popes and received their submission as vassals.[102] Here he was replicating old controversies between the temporal and spiritual powers. The essential question in the seventeenth century as in those earlier centuries had nothing to do with self-government. The issue was which power—pope or emperor, prince or prelate—would have the primacy in a hierarchically ordered society.

Although ideas about the hierarchic nature of authority and its natural and divine foundation were widely shared, they did not save James from the encroaching claims of his increasingly aggressive parliaments. Under the Tudors the great questions of common good were the Crown's preserve, entrenched in its prerogative. At the opening of the parliament of 1571, the Lord Keeper, speaking the Queen's mind, warned the commons that "they should do well to meddle with no matters of state but such as should be proponed unto them."[103] During most of her reign, Elizabeth succeeded in denying to the commons the initiative in such "matters of state" as the religious settlement, the royal succession, and war and peace. By the end of her reign attempts to draw these questions into discussion by the house had been launched by what Neale calls "the Puritan Party."[104] Differences over Church doctrine and organization caused increasing friction. What parliament could and could not discuss became a major constitutional issue. A crisis was reached in 1621 when the commons asserted their "birthright" freely to discuss religion and related matters of state. In response the king dissolved parliament and tore the offending pages from their journal.[105]

As these apologies for the old regime revealed, the hierarchic tradition had been badly knocked about since the days of the serene synthesis of Saint Thomas. Yet the theory of Stuart monarchy set forth by James was still informed by the age-old principles of authoritative virtue and deferential consent. Their long-lasting power was a source of frustration and fury to the early English republicans. In February 1649, within a week of the execution of Charles I, an account of the king's last days, presumably written by him, was published in London under the title of *Eikon Basilike (The Royal Image)*.[106] A modern reader may well think that "its intellectual content is nil."[107] When one looks at this work from the viewpoint of the tradition of Western political thought, one can see how it might make a powerful appeal to ancient and honored sentiments. As the title suggests, the book called up the old associations of royalty and divinity, making the analogy between the King and Christ a central theme. Understandably, John Milton felt obliged to reply, which he did in *Eikonoklastes (The Image Breaker)*.[108] In spite of the violent rhetoric which that work unleashed against the ancient similitudes, the apology for the martyred king was an instant and enormous success, thirty-five editions being published in London within a year and twenty-five more elsewhere. Its popularity among

Englishmen of all classes was a major reason for Milton's disillusionment with "the common people," from whom he had originally expected wide support for the republican cause. As late as the mid-seventeenth century, in short, the hierarchic tradition in politics still flourished. Even a hundred years later and more, as we have seen, it was still strong enough in Britain to arouse the fear and sharpen the scorn of the young John Adams.

The medieval synthesis of classical and Christian thought locked Western man into political inequality by a double lock, one philosophical, the other religious. The key to each lock was the principle of inclusive hierarchy, or, if you prefer, Aristotle's principle of unilinear gradation. In each scheme, whether by natural virtue or divine grace, the ruler was endowed with powers of the soul that set him off from and over the ruled. The opposition of this scheme to the ideas of free thought, free government, and a free economy introduced by the republican theory was fundamental.

In the hierarchical tradition, both secular and ecclesiastical government enjoyed the consent of the governed, but it was the consent of deference, not self-government. In overturning the old outlook, the task of republicanism was to convert the passive consent of deference into the active consent of self-government. In accomplishing this, their practical task, the republican theorists advanced the subversive idea that the ordinary individual could contribute to the discovery of the common good by his own rational powers. This new moral individualism confronted republican theory with two great questions: how to establish authority over such individuals, and how to define the purpose of that authority in a world in which the standards themselves would be changing. Ultimately, the republicans found their answer to both questions in the concept of the nation. This new political entity, the nation, was at once the people as the source of authority and the people as the substance of history, whose perfecting was the purpose of that authority. The government it established was government of the people because it was both government by the people and government for the people.

That double work of destroying the old doctrines of virtue and grace and conceiving a new rationale for authority and purpose laid the intellectual foundations for the American republic. Many thinkers contributed to that outcome: Machiavelli and Montaigne, Copernicus and Galileo, Luther and Calvin, Bacon and Knox. It was, however, the Commonwealthmen of the seventeenth century who set forth the republican alternative that informed the great American break with the Western tradition.

CHAPTER 2

The Idea of the National Republic: John Milton

IF ONE IS LOOKING for the single work that most fully illuminates the breach between the republican and the hierarchic outlooks, it would be hard to make a more revealing choice than Milton's *Areopagitica*. In this famous tract the great champion of the Commonwealth in the field of thought scornfully rejects the rule of the wise and the holy. As an alternative he presents in essentials the idea of the national republic.

Areopagitica is not a treatise on political philosophy but a red-hot pamphlet against government intervention with the first freedom. The argument is laden with the specificities of time and place. Milton is mainly concerned with religious liberty of conscience. The scope he would allow free speech is far too narrow for a present-day liberal democrat, as are the boundaries he would set to the right to vote. Yet his argument conveys a message of liberation that has lived on and extended its influence over succeeding centuries as a rationale for popular government in a free society. For Milton's defense of liberty of conscience also makes the case for government by discussion[1] among the many as against government by the authority of the gracious and virtuous few.

If we are to get at his enduring thought, we need to take a close look at the text, unbraiding its knotted metaphors and cooling off its fiery prose. It will help to introduce the idea we are seeking to elucidate if we first look briefly at how it was used by a skeptical American of the twentieth century.

In his classic dissent in the Abrams case (1919), Justice Holmes found that even in time of war the Constitution severely limits the power of the federal government to interfere with the individual's right of free speech. Setting forth his interpretation of the First Amendment, he echoes the Miltonian argument:

> Persecution for the expression of opinions seems to me perfectly logical. If you have no doubt of your premises or your power and want a certain result with all your heart, you naturally express your wishes in law and sweep away all opposition . . . But when men have realized that time has upset many fighting faiths, they may come to believe even more than they believe the very foundations of their own conduct that the ultimate good desired is better reached by free trade in ideas—that the best test of truth is the power of the thought to get itself accepted in the competition of the market, and that truth is the only ground upon which their wishes safely can be carried out. That at any rate is the theory of our Constitution.[2]

Holmes was defending the right of free speech against the claims of the war-making power. He defended that right not merely as an individual right but especially as a necessity of government itself. In his view, government needs the truth because it needs to know what the wishes of the public are and how in a complicated social and natural world those wishes may be carried out. Truth is most likely to be reached not by the fiat of authority but by free debate among diverse opinions. Diversity of opinion, therefore, is not to be suppressed but welcomed as a condition for arriving at the truth. This reflection of seventeenth-century republicanism Holmes called "the theory of our Constitution."

In modern thought this political function of free speech and public debate has been perceived and appraised with favor by a long line of writers and leaders. They can be found in many countries and generations. In later pages we will look at what some of them said and did. The names of a few of the more notable will suggest the thrust of the analysis and the spread of its advocacy: on the British side, Harrington, Locke, Bentham, John Stuart Mill, Walter Bagehot; on the American side, Franklin, James Wilson, Madison, Jefferson; in France, Voltaire, Condorcet, Helvétius, Constant. In our own time the essentials of the analysis have been restated and put to use by political scientists who have shown how democratic policy-making can be a process of "social learning" in which outcomes are determined not by "the bumping of inpenetrable billiard balls of power, but by men who could learn and whose viewpoints could change."[3]

The Masterless Man

Although Milton's argument was wide-ranging and long-lived, the occasion for *Areopagitica* was quite specific. It was published in November 1644, two years after the outbreak of the civil war. The royalist members of both houses of parliament had followed the king to Oxford, and the government in London was now entirely in the hands of the men who had formed the opposition to Charles. Under their guidance the parliament in the previous year had ordered that all books and pamphlets be submitted to a board of licensers before being printed. This practice had been usual under Elizabeth and the Stuarts, and the powers of the board were much the same as those which the Star Chamber had given to the comparable body under Charles in defense of "the peace of the Church and State" against "divers libellous, seditious, and mutinous books." Alarmed by what it saw as "the great defamation of Religion and Government" which resulted from unlicensed printing, the parliament had simply adapted the old machinery of control and suppression to a different political and religious cause.[4]

Milton's tract was directed specifically at such previous censorship of printed matter. The premises from which he drew his conclusions were so broad, however, as to embrace principles radically opposed to the old hierarchic orthodoxies. The heart of the conflict was a new view of the individual. In the older view, the defining characteristic of man was that he could choose whether or not to abide by the truth, natural and divine. So also could man as Milton saw him. In Milton's view, the individual also could and should decide for himself what that truth is. As moral beings, our essential humanity is not merely to choose whether to obey the moral law but above all to choose the law to obey. In matters of religious belief, for instance, the Miltonian individual can and must make up his mind not only as to whether he will abide by the dictates of his faith but also as to what faith he will adopt. This view of the individual—his powers, rights, and duties—is the main premise of the argument in

Areopagitica for freedom of thought and expression. It is also the foundation for a theory of self-government which distributes widely throughout society the function of deciding on the common good and which holds that deliberation by the many is superior to the judgment of the few.

A concern with freedom of choice runs through the whole of *Areopagitica*. Near its start Milton, laying down the principles of his case, exclaims grandly: "Many there be that complain of divine Providence for suffering Adam to transgress. Foolish tongues! when God gave him reason, he gave him freedom to choose, for reason is but choosing."[5] With those words Aquinas would not disagree. In a similar vein in his treatise on man, Aquinas asks "whether man has free choice" and replies: "It is written (*Ecclesiasticus,* xv, 14) 'God made man from the beginning and left him in the hand of his own counsel' . . . That is, in the liberty of choice."[6]

The possession of this power, Aquinas goes on to explain, distinguishes man from other creatures of the sublunary world. For they act in accordance with the eternal law without judgment, as a stone moves downward, or without free judgment, as a sheep shuns the wolf from instinct. In contrast man chooses "from some act of comparison in the reason . . . and retains the power to be inclined to various things." "In that man is rational," he concludes, "it is necessary that he have free choice."

So far Aquinas and Milton agree. For each, "reasoning" is "choosing." It is when one asks how the individual gains his knowledge of the truth that their fundamental conflict appears. For Aquinas, as we have seen, that truth is made known to him by the wise and the holy. If the individual himself belongs to that order, there will always be some person within it possessing higher authority who will instruct him in the more universal demands of the truth. In the church, for instance, priests must "know what the people have to believe and fulfill in the law," and the bishops must know "even those points of law which may offer some difficulty and know them more perfectly according as they are in a higher position."[7]

Given this conception of how people ascertain the truth, as belief and as morality, it makes sense to conclude, as Aquinas did, that conformity should be backed with physical and spiritual coercions.

The demands of the truth, as the law of virtuous conduct, are known. Individuals who are good thanks to natural and supernatural causes choose to obey voluntarily, while those who are "prone to vice" may be rendered less vicious by the habits induced by the threat of punishment. Therefore, when we consider how the ignorant may be misled by false and immoral teachings, there is good reason to prevent such teaching by previous censorship. If there is a known truth, coercive action by state and church to protect it, as Justice Holmes acknowledged in the Abrams dissent, is a logical requirement of the common good, as defined by that truth.

In some passages Milton may seem to accept the premise of that conclusion—that there is known truth that needs to be maintained and strengthened. To start from this seeming agreement with Aquinas will help illuminate his basic disagreement.

Milton summarizes his case against previous censorship in two allegations directed against its bad effects: first, its "disexercising and blunting our abilities in what we know already," and second, its "hindering and cropping the discovery that might yet be further made both in religious and civil wisdom." He supports his first allegation with a plea for what he calls "the trial of virtue and exercise of truth." Emphasizing the moral aspect, he asks rhetorically, "What wisdom can there be to choose, what continence to forbear, without the knowledge of evil?" Then, after launching his contemptuous thrust against "a fugitive and cloistered virtue unexercised and unbreathed, that never sallies out and seeks her adversary," he declares that what "purifies us is trial and trial is by what is contrary." What "trial" is for virtue, "exercise" is for knowledge. So he concludes: "Since . . . the knowledge and survey of vice is in this world so necessary to the constituting of human virtue, and the scanning of error to the confirmation of truth, how can we more safely, and with less danger, scout into the regions of sin and falsity, than by reading all manner of tractates and hearing all manner of reason?"[8]

This line of thought was not entirely alien to Aquinas. Indeed, his method of inquiry hinged on confronting the known truth with its "contraries" and from this "trial" reconfirming that truth. In order to clarify and confirm the received opinion, Aquinas could examine the views of the heretic Pelagius or the Jew Maimonides, not to mention the views of pagan thinkers among contemporary Arabs or among ancient Greeks and Romans. Scholastic method would seem to follow the Miltonian rule: to take "what we know already" and by comparison and contrast to "exercise" and "sharpen" our ability to hold it.

To be sure, in Aquinas's day this method of inquiry was open only to members of the *studium,* its exercise by them, moreover, being subject to approval and correction by higher authority. In the treatise on law, Aquinas observes that while the natural law remains always the same, the human law by which it is applied to communities may be "justly changed." This may occur not only because conditions have changed but also because "it is natural to human reason to advance gradually from the imperfect to the perfect." And he cites the case of "the teaching of the early philosophers . . . that was afterwards perfected by those who succeeded them."[9]

According to Aquinas, however, human reason will err unless guided by faith.[10] Hence, the demonstrations of reason depend upon the revelations of faith and the advances of philosophy are limited by the dogmas of theology.[11] Yet, although the faith itself does not change, its "symbol," consisting of "collections of its truth," may be changed "in order to set aside the errors that may arise." Such change can be authorized only by the pope. "It belongs to the sole authority of the Soverign Pontiff," Aquinas declares, "to publish a new edition of the symbol, as do all other matters which concern the whole church, such as to convoke a general council, and so forth." Thus, reason advances according to its "nature," but subject to such inner guidance and external control.[12] The truths of the faith do not change, only their "symbol," and that only at the behest of the pope.

Are we to conclude then that the republican innovation represented by Milton was simply to free Thomistic "liberty of choice" from hierarchic authority, while leaving unchanged the substance of that liberty? This cannot be what Milton meant. For to eliminate authority over freedom of choice is radically to change the nature of choosing.

To the Thomistic believer, the known truth is known thanks to its acceptance by authority. To remove that authority over thought and expression is to deprive the believer of that knowledge. He will no longer have a known truth on which to practice the method of confrontation by "contraries." If he is to acquire such a truth, without the guidance of authority, old or new, he must rely on his own reasoning, as it may be enlightened by the reasoning of others. His choosing therefore is no longer merely deciding whether or not to accept the known truth but above all deciding what that truth is. The removal of authority over thought and expression for which Milton pleads fundamentally alters the nature of "reasoning" and "choosing."

Milton's first objection to censorship is that it blocks the individual's ability to confirm what he already knows. Yet if the individual is to make this trial in the absence of authority, he must already have ventured on the far more demanding task of judging what is true. Indeed, the two processes cannot be separated. When a person sets out on the first sort of exercise, he must consider the "contraries" on their merits. He must keep his mind open to the possibility that these opinions and not his current beliefs may have reason on their side. He cannot fail to consider that there may be other "contraries" against which he must test his opinion. In seeking to maintain old truth, he has embarked upon the task of discovering new truth. Milton's first objection to censorship merges with his second.

Milton elaborates this connection between the maintenance and the discovery of truth in an argument that leads to his theory of republican government. Declaring that he will "easily show" how censorship is "a step-dame to truth: and first, by disenabling us to the maintenance of what is known already," he writes:

> Well knows he who uses to consider, that our faith and knowledge thrive by exercise, as well as our limbs and complexion. Truth is compared in Scripture to a streaming fountain; if her waters flow not in a perpetual progression, they sicken into a muddy pool of conformity and tradition. A man may be a heretic in the truth; and if he believe things only because his pastor says so, or the Assembly so determines, without knowing other reason, though his belief be true, yet the very truth he holds becomes his heresy.[13]

The "heretic in the truth" is the person who because of censorship or his own failure of will has not engaged in "the trial of virtue or the exercise of truth" and who therefore lacks "the true knowledge of what we seem to know." As Milton's metaphor indicates, however, the known truth cannot be maintained without change but must like "a streaming fountain" flow in "a perpetual progression." Altering his metaphor and elaborating his thought, he writes: "The light which we have gained was given us, not to be ever staring on, but by it to discover onward things more remote from our knowledge."[14] To continue to look upon even the advanced truth we now possess, he warns, will make us "stark blind."

Truth itself impels us into a further search for truth; to halt inquiry is to lose what we have; we keep it only by further increase. Milton's individual not only chooses whether to abide by the known truth. He must also decide what that truth is. And, moreover, that choosing is also a seeking which tries continually to correct and amplify its grasp.

The truth that especially concerned Milton was religious truth. When he urged his readers: "To be still searching what we know not by what we know, still closing up truth to truth as we find it," he was laying down, he said, "the golden rule for theology." When attacking "heretics in the truth," he made their chief offense that they "post off to another . . . the charge and care of their religion." The truth that Milton sought to maintain was the truth brought by the Reformation. He saw that new truth itself leading toward further reformation which the old reformers, entrenched in the Westminster Assembly and the Presbyterian Parliament, were attempting to impede.[15]

That further reformation, however, was not conceived as narrowly concerned only with doctrine or worship in the church. For his times and certainly in his thought, the truths of religion penetrated widely and deeply into the secular realm. The advance he sought embraced both "religious and civil wisdom." Rejoicing over the removal of sacerdotal authority, he asked for further reform "as great" not only "in the Church" but also "in the rule of life both economical and political."[16] From the truth so conceived, opinions regarding the private good of the individuals and the common good of society were derived. To argue as Milton did that the individual could recognize and contribute to the discovery of the truth was also to give him a role in deciding on the common good. As an offshoot of the truth, that deciding was not only a choosing but also a constant "searching what we know not by what we know."

Government by Discussion

This new view of the individual leads to a new view of society, history, and government. Looked at in one way, Milton's individual is painfully isolated. He no longer enjoys the moral and intellectual security that came from the deference of his inferiors and the guidance of his superiors. Deprived of these vertical supports of the great chain of being, he confronts the enormous questions of belief and conduct, of good and evil, alone with his reason and his God. On the other hand, since his fellows have similar powers which they are exercising in the same quest, he can and must look to them for counsel. From this collateral intercourse with others he receives a kind of assistance that was rare in the world of Aquinas. In the England of his day Milton saw "the people, or the greater part, more than at other times, wholly taken up with the study of highest and most important matters to be reformed . . . disrupting, reasoning, reading, inventing, discoursing, even to a rarity and admiration, things not before discoursed or written of." In this "mansion house of liberty," he reported, "there be pens and heads . . . sitting by their studious lamps, musing, searching, revolving new notions and ideas" and "others as fast reading, trying all things, assenting to the force of reason and convincement."[17]

From "much desire to learn," he granted, there arose "of necessity . . . much arguing, much writing, many opinions." According to the centuries-old orthodoxy of the West, such diversity of thought and expression must lead to chaotic conflict in opinion and ultimately in behavior. A government which responded to this exuberant pluralism would not be effective. It could not achieve that "cohesion," that "unity, or peace" which Aquinas made a primary end of government. For Milton, however, this kinetic diversity is all to the good and is indeed a source of the superiority of government by the people. Given the partial and progressive nature of truth, "new notions and ideas" must be put forward if there is to be advance. Controversy will surely arise. The way to truth, however—to holding what is sound, purging old and rejecting new error, while advancing to wider and firmer knowledge—is not the method of authority but the method of free debate. For, declares Milton in a startling assertion which became an axiom of modern freedom, "though all the winds of doctrine were let loose to play upon the earth, so let Truth be in the field, we do injuriously by licensing and prohibiting to misdoubt her strength. Let her and Falsehood grapple; who ever knew Truth put to the worse, in a free and open encounter?"[18]

Liberty of conscience is first of all an individual right. It is also a social necessity. It is a right against society in so far as society tries to impede its exercise. It is also a right for society in that freedom of thought and expression provides society with something it profoundly needs—progress in the truth. Between the individual and society there is the opposition of polarity, not contradiction. Since no authority can certify the truth for the individual, he must rely on his own reason to ascertain the truth and judge the common good. Yet that same reason tells him that since others also enjoy this gift, he will need to know what they think. Their rational deliberation can test, correct, and amplify his conclusions, by which exchange he serves others while they also serve him.

If and as reason prevails, general agreement will arise. Not that consensus can last. The "light we have gained" is given us "to discover onward things more remote from our knowledge." We will be "searching that we know not by what we know." In conditions of Miltonian freedom, truth continually produces the criticism that displaces it. The polarity persists, renewed as it is overcome. That interdependence of individual and society, his need for society and its need for him, is expressed in the way Milton formulates his demand for liberty of conscience: "Give me the liberty to know, to utter, and to argue freely according to conscience, above all liberties."[19] The free thought and free debate that result from the exercise of this liberty will for the individual members of society heighten their grasp of truth and also bring them into agreement upon it.

Implicit in this defense of liberty of conscience are conceptions of authority and purpose which legitimate popular government. We will first look at the theory of republican authority and then at the purpose which this authority would serve.

At first glance the suggestion that a polity based on Miltonian principles can generate authority is implausible. The right, indeed, the duty of each individual to find the truth by which he will abide surely sounds like the negation of authority and the vindication of anarchism. And, needless to say, the right of private judgment is deeply rooted in Milton's thought and could in certain situations justify conscientious objection, resistance, or rebellion. At the same time, Milton had great admiration for the Englishmen of his day, not just as individuals but also as "the people . . . disputing, reasoning, inventing, discoursing." It was from their joint endeavor—preferably "one general and brotherly search after truth"—that he expected further reformation, ecclesiastical, economical, and political.[20] The polarity of individual and society has implications for the republican polity. For the same reason that the individual must seek counsel from his fellow citizens, he must also respect the outcome of free debate among them.

The problem can be focused if one asks: on what ethical grounds could a person who conscientiously dissented from the commands of the Miltonian republic feel obliged to obey them? The short answer is that whether or not he disagrees with this or that decision of government, he believes in the system—Justice Holmes would say "the constitution"—under which those decisions have been made. He believes that the people—freely speaking and writing, freely listening, reading, and criticizing—are more likely to get at the truth of a matter than any other claimant to authority. The people are not infallible. In Milton's world no one is. But the probabilities are on their side when they are compared with the old princes and prelates or the new presbyters and parliamentmen.

The main ground of this probabilistic claim for popular authority is the rational capacity displayed by the individual citizen in personal reflection and public debate. Paradoxically, moreover, that claim is strengthened by their very diversity of opinion. As Milton continually emphasizes, a wider spectrum of opinion can increase the chances of public judgment's reaching new and broader truth. He pleads with the parliament not to suppress "all this flowery crop of knowledge and new light sprung up and yet springing daily in this city." He deplores the contemporary "terrors of sect and schism," declaring that the "many opinions" result from the "desire to learn" and will lead to new knowledge, since "opinion in good men is but knowledge in the making." No Platonist ever took greater pleasure in the cosmic plenitude than Milton did in the abundance of "new notions and ideas" in his England.[21] But for him that diversity did not need to have order imposed upon it from above; it could create its own order from below. Milton's radical individualism can generate authority, thanks to government by discussion.

Elite and People

In *Areopagitica* Milton lays the foundation for a theory of government by the many. But how many? The answer has two aspects. One is the question of scale. The Miltonian republic would embrace a population consisting not of thousands, like the Greek city-states of ancient times, or the Italian republics of the Renaissance, but rather of the millions living in England in the mid-seventeenth century. Milton conceived free and rational debate as working itself out successfully in a forum on the scale of the modern nation-state. A republic based on Miltonian principles would be a national republic. That bold presumption, following from his perception of the power of free speech, is Milton's most original contribution to republican thought. To make it plausible one must specify the institutions which would enable so large a populace to govern itself effectively. That question will be the subject of the next chapter. Here we will consider a preceding question of principle: what fraction of this numerous population would actually have a part in governance? Milton has often been called an "aristocrat" or an "elitist." He himself said that new presbyter was old priest writ large. Would his new republic be in effect simply the old elite, only without pope or king?

In a brief reference to the Mosaic regime, Milton indicates a preference among forms of government. Unlike Aquinas, he does not find in that example an enduring model of the best regime. On the contrary, in place of the rule of "Moses, the great prophet," he proclaims that "now the time seems come . . . when not only our seventy elders, but all the Lord's people are become prophets."[22] For a Calvinist, however, that eventuality might mean only a slight quantitative advance toward republican rule. The term "the Lord's people" could refer to only those few who are predestinated to salvation—and who know it. In Calvin's theology, these are the elect—the knowing and visible saints.

The certainty of their knowledge of election is a crucial qualification. For John Calvin had departed from the sensible doctrine of Aquinas and his church that no man can be certain of salvation. Faith, he declared in a climactic annunciation, is "a steady and certain knowledge of the Divine benevolence toward us" *(une ferme et certaine cognoissance de la bonne volunté de Dieu envers nous).* He emphasized the certainty, referring to "confidence," "full assurance," "a full and fixed certainty."[23] And starting from this view of election, some Calvinists claimed for the saints a special authority in church and state to declare and enforce the laws of God laid down in Scripture.[24] Among Milton's Puritan contemporaries, the Fifth Monarchy men carried this claim to the extreme of imagining themselves the saints, whose rule, according to the Book of Revelations, would usher in the thousand-year reign of King Jesus.[25]

The premise of this politics, the certainty of election, was not, however, inherent in Reformation doctrine. There were always some Protestants who denied predestination of the few and thought that all persons shared equally in the grace of atonement.[26] Even when certainty was affirmed, the identity of the elect could be so qualified as to open wide the opportunity for dissenting opinion. For example, the Second Helvetic Confession of 1566, the most widely received statement of faith in the Reformation period, declared that although "here and there [in Scripture] mention is made of the small number of the elect, yet we must hope well of all, and not rashly judge any man to be a reprobate." In the spirit of *Areopagitica,* toleration of dissent was seen as a means to the manifestation of truth. For, continued the Confession, recalling that "there have at all times been great contentions in the Church," "it pleases God to use the dissensions that arise in the Church to the glory of his name, to illustrate the truth, and in order that those who are in the right might be manifest."[27]

Another notable statement of the Calvinist faith, while also affirming the predestination of the elect, explicitly ruled out certainty.

The Scots Confession of 1560, composed by John Knox and five associates, declared flatly that the church of the elect is "invisible, known only to God, who alone knows whom he has chosen." Inevitably, therefore, in the church "the reprobate may be found in the fellowship of the chosen."[28] This statement of faith was accepted by the Church of Scotland until 1647 when it adopted the confession drawn up by the Westminister Assembly, which, composed largely of Puritan ministers, had been called by the parliament in 1643 to reform church organization and doctrine. The new confession reaffirmed at length the belief in "the infallible assurance of faith."[29]

If election is unknowable, the rule of the knowing and visible saints is excluded and the way is paved for a broader toleration of religious belief. Liberty of conscience would be extended to all—the reprobate as well as the elect. A different route to the same result was taken by the Arminians. Denying the predestination of the elect, they held that Christ died not only for the elect but rather for all men. Redemption, therefore, depended not only on grace but also on free choice and, although all would not actually be saved, salvation was open to all. Not accidentally the adherents of Arminius belonged to the republican faction in Holland, and their views were taken up by republicans among English Puritans.[30] Milton was one of these. While not a pelagian or rationalist, Milton had moved toward the Arminian position by the time he wrote *Areopagitica,* as one might infer from his celebration of freedom of choice in "the trial of virtue" and "the exercise of truth." His republic would be ruled no more by a new than by the old priesthood.

Nor did he look to an aristocracy of natural virtue on classical lines for the rulers of his republic. Striking directly at the source of the hierarchic tradition, he ridiculed Plato's "Commonwealth" with its regime of "airy burgomasters" who "by unalterable decree" so narrowly limited the body of permissible knowledge that it could be contained in "a library of smaller bulk than his own Dialogues."[31] To be sure, Milton's republic was not a twentieth-century liberal democracy. His doctrine would permit the suppression of books after publication on such grounds as "popery or open superstition."[32] In effect, therefore, spokesmen for such ideas, once they had had their first say, would be excluded from the self-governing people. Moreover, in the last days of the Puritan Commonwealth, desperately attempting to ward off the restoration of monarchy, Milton proposed a republic governed in the counties by the nobility and gentry and at the center by a senate chosen for life from these same classes.[33] Yet, it is important to note, he did not make these concessions because he trusted the upper more than the lower classes. The disorders of the Commonwealth had indeed disillusioned him with the common people.[34] But in his eyes the leaders also had failed the cause by yielding to "avarice and ambition."

In those earlier years of hope, however, when he wrote *Areopagitica* and when the question of the franchise was being agitated by the Levellers, he took a much broader view, which put him somewhere between Rainborough and Ireton.[35] In *Areopagitica,* when indicating who would take an active part in freely reading, speaking, and debating, his language is inclusive. To license books, he says, is "an undervaluating and villifying of the whole nation," and he takes care specifically to include "the common people" in that whole. Again, it is "the people, or the greater part," whom he praises as "wholly taken up with the study of highest and most important matters to be reformed . . . disputing, reasoning, reading, inventing, discoursing."[36] The people: that is where the power lies in the Miltonian polity.

Milton is not so unobservant as to suppose that all persons contribute equally to public debate. He finds great variety in gifts of mind and will among his fellow Englishmen. In the discovery of new truth, an elite gives the lead. They are those "men of rare abilities and more than common industry" whom "God raises to his own work," "not only to look back and revive what hath been taught heretofore, but to gain further, and to go on some new enlightened steps in the discovery of truth." Presumably it is they who "sitting by their studious lamps" revolve "new notions and ideas" that present "the approaching reformation." Authors must, however, submit their initiatives to readers, who, "trying all things," assent only to "the force of reason and convincement." Nor do the members of the elite come from some established rank or order in church or state or society. Milton emphatically warns against that supposition, "lest we should devote ourselves again to set places and assemblies and outward callings of men."[37]

This relationship of authors and readers suggests how in a general sense leaders and followers would interact in the Miltonian republic. Leaders perform a crucial role by initiating proposals for the common good. When they win acceptance of their views, however, they do so thanks not to charisma of person or office but to rational persuasion of followers. Indeed, the followers decide who will become the leaders by choosing between the champions of truth and of falsehood in those grand Miltonian encounters. For not all initiatives have the truth in them; "many sectaries and false teachers" also contend for a following.[38] One cannot, however, know ahead of time by "place," "assembly," or "outward calling" who is the spokesman for truth. Repeatedly what seemed on the first encounter to be false has proved to be true after testing. That testing is precisely the function of the free and open confrontations of public debate. In this debate, those who listen and read, who criticize and dispute, who reject and accept, are those who decide whose "new notions and ideas" will become part of the emerging consensus. These contests for leadership, we might say, are decided on the "issues."

In the Miltonian republic, as in the Thomistic monarchy, there are inequalities of ability and good will. Ideally also, in each case the polity is unified by a conception of the common good. Unlike the Thomistic community, however, the unity of the Miltonian republic consists not in deference to a ruler, whose reasons the ruled can never understand, but in consent to proposals for the common good which all members of the polity have helped formulate. As for Aquinas, the conception of the common good is in the mind and will of the ruler, but for Milton the ruler is the people.

Nation and Purpose

Milton's elitism, religious or secular, sets no narrow limits to his conception of the actively self-governing people. The free and open encounters would be conducted not merely among an elite of grace or virtue, or within the walls of a representative parliament or ecclesiastical assembly, but among "the whole nation." The people would not merely choose those who would govern them but would govern themselves. That breadth of view came from the new individualism; it also arose from Milton's trust in his fellow countrymen.

His broad republicanism was rooted in a deep nationalism. "Lords and Commons of England," he admonished the parliament, "consider what a nation it is whereof ye are, and whereof ye are the governors: a nation not slow and dull, but of a quick, ingenious, and piercing spirit; acute to invent, subtile and sinewy in discourse, not beneath the reach of any point the highest that human capacity can soar to."[39]

Free and open debate among this remarkable people would lend authority to their government. That government would also have an overriding purpose from which it gained legitimacy: to protect and promote the first freedom, the exercise of liberty of conscience by which Englishmen and England might advance in truth and virtue, rising toward "any point the highest that human capacity can soar to." England had a mission for itself and for mankind. God, wrote Milton, reveals himself "first to his Englishmen." In the appearance of Wyclif "this nation [was] chosen before any other" to proclaim and sound forth "the first tidings and trumpet of reformation." And now, he continued, "God is decreeing to begin some new and great period in His Church, even to the reforming of reformation itself."[40]

That advance would define the purpose of the Miltonian republic. It would include great changes, ecclesiastical, political, and economical. Neither an ascetic nor a pacifist, Milton did not disdain opulence and power as objects of republican statecraft but rather foresaw England "entering the glorious ways of truth and prosperous virtue, destined to become great and honourable in these latter ages." "Methinks," he continued with imperial pride, "I see in my mind a noble and puissant nation rousing herself like a strong man after sleep, and shaking her invincible locks. Methinks I see her as an eagle mewing her mighty youth, and kindling her undazzled eyes at the full midday beam; purging and unscaling her long-abused sight at the fountain itself of heavenly radiance."[41]

This powerful, progressive, and reformist republic would have an active government. A principal task would be education. Even in the days of failure Milton could write with glowing optimism of the effects of public education upon the people of a free commonwealth. "Schools and Academies" in the counties, he predicted, "by communicating the natural heat of government and culture more distributively to all extreme parts . . . would soon make the whole nation more industrious, more ingenious at home, more potent and honourable abroad." He hoped, above all, to see the people "flourishing, virtuous, noble and high spirited." He sought a "commonwealth for increase," to use Harrington's later phrase. But first and last the increase he sought, and which liberty and self-government would serve, was the inward perfecting of individual consciences in fellowship with one another: the national *paideia* for "the constituting of virtue" and "the confirmation of truth."

Milton did not shirk the problem of pluralism, namely, how to reconcile social diversity with the order necessary for social survival. In a real sense, his radical individualism makes that problem more acute by charging each person with the duty to decide for himself the moral and natural truth by which he would live. One might well conclude that a people who acted on these principles could survive only under a sovereignty far more authoritarian than any conceived by the champions of the old hierarchies. Hobbes offered counsel along these lines, as did other absolutists of the age. Yet as Milton understood the operation of that individualism, it implied a collective rationality which held out the promise of order with freedom.

In that polity the powers of the individual which enabled him to depend on himself also led the individual to utilize and respect those same powers in his fellow citizens. The results of free discussion and the respect for the system that produced them justified obedience and kept the peace. This republic could do without the vertical differentiation that ordered the plenitude of the old world. No less richly diversified, its differences drew it together in the collateral intercourse and interdependence of self-government.

Yet this new political world could never offer quite the same assurance of order, peace, and unity promised in theory by that old world, where change took place not at all or only under beneficent guidance from above. The nation had begun to engage public affections in place of king and pope and to define the purpose of the political order. But that purpose was not fixed in quantity or quality, but like the truth of which it was an aspect, was the object of a constant "searching what we know not by what we know." A polity that lived by this vision would be a "commonwealth for increase." The kinetic future that would unfold in America was being prepared.

CHAPTER 3

A Constitution for
the National Republic:
James Harrington

LIKE MILTON, James Harrington rejected the claims of the gracious and virtuous few to rule. Like Milton, he would base authority upon discussion among the many. "Truth," he wrote, in the authentic Miltonian spirit, "is a spark whereunto objections are like a bellows."[1] He had the same ardent faith in the capacity of the people, specifically the English people, to discover the common good and continuously and actively to govern themselves by its light. Unlike Milton, however, he did not trust solely to free speech among an educated and well-led citizenry to bring about this happy result. He labored—and that is the right word for his earnest, scholarly, prolonged, involved lucubrations—to find the institutions that would close the gap between the bright promise of this free people and self-government that worked.

Republican enthusiasms had widened that gap to tragic proportions in the years leading up to the publication of *Oceana* in 1656.[2] Liberty of conscience had created not consensus but a cacophony of dissent which frequently clothed with a religious gloss miscellaneous efforts of sedition. The consequent collapse into the arms of a Caesar was preparing the way for an ignominious scuttle back to monarchy. Once again the Platonic cycle among forms of government was being exemplified. For some the failure of the Commonwealth was not a tragedy but a farce, symbolized by the name "Barebones Parliament" given to one of Cromwell's futile attempts to restore representative government. "A very droll spectacle it was," commented the aristocratic Montesquieu some hundred years later, " . . . to behold the impotent efforts of the English towards the establishment of democracy."[3]

In spite of living through such a crushing vindication of the age-old prejudice against popular government, Harrington championed with high hope the idea of the national republic. For a panacea, he looked to institutions set up by the thirty "orders" of Oceana. They would avoid the "confusions" of the Commonwealth, lend stability, indeed, "immortality" to the state, and realize the common good far more fully than could be done by monarchy or aristocracy. "Popular government," he wrote, "reaching the perfection of the kind, reaches the perfection of government, and has no flaw in it."[4]

Under this constitution the people of Oceana would govern as well as it was formerly thought only the wise and the holy could do. In that older view it was the virtue of the ruler or rulers that enabled government to bring the people together in peace and unity and to guide them toward the common good. Harrington expected his republican regime to achieve even better results. But for the opposite reason. "'Give us good men and they will make us good laws,'" he wrote, "is the maxim of a demagogue, and . . . exceeding fallible. But 'give us good orders, and they will make us good men' is the maxim of a legislator and the most infallible in politics."[5] For the regime of virtue in classical and medieval thought, Harrington would substitute constitutionally ordered government by discussion.

One element in this constitutional order was a vertical distribution of powers between center and periphery, protected by fundamental law. This scheme of constitutional decentralization foreshadows the federal structure adopted by the Americans in 1787. We need to look at it in the context of Harrington's whole system of thought, if we wish to see the contribution to popular government that this early republican expected from what Americans later came to call "federalism."

His system is not easily grasped. Reading *Oceana* is hard work. Its sentences are awkward, its meanings often obscure, its proposals sometimes unworkable and fantastic. Even Harrington's staid biographer in the *Encyclopaedia Britannica* of 1911 found the work "irretrievably dull." Yet when one penetrates through the prolixity of his text and its absurd adornment with detail about architecture, nomenclature, costume, and protocol and gets at the points he is trying to make, the substance is familiar and relevant. The main thoughts still live in democratic theory and practice. The tedious complexity itself of the proposals strikes a responsive chord in the mind of anyone who has struggled to comprehend the law of American elections to party and public office, or the rules of procedure of our legislative bodies. No less familiar is the air of earnest effort to avoid fraud and abuse and to elicit the conscientious choice of the people. Gradually one begins to understand how Harrington came to inspire generations of republican constitution-makers, not least in America.

The Dilemma of Scale: Machiavelli

Harrington not only maintained his high hopes for popular government in the teeth of bitter failure; he also elaborated a theory which he believed would realize these hopes despite the conclusions of the foremost political philosopher of the age. What Machiavelli had said was a threat not, of course, because he supported the old regime, since he, like Harrington, also spurned the rule of the wise and the holy and praised the judgment of the people. Harrington, indeed, admired Machiavelli for his understanding of politics and cited him frequently as an authority, terming him "the prince of politicians" (that is, political theorists) and the "incomparable patron of the people."[6]

The conflict between them, nevertheless, went to a fundamental issue, the problem of scale. This issue was focused by the different answers they gave to a specific historical question, namely, what caused the fatal conflict between the senate and the people of Rome, and could it have been averted and the republic saved? Their differences on this point brought out a basic opposition between the two systems of thought. As Harrington remarked, if Machiavelli's "judgement" on this historical question were to stand, "our commonwealth faileth." He, therefore, advanced an explanation of the fall of the Roman republic based on "other principles."[7]

Taking up this historical question in *The Discourses* (1513),

Machiavelli had organized his evidence by means of a twofold classification of regimes, which Harrington later termed "commonwealths for preservation" and "commonwealths for increase."[8] Using Sparta and Venice as examples of the former, Machiavelli considered various explanations of why their republics endured and that of Rome failed. In Sparta he found a king and a small senate ruling a small population devoted to the laws of Lycurgus. The equality of property provided by these laws made inequality of rank more tolerable to the plebs, while the king held the nobles in check. The main reason for the survival of popular government, however, was "the smallness of Sparta's population," maintained by exclusion of foreigners, which prevented the republic from becoming so large that it was "ungovernable by few." Venice achieved a similar effect by reason of the small number of its inhabitants.[9] While both republics kept the peace at home thanks to their small populations and governing bodies, *a fortiori* both were externally weak, whether for defense or for conquest.

Rome, on the other hand, enjoyed a form of government suitable for expansion, making it a "commonwealth for increase." Authority was shared by the senate with the plebs, who provided the armed strength to win and hold "a great empire." This "large population," however, was hard to manage and produced the "commotions and disputes of all kinds" which were "Rome's undoing" as a republic.[10]

From this historical comparison followed the dilemma of scale for popular governments. On the one hand, if a state—any state—is to avoid internal disruption, its governing body must be small. On the other hand, if it is to be strong enough to cope with external threats, it must be able to summon large numbers to its defense. For republics, which by definition are governed by the people, these imperatives of scale create an insuperable dilemma. If the republic is small enough to govern itself peaceably, it will be too weak to defend itself, while if its numbers are great enough for defense, they will be too many for self-government. Faced with a choice between the two types of republic, Machiavelli preferred "the greatness of Rome."[11] Such a "commonwealth for increase" would, of course, sooner or later, like Rome, become a republic in name only.

Machiavelli's analysis consists of two lines of reasoning elaborate enough to be called theories: the small state theory of democracy and the big state theory of tyranny. Both are founded on a common premise which we may call Machiavelli's law of political number and which may be approached by further examination of the small state theory of democracy.

What is the ground of Machiavelli's conclusion that in order to avoid internal disruption, the governing body of a state must be small? If we could trace the origin of this small state theory to an earlier source, we might get light on its rationale. Some scholars find its origins in classical thought.[12] But, although Machiavelli cites evidence from classical history to support his analysis, he refers to no earlier theoretical source. Nor does Harrington, despite his commitment to "ancient prudence."

Both Plato and Aristotle did take up the question of scale, and both came down emphatically on the side of the small polity. Their concern, however, was not for democracy but for community. In their opinion, therefore, the restriction on numbers applied not merely to republics but to all forms of government, whether by one, the few, the many, or a mixture. Setting out his reasons in an extravagant version of the organic analogy, Plato argued that "that city is best governed which is most like a single human being." This meant that its "greatest good" would be a "community of pain and pleasure" among its members so total that they would suffer no private, but only common, joys or sorrows.[13] Without deciding whether a common life so dense is possible, let alone desirable, we must grant that any approach to it would require intercourse among individuals so close and comprehensive that only a small number could take part. Plato's ideal total of 5,040 heads of families, as set forth in *The Laws,* may well seem too many to us, as it did to Aristotle.[14] Plato himself preferred a smaller number when in *The Republic* he said that a population with a thousand arms-bearing men would be "the best size for our city."[15]

Aristotle also approached the question of scale from a recognition of the need for community. Rejecting Plato's visionary proposals as counterproductive, he held that a common life which respected the privacy of family and property would in fact engender a greater "spirit of fraternity" and so greater unity in the behavior of citizens.[16]

Yet his conception of that common life would restrict its scale no less severely than Plato's. It must be such a face-to-face relationship that all citizens could have personal knowledge of one another's characters. For only if the rulers, whether few or many, had such personal knowledge of the ruled could they properly perform the civic function of judging litigants and choosing office-holders. Only under these conditions of thought and sentiment could there ensue that habitual obedience to the law that Aristotle identified with order.[17]

The classical Greeks gave us not the small state theory of republicanism but the small state theory of community. They did not hold, as Machiavelli did, that only republics must be small in order to enjoy internal quiet. They argued rather that whatever the regime, only if numbers are small enough for close personal intercourse can that "spirit of fraternity" arise which makes possible an acceptable and accepted mode of government. This requirement would rule out as unstable (as well as undesirable) the large polities of later ages, including imperial Rome.[18] In Machiavelli's twofold typology, however, imperial Rome was a regime which was stable and strong enough to realize the "greatness" that he so much admired.

The thoughts of the ancient Greeks do little to uncover the grounds for Machiavelli's small state theory of democracy. We get more light from a close reading of his text by a modern scholar. In his commentary on *The Discourses,* Professor Harvey Mansfield, Jr., takes up Machiavelli's comparison of the two types of commonwealth, the large and small, and various explanations of their differing fates. Among these explanations, Mansfield observes, Machiavelli's sovereign principle is number.[19] The hypothesis that a state must be governed by "a few" if it is to avoid internal disruption does not mean that, as the ancients would say, government requires wisdom, and only "the few" are wise. Machiavelli disdained these qualitative distinctions of the old virtue philosophy. For him, as Mansfield writes in his comment on this passage, "nothing can be found in the quality of being gentle or noble for which rank might be given and government be formed. Number, not quality, is sovereign in politics and perhaps in all things."[20]

In behavioral terms, this law of political number is fairly rendered by saying that when the governing body is small, orderly government is likely; when it is large, orderly government is unlikely. Or, more precisely, as a relation between variables, that the chances of orderly government vary inversely with the size of the governing body.

The reason why number makes this difference is that it means diversity. For Machiavelli as for Montesquieu, the greater the number of participants in a governing body, the greater the diversity of views; the fewer the participants, the greater the uniformity. This insight, which for the sake of brevity we may call Machiavelli's law of political number, did not exclude other considerations, such as the role of class conflict, in the fall of the Roman Republic. But the root of the trouble, as Mansfield's generalization indicates, was not the polarity of class conflict but the pluralism of "commotions and tumults of all kinds." The expanding republic was not simply divided by the struggle between plebs and patricians, which, indeed, in its earlier days as a small city-state had been healthy. It was made "unwieldy" and hard to "manage" by the "animosities and tumults" of too many participants.[21] The fundamental problem was not class conflict but pluralism.

From this law of political number it follows that only a small state can enjoy that homogeneity of views necessary for popular government. As Machiavelli said, it was "the smallness of Sparta's population" that enabled the republic to achieve that "union" in which its citizens lived for so long a time. The same premise, of course, subjects the big republic to the danger of tyranny. For it is the excessive pluralism of a large state that brings on those "commotions and tumults" which are the opportunity for the man of vaulting ambition, as the disturbances raised by the Gracchi prepared the way for the usurpation of Marius.[22] The law of political number, in short, leads both to the small state theory of democracy and the big-state theory of tyranny and so to the dilemma for republican government from which Machiavelli saw no escape.

Machiavelli's dilemma does not follow solely from law of political number. The greater the diversity of views in a governing body, he is saying, the more difficult it will be to reach agreement and so the greater the chance of disorder and confusion in government action. Moreover, he then concludes, such incoherence will prompt citizens to welcome an authoritarian leader and the ambitious man to take advantage of that opportunity.

These further inferences—that diversity leads to disorder and that disorder leads to tyranny—are separable from the premise that number leads to diversity, but they are necessary to Machiavelli's conclusion that the commonwealth for increase, because it is big enough for defense or conquest, will be no commonwealth. In this sequence, these three propositions constitute what we may call the big state theory of tyranny. It follows from the same line of argument as the small state theory of democracy. In that case, the law of number is taken to mean that the fewer the members of the self-governing polity, the greater will probably be the homogeneity of their views. That greater homogeneity in turn is thought to enhance the chances for agreement and so for orderly government in the republic.

Political theorists of quite different persuasions have accepted the Machiavellian premise. Thomas Aquinas, the authoritarian, said as much when laying out the necessity for government. "Even in a state of innocence," he wrote, "a social life cannot exist among a number of people unless under the governance of one to look after the common good; for many, as such, seek many things, whereas one attends only to one."[23] Like the small state theory of democracy, the big state theory of tyranny was adopted and elaborated by Montesquieu.[24] In a modified form, it was often used by republican critics of unitary government and of centralization in large states. Madison, the republican, also agreed that in a popular government, the diversity of views will vary with the number of citizens. He rejected, however, the further inferences of the Machiavellian argument that diversity would lead to disorder and to tyranny. Turning that reasoning on its head, he defended the "extended republic," arguing in the spirit of the early Milton that diversity could lead to more just and stable government.[25] Likewise granting that diversity varied directly with scale, Harrington escaped from the Machiavellian dilemma by a solution which in fundamental respects anticipated Madison's defense of the "extended republic."

Harrington's "model" (his term) was based on "other principles" than those which led Machiavelli to his dilemma. So constituted, the commonwealth of Oceana was popular, constitutional, representative, deliberative, national, and, not least, federal.

Constitutionalism and the Public Interest

Harrington's federalism presupposed a certain kind of constitutionalism which can be best described by comparison of the American with the British example. In the American federal system, each level of government derives its authority from the same supreme law-making power, the people of the United States. Since each level of government derives its powers from the same source, both are legally coordinate with one another and neither is subordinate to the other. National federalism is possible because of these two key features: the people are the supreme law-making power, and the law they make is superior to the law of both federal and state governments.

This American conception of constitutionalism was radically in conflict with the doctrine, which had come to prevail in Britain by the time of the American Revolution and the framing of the Constitution, that the legal power of parliament was unlimited. In this view, not the people but parliament was the supreme law-making power, the classic formulation being set forth in 1765 in Blackstone's *Commentaries*. Under the British "constitution," wrote Blackstone, "that absolute despotic power, which must in all governments reside somewhere" was entrusted to parliament, which therefore had "sovereign and uncontrollable authority" to make or unmake all man-made laws, including those deemed "fundamental."[26]

On this understanding, the term "constitution" meant simply the main authoritative rules by which Britain was governed. As an American tory, reflecting the orthodoxy of his day, put it in 1776, the British constitution was "that assemblage of laws, customs and institutions, which form the general system; according to which the several powers of the state are distributed and their respective rights are secured to the different members of the community."[27] Since the first among these authoritative rules was that parliament was sovereign, that body could make or unmake any rule, constitutional or statutory, except of course the principle of its sovereignty. Hence, its rule-making could override any rule-making by local governments and was indeed itself the source of their powers. Whatever powers parliament might give other governing bodies in Britain or the colonies it could also take away. Such governments therefore were inescapably subordinate to the central government and could not be legally coordinate with it. On this view of constitutionalism and sovereignty, national federalism on American lines was impossible.

This doctrine, which the term "parliamentary sovereignty" came to designate, had emerged from the conflicts of the seventeenth century. In Harrington's time the terms "sovereign" and "sovereignty" were beginning to acquire their later meaning of the legal omnipotence of a governmental body. The most notable source was Hobbes's *Leviathan* (1651). There, especially in Book 2, chapter 18, Hobbes argued that any government, whatever its composition, must be "sovereign" and that "sovereignty" by its nature was legally unlimited.

Harrington also frequently used these terms, taking them to indicate the higher authority of some thing, institution, or person over others, as when he said, for instance, that the parliament of Oceana had "sovereign power." His thought, however, did not move toward the Hobbesian position but rather toward the later American idea of constitutionalism. In a fierce attack on Hobbes near the start of his treatise, he contended that the very Roman history cited by Hobbes actually showed that a governing body can be made sovereign "upon conditions," and he heaped scorn on Hobbes for denying this as a fact of Roman history and a principle of political theory. Harrington's usage was such as to admit, indeed to require, that the "sovereign power" of the parliament of Oceana was not unlimited but was exercised "upon conditions."[28]

Like the American Constitution, the thirty orders of Oceana prescribe those "conditions." We can see this in Harrington's terminology. As we today distinguish "constitutional" from "statutory" law, he distinguished the "orders" from the "laws" made under the authority of those orders, as, for instance, in "orders" 19, 20, and 23 which state the procedure by which a "law" is made.[29] Again, the oath which the twelfth order requires all members of parliament to take before entering on their tasks of law-making specifically obliges them to "well and truly observe and keep the orders and customs of this commonwealth which the people have chosen."[30] The same background of thought is reflected in the requirement of the American Constitution that members of Congress take an oath to "support this Constitution" in contrast with the British requirement of only a pledge of allegiance from members of parliament to the reigning monarch and his or her successors.[31] In Oceana, the power to govern, whether called sovereign or not, is subordinate to a superior body of rules which authorizes and thereby limits it. Harrington uses the term "constitution" in a narrower sense than the Americans did and do. The legal status he gave to the "orders" of Oceana nevertheless make them a constitution in the American sense of the word.

At that time, like Harrington, other republicans were distinguishing between two sorts of law and, like him, attempting to set out the fundamental law in a written document. While Harrington was composing his great work, Cromwell was trying to govern England under the first written constitution of modern times, *The Instrument of Government* of 1653. In a characterization that became famous in the history of constitutionalism, he had warned the first parliament called under that constitution to respect the distinction between one sort of law which was "somewhat fundamental, somewhat like a Magna Charta, that should be standing, be unalterable,"[32] in contrast with another sort which dealt with the "circumstantials" of government organization and might be made and unmade by the legislature. A few years earlier the Levellers had put forward *The Agreement of the People,* which in its several versions laid down what its advocates had hoped would become the fundamental law of a new republican regime. Like Oceana, this regime would be federal, not on the confederate but on the national model. What the Levellers sought was a compact not among governments or communities but among individuals, stating the powers and limits of government at all levels. Within this framework of a national republic, some of their leaders, principally Richard Overton, pressed for measures of radical decentralization. These appear especially in the third agreement of 1649, which would endow local governments with wide military, judicial, and administrative powers, very much along the lines of Harrington's model.[33]

In Oceana, as the oath imposed on law-makers explicitly recognizes, the orders, like the American Constitution, derive their superior legal status from the will of the people. This is a complicated transaction. Harrington does not imagine, as does Locke, that a form of government can be brought into existence directly by the people acting as "a perfect *Democracy*" under majority rule.[34] He sees the need for intermediary bodies and persons, such as his "council of prytans," a small committee to review suggestions from the public and pass them on to its parent body of learned counselors, the "council of legislators," who under the direction of an exceptional figure, the "legislator," actually discuss and "upon mature debate" draft the document.[35] The American Constitution, likewise, did not spring directly from public discussion and decision but was framed, in even greater privacy, by that famous body of fifty-five, incidentally almost exactly the same size as Harrington's council of legislators, which numbered fifty.

In neither case did this recognition of the realities of making a constitution deprive it of a popular foundation. In Harrington's republic, the legislator, being modeled on ancient state-founders such as Lycurgus and Moses, took the initiative in the reconstitution of the state and exercised an undefined but leading role in the decisions of the council. Yet the will of the people intervened at two critical points. Democratic legitimacy was lent to his initiative when "the universal suffrage of the army" "created" him "sole [sic] legislator," since this army was in fact "the people in arms."[36] Moreover, although the people at large played only an occasional part in the debate and the drafting of the thirty orders, their constituent sovereignty was asserted when the final document was "ratified and established by the whole body of the people."[37] This is entirely in accord with Harrington's reading of Roman constitutional history to show that "the people, who only were sovereign, were such from the beginning" and so could establish and grant authority to governing bodies "upon conditions."[38] In Oceana as in the United States, therefore, the constitution was not the outcome of a compact among a number of provincial governments. On the contrary, it was the constitution which established and authorized these governments, as well as the central government.

Under the constitution of Oceana, local government has three levels: the parish, the hundred, and the "tribe," or shire, of which the latter is the principal jurisdiction. Shire governments function as parts of the system of indirect election of members of parliament. They are also administrative organs of the central government, which, having almost no bureaucracy, must depend upon local governments for virtually all tasks of execution and adjudication. These governments would also seem to have some autonomous powers of taxation and legislation. The precise assignment of powers to the central and local governments is not entirely clear in part at least because Harrington himself was not of one mind on the question.[39] It is obvious at any rate that the government of Oceana is highly decentralized in administration, although not in legislation, and that the basis for this decentralization is constitutional. In this broad sense, Oceana fits the model of national federalism.

Why at this early stage of modern thinking about popular government should an advocate such as Harrington favor a federal division of power? What larger purpose of political theory did he think it would serve? Needless to say, if we are to get at this question, we cannot look at his federal scheme in isolation. With regard to both form and function, to both the legal structure and the possible reasons for that structure, the federal system must be considered as part of Harrington's whole scheme.

His great theme was how to make government by discussion viable in the extended republic. This meant not merely avoiding the abuses to which popular government is prone but above all realizing the excellence of which he believed it capable. In contrast with the old regime of virtue, the constitutional order that would make this possible would say not who were to be the rulers who governed the commonwealth but rather what were the rules by which it would be governed. Harrington looked not to "good men" to "make us good laws" but to "good orders" to "make us good men." A constitution on these lines could make men "good" as law-makers and self-governing citizens in various ways. One way would be by rules to prevent them from governing oppressively. In this vein it is sometimes said that the main purpose of the American constitution is the restraint of governmental power and that its achievement is "limited government." This is done partly by outright prohibitions, as in the case of most clauses of the Bill of Rights. The separation of powers at the center and the division of power between the federal and the state governments are held to do the same thing. In these instances the rules create conditions—the celebrated "checks and balances" of our system—which serve the same restrictive purpose as the outright prohibitions. Carl Friedrich put this restrictive view in a general form when he said that the essence of constitutionalism is the division of power, and accordingly he defined a constitution as a system of effective regularized restraints on government for the protection of individual rights.[40]

In a sense the orders of Oceana fit this restrictive concept of constitutionalism. Harrington does expect that they will enable his commonwealth to avoid the "confusions" common to republics and the consequent danger of tyranny. But this avoidance is only a side-effect of his main object, the realization of the perfections of popular government. Certain rights are indeed protected. The orders explicitly safeguard liberty of conscience. Private property is presumed by the two "fundamentals" of the constitution, "the agrarian" and "the ballot." Yet in the orders dealing with these rights of conscience and property the governmental purpose is controlling. The agrarian presupposes private property only in the course of limiting the size of landed estates, and the reason for that limitation is to protect the popular basis of the state. The order defining the franchise establishes a property qualification so that the voter will be able to provide himself with arms and to think independently about politics. In so far as the constitution of Oceana prevents confusion and oppression, it does so in the course of achieving Harrington's great end, government in "the public interest." The orders are not denials of power but grants of power; not disabling but enabling; not restrictive but directive.

Harrington takes pains to make this distinction. Likening sovereignty to gunpowder, which is at once a source of "danger" and "safety," he observes that the power of governing must be so "distributed" as not to blow up the "magazine," yet also so "collected" as to be "in full force and vigour." He avoids the connotation of mere restraint by saying that sovereign power in the state is not "bounded" or "straightened." Rather, he says, it is "balanced" like the power of the eagle in flight, which, as in the case of Rome, was thereby enabled to "spread her wings from the ocean to Euphrates." As these martial and imperial metaphors suggest, the "balance" of the constitution does not reduce the power of government but enables it to act with "full force and vigour" across a wide front of domestic and foreign concerns.[41] To think of his guiding purpose as the restraint of power and the establishment of "limited government" is to mistake his meaning and to misjudge his influence on later champions of republicanism in England and America. Harrington was not concerned merely with preventing the abuses of popular government but above all with eliciting its perfections.

The constitution of Oceana takes this positive stance by affirming, like the Preamble of the American Constitution, certain broad purposes of the state. In general terms certain orders, such as 26 and 27, define the public interest by directing the government toward making the nation rich, powerful, and virtuous.[42] Since, however, this government is popular not only in its foundation but also in its operation, the laws which achieve these ends must be the voluntary outcome of the people's deliberations. For the most part, therefore, the orders specify not the outcome of these deliberations but the conditions under which they are conducted. Nor are these conditions usually restraints but rather incentives to "reason" and "virtue." They presume to make men "good" not by restraining their bad motives but by eliciting their better motives. In this sense constitutionalism in Harrington's thought appears as an instrument of popular government, not a restraint upon it. Adapting Friedrich's formulation to accord with this meaning, we would define a constitution as a system of effective regularized incentives to government in the public interest.

As Blitzer has observed, the fathers of the American republic greatly admired *Oceana* "as an eloquent and persuasive vindication of government by law, not men."[43] What Harrington meant by this ancient and ambiguous expression was specific to his conception of popular government. He did not mean government by a few wise and holy men whose grasp of a higher law enabled them deductively to determine the common good for the many. He meant rather government by the many by laws expressing the "public interest," or as he sometimes put it the "national interest."[44]

His use of the term "interest" is crucial to this conception of government not from the top down but from the bottom up. As Gunn has pointed out, the term came to be used in the seventeenth century in reaction to older authoritarian ideas.[45] It was a way of saying that the proper starting point for the search for the common good was each man's concern for his safety and property. According to the older view, it was the wisdom and sanctity of the few which entitled and indeed obliged them to impose their idea of the common good upon the many. It followed, as Pocock has noted, that the decline of virtue had as its logical corollary the rise of interest.[46] The subversive thesis implicit in this usage was that the ordinary person had something to say about the common good which the elite did not know and could only learn from him. The "essence" of Harrington's conception of the public interest, writes Gunn, "is the classical liberal view that the raw materials for discovering the public interest are the concerns of private men as understood by those men themselves."[47]

The concerns of "private interest" were only the starting point. The task of the republican constitution was precisely to lay down "such orders of government" as would constrain mere men to turn away from their "private interest" and toward "that which regards the common good and interest." As conceived by Harrington, this transformation did not necessitate altruistic self-denial. Nor did it mean that, on the model of the old virtue philosophy, the commonwealth would impose upon the citizens a conception of the public interest which was alien to or destructive of their private interests. Its task was rather to discern and promote those concerns which individuals had in common with one another. Harrington, therefore, could reply to a critic who charged that the government of Oceana would rule "against private utility" that on the contrary it would not only "fit private unto the public, but even public unto private utility."[48]

He occasionally gives examples which make his meaning more specific. Among property owners, for instance, if one is a thief, that gives him a private interest distinct from the interests of the others. Punishment for stealing, therefore, observes Harrington, is "certainly none of his private interest." Yet, when the matter is viewed on a plane of broader generality, all, including the thief, have a common interest in the protection of their possessions against theft.[49] Another example illustrates the commonality of interests which are not identical but complementary. Against the charge that "the lower sort of people" would follow a "King Piper" who proposed to rob the rich for the benefit of the poor, Harrington countered that even the footman or peasant would understand that making war on the rich would "obstruct their own livelihood."[50]

The perception of such commonalities, it must be emphasized, is not achieved solely thanks to the incentive system of government by discussion. Harrington does not suppose that the will for private advantage can be converted into action for the public interest by institutions alone. The capacities that the citizens bring to government enable these institutions to work their beneficent transformation. These capacities are mixed, the human soul, according to Harrington, being divided by a conflict between reason and passion, with passion inclining it to sin and reason to virtue.[51] Yet the will is moved by neither one alone but by a compound of both. It is this joint source of motivation that Harrington terms "interest." And, he declares, "the mover of the will is interest."[52]

Reason directs the individual soul toward ends ranging from personal advantage through more inclusive communities, such as family and commonwealth, and finally embracing "the interest of mankind or the whole." The task of the incentive system of government by discussion is to elicit these more inclusive preferences. As passion fully rationalized, now called "virtue," interest moves the will toward the public interest. One could call this process the rationalization of interest. Pocock's term is the "mechanization of virtue."[53] In this process, as Gunn observes, although there is a public interest distinct from that of the citizens individually, a conception of the public interest emerges from the expression of particular private interests and can be known only by reference to them.

In this larger sense, Harrington speaks of interest as "right reason," "common right, law of nature or interest of the whole." Quoting Hooker, he can say that "reason" binds "each to serve others' good and all to prefer the good of the whole, before whatsoever of their own particular."[54] Politically, the great difference between the two philosophers is, of course, that for the achievement of this higher good Hooker relied upon the rule of the wise and the holy, whereas Harrington relied upon government by the people.

Harrington rejects the notion that not the institutions of the state but the personal qualities of the high-minded few enable them, as well as entitle them, to rule. As Hume later commented approvingly, Harrington, unlike other framers of utopias, does not require any great reformation of manners.[55] No more would he attempt the impossible alchemy of converting an aggregate of wholly egoistic atoms into a coherent public by means of constitutional machinery. He premises the constitution for Oceana on an intermediate view of human potentialities: that all men acknowledge and are moved by "the interest of the whole," yet any may be diverted from that end by folly or vice. Temptation, so to speak, cuts both ways. Opportunities for private advantage tempt men to deviate from the public interest. Interest in the common good tempts them to disavow private advantage. Institutions can tip the balance one way or the other. If sole authority is entrusted to one or to a few, private interest will win out. Monarchy and aristocracy must therefore be rejected.[56] If the public interest is to prevail, the sovereign power must be exercised by the people. The task of the orders of Oceana accordingly is to set in motion a process of discussion and decision that will elicit and inform their preference for the public interest.

Representation from the Bottom Up

The orders of Oceana that set this process in motion are of two sorts. First, they provide for that participation of many which makes the regime republican. Harrington called this first range of orders the "institution" of the commonwealth. Second, thanks mainly to the orders which he termed the "constitution," the participation of the many is so structured that the laws they make will be in the public interest.

The first range of orders, the "institution," provided for "equality" in the economic base and in the political superstructure. "An equal commonwealth," he wrote, "is such a one as is equal in both the balance or foundation, and in the superstructure; that is to say, in her Agrarian law and in her rotation."[57] The order setting out the agrarian law would so radically modify primogeniture that ultimately in England no one could possess lands yielding more than £2,000 a year.[58] Such a distribution would permit considerable disparities. It would, however, eliminate the very large landowners—Harrington estimates that in England about three hundred estates exceeded the maximum—who, he feared, might "overpower" or "eat out" the lesser proprietors.[59] The agrarian law would eliminate this opportunity and temptation. Looking ahead, one can safely surmise that such a restriction would have decimated the Whig oligarchy which ruled England in the time of the American Revolution.

Within the population defined by the agrarian, the right to vote and to hold office was limited by qualifications of gender, age, and property, being confined to the "elders," men over thirty with an economic status that would enable them to provide themselves with arms and to exercise independence in their political judgment.[60] Religion also in effect entered into these limitations, since by the orders toleration was extended only to Protestants. In comparison with the demands of other republicans of the time, his definition of the franchise was not unduly narrow and would put him among the moderate Levellers. Harrington estimates that the total number of citizens would be one million, divided evenly between the "youth," eighteen to thirty, who were subject to regular military service but could not vote or hold office, and the "elders." The total citizenry made up about a quarter of what he took the whole population of England to be.[61]

For certain more important offices, such as membership in the senate, Harrington established a higher property qualification of land, goods, or money worth at least £100 per year, the same qualification, incidentally, required of justices of the peace under the Stuart monarchy. These constituted the "horse" or "knightly order" among the armed people, in contrast with the less propertied, who were the "foot."[62] Yet this effort to give institutional form to a political elite was not imposed on the first stages of the "institution" of the commonwealth. Free of any formal requirement to favor members of the knightly order, the elders of the parishes annually elected from their ranks the "deputies," who, constituting in Harrington's words "the *primum mobile,* or first mover of the commonwealth," in turn chose the principal members of the local, provincial, and national governments.[63]

While Harrington agreed that "riches are power,"[64] he was not an economic determinist. He did not think that changes in the state arose monocausally from economic development. Indeed, he hardly seems aware of the possibility of economic growth on a large scale, such as the vast expansion that set in during the next century with the rise of commercial and industrial capitalism.[65] The collapse of the "Gothic Constitution," which he traced to the reign of Henry VII, had been initiated not by developments in the economy but by changes in the law relating to alienation of property.[66] From these legal changes came the great extension of landownership which, in his view, propelled England toward republicanism. As in that sequence, the form of the polity generally, according to his thought, did not merely reflect the form of the economy. Quite the contrary. In Oceana, as in every state, the distribution of property was determined by law. For that reason state-making, which included the adoption of an agrarian law, was feasible and important. Harrington was among the first in that line of modern thinkers who sought, as Alexander Hamilton said in *Federalist Paper* 1, to establish "good government by reflection and choice," rather than trusting to "accident" and "force."

The "institution" set out not only who would be entitled to participate but also how they would participate. This was by means of the "ballot" or "rotation."[67] In its specific meaning the ballot was a method of voting by balls and urns copied from Venetian practice and designed to prevent corruption and to ensure good order in the exercise of the franchise. The offices so filled were subject to rotation, membership in the various governing bodies being renewed by one third every year, persons ending one term of office being ineligible for re-election for two years.

In a wider sense, the ballot/rotation not only laid down how the voting was to be conducted but also provided for equal apportionment of representatives to voters.[68] The order for the ballot of the basic constituency, the parish, required that one deputy be elected for each five voters. The parishes were grouped so that in each shire, of which there were fifty, the same number of deputies, two thousand, representing the same number of voters, one hundred thousand, chose the same number of members of the parliament, nine. At the same time, however, the deputies were required to choose from the knightly class all members of the senate and a minor proportion, two sevenths, of the members of the assembly. In this way, the system of election gave a political elite exceptional representation in the central legislature, whose members were, nonetheless, equally apportioned to a fairly broad electorate, defined by an identical franchise throughout the nation.

While "party" and "faction" were among the evils which the system was specially designed to guard against, republican thought had already begun to recognize the need for institutionalized opposition, and the orders of Oceana expressly arranged for a choice among candidates. Typically, a body of "electors" chosen by lot would nominate "competitors" among whom the electing body would choose, a majority vote being required for election.[69] Legislators, moreover, would be paid, a reform not accomplished in Britain until 1911 for the House of Commons.

The departures from the old system of corporate representation were radical. In that system, which arose during the Middle Ages and lasted until the great reform act of 1832, the franchise varied among constituencies, each of which elected the same number of MPs regardless of the size of its electorate, or indeed its population, wealth, or territorial extent. The new commitment to individual rather than corporate representation was shared by Harrington with other republicans of his day. *The Agreement of the People* of 1648, for instance, included a table setting out the number of MPs to be elected by each constituency, the numbers varying, it would seem, roughly in proportion to population.[70] The demand that "everyman that is an inhabitant" should have "an equal voice" set off the famous debate between Rainborough and Ireton. Both sides in that debate, however, like Harrington, rejected corporate representation in favor of arithmetical representation, their differences, familiar among early republicans, centering on how big the individual property qualification for the franchise was to be.

According to Harrington's Victorian editor, the system of election was designed to keep the legislature "true as a reflection of the public mind."[71] This injection of latter-day Liberalism was not unfaithful to the spirit of Harrington's regime. The popular assembly, he wrote, would be "such a representative as may be equal, and so constituted as can never contract any other interest than that of the whole people."[72] It had this grasp of the public interest to begin with, because the active citizenry could at frequent intervals communicate their private and particular interests to the legislature through their choice of representatives. Rotation enabled "every hand that is fit" to have a chance to enjoy public office. But Harrington wanted to do more than enable citizens to display and develop their "virtue" by having a turn at governing. That could have been accomplished by representation "by lots," that is, by chance, as in many ancient republics. Harrington preferred representation "by suffrage," that is, by choice, which he attributed to the Athenians and which, he observed, had been used by "the late house of commons."[73] By this means the interests of the people at large could be brought together in the central forum where the public interest was determined. When "taken apart," wrote Harrington, the people are "very simple" and "but so many private interests." When brought together, however, "they see and know something . . . they are the public interest."[74] Participation by means of the ballot made possible this collection of power and interests at the center.

Nor was the system of representation the only way that the thoughts and feelings of the people could influence what government did. By constitutional provision, the deliberations of parliament would also draw upon daily "conversations" of officials with "all sorts of company," the advice of "any man" by letter or in person, and petitions from local governments. By these means, Harrington declared, "the ear of the commonwealth" would be "open to all."[75]

Popular participation, moreover, was not confined to voting, office-holding, and petition. The voice of the people was also brought to bear directly on law-making. No measure could be enacted into law unless it had been "printed and published to the whole nation" for a period of six weeks before the conclusive vote of the assembly. By this means, the people and their representatives would "both by discourse and letters, debate six weeks together upon the matter."

And so populistic was this appeal to the people that Harrington could declare that "the representative is nothing else but an instrument or method, whereby to receive the result [that is, the decision] of the whole nation, with order and expedition and without any manner of tumult or confusion."[76]

"The multitude," declared Harrington, again quoting Machiavelli, "is wiser and more constant in their resolutions than a prince." Taken individually, the senators are "wiser" than the members of the assembly, but taken together the latter have "the prerogative"—that is, the exclusive function—of expressing the wisdom of the commonwealth. "And hence it is," he writes, "that the prerogative of your commonwealth, as for wisdom so for power, is in the people which . . . gives the denomination [that is, the name] to your prerogative tribe."[77]

This system of representation was designed to cope with the problem of scale, not the problem of virtue. Although committed to the big republic, "the commonwealth for increase," Harrington recognized the danger of large numbers. Making no reference, however, to Machiavelli's use of this hypothesis, he held, in his free and easy way with historical fact, that it reflected the experience of the republics of ancient times. Those polities, he asserted, were not small, consisting of only "one town," as commonly believed, but embraced large territories and populations. In the absence of representation, large numbers led to breakup or to oligarchy. In ancient Israel, for example, the "assembly of the people," consisting of the twelve tribes, was so "vast and slow" that it became "a great cause of the breaking of that commonwealth." By contrast, as the "rustic tribes" of Rome extended their rule, they coped with scale by inventing a method of representation "by lots." Since Harrington wished to bring the interests of the people to bear upon central decision-making, he preferred representation "by suffrage,"[78] coupled with equal national apportionment. He was proposing what American whigs later called "actual representation."

Harrington could find practices in ancient times which resembled the institutions by which office-holders were to be chosen in Oceana.[79] The meaning he gave to these institutions, however, was not derived from the hierarchic tradition. In the old view, virtue, as a power of the soul of a superior person, could not be represented "by suffrage." That is, it could not be conveyed by the superior person to another person by a mere act of choice or delegation or mutual agreement. The general of an army could no more delegate his courage to his soldiers than the cobbler could delegate his craft to the unskilled peasant. The natural ruler could communicate his wise commands to his subordinates and subjects, but he could not impart to them the power of his wisdom.

Bringing up people to be virtuous was another matter. The ruler could lead the ruled to the virtue for which they had the inherent capacity. But in that relation it was the teacher, not the taught, who was the representative of the wider humanity to which the taught aspired. In accord with the principle of inclusive hierarchy, the natural ruler "represented" his people because he embraced the whole panoply of virtues which one of the ruled could possess only in part. As Aristotle wrote, a king "must excel his subjects in every quality"; otherwise "he will only be a king by chance." Similarly, King James could advise his fellow monarchs that their "craft" as kings meant "know[ing] all crafts, for except ye know every one how can ye control everyone, which is your office?"[80]

The possession of such all-inclusive intellectual and moral powers is no more than one would expect of the "head" of the body politic. In his later pro-papalist phase Nicholas of Cusa had described both the pope and the emperor as "containing" (complicatio) all those subject to them. Members of the general council of the church were said to represent lesser hierarchical groupings in a similar manner. In his account of the political thought of Nicholas of Cusa, Paul Sigmund brings out the similarity of these medieval notions to the later idea of virtual representation. Characterizing the authority of the general council of the church, Cusanus said the council was made up of priests and bishops gathered together "directly or through representatives" (actu vel virtualiter). The persons attending the council "figure" or "personify" the lower ranks and orders. They are "personally identified with all those below them," concludes Sigmund, "in a manner akin to Burke's view of virtual representation." The Latin does indeed strikingly parallel the later distinction between "actual" and "virtual" representation.[81]

Similarly, in England in the early sixteenth century, as Hanna Pitkin writes, it was thought that "the whole nation is somehow embodied in its ruler, as the church is in Christ or in the Pope after him. It is a medieval and mystical conception: the king is not merely the head of the national body, not merely the owner of the realm, but he *is* the crown, the realm, the nation."[82] To such ideas De Grazia traces the origin of the later concept of "virtual representation," finding that the notion of the Crown as the "virtual representative" of a corporate community matured between the time of Henry VIII and Elizabeth.[83] The term is suggestive: the higher authority embodied not the wishes or interests of the lesser orders but the whole array of their virtues. This is representation not from the bottom up but from the top down; not delegation but "impersonation," in which the ruler is conceived as personifying or "bearing the person" of the community he rules.

Representation from the top down is the natural consequence of the conception of virtue embodied in the hierarchic tradition. Representation from the bottom up becomes feasible if, as in Harrington's thought, the moving force in government is taken to be virtue as rationalized interest, not virtue as power of the soul. Bringing together the interests of the whole nation, representation by suffrage would make possible government by discussion in the extended republic.

Yet a representative system of election alone did not qualify the popular assembly to govern Oceana. If it were left to act on its own initiative and to exercise unlimited powers of debate and amendment, that large body, Harrington believed, would fall into hopeless confusion and would ultimately succumb to tyranny. The preference for the national interest entertained by the people had to be elicited by corresponding proposals coming from the senate. To this end Harrington designed the procedures of central deliberation.

The Machinery of Rational Deliberation

Taking up what he terms the "constitution," Harrington turns to the "use of the parts" brought into existence by the "institution."[84] He mentions executive and judicial functions, but he is mainly concerned with legislation. The legislature is bicameral, consisting of the senate and a larger popular assembly, which he sometimes calls "the prerogative tribe" and sometimes simply "the people." A proposal originates in the senate, proceeds through a number of specialized committees, and comes up for discussion by the whole body, which by majority vote may pass it as a "decree." The senatorial decree then goes to the popular assembly, which after a lapse of six weeks, but without debate in the assembly, votes it up or down.

The senate and the assembly together constitute "the sovereign power, or parliament."[85] Its ear being open directly or indirectly to the voices of the whole citizen body, the parliament by its deliberations ascertains the "public interest." That the public interest prevails makes the commonwealth "an empire of laws, and not of men."[86] The proximate grounds for this happy outcome of parliamentary deliberation are the division of functions between senate and assembly and the property qualification for the senate. How according to Harrington do these two pieces of constitutional machinery operate so as to ensure law-making in the public interest?

By the first of these devices, Harrington assigns "debate" to the senate and "resolution" to the assembly;[87] that is, the senate discusses and proposes, the assembly listens and decides. In the homely example with which he introduces the discussion of the "principles" of his scheme, he illustrates by analogy the strategy of this division of functions.[88] Two girls have a cake. If one cuts and also has first choice, the outcome will be unfair, since she will see to it that she gets the bigger piece. Because both understand that this is what would happen, however, they agree to have one girl cut and the other choose, a separation of tasks which will ensure an equal division of the cake, the outcome which, according to Harrington, expresses their "common interest."[89] And since, according to Harrington, proposing and deciding by the two houses of the parliament is analogous to dividing and choosing by the two girls, the parliamentary division of functions will similarly ensure decisions in the public interest.

As public choice theory, the analogy is rudimentary, but it is instructive enough still to be used today by philosophers when analyzing concepts of distributive justice.[90] It does illustrate Harrington's constitutional strategy of how to make men "good" not by commands but by incentives. Or, to elaborate the point, it shows how an equitable outcome of collective action can in some circumstances be secured not by a substantive rule requiring the actors to accept a predetermined outcome but by a procedural rule which leads them voluntarily to seek out and adopt such an outcome. Moreover, as in the example, this procedural rule frames the option in such a way that the choice made by the initiating actor will anticipate the reaction to it of the responding actor. Hence, if we can assume that the assembly will accept only a proposal which is in the public interest, we may infer that the senate, anticipating this reaction, will avoid proposals serving factional interests among their order or among the people and will put forward only proposals in the public interest.

That was precisely what Harrington assumed and inferred. The people, he believed, would not consent to measures damaging to their interests. The senate, therefore, "perceiving," as he wrote, "that they cannot impair the common interest, have no other interest left but to improve it."[91] That being the case, the senate, like the girl who cuts, will submit an equitable proposal, which the assembly, like the other girl, will also find suits its preference. And so Harrington sees the parliamentary process. He does not suppose that the senate will propose a series of options among which the assembly chooses. Rather, after debate, it will put forward a decree which the assembly, recognizing its conformity with the public interest, then accepts and enacts into law.

But whence comes Harrington's assurance that the senate can discern the public interest and that the assembly will recognize and adhere to it? One safeguard is the prohibition of discussion or amendment by the assembly, whose business is thereby confined to "resolution" without the opportunity of initiation in either discussion or legislative action.[92] In defense of this wildly impractical proposal one may compare it with the "closed rule" of the American House of Representatives which can be used to protect the coherence of a bill by obliging the house to vote it up or down without amendment. A main purpose of such rules of parliamentary procedure is to prevent factious combinations, as when shifting majorities destroy the sense of a proposal by a series of disconnected amendments. It is not unduly kind to Harrington to suppose that he had a similar sensible purpose when he outlawed amendments and even criticism of senatorial proposals by the assembly. Obviously, however, if we are to grant any credence to his high claims for his parliament's law-making, we must go beyond the division of functions and consider the individual and collective capacities of the members of the two branches. And so Harrington does by introducing a second piece of constitutional machinery.

By the £100 property qualification for membership in the knightly order from which senators were drawn, Harrington thought he could sort out individuals with a special capacity for discerning the public interest. He suggests the nature of this capacity by another analogy. If we take "any number of men (as twenty)," he supposes, and imagine them having to govern themselves, we shall find that "about a third will be wiser, or at least less foolish, than all the rest." As the fourteen more simple listen to the wiser six "discoursing and arguing with one another," they will "discover things which they never thought on; or are cleared in diverse truths which formerly perplexed them." Therefore, "in matter of common concernment," they will look to the six as "guides."[93]

By analogy this example tells us what each house will do and how they will be related to one another. As the wiser six in the example are "guides," so in the parliament "the senate is to be not commanders, but counsellors of the people."[94] Like the fourteen, the assembly accepts this guidance not by deferentially surrendering power to the few but by rationally being persuaded of the "truths" put forward by their senatorial "counselors." This is popular government by rational discussion. Yet in contrast with the first analogy, there is now inequality of some sort between the two parties to the interaction. Harrington has introduced an elite into the system.

Although he continually refers to the knightly order as "virtuous" and "wise" and calls them a "natural aristocracy," his £100 landowners cannot and do not do for the state what the few wise and holy of classical and medieval theory were supposed to do. The tip-off is that unlike the true believer in hierarchy, Harrington would not trust them with the sole power to rule. On the contrary, he foresees that if the senate alone were to be the governing body, it would become nothing more than a "foul oligarchy" to the rest of the state and within its own ranks would succumb to a "scramble" for individual advantage.[95] To avoid such self-destruction the senate needs the people as much as the assembly needs the senate. For it is the assembly's firm commitment to the public interest which makes it futile for the senate to attempt self-serving options.

The contrast with what Burke a century later also called the *"natural aristocracy"* brings out the modest role of Harrington's elite. In Burke's rhapsodic account the governing class of eighteenth-century England were superior in both understanding and will, being not only formed "to take a large view of the widespread and infinitely diversified combinations of men in a large society" but also "habituated in the pursuit of honor and duty" and moved by "sublime principles" instilled in "persons of exalted station" by the established church. Unlike Harrington's elite, they were commanders of the people, imposing on them a "habitual social discipline, in which the wise, the more expert and the more opulent conduct, and by conducting, enlighten and protect, the weaker, the less knowing, and the less provided with the goods of fortune." To the few who "conducted" them with such farsighted understanding and kindly good will, the many returned deference, electing them to the parliament where, in Burke's words, the "widespread interests" of nation and empire "must be considered—must be compared—must be reconciled, if possible."[96]

In contrast with these enormous gifts of a true aristocracy, the senatorial elite contribute to government by discussion what Harrington called "the genius of a gentleman."[97] The nature of that capacity appears in the contrast he draws with two other social types: mechanics and professional men, both of whom in comparison with the gentry have a common failing. The variable is not wealth, since like the gentry the "great lawyers, great divines and great men of all professions" are well-off. Harrington thinks poorly of such professional men for "running on a narrow bias" and having no better judgment than "so many other tradesmen." The deficiency of the mechanics is similar in that they are "so busied in their private concernments" that they do not have "the leisure to study the public" concernments.[98] For both, narrowness is the flaw.

"The genius of a gentleman" is breadth—the capacity to see things as a whole. In contrast with the two sorts of specialists, he is the generalist. Referring to the "choices" made by the parliament, Harrington writes that "that choice which suiteth with every man's interest excludeth the distinct or private interest or passion of any man, and so cometh up to the common and public interest or reason."[99] The parliament does not do this by imposing upon the citizens a conception of the common good which is alien or hostile to their interests. Rather it seeks out that interest which each has in common with others: "everyman's interest." Its task is to perceive such commonalities and make them the basis of the law. The contribution of the senate to this outcome is by its debate to see the general in the particular and by its decrees to show how the particular can be subsumed under the general.

The law, therefore, has coherence, but it is a coherence derived from the interests brought forward by the representative system of the ballot. While the public interest is distinct from the interests of citizens taken individually, it is derived from their particular and private interests. Hence, the law which emerges from the deliberative process has relevance as well as coherence. To use a word later employed by Milton, Hume, and Madison to characterize this process, the generalists would "refine" the private interests of their constituents. They proceed, however, inductively from those interests as known and felt by their constituents, and not deductively from a superior knowledge of the common good.

In stating the need for the generalist, Harrington was saying nothing new. That the polity needs an elite which performs such a function is a common theme in the history of political thought. In contrast with advocates of a truly aristocratic regime, however, he gave his elite a far more modest role which fits easily with the practice of popular government. Radically differing from Aristotle and Thomas—or, indeed, from Hegel and Burke—Harrington attributed to his elite a superiority that was confined to qualities of mind, not will: wider understanding, not greater devotion to the public interest. In contrast with the older view of wisdom as both cognitive and normative, Harrington supposed that the two functions, the intellectual and the volitional, could and should be performed by different governmental bodies. Praising "a commonwealth, where the wisdom of the nation proposeth and the interest of the people resolveth," Harrington characterized this institutional separation as follows: "Two assemblies, thus constituted, must necessarily amount unto the understanding and the will, unto the wisdom and the interest of the whole nation."[100] His elite had property and brains, but not *noblesse oblige.*

Nor did the senatorial elite have a monopoly on understanding. Their special capacity entitled them only to the initiative in seeking out and proposing what was in the public interest. The response of the assembly was certain both in its grasp of, and preference for, the public interest. Its will was not an arbitrary will. The people did not, like some Occamite deity, make a proposal good merely because they preferred it. Their inherent capacities and the manner in which they formulated their preferences under the constitution ensured that their will would embrace the common good. Harrington could therefore conclude that "the prerogative of the commonwealth, as for wisdom as for power, is in the people."[101]

The senate does not overwhelm the assembly by the charisma of its members. While the assembly is forbidden to debate, it is not forbidden to think. Like the fourteen in the homely example, the assembly as a whole, including those from the "foot" as well as the "horse," understands what the senatorial elite proposes and can judge whether or not it is in the public interest. So also presumably do the citizens who with their representatives have debated the proposed legislation during the six weeks appeal to the people. In Harrington's opinion, observes Pocock, "the power of judgement" of the people at large "in the long run exceeded that of any aristocracy and approached the borders of infallibility."[102]

Harrington's analysis tells us a good deal about how government by discussion can be successfully carried on. For that purpose, however, we do better to look at the process he is describing rather than the structure he designed to elicit this process. His bicameral design may suggest models of mixed government in which the two houses are intended to balance against one another two social orders or sets of diverse interests, such as plebs and patricians, lords and commoners, landowners and bourgeoisie. This rationale, reflecting the themes of restrictive constitutionalism, does not fit with Harrington's account. He vehemently criticized the "wrestling match" between monarch and estates generated by the "Gothic Constitution." To be sure, the elite from which the senate is drawn could be regarded as a social order, in so far as it consists of a body of persons with substantial property and exceptional qualities of mind. Its collective quality as a social order, however, is not what Harrington wishes to introduce into the process of government. On the contrary, he fears this influence as oligarchic and seeks to neutralize it by institutional arrangements. He values the senators not as a collectivity but as individuals, and it is only in this respect that he finds them "wise."

The assembly likewise does not represent a separate social order. It is chosen by the people at large and includes members from the greater as well as the lesser proprietors. The senate is deeply dependent upon the people. It comes into existence when some of the elite are drawn off by election from the citizen body, but without changing the composition of that body, and are set apart to perform a limited but crucial function. The actions of this portion of the people are not balanced against the actions of the whole. They are rather integrated with them. Barred from acting on its separate interest, the senate cannot check, but only enlighten, the assembly, itself instructed by the appeal to the people. The object is not preventative but constructive, a single process to which both actors contribute, as in the paradigmatic analogies of the two girls and the twenty men.

Harrington held that a limit on economic inequality was a necessary condition for the survival of republican government. His integration of the knightly order into the popular polity was a way of limiting political inequality. Perceiving the need for a political elite such as the knightly generalists of his senate, he also recognized the danger of letting this social order acquire independent governmental power. That, he held, was a fundamental flaw of the Roman Republic, going back to its very origins. Long before Rome's great increase in scale, Romulus had committed the grave mistake of giving the election of the senate not to the people as a whole but to the patricians, "a distinct and hereditary order," separate from the plebs. From this creation of "two contrary interests or roots," he argued, flowed oligarchic oppression by the patricians, leading to anarchic resistance by the plebs, in the face of which conflict and confusion the enforcement of the agrarian law of Rome was neglected.[103] The institutionalization of political inequality had engendered a destructive economic inequality.

Illustrating the same principles of political science, but with the opposite result, Sparta achieved internal quiet. Its senate was elected not by a separate order but by the people, and its agrarian law was enforced. Similarly with Venice, which in Harrington's words, was "the most quiet, so also the most equal commonwealth."[104] By following the same republican prescriptions, Rome could have survived, and Oceana would survive as a commonwealth for increase, externally strong and internally at peace. In the light of Harrington's "other principles" of political science, Machiavelli's despair of the extended republic was unfounded.

Government is not a seminar and political debate is not some sort of scientific or scholarly inquiry. Yet government decisions do have an intellectual dimension, and when they fail to express the public interest it is often because of vagueness, inconsistency, discontinuity, ambiguity, and other forms of incoherence. Harrington was right to emphasize this aspect of decisions and decision-making and to direct attention to the kind of persons who might be specially responsible for seeing that government and politics met the intellectual criterion.

As later attempts to put his ideas into practice showed, he went astray in thinking that he could identify an intellectual elite for the polity by means of a property qualification and especially in believing that he could constitute from such an elite a popularly elected branch of the legislature. The Americans were taught these lessons by the failures of the political science of John Adams. On the eve of the revolution and the period of constitution-making in the new states, this close student and admirer of Harrington took the lead in proposing that the new governments include an "aristocratic" element in the form of a second chamber.[105] According to Adams, the consequent bicameralism of the states was based upon the "principles" set forth in *Oceana*. The second chamber established by their constitutions was commonly called the "senate," and, while the electorate was usually the same for both houses, nearly all states required senatorial candidates to meet a property qualification higher than that imposed on candidates for the lower house. Also in harmony with Harringtonian doctrine, advocates of the second chamber expected it to attract a special kind of person—in Adams's rhetoric, "the wise and the learned," "the contemplative and well-informed," those with "wisdom and foresight . . . who have a long acquaintance with the history and manners of mankind."[106]

These institutional arrangements, however, failed to produce second chambers of Harringtonian generalists, even less a New World surrogate of the Whig governing class. The voters, being normally the same for each house, chose the same sort of persons for each. Accordingly, the conduct of each was similar, the senates, according to critics, displaying the same lack of "firmness" and "steadiness" that was thought to be peculiar to more popular assemblies. A historian of that time summarized what must seem to us the inevitable result. If both houses were elected "out of a homogeneous mass of people," wrote David Ramsay, "this rather made two coordinate houses of representatives than a check on a single one, by the moderation of a select few."[107] Then as now when voters chose a representative, they did not, as Harrington expected, so much look for someone with intellectual distinction as for someone who would stand up for their interests.

Yet in this process of electoral choice, American politics has not neglected the intellectual criterion but has met the need for the generalist in a manner in keeping with its self-governing genius. If we look over the political scene, we can find individuals with power or influence who, in the manner of the Harringtonian senator, respond to the interests of the voters, yet at the same time put these interests in a perspective which clarifies their meaning for the voters themselves. We find such people in various walks of life and all branches of government, but especially among those holding or aspiring to elective office. What these political leaders say and do responds to the wishes of their constituents. It also expresses something those diverse particulars have in common. One can think of memorable examples from the words and deeds of presidents at times of crisis or high decision. But this Harringtonian manner of stating a view of the public interest does not require an elegant rhetoric. It can take the form of the catchwords of the political campaign: "the full dinner pail," "the Square Deal," "Back to Normalcy," "the forgotten man," "the economic royalist," "government is not the solution; government is the problem," summarizing a set of interconnected grievances and aspirations and giving direction to subsequent government action.

This kind of leadership arises from a kind of politics which has flourished since our beginnings. Madison caught the character of that politics in *Federalist* 10. There he saw and favored a great diversity of interests from which majorities could be formed only by the discovery of interests common to so many that the resulting action would meet with general approval. For such majorities to arise in the ordered debate of constitutional self-government requires the kind of leader who can elicit the commonalities of a diverse people. His function is not mere brokerage, which may accomplish nothing more than the piecing together of an inwardly incoherent and possibly self-defeating coalition. Nor is he a charismatic leader who wins consent for a new departure of his own concoction. Both brokers and visionaries can be found in American politics, and each may at times serve the public interest. Our Madisonian style of popular government also produces a Madisonian type of leader. We may call him "representative" in Harrington's sense of the word. While serving the interests of the people, he also elicits coherence from these interests. We will not share the exuberant confidence of Harrington that success in this task guarantees good government and inevitably agrees with the right reason of mankind. Such representative leadership, however, is genuinely popular. Moreover, it expresses the spirit, if not letter, of *Oceana* and marks the continuity of our republican experience with his republican thought.

Harrington's elitism is entirely compatible with republican doctrine. He maintains the fundamental proposition of self-government that the ordinary individual can contribute to the determination of the public interest. He holds that this is done by debate among "the whole nation." That does not mean simply miscellaneous mass intercommunication. Nor, while the leadership of the generalists is necessary, does the exchange of ideas between the voters and this elite suffice: the institutions of representative constitutional government provide an indispensable structure. Within that structure, the determination of the public interest starts from the interests of individuals.

Proposals seizing on the commonalities that will satisfy those interests are initiated by the elite, according to Harrington. They are then debated within the legislature and between the legislators and the people. Reflecting the outcome of that debate, the popular assembly enacts the informed will of the people.

Federalism for Utility or for Liberty?

The form of government established by the constitution of Oceana is popular, constitutional, representative, and deliberative. It is also federal in some sense. In what sense and for what purpose? How does Harrington's federalism contribute to solving the dilemma of scale—that is, to offsetting the weaknesses and eliciting the strengths of popular government in the extended republic?

Harrington did not use the term "federal," but he was fully aware of the idea. When considering how this commonwealth for increase might extend its dominion, he took up and rejected the confederate option, which like Montesquieu a century later he found exemplified in the governments of the United Provinces and Switzerland. Much as he admired the Dutch and the Swiss for their virtues as individuals, he scornfully dismissed their "equal leagues" as "useless to the world" because they did nothing to spread "the empire of liberty," and "dangerous to themselves" because of the weakness of their central organs.[108]

His preferred vehicle for expanding the "the liberty of mankind" was the Roman instrument of "unequal leagues." Provinces acquired in this way would be guaranteed a regime of liberty by the imperial power and would enjoy a limited degree of self-government. But, although they would not be reduced to the "bondage" imposed on territorial acquisitions by monarchs, they would remain subject to the overriding authority and military presence of the center. In accord with his own theory of the relation of property to power, Harrington recognized that such an arrangement could not last. For, as he pointed out, if the regime of liberty enabled the propertied class to win and exercise provincial authority, the balance of power would shift away from the imperial center, changing the government of the province from "provincial and dependent to national and indepen-

dent." Even in colonies originally sent out from the center Harrington foresaw this erosion of authority "when they came of age." "For
men," he wrote, "like flowers or roots, being transplanted take after
the soil wherein they grow." Not a bad analysis of the American
break with Britain, as John Adams later recognized in his comments
on Harrington's system.[109]

Federalism on neither the confederate nor the imperial model met
the needs of a commonwealth for increase. The scheme of national
federalism implicit in the model of Oceana had greater promise, not
least for a country like the early American republic confronting the
task of continental expansion. In Oceana governments below the
national level were not established by and under the authority of the
central government, as they had been and continued to be in England. Nor were they, of course, as in compact theory, the sovereign
authors of the confederation. Neither unitary nor confederate, the
vertical distribution of authority in Oceana gave local as well as
central government a legal status which, being founded on the same
"unalterable" law of the constitution, made it broadly speaking a
system of national federalism. In that sense, Harrington anticipates
the vertical allocation of authority adopted by the Americans in
1787.

In contrast with central–local relations under the Stuarts, Harrington's system was radically democratized and decentralized. One sees
this when one considers the role he assigned to the parish, a tiny
jurisdiction which in Oceana would have on average only four hundred inhabitants, of whom fifty were entitled to vote. In the old
regime, parish officers were appointed by appointees of the crown,
the justices of the peace. In Oceana they would be elected annually
by secret ballot by the voters. As "deputies" they would also constitute the electoral colleges which chose the governing persons and
bodies at higher levels of government, culminating in their annual
gatherings at the shire to choose members of the central legislature.[110]

Harrington saw a connection between popular government and
decentralization. But although decentralization was necessary for a
more perfect democracy, decentralized government was not the
forum where democracy would be perfected. Like Machiavelli, Harrington acknowledged that the small republic would be less "un-

wieldy" than the large. Yet in spite of its advantage of small numbers, Harrington like Hume and Madison after him displayed a profound distrust of the small self-governing polity. This is seen in the ban the constitution of Oceana puts on "debate" at all gatherings below the national level.[111] That indispensable process in the making of general law was confined to the central legislature where alone the public interest was discerned and where "reason" and "virtue" reached their highest expression.

Harrington suggests that scale makes the difference by his one exception to the ban, the government of London (Emporium).[112] At that time, London had a population of more than 300,000, three times the size of Oceana's average shire and far larger than any other English town, Norwich, the next largest, having only 15,000 inhabitants. In contrast with the unicameralism of the other governments of Oceana at this level, the orders gave London not only a popular assembly but also a senate, in which debate was an essential process. In the metropolis, in short, as in the nation as a whole, scale and the diversity of interests that went with it—Harrington termed the sixty "companies" of tradesmen "the roots of the whole government of the city"[113]—could be expected to raise questions of a magnitude that would require the grand reconciling procedures of debate and resolution.

Not Machiavelli's law of political number, but Harrington's own theory of interest representation, provides a rationale for decentralized democracy. In a representative system designed to take its primary impulse from the private and particular interests of individuals, it makes sense to start from a constituency so small as to give discernible weight to the preferences of every voter. Such a small and therefore more homogeneous body could readily express its collective interests in its choice of representatives without need for special procedures of aggregation. Precisely this "closeness" of voter to representative enabled the local community to turn not inward on itself but outward toward the larger public. Bearing these interests from the localities, the representative system was perfected by the deliberations of the center, where the diversities of the nation were aggregated in general laws expressing the public interest. Harrington emphasized this centralizing function of the representative system when he compared elections in the commonwealth to the stairs in a house, saying "not that Stairs are in themselves desirable, but that without them there is no getting into the Chambers."[114] Essential to a representative system based on interest and so properly fortified by a constitutional guarantee, decentralization led not to isolation but to aggregation. The function of federalism in this instance was not segregation but integration. To adapt a concept of Max Weber's, we may say that the local community in Oceana was not a closed arena but an open gate, communicating its preferences to the center by the system of representation and receiving direction from the center by the system of administration.[115]

While the representative system was centralizing, the administrative system was decentralizing. But, also in contrast with the former, the latter was set in motion by a large centralized body, the parliament, which exercised wide law-making powers over foreign affairs, defense, religion, and trade. A paradoxical feature of this powerful central government was its lack of instruments, military and civilian, to execute its decisions. It did have at its command a large military force. What Harrington oddly called the "standing army," however, included no long-term professional component, but was recruited anew every year at the parish level.[116] Elected on a rotating basis by the citizen youth from their own number, nearly all of whom were obliged to do military service, its contingents chose their own officers at the lower ranks and met at annual musters for training at the three levels of local government. Thinking of the difficulties of our Continental Congress in the later years of the Revolution, one may wonder how the central government of Oceana could enforce its large constitutional sanctions against localities reluctant to provide their quotas. Surely a citizen army so democratized and decentralized constituted a formidable set of checks upon unwelcome interventions by central authority. Montesquieu thought such a devolution of military force was a main advantage of his confederate republic. Madison saw that also under a system of national federalism, the state militias authorized by the constitution could similarly be used against "encroachments" by the federal government if and when that government brought on "a trial by force."[117]

The congruent decentralization of civilian with military administration enhanced still further this counterbalancing capacity. In the judicial sphere, the itinerant justices, those agents of powerful but intermittent intervention, continued their circuits. But otherwise the central government had almost no bureaucracy, the entire personnel of the permanent civil service numbering only twenty-four.[118] This meant that virtually the whole burden and power of administration rested with locally elected officials and councils. Central taxation, for instance, would be levied upon the phylarch, a body of sixty-six of the officials elected by the deputies at the hundred and the shire, the levy being passed on to the hundred and then to the parish for assessment and collection.[119] At these levels, although officials were to a great extent the same in name and function as those who had carried on government under the old regime, central–local relations were radically transformed. Under the monarchy, local officials had been appointed by the crown, as with justices of the peace, lords lieutenant, and sheriffs, or appointed by appointees of the crown, as with parish constables or persons called for jury service. In Oceana all such officials were elected directly or indirectly.

The change in the status of the justices of the peace marked a particularly important shift of power downward and outward. They had always been local gentry and by no means *intendants* in the French style. As appointees of the crown, however, they had been used for more and more tasks by the central administration, and meeting together as quarter sessions had become the main governing power in the respective shires. In Oceana, by contrast, the justices were annually elected at the hundred by the parish deputies from the members of the knightly order in their own ranks.[120]

Thus we find a federal division of functions serving the ends of a constitutionalism of incentives in the representative system and the ends of a constitutionalism of restraints in the administrative system. Constitutional protection was necessary if local government was to perform either role. A central government that could intervene *ad lib* with local governance could impair the collection and transmission of interests to the national legislature and could prevent the local citizenry from using their administrative powers to check abuses by the center.

While the broad scope of the national legislature reflected the centralizing design of the representative system, there was also a federal element in the division of legislative power since local government, especially the shires, had some constitutionally assigned rule-making authority. Among the powers of the new governing council of the shire, the phylarch, was the charge to hold "the quarter-sessions according unto the ancient custom."[121] In England at that time, when law-making was not yet fully distinguished from law-declaring, the powers of this "court" included in effect some authority to make rules with a local import, as when, for instance, quarter sessions set the rates for poor relief and public works. The orders also gave this body new rule-making authority, such as the charge to make "rules and orders" regarding the conduct of elections by parish and hundred. In a later revision of his model, Harrington added a new and smaller governing body of the shire, which he empowered to make "orders and instructions" when acting as the agent of the parliament in the "reformation" of the law.[122]

Can we detect in Harrington's account the rationale that he followed in his federal division of law-making power? Among the possibilities made familiar in the history of federal theory are two criteria reflecting different philosophical values and projecting markedly different political consequences. These may be tagged "utility" and "liberty."

To say, as Harrington does, that the public interest can be expressed only by the national parliament suggests that there may be lesser interests which entail rule-making by lesser governments congruent with them. Theories of federalism have sometimes put forward this justification, as when Madison defended the constitutionally protected powers of the states as necessary to cope with the "local circumstances and lesser interests" which the general government might neglect because of its concern for "the great and national objects."[123] This criterion of more and less comprehensive interests can be supported and simplified by sound utilitarian reasoning, and in later times economists and political scientists in the spirit of rational choice theory have made much of it when trying to define the proper spheres of different levels of government.

In a highly interdependent society, where virtually all local activities, whether in the public or the private sectors, have substantial spillovers into the whole territory, such considerations of utility leave little room for local autonomy. In this situation, however, the demands of liberty—individual and political—may have contrary implications. Even though it were granted that a highly centralized government was needed to regulate the nationwide impacts of local activities, one could argue on the other side, that such an imbalance of power was a danger to individual rights and to the valuable exercise of local self-government.

This question is raised by the way Harrington deals with education. An instance in which he severely and deliberately weakens the central government, these provisions oblige one to ask whether his rationale is utility or liberty. Both criteria are relevant, but when one considers other Commonwealth thought on this question, in particular what Milton has to say, the argument from liberty seems to be by far the more important.

Seeing in education a means of enhancing the power and virtue of the people, Harrington treated it as a matter of great national importance for government and laid down in the orders a fairly elaborate scheme for compulsory compliance and substantial public support. For males between the ages of nine and fifteen, schools were to be "erected and endowed" in each shire, whose officials were also to supervise the later stages of preparation for manual occupations and for the professions.[124] Even the parish had a constitutionally defined role, since it would choose the pastors who would also be teachers in the schools. In laying out this scheme, however, the orders said nothing about the role of parliament, but put the whole responsibility on local government. This by-passing of parliament was too conspicuous not to be deliberate. It breaks sharply with the usual pattern of giving parliament controlling authority over matters of national importance. Surely if utility were the main consideration, the national legislature would have the principal voice in saying how the constitutional mandate for providing this nationwide collective good would be carried out. Milton's treatment of education and of the central–local problem generally in his adaptation of Harrington's model suggests the reasons Harrington may have entertained for this tilt of the system away from the center.

In 1660, in a last desperate throw to avert the restoration, Milton advanced a less democratic and more decentralized version of *Oceana*, entitled *The Readie and Easie Way to Establish a Free Commonwealth*. Like Harrington, sobered though not daunted by "the confusion . . . of factions"[125] into which the Commonwealth had fallen, he too was greatly concerned with protecting popular government from self-destruction. Rejecting king and lords, he would found government upon "the People." But the distance he put between them and their governors was much greater than in Oceana. The people's choice of the central governing body, the "grand Council" was "refined" (Milton's term) by indirect election by a restricted electorate; moreover, its members for life were not obliged to face reelection.[126]

Milton also proposed a scheme of constitutional decentralization on the lines of national federalism. Within the Commonwealth of England, each county would become "a kind of subordinate commonality or commonwealth," possessing wide law-making powers and governed by the "local nobility and chief gentry." Although Milton condemned Harrington's popular assembly as "unwieldy," he gave to local representatives powers over central legislation not greatly different from those entrusted to that body in Oceana. Like Harrington's senate, the central council had the initiative in law-making, its proposed laws being subject to approval or disapproval by local assemblies acting through "deputies."[127]

Like Harrington, Milton expressly rejected the confederate model exemplified by the Dutch republic. When the counties expressed their assent or dissent to central proposals, the vote of a majority of them would be binding on all, none having the right to exempt itself, as in the case of the "sovereign" communities of the United Provinces. In a pejorative contrast with that system, Milton declared that his republic would consist of not "many sovereignties united in one Commonwealth, but many commonwealths under one united and intrusted sovereignty."[128]

While this federal republic, like Oceana, would be national, its design reflected a notably greater fear of overcentralization than Harrington's model. And more clearly than Harrington, Milton suggests his principal criterion for the federal division of power. It is not utility but liberty, as one sees in his provisions for public education.

Like Harrington a nationalist, Milton had high hopes for education, which he prophesied would "make the whole nation more industrious, more ingenious at home, more potent, more honourable abroad." But again as in Oceana, control over this great national enterprise, producing a nationwide public good, would be vested in the local citizenry. The schools would therefore, be "at their own choice"—that is, the citizens' choice—and would bring up their children "in their own sight," so that, as he said of local self-government in general, "they shall have none then to blame but themselves, if it be not well-administered." The smaller constituency, in other words, would enhance the citizen's sense of efficacy and so of responsibility. Moreover, not only local self-government but also central self-government would benefit. Participation locally would give citizens the opportunity to "exercise and fit themselves" for higher office at the center and to display their relative "worth and merit" before the electorate that would send them there. Decentralization would help with both the preparation and the selection of better governors for the center.[129]

In Milton's scheme the federal division of power would make local and central self-government more effective; its bias in favor of the periphery would also presumably protect individual liberties against abuse by the central government. The recent experience of caesarism rising out of confusion and faction at the center was a prime reason for these precautions. Aware of the parallel with the fall of the Roman republic, Milton, like Machiavelli, identified the rise of Marius with the turning point toward tyranny in that cautionary tale. Urging the merits of his scheme, Milton emphasized how the devolution of power would be a safeguard against central oppression. On this ground he argued that the "grand council," although "perpetual," would not "endanger our Liberty," since the scope of central government under the proposed division of powers was so limited in comparison with the power of "the People" consisting in the wide authority of local assemblies and their right of veto over laws proposed by the council. Against the possible abuses of the elitism produced by his fear of "licentious democracy" at the center, he turned to a severely decentralized version of national federalism.[130]

There is a local interest at work here, the concern of parents and of the local citizenry for the upbringing of their young people. The preservation of the free commonwealth, however, was the principal ground for the tilt against the center. The purpose is staunchly national, although local government is the chosen instrument of action. Commonwealth nationalism did not imply unmitigated centralization.

A Commonwealth for Increase

Whether acting through central or local authority, the government of Oceana would be activist. The "balance" of the constitution did not reduce the power of government, but enabled it to act with "full force and vigour" across a wide range of domestic and foreign concerns. This commonwealth had a purpose: "increase."

For Harrington as for Milton, "increase" had ideal as well as material dimensions, but he reversed the priorities. He would have government patronize religion and education not merely because truth and virtue were valuable in themselves, which he no doubt believed, but especially because they were valuable to the state. Christianity of a broadly Puritan variety was fostered by a nationally established and publicly supported church, which vested the right of ordination in local congregations but which looked for its doctrine to the declarations of a council of the senate.[131] Outside this establishment, liberty of conscience was extended to what was for that day a fairly broad spectrum of beliefs. It was also limited for reasons of state. Catholics were excluded, because of their connection with a foreign power; so also were non-Christians, because they could not be trusted to keep oaths, then commonly sworn in the name of the Christian God.[132] Ministers were charged with pastoral and educational duties, but in reaction to the disorder fomented by the saints and other sectaries, they were sternly forbidden "to meddle with matters of state."[133] Yet the settlement was designed not only to protect against disorder and subversion but also to strengthen the bonds of national unity. In their common Christianity Harrington saw grounds for the reconciliation of royalist and commonwealthsman.[134]

Also, like Milton, Harrington saw in public education the means of cultivating the culture and character of the English people. He was, however, more concerned than Milton with the contribution of education to the power of the state. Holding that virtue was the product of upbringing rather than nature, he looked to public education—"the plastik art of government"—for the cultivation in the young of the courage and wisdom necessary for a commonwealth "constituted especially of two elements, arms and councils."[135] Thanks to the supervision of public magistrates, pupils, he expected, would imbibe patriotic sentiments on the Roman model.[136] One can also see his purpose from the context. The twenty-sixth order which provides for education also provides for universal compulsory military training, and the ensuing discussion culminates in Harrington's famed program of benevolent imperialism. The old Gothic kingdoms were dying—"France, Italy and Spain . . . all sick, all corrupted together." Oceana could look forward to extending its sway without limit toward "the empire of the world."[137]

This increase would be accomplished by arms, but also by the attractions of external security and internal liberty brought by empire. Oceana would not simply impose its "yoke," for that would contradict its "principles" and lead to its own destruction.[138] Following the Roman example, it would rather extend its rule by "unequal leagues." These would secure to those conquered people deemed "capable of liberty" a republican regime, including the fundamental laws of the agrarian and the ballot, which would give them wide powers and self-rule by their own laws under their own magistrates. Provinces, however, would be subject to the substantial authority of the imperial center in such matters as defense and tribute.[139]

For Harrington as for Milton, God had a mission for England. Oceana, he wrote, "is not made for herself only, but given as a magistrate of God unto mankind, for the vindication of common right and the law of nature." In a final burst of patriotic fervor, he saw the "increase" of the commonwealth culminating in a political millennium for the world.[140]

What the American student of federalism must find especially illuminating in Harrington's thought is how vividly it brings out the nationalist emphasis of the republican tradition. His advocacy is all the more convincing because he considered other possibilities. He considered and rejected the small state theory of republicanism advanced by Machiavelli. He repeatedly spurned the confederate model later popularized by Montesquieu and adopted by many Anti-Federalists. Nor did he find in local government, but in central government, the forum where virtue, as he understood it, might be more fully exercised and the public interest more adequately set forth. In his nationalism Harrington was typical of republican thought. His commitment to the extended republic was shared by all contemporary supporters of popular government, whether they preferred, like Harrington, Milton, and the Levellers, a federal or, like Sidney, a unitary system.

Harrington's republic was big because it was national. Unlike nationalists of a later age, he did not theorize about the relation of state and nation. But the main body of their doctrine is implicit in what he said. Like them, he would make the political and the national unit congruent. Like them, he rejected the rule of the wise and the holy and held that government derives its authority and purpose from the nation. In his scheme the people of England were both constituent and governmental sovereign. They ratified and established the constitution, and they governed themselves under it. Thanks to the rational deliberation of democratic constitutionalism, they avoided the dangers and realized the advantages of the pluralism of the extended republic. From the many they made one. Their concern for the common good being elicited by the procedures of the constitutional order, they derived from the manifold of private interests a relevant and coherent conception of the "national interest."[141]

This happy result was not the consequence solely of republican institutions. It also depended upon the capacities which the English nation brought to the tasks of self-government. When Harrington said, as he repeatedly did, that government must be founded on "the People," he was not making some universal reference to any aggregate of persons anywhere anytime. Nor did he mean simply a number of hitherto isolated beings who had voluntarily joined together to form "a people." Harrington made no use of the myth of social contract in order to account for the body which authorized and utilized the commonwealth. His model assumed the existence of a specific people, the English, such as they were, the products of nature and history, in the mid-seventeenth century.

This people shared a mixed rational and passionate nature which, being common to all mankind, meant that "the commonwealth (though they do not see it) is already in the nature of them." As virtue, this rationalized passion inclined them to seek the public interest. History had defined that public by making a nation of the inhabitants of England. They shared a common descent, being near "of blood" and "flesh of your flesh," giving rise to "natural affection" which made the commonwealth "a great family." They had a common faith, Puritan Christianity, which their national religious establishment would maintain. And to these commonalities of ethnicity and religion, Harrington appealed as grounds on which to reconcile even their bitterest disputes. This people, moreover, had undergone a wide diffusion of proprietorship which, although dividing them into the contending "parties" of royalist and commonwealthsman, had left all with the common "cause" of private property. The change in the economic "balance" had also dissolved the old conceptions of authority—"the right of kings, the obligation of former laws, or of the oath of allegiance"—and had brought about "such a reformation of manners" that the people would "bear no other kind of government" than a commonwealth.[142]

Although Harrington did not say so in formal propositions of political theory, he was as aware as any modern student of nationalism that such common social conditions and common values, interests, and affections prepare a people for common political action. Yet he rejected not only the small state theory of republicanism but also the small state theory of community. In his thought the modern republic was made legitimate and possible by the modern nation.

PART TWO

THE NATIONAL AND
REPUBLICAN REVOLUTION

I N   T H E   F O U N D I N G of a state that claims to be both a democracy and a nation, one claim may have priority over the other. Even in the American case, argued Joseph Schumpeter in a typically perceptive and irreverent aside of his classic, *Capitalism, Socialism and Democracy*, the principal motive was nationalism. By the middle of the eighteenth century, he declared, most colonists had ceased to look upon "the English monarch as *their* monarch and the English aristocracy as *their* aristocracy," regarding them rather as "foreigners" who were interfering with American "political and economic interests." In the war of independence, however, the colonists, according to Schumpeter, sought to legitimate with democratic rhetoric what was in fact a national uprising. "From an early stage of the troubles," he concluded, "they presented their case, which really was a national one, as a case of the 'people' against its 'rulers' . . . The wording of the Declaration of Independence and of the Constitution adopted these principles. A prodigious development followed that absorbed and satisfied most people and thereby seemed to verify the doctrine embalmed in the sacred documents of the nation."[1]

Nationalism and democracy are indeed quite different motives of political action. To want to be governed as an independent nation is not the same as to want to be governed democratically. The concept of authority of a state must answer two questions: how is the state to be governed, and who is to be included in the state? A definition of the mode of government does not also identify the unit of government. A commitment to democracy answers the first question but not the second. Democracy, let us grant for the sake of brevity, means the rule of the majority. That does not identify the set of people within which the rule is to apply. Some of the more intractable conflicts of modern politics flow from ambiguous or incompatible answers to that second question. In Ulster, Protestants insist on majority rule in Northern Ireland, while Catholics call for majority rule in the whole island. In a modern democratic state, for the sake of ideological coherence and domestic tranquility, there must be a generally accepted answer to the question of boundaries: what territory and what persons are included in the unit of government? Nationhood provides that answer.

Schumpeter's distinction is sound political science. The hypothesis that in the process of state-making, nationalism may take precedence over democracy is supported by the experience of many new states in recent decades. It does not, however, fit the facts of the American case—fortunately, since that beginning has helped make and keep our idea of the nation democratic. During the decade or so of agitation that led to the break with Britain, the demand for representation made the running far ahead of the demand for separation. The colonists began as Englishmen demanding a greater degree of self-government and ended as Americans declaring their independence.

Drawing especially upon the republican tradition that had come down to them from the Commonwealth, the American dissidents gradually worked out an idea of the national republic which foreshadowed their political future. Given the depth of the conflict between American and British principles, we may think that a decision for independence was inevitable. Some colonial leaders came to that conclusion rather sooner than others. We need not doubt, however, the sincerity of those many dissidents who repeatedly maintained that they sought only freedom within the British empire, not freedom from it. "In the closing months of 1775," writes Marcus Cunliffe, "only an extremist minority favored independence." For months after Washington took command of the Continental Army in 1775, he and his officers daily drank the king's health, as was the custom in a British officers' mess.[2]

If independence was to be declared, and certainly if it was to be secured, the national question had to be decided. In the event this was less a decision than a discovery. During the decade or so of agitation leading to independence, among the scattered dominions of Great Britain in the New World, a large part of the inhabitants of thirteen contiguous colonies along the North American coast demonstrated with increasing credibility their capacity for unified political action in support of a demand for greater self-government. Around that growing demand for self-government a new nation coalesced, and thereupon "the thirteen United States of America" could give a plausible and decisive answer to the national question when they declared that they were "one people" who found it necessary to assume "among the Powers of the Earth, the separate and equal station to which the Laws of Nature and Nature's God entitle them."

Unlike many new nations which have emerged from empires in recent times, the boundary of the new American nation had not been previously defined as an area of imperial governance. The old jurisdictions of British colonialism were the arenas within which the American dissidents resisted imperial rule. But the thirteen were only a fraction of the two dozen or so British colonies in North America and the West Indies. In some other British colonies beside the thirteen, similar conditions gave rise to similar whiggish sentiments.[3] Only in the thirteen, however, were the rebels strong enough to successfully challenge British power. It was this movement, organized throughout the continent and acting through the several colonial governments and independently through its own organs of resistance and revolution, which established the new state. It was this whig movement which created and governed the national republic.

Schumpeter, therefore, did not get the American case quite right. The dissident colonists had come to look on the British monarchy and aristocracy as "foreigners," but not because they were British; rather, because they were monarchic and aristocratic. That alienation of the Americans from the British sprang in large part from a conflict between two irreconcilable conceptions of authority. If we are to understand what the Americans were for, we must first see what they were against. That means looking at the Old Whig constitution through the eyes of Edmund Burke and William Blackstone. From the fundamental opposition of government by the many to government by the few followed the differing American and British views of sovereignty, constitutionalism, and representation. The long controversy over actual vs. virtual representation brought out these differences and obliged the Americans to elaborate their idea of the national republic.

While Schumpeter missed the power of this republican thrust, from another angle he was on target. He rightly recognized that American nationalism was also informed by a sense of the purposes which republican government would serve. The whig dissidents were moved to resistance and ultimately to revolution not only by convictions of their rights but also by calculations of their interests. These embraced but were not confined to such concerns as the profits of colonial merchants and the debts of southern planters.[4] This coalition of interests was given coherence by a vision of continental expansion, which led to that "prodigious development" of which Schumpeter wrote. It was, moreover, a distinctively American vision, increasingly at odds with the British imperial view. We will get at its meaning if we look at its emergence from British sources in the early thought of Benjamin Franklin.

The cry of "no taxation without representation" embodied both aspects of the conflict of ideas, both purpose and authority, policy and process. In the shifting American positions, sometimes policy and sometimes process was the leading motif of their complaint. And from the years of controversy over these two issues arose the idea of the nation as one people, at once sovereign and subject, the source of authority and the substance of history.

During this agitation, the argument was conducted for most of the time on the presumption, shared by both sides, that they belonged to "one state," "one nation," "the same people." The attempt to find a solution by sending American MPs to Britain—the parliamentary option—obviously took this for granted. The other main proposal, which I have termed the federal option, also assumed that there would continue to be one state. Within it, however, a constitutionally protected division of authority would in some fashion be arranged between the center and the periphery. Given the fundamental ideological conflict, the federal no more than the parliamentary option could lead to a solution acceptable to both sides. Yet the notion of such a vertical division of authority, harking back to the federalist ideas of the Commonwealth, prepared the way for the national federalism of 1787.

The federal decision had not yet been taken in 1776, but the way to it had been opened. The key was the idea of popular sovereignty. Once it is granted that the people establish and may alter the frame of government, the ground is prepared for this authoritative power to set up a federal system. Acting in their constituent capacity, the people make a territorial allocation of power, authorizing governments for the parts and a government for the whole, the government of each sort having coordinate legal status with the other.

This was in fact how our system of national federalism came into existence. During the months before and after independence, the American people, acting through the Continental Congress, authorized governments for the provinces which had previously been ruled by colonial governments established by the British crown. From 1774 to 1781, however, the Continental Congress acted without benefit of a constitution. That came later when the people of the United States established a general government by the Articles of Confederation of 1781 and then by the Constitution of 1787. Very much in accord with republican doctrine, the sovereign people, acting in their constituent capacity, authorized governments for the states and for the nation. The national theory of American federalism was formulated as an account of this historical process.

The principle that made possible the distinctively American form of constitutionalism and so of federalism was popular sovereignty. This fundamental principle of American republicanism was irreconcilably in conflict with the principle of hierarchy which, as embodied in the Old Whig constitution, necessarily implied parliamentary sovereignty over a unitary system.

CHAPTER 4

The Conflict
of Ideas

IN 1776 the American rebels chose not only independence but also popular government. In making that choice, they turned their backs on one of the main lessons of the Western political tradition. For more than two thousand years, nearly all leading minds had rejected government by the people.[1] Classical philosophy had taught the rule of the wise, Christian theology the rule of the holy. Medieval thinkers had combined the two ideas, vesting authority in a hierarchy of natural virtue and a hierarchy of divine ordination. They differed over the relation of secular and sacerdotal power. They did not doubt that the ruler, whether prince or prelate, knew what was good for the ruled and therefore had the right, indeed the duty, to direct them toward that good.

By the time the Americans made their audacious choice, the intellectual foundations of the classical and medieval idea of government had been fatally weakened by new views of God, man, and nature. In a neoclassical version, however, its principles were being reaffirmed in more empirical formulations. The argument for hierarchy had shifted from cosmological and theological speculation toward sociological and historical scholarship. Both Montesquieu and Burke, for instance, greatly admired the government of Great Britain for its preservation of liberty, order, and the rule of law. They found the reasons for these merits not in the inherent wisdom of its rulers or their gifts of grace, however, but in the balance of powers of its constitution and the breeding of its governing class.

Edmund Burke was the most eloquent spokesman and acute analyst of the Old Whig outlook. What he said and wrote about politics shows how the old superstructure of hierarchic doctrine was being refounded on a substructure of modern thought. Because he personally also displayed greater understanding of the American claims than most British statesmen, his exposition of the reigning outlook is an even more convincing demonstration of the ideological chasm between mother country and colonies.

Edmund Burke and the Old Whig Constitution

The Old Whig regime had departed from the classical and medieval ideals of Old Tory politics in quite fundamental ways.[2] In defense of Britain's hereditary monarchy, for instance, Burke dismissed as foolish, even impious, the notion that monarchy has "more of a divine sanction than any other mode of justification." Its true defense was pragmatic and historical:

> No experience has taught us, that in any other course or method than that of an *hereditary crown* our liberties can be regularly perpetuated and preserved sacred as our *hereditary right* . . . the undisturbed succession of the crown [is] a pledge of the stability and perpetuity of all the other members of the constitution.[3]

In a similarly secular spirit he justified Britain's aristocracy by its public service and found its source in social and political institutions. In his eyes the governing classes were not a God-given body of men with inherent, superior virtue. They were formed and sustained by favorable circumstances of breeding, education, and milieu, which Burke describes at great length and in detail. Thanks to that environment, the governing classes acquired and cultivated those capacities which enabled them to perform the function that justified their power and privilege.

Likewise, there was no one "best model" for all states. In his arraignment of Warren Hastings and the East India Company Burke objected that India should be governed "upon their own principles and not upon ours." At times "constitutions" need to be restored or even improved. On these occasions a nation should, as Burke advised the French, and as they failed to do, consult its past and build on the old foundations. In the course of its history each nation works out the form of government and society appropriate to it. In this sense, government is an "experimental," not a "theoretical," science.

Burke's historical method opened the way for "reflection and choice" to play a large part in the development of the state. On the one hand, it led governments to look not to "abstract right" and "general theories," philosophical or theological, for constitutional guidance but to the precedents of their own history. On the other hand, it also taught that they must accommodate their institutions and their policies to history. "We must all obey the great law of change," wrote Burke. "All we can do, and all that human wisdom can do, is to provide that the change shall proceed by insensible degrees."[4] Burke was one of the first political thinkers to recommend prudent, gradual, but continual adaptation and improvement. His traditionalism made him also a reformer.

Old Whig differed from Old Tory ideas not only on this high philosophical plane but also in their view of political institutions. The great change was, of course, in the relations of king and parliament. Under the Tudors, as we have seen, the initiative and decisive influence in regard to the great questions of the common good were the Crown's preserve.[5] By the eighteenth century, in contrast with the time when the House of Commons fought bitterly with James I for the right to discuss "matters of state," all three branches, not least the Commons, took part in deliberating on the public interest and the common good. In 1716 one authority wrote:

> Our three estates of King, Lords and Commons, making up the supreme Legislative power of the nation . . . as they are mutual checks and awes to one another so they are to one another mutual lights and assistants. In the equilibrium of this body and the unanimity of their deliberations, consists our greatest happiness.[6]

Government by discussion was institutionalized in parliament. Forces of protest and reform, even when aimed at the oligarchic constitution itself, could at times win a hearing there. Freedom of the press was shaking off censorship and slowly but perceptibly growing up as the right to do in public what was already being done in parliament. Liberty of conscience was exercised with an amplitude that would have horrified Saint Thomas or Laud. Personal freedom before the law was protected by procedures such as *habeas corpus* and trial by jury, which the American dissidents prized and claimed as their own.

These departures from Old Tory principles greatly narrowed the gap between the British regime and the republican ideal. Certainly, the reduction, if not the removal, of the religious issue eliminated much of the bitterness of the earlier antagonism. Yet John Adams was right to see the American uprising as continuous with the struggle against "the execrable race of Stuarts." He correctly identified the underlying issue: on the one side, the idea that the many must look to the few for instruction in and guidance toward the common good, and on the other side, the idea that the many can themselves determine the common good and direct the polity toward its realization. The enemy against which the Americans rose was the age-old hierarchic tradition of the West in a modernized version.

One should not force these attitudes into the neat categories of political philosophy. It was an aristocratic age when the rule of the few was so widely accepted and so inexorably exerted that the governing classes could feel no need for elaborate justifications of their power. Elitism is the term with which political science characterizes such a regime. But the word is so bland as to miss the point. A few great families—Russell, Pelham-Holles, Watson-Wentworth, Bentinck, Petty, Cavendish, Fox, Stanley, Seymour, and so on—dominated the nation at the capital and in the shires, enjoying a princely status, founded on wealth, power, and prestige, with which the elites of the American colonies could not faintly compare. There is something pitiful in John Adams's effort to find an equivalent in the first families of Boston (population 16,000) and of the countryside, where their superior status was measured by the leading member of each generation being made a justice of the peace.[7] Yet the attitudes which supported this regime of "civilian feudalism" in Britain, as Namier called it,[8] were not a mere miscellany of legitimizing sentiments. They had a coherent structure. They were a "mentality," which an outsider like Burke could more readily perceive than the beneficiaries themselves. This structure of thought appears in bits and pieces, becoming more clearly defined as the controversy over representation progressed during the hundred years or more from the debates about instructions and shorter parliaments in the early eighteenth century to the great reform act of 1832.

The hierarchic ideal pervaded Burke's thought even when, in one of his most liberal moments, *Thoughts on the Present Discontents* (1770), he called upon "the people" to help throw back encroachments of royal power. In a memorable phrase he declared that the House of Commons should be "the express image of the feelings of the nation." This, however, was no appeal for instructions from the voters. Burke expressed the received opinion when, as an MP, he repudiated "authoritative instructions" or "mandates" from his constituents. When he called on "the people" to interpose itself against royal power, the political force that he wished to bring into play was "the natural strength of the kingdom: the great peers, the leading landed gentlemen, the opulent merchants and manufacturers, the substantial yeomanry." It was through such natural leaders, themselves hierarchically ordered, that "the people" entered the process of government. Above all, they acted and spoke through the great Whig families, rooted in the country by a "more natural and fixed influence."[9]

In Burke's view, only when "the multitude" acted under an "habitual social discipline in which the wiser, the more expert, and the more opulent conduct, and by conducting enlighten and protect, the weaker, the less knowing, and the less provided with the goods of fortune" did he recognize "the venerable object called the people." In England, he said, no "original or any subsequent compact of the state, expressed or implied, constituted *a majority of men, told by the head,* to be the acting people." On the contrary, "for their own benefit, [this discipline] postpones, not the interest, but the judgement, of those who are *numero plures,* to those who are *virtute et honore majores.*"[10] In Old Whig as in Old Tory England, the less endowed many deferred to rule by the virtuous few. In contrast with Old Tory usage, the idea of virtue had been transformed to allow for the influence of environment and the necessities of changing times. The term still stood for certain qualities of mind and character which were a title to deference and a justification of authority.

In their various ranks and orders, "the wise, the more expert, and the more opulent" performed what Burke called their "integrant" function in many spheres of civil society. At the center of realm and empire, they governed through parliament. The peers were directly present in the lords; otherwise, "the people" were represented in the commons by MPs elected from the ancient communities of borough and shire. Such representation was not "actual" but "virtual." In Burke's exposition the authority which parliament drew from virtual representation had two sources. In harmony with Old Tory usage, one was the qualities of mind and character—the virtues—of its members. The other was "a communion of interests and a sympathy of feelings and desires" with the various classes, or, in Burke's term, "several descriptions," of the people. In neither respect was the representativeness of the MP derived from his being "actually chosen" by those he represented. That would be actual representation. In comparison, continues Burke, virtual representation is better, since it "corrects the irregularities in the literal representation" which arise because "the people may err in their choice."[11]

Burke does grant that there must be some "substratum" of actual representation. "The member must have some relation to the constituent." If he is to be acquainted with and attend to the interests and feelings of that "description of people" to which his constituents belong, it is expedient that he apply for their favor from time to time. Yet such participation must be severely limited. To ensure a responsible use of electoral power, only those who meet qualifications of property, training, and the like should be admitted to the franchise.[12]

While the member was accountable to the electors in only this attenuated sense, he might well be called strictly to account by an outside person, his patron, if like a large proportion of MPs he had one.[13] The Old Whig code required the member to resign his seat if he parted company from his patron in his voting of parliament. No less a whig than Charles James Fox declared of the obligation of the MP to his patron: "If he does not obey the instructions he receives, he is not to be considered a man of honor and a gentleman."[14] While reformers called such patronage "corruption," the orthodox regarded it as benign and necessary "influence."[15]

Thanks to such connections with outside persons and bodies, the House of Commons represented the "great interests" of the country, as well as its virtue. Burke linked these two aspects of virtual representation when he observed that "a great official, a great professional, a great military and naval interest, all necessarily comprehending many people of the first weight, ability, wealth and spirit has been formed in the kingdom," and went on to argue that they along with the landed and the commercial interests should be assured a share of parliamentary power.[16] These broad functional groupings of British society provided starting points for government by debate in parliament, where, as Burke said, the "widespread interests" of nation and empire "must be considered—must be compared—must be reconciled, if possible." In these deliberations presumably men of wisdom and beneficence would be guided not by "local prejudices" but by "the general good resulting from the general reason of the whole."[17]

From the hierarchic premise, virtual representation followed unavoidably, and from virtual representation followed parliamentary sovereignty. If the many had been enfranchised and deference abolished, the rule of the virtuous few would have collapsed into popular government.[18] The great interests of realm and empire and the various ranks and orders of the governing class would have no longer been assured of their proper weight and voice in government. For that reason, sovereign authority could not be vested in the people but only in that complex body, the parliament, which, including king, lords, and commons, brought all virtues and all interests into a common deliberation in their proper ordering. On Old Whig premises, if there was to be sovereignty in Britain, that "absolute despotic power," which according to Blackstone had to be lodged in some organ of every government, could belong only to parliament. In this sense, the neoclassical remnants of the old virtue philosophy provided the intellectual foundation of parliamentary sovereignty.

Given the premise of parliamentary sovereignty, the British could not accept the idea of constitutionalism emerging in America. For the Americans, the power of governing bodies, like certain rights and liberties of individuals, depended upon a man-made law superior to the law made by those bodies. Governments therefore could not violate the imperatives of this superior law without undermining their own authority. If asked what human authority made and unmade that superior law, the Americans, like the republicans of the seventeenth century, could, and ultimately did, reply, "the People." The presumption of popular sovereignty, coming down with the republican tradition, made possible the two-tiered American conception of constitutionalism.

That path of thought was barred to the British. Like Burke, they could hold that certain rights and liberties, certain institutions and procedures should be cherished and maintained. Like Burke, however, they could not grant that these cherished rights and institutions were safeguarded by a man-made law superior to the law of parliament. In words matching Blackstone's hyperbole, Burke said of parliament that "her powers must be boundless," and he saved some of his sternest rhetoric to denounce the doctrine that "the *people*," having formed a state, retain the power to change it. In his view the parliament acted in a twofold capacity. One was as "the local legislature of this island, providing for all things at home." There was also "an *imperial character;* in which, as from the throne of heaven, she superintends all the several inferior legislatures." In language echoing his appreciation of the "natural aristocracy" he characterized this role in colonial affairs: "It is necessary to coerce the negligent, to restrain the violent, and to aid the weak and deficient, by the overruling plenitude of her power."[19] Warm as he was for conciliating America on grounds of policy, he rejected the American views of representation, sovereignty, and *a fortiori* constitutionalism.

These British ideas of sovereignty and constitutionalism ruled out federalism as a solution to the conflict with the colonies. We need to look more closely at them in order to see where they differed from American views and why this difference made federalism possible within America but not between Britain and America.

Blackstone and Sovereignty

The eighteenth-century doctrine of sovereignty can be made to look ridiculous. When Blackstone speaks of "absolute despotic power" as a necessity of all governments and an actuality of the regime of liberty-loving Britons, it does seem an affront to decency and to fact.[20] Yet what he and other exponents of the idea were saying was not as new or obnoxious or foolish as such isolated quotations suggest. To begin with, they did not mean that the sovereign power—in the British case, the parliament—was free of moral constraints.[21] On the contrary, as Blackstone said in the Introduction to his *Commentaries,* "the law of nature," consisting of "the immutable laws of good and evil," is "binding over all of the globe, in all countries and at all times." It followed that "no human laws are of any validity, if contrary to this [law]," and "with regard to such points as are not indifferent, human laws are only declaratory of, and act in subordination, to the former." Making more specific the general precepts of the law of nature, "the revealed or divine law" was the other foundation on which "depended all human laws."[22]

The law of nature included certain "absolute rights" to life, liberty, and property "which every man is entitled to enjoy, whether out of society or in it." In so far as human laws embodied these norms, they carried a direct moral obligation. With regard to the many points which are morally "indifferent," human law establishes what is "right or wrong" in the light of what the legislator sees as "proper for promoting the welfare of society and more effectually carrying out the purposes of civil life." Since "the principal aim of human society is to protect individuals in the enjoyment of [their] absolute rights," even legislation on indifferent points has a moral claim to obedience.[23]

Although the law of nature is binding on conscience, moral obligation alone does not ensure that men in society will respect its norms. Government, the agency by which coercive human law is made and enforced, is therefore a necessity if the social order defined by the law of nature is to be preserved. Accordingly, as Blackstone says, the British constitution "intrusted" parliament with "sovereign and uncontrollable authority" to make and unmake all laws, including those called "fundamental." Quite properly, he did not call this principle of the constitution a law, since it was itself the source of the authority to make law.[24] Not itself a law, the principle of parliamentary sovereignty was a conclusion of Old Whig political theory, following from the purpose of government in the face of the necessities of social union. For if government was to guard "the rights of each individual member," then "each individual should submit to the laws of the community; without which submission of all it was impossible that protection should be certainly extended to any." That is, if there were someone who was not obliged to submit, he would be legally free to harm anyone and everyone.[25]

To say that everyone must submit to all laws is to say that the law-making power is unlimited. "Unless some superior be constituted," wrote Blackstone, "whose commands and decisions all the members are bound to obey, they would still remain in the state of nature, without any judge upon earth to define their several rights, and redress their several wrongs."[26] Such a government would claim a monopoly of coercive force. It was not the monopoly of force which made it sovereign, but its sovereignty that entitled it to claim a monopoly of force.[27] The legal authority to demand and to enforce such universal obedience was sovereignty.

If lesser law-making bodies, such as colonial legislatures, or worse, if individual subjects or self-constituted committees of subjects, were to be allowed the right to disobey laws of parliament which they found to be "invalid" in the light of God or nature, then the legal foundation of the social order would have been destroyed. Laws contrary to the law of nature were indeed "invalid," but according to the British constitution, the body that was to determine that question was the parliament. And therein lay its sovereignty.

The argument leading to this conclusion is not without merit and certainly not without pedigree. The question it addresses is the old problem of how to reconcile the diversity of any social aggregate with the unity necessary for its survival as a social order. Addressing this problem, Aquinas had concluded that "a social life cannot exist among a number of people unless under the governance of one to look after the common good; for many as such, seek many things, whereas one attends only to one."[28] Similarly, Old Whigs of the eighteenth century such as Blackstone and Burke held that there must be an ultimate authority in the state which was unitary. Thanks, however, to their theory of mixed government and to the lessons they drew from English history, they concluded that the sovereign power was properly not a single person but that complex and balanced entity, the king-in-parliament.

Why should such arrangements have the capacity to cope with the problem of order? Like their predecessors in the hierarchic tradition,

Old Whig theorists grounded this capacity of government in the superior virtue of its members. In any "well-constituted frame of government," according to Blackstone, this sovereign power should be entrusted only to "such persons" as have the qualities which in their "perfection" are found in "the Supreme Being," namely, "wisdom to discern the real interest of the community; goodness, to endeavor always to pursue that real interest; and strength, or power, to carry this knowledge and intention into action." For Blackstone as for Burke, the constitution was balanced within the charmed circle of the virtuous few. Democracy, while well-intentioned, was not "well-constituted."[29]

Any exercise of the coercive force of the state was constitutional, that is, legal, only if authorized directly or indirectly by this ultimate power. The authority which Aquinas gave to the monarch, subject to the pope, and which James I claimed for himself, subject to neither pope nor presbyter, Blackstone found in the parliament. Did that mean there was no check on power? Not at all. The outcome of the long struggle with royal pretensions had been precisely to establish a system of checks and balances among the three estates such that no one of them could overawe the others and all might contribute to the enlightenment of the whole. The division of power which some scholars have held to be the core of constitutionalism was built into the "balanced constitution."

This separation of powers made talk of the sovereignty of parliament as an "indivisible" power slightly bogus.[30] For if the social order were disrupted and the three estates could not agree on what to do, there would be no rule to which the obedience of all could be demanded and upon which order could be restored. In short, a sovereign composed of two or more voices, all of which must agree if the sovereign is to act, raises the possibility of stalemate and a consequent inability to maintain order. It would seem that the guarantee of order could be "certain" only if the sovereign were one person—with an undivided mind. Parliament was a single power, however, in the sense that, once these separate bodies had come to agreement, no other human agency could nullify that decision. To vest such authority of review in a further body, such as the judiciary or the people, as radicals at home and in the colonies sometimes urged, would destroy the very balance upon which respect for the law of nature and the maintenance of social order depended.[31]

To say that parliament was the sole ultimate authority was to say that no other human agency—no pope or presbyter, no court, corporation, or magnate, no other nation or ruler—could nullify the legal obligation of a parliamentary statute. In relation to such other bodies, its legal competence was "boundless" (Burke) and "absolute" (Blackstone). Seeming violations of the law of nature had to be endured, if the social order defined by the law of nature was to be maintained. The reasoning appealed to consequences: as Blackstone said, "without [the] submission of all, it [is] impossible that protection should be certainly extended to any." There was, of course, a limit to submission. No whig of any stripe could stand for absolute passive obedience, even to parliament. At some point, such actions by government justified resistance.[32]

The right of resistance, however, was a moral and political, not a legal or constitutional, right. Necessarily, according to Blackstone, "oppression" by "the sovereign power" would be "out of the reach of any *stated rule,* or *express legal* provision." In the case of "unconstitutional oppression" advancing by "gigantic strides," however, "mankind will not be reasoned out of its humanity" and may resort to "those inherent, though latent, powers of society which no climate, no time, no constitution, no contract, can ever destroy or diminish."[33] This may seem to suggest a right of revolution. It is, however, by no means an appeal to "the People" in the Lockean sense of a coherent authoritative power standing outside and over government.[34] It is rather a realistic recognition that at some point an oppressive government will meet with what Barker calls "civic resistance,"[35] of some unpredictable and irregular character, unformed by any constitution, human law, or "express legal provision."

Republicans did not deny the political problem of pluralism. They proposed a radically different solution, however, from that of Old Tories and Old Whigs. They agreed that there must be an ultimate authority that was unitary. Their enormous claim was that the many could act as this final judge and power. While it was conceded that the many did seek many things, it was further argued that they could also bring themselves to act as one without calling in the rule of the few. Such was "the People" of the doctrine of popular sovereignty. As the constituent authority in the state, the people laid down the fundamental law of the constitution and could intervene to maintain the constitutional order.

Blackstone rejected this possibility. Like Burke, he vigorously took issue with Locke's assertion that "there remains still inherent in the people a supreme power to remove or alter the legislative, when they find the legislative act contrary to the trust reposed in them; for, when such trust is abused, it is thereby forfeited, and devolves to those who gave it."[36] Blackstone's criticism was that such a procedure was impractical. Such a devolution of power, he claimed, would not only dissolve the government but would also reduce the members of the society to "their original state of equality" with no authority over them.[37] Blackstone was as certain as Burke that, however the government may have come into existence historically, the people could not reclaim or exercise sovereign power. They could annihilate government, but they could not themselves govern. On this question Blackstone adheres to that fundamental proposition of the hierarchic tradition: government endures only where the few rule over the many.

Here was the underlying issue between the Americans and the British which emerged in the course of the long controversy leading to independence. Otherwise, on these questions of sovereignty and constitutionalism, they had a great deal more in common than their spokesmen were usually ready to grant in the heat and confusion of debate. Both sides recognized that government was morally subject to the constraints of the law of nature. Both recognized life, liberty, and property as "the great and primary rights" enshrined in the higher law. Both agreed that the British constitution included a "fundamental law" asserting these rights in general and protecting them in specific ways. They agreed that there was an ultimate authority in society which established this fundamental law of the constitution and which could change it.[38] Their great and unbridgeable disagreement was over the location of this ultimate authority. For the British it was parliament; for the Americans it was "the People."

Given this conception of popular sovereignty, the Americans necessarily conceived of two sorts of human law: on the one hand, a fundamental law made by the sovereign people which authorized government and defined individual rights and, on the other hand, another sort of law made by bodies authorized by this fundamental law. Needless to say, if the rules made by such inferior law-making bodies breached the fundamental law, these rules were invalid not merely morally but legally, since the law giving these bodies authority at the same time limited that authority. Above these inferior law-making bodies was a sovereign power which had authorized them and which watched over them and could intervene to correct them. To appeal to this superior authority against transgressions of the fundamental law did not disrupt the social order or send society back into the state of nature but rather called into action the sovereign law-making power, the people.

The existence of such a continuing constituent sovereignty made national federalism possible. Possessing the whole of that "absolute despotic power" of Blackstonian doctrine, the people could delegate some powers to the state governments, some to the federal government, and, if they preferred, reserve the rest to themselves, as in the Tenth Amendment to the Constitution. Neither level of government would be subordinate to the other; both would be subordinate to the same sovereign source. By contrast in the British case, such a federal arrangement was ruled out by parliamentary sovereignty. Parliament could authorize lesser governments, as it did in abundance in the highly decentralized system of realm and empire. It could embody this act of devolution in a statute, a convention, or an express commitment of British administrations. But such a government would remain subordinate to the British parliament. Its continuing autonomy, therefore, would depend upon the self-restraint of parliament—in other words, upon the good will of the British governing class.

No matter, therefore, how generous the British proposals of home rule for the colonies might be, the reservation of parliamentary sovereignty made them unacceptable to American whigs. They were no longer content, as they had once been, to entrust the protection of their liberties to the virtue of the few. None of the various schemes

of imperial reorganization could solve the conflict over authority—
for the simple reason that that conflict was not about the territorial
division of sovereignty but about the democratic basis of sovereignty.

Benjamin Franklin and National Purpose

That conflict was over representation. But representation for what?
When the American whigs sought government by the many, they
were not unmindful of the kind of governance the many would
render. The clash of ideas was over purpose as well as authority. This
purposive aspect of colonial motivation was expressed, enlarged, and
put in context by the developing thought of Benjamin Franklin.

Franklin has been called the least philosophical of the Fathers,[39]
but his thinking, while practical, worldly, and often quantified, was
on a grand scale in space and time. In his politics as in his science,
he displayed that power of imagination which, as Alfred North
Whitehead has observed, one often finds among a commercial people.[40] His genius was to see the possibilities latent in particular
circumstances, such as those that occasioned the Albany conference
of 1754. In comment of this sort, dating mainly from the 1750s, he
set out a powerful conception of the future of the British empire: a
future of power, opulence, and liberty, increasingly realized in an
expanding America.

Until its later years, the eighteenth century in Britain, as in Europe
generally, was a time not of increasing liberty but of growing state
power.[41] In his appreciation of power, Franklin had much in common
with the state-makers and empire-builders of those days—uneasy as
it might have made him to find himself classified with enlightened
despots and aristocratic imperialists. At the climax of his famous
paper of 1751, *Observations Concerning the Increase of Mankind*,
foreseeing an America raised to such a height of prosperity by the
abundance of unsettled land that its population would double in
twenty-five years, he exclaimed:

What an Accession of Power to the British Empire by Sea as well as
Land: What Increase of Trade and Navigation! What Numbers of
Ships and Seamen! We have been here but little more than 100 Years,

and yet the Force of our Privateers in the late War, united, was greater, both in Men and Guns, than that of the whole British Navy in Queen Elizabeth's Time.[42]

Unlike the typical statesman of his day, Franklin also concluded that civil and political liberty were conditions of that greater prosperity and power. Not only fertile land and great open spaces were necessary but also the freedom for the laborer to leave his employment and, setting up for himself as a farmer or craftsman, so to prosper that he could marry early and raise a big family.[43] As a taxpayer, moreover, he would more willingly and more effectively share his abundance with the state, if he had a voice in deciding what it did. As early as 1754 Franklin set out the twofold issue around which the great quarrel with Britain later revolved, declaring that it was the "undoubted Right of Englishmen not to be taxed but by their own Consent given thro' their Representatives."[44] When he elaborated the grounds of this right, however, his characteristic reasons were not legal or ethical but pragmatic: an appeal to the consequences for state and nation. Passing over in silence any claim of the British parliament to greater wisdom or virtue, he argued that the colonists themselves had a better understanding of the need for taxation and of their ability to bear it. In accord likewise with his belief in government by discussion, he also saw in representative government a means of enlisting not only the understanding but also the will of the people in the decisions on the common good. For, he wrote, "where heavy burthens are to be laid on them, it has been found useful to make it, as much as possible, their own act; for they fare better when they have, or think they have some share in the direction."[45]

Like other imperialists of the age, Franklin accepted the general mercantilist framework of state intervention for the sake of greater wealth and power. His means, however, were increasingly less restrictive and more liberal. The 1751 paper itself was called forth in protest against the Iron Act of 1750, which imposed new constraints on the industry in America. In later years, while never a convert to laissez faire, he moved toward still greater economic freedom, in 1760 hailing as an "excellent Essay" Hume's *Jealousy of Commerce,* which anticipated many of the arguments for free trade.[46] As one of his biographers has remarked, Franklin was among the first to perceive "the function of the American frontier" and how its abundance of cheap and fertile land could open the way for generations of "unchecked human increase and prosperity."[47] He also understood that this material base could produce those results because, to use his words, "the seeds of liberty" had been planted there.[48]

The republican strain in Franklin's thought set him apart from the imperialists of England, as well as from the state-makers of enlightened despotism. His liberal imperialism was unusual to the point of being unique in his age. Indeed, one finds a better likeness to it at an earlier time in the republican expansionism of Harrington. Shading out the element of British rule in Franklin's early vision, one can readily see in his prospect for America a "commonwealth for increase." In contrast with the expansion of Oceana, however, the process of American increase would be less martial and more economic. Harrington had not grasped the possibility of economic growth on a large scale, such as the vast expansion that set in during the eighteenth century. Franklin vividly experienced that expansion and had begun to understand its causes. He perceived the general importance of freedom of employment and movement for economic growth and sensed how the specific mechanism of the division of labor worked in a large and widening market.[49]

Although toning down the martial emphasis of orthodox mercantilism, Franklin saw the need of a strong state with an active central power to protect and to promote that process of increase, if necessary by force of arms. The constitution of this state, therefore, would be an imperial union, not an imperial federation. No more than Oceana would it be based on "equal leagues." From his early failures to get the colonies to unite, Franklin concluded that a union by voluntary compact was impossible. The problem was not simply conflicting interests. Even where common interests indicated cooperation, the free rider temptation led people astray, "one assembly waiting to see what another will do, being afraid of doing more than its share, or desirous of doing less."[50] And even if voluntary union were possible, Franklin thought it inexpedient, since accession at the will of each colony opened the way to secession on the same ground.[51] For both reasons, Franklin urged that union be imposed on the colonies by an outside authority. For one who still fervently accepted the British regime, that authority could be only the sovereign parliament.

In this imperial constitution, however, union would be strengthened by two measures of popular government. According to the Albany Plan of 1754, which was almost entirely Franklin's brain child, an act of parliament would bring the colonies together under a "general government" for purposes of defense and expansion. Consisting of a council of representatives, who were chosen not *ex officio* but by vote of the colonial assemblies, and a president with a veto, who was appointed by the crown, this government would have the authority to tax directly the inhabitants of the colonies. At about the same time Franklin adopted Governor Shirley's proposal that American members be admitted to the British parliament. This would meet the objection to colonial taxation by parliament, since now the colonies would have representatives there. In both the colonial union and the imperial union, representation in a common legislature would perform similar functions, legitimating and facilitating taxation of the represented and further uniting them in sentiment and action. In America the colonists would learn from their representation in a common legislature to consider themselves "not so many independent states, but members of the same body and thence be more ready to afford assistance and support to one another."[52] By their union in the imperial parliament the people of Great Britain and the people of the colonies would likewise "learn to consider themselves, not as belonging to different Communities with different interests, but to one Community with one Interest which . . . would contribute to strengthen the whole, and greatly lessen the danger of future separations."[53]

In these early thoughts on constitutional reform, Franklin projected a unitary regime under a sovereign parliament over a vast Anglo-American empire, the crucial provision being actual representation of the colonies at the center. Yet this big state also had federal features. Strictly, the imperial union was not federal, since the devolution of power to the colonies was enacted, and so could be modified or withdrawn, by the imperial parliament. Within the colonial union, however, authority would be divided between the general government and the several colonial governments by a man-made law superior to both.

A scheme concocted by Franklin in connection with the Albany Plan is still more suggestive of how in later generations federalism actually did function in the growth of the American republic. This was a proposal to establish two new colonies in the Ohio country into which, Franklin predicted in the spirit of his 1751 paper, "thousands of families would swarm" and so lay the foundation for "a populous and powerful dominion" beyond the Appalachians.[54]

An early expression of Franklin's life-long concern with western expansion—he was himself a land speculator[55]—this scheme shows how a republican form of government could at once expand in territory and power and yet remain republican. The difficulty of that problem and Franklin's ingenuity in suggesting a solution appear if we consider Harrington's inability to deal with it. In his critique of equal and unequal leagues as vehicles of imperial expansion, Harrington had observed that equal leagues have the advantage of being voluntary and so of enjoying the consent of their members, but the disadvantage of facilitating secession and of lacking strength to expand. Unequal leagues, on the other hand, are better able, he thought, to expand the commonwealth and to restrain secession, but by the imposition of their "yoke" they will arouse resistance and weaken cohesion.[56]

Franklin's scheme would combine the advantages of equal and unequal leagues in the manner of national federalism under the constitution of 1787. Certain of the old colonies claimed jurisdiction over the western lands.[57] Acting separately, however, the old colonies were not suitable instruments of expansion. "A single old colony," wrote Franklin, "does not seem strong enough to extend itself otherwise than inch by inch." The crown could undertake the task. Franklin perceived—and here was his originality—that this could also be done by the old colonies acting in concert under the Albany Plan. Indeed, one of the main things that colonial union was intended to do was to initiate, direct, and supervise new settlements. Through its general government it would purchase lands from the Indians, grant land to settlers, and make laws for governing the settlements, until the crown authorized particular governments for them.[58]

Up to this point the relationship between the union and new

colonies would be that of an unequal league. Once the new colony had a government, however, the arguments against separation mustered by Franklin on behalf of the Albany Plan would require that it be admitted to the union on a basis of equality with its other members.[59] Franklin's thoughts on government in the America colonies were firm and clear on two main points: that the colonies should enjoy rights of self-government and individual freedom and that they should be united with one another under a representative government. Unequal in the process of colonization, the colonies of this expanding empire would become equal members of the union which exercised those superior powers. In this scheme, the equality of states in the American union along with its guidance and protection by the federal government was foreshadowed, and the inferior position in which the British kept their colonies was avoided. In comparing Franklin's and Harrington's thoughts on the constitution of a commonwealth for increase, one can measure Franklin's advance by noting that he applied to the expanding empire the scheme of national federalism which Harrington confined to Oceana.

Franklin valued economic growth and national power and stood ready to adapt the forms of government to the enhancement of these values. He also was concerned with the opportunity which land and liberty would give to individuals generally to share in these values. But "opulence" and "power" and "equality of opportunity" would not fully describe what he saw as the promise of American life. He also looked to the character of the people. He wanted this nation to be not only "populous and mighty" but also "virtuous." He looked forward, in Esmond Wright's words, to "an expanding Anglo-American empire of power and culture."[60]

Franklin wrote a great deal about virtue and even in his old age recalled with approval the earnest self-examination of his very early years.[61] What he wrote then has often been taken to be hypocritical, and one cannot deny that it does at times reflect a Babbitry which is puzzling in a person of such skepticism and intelligence. That ethical teaching has been severely judged. D. H. Lawrence denounced "this dry, moral, utilitarian democrat" because "he tries to take away my wholeness and my dark forest, my freedom."[62] St. Beuve with a rather different gravamen accused him of "a lack of sentiment, honor, chivalry, religion," declaring that "an ideal is lacking . . . The useful is always preferably his measure."[63] One can quarrel with the details, but in essence both criticisms are right. Franklin had neither a romantic nor a classical sensibility. His lack of the first is evident and was inevitable. In his time the romantic dimension in man and nature was just beginning to be appreciated.

He distanced himself even further from the classical tradition of virtue and the metaphysics of being which it expressed. His famous table of virtues, drawn up around 1735, in which he finds that the right number is thirteen can easily be taken as deliberate mockery of the Platonic four, the Christian seven, or the Aristotelian ten. As expounded with his approval many years later, they still seem to be little more than a set of maxims of enlightened self-interest, pointing the way to economic, social, and political success.[64]

"Nothing," he observed in a marginal note to his autobiography, "so likely to make a man's fortune as virtue."[65] His *Advice to a Young Tradesman* (1748), of which Max Weber makes so much as a reflection of the spirit of capitalism, was hard-nosed practical advice on how to make money and accumulate wealth as a craftsman or storekeeper.[66] *Poor Richard's Almanac* conveyed much the same message.[67] Needless to say, this businessman's ethic with its high regard for manual labor, trade, and money-making would have appalled Aristotle and Aquinas. Nothing strange in that. Standards of virtue change from age to age.

If Franklin's emphasis on results was a reaction, it was not, however, against classical philosophy but against an exaggeration much closer home, namely, the church-bound piety and social passivity which some readings of Luther imparted to Protestantism. A vivid and feeling anecdote from Franklin's autobiography illuminates the psychology. Explaining why he deserted the worship in which he had been brought up, he recalls the climax when his minister in Philadelphia, choosing to sermonize on "virtue," confined its meaning to church-going, Bible-reading, Sabbath-keeping, and purely ecclesiastical exercises.[68] It was at about the same time, Franklin goes on to note, that he set about drawing up his table of virtues, oriented toward "moral perfection" in his daily individual and social behavior.

The biographical origins of his ethic confirm what one senses from the content of its imperatives: its author is neither romantic nor classical but Puritan. As Weber rightly emphasized, Franklin's ethic is not a mere doctrine of self-interest. On the contrary, it would inculcate a duty to practice the virtues he preaches. These duties, moreover, were not only a discipline of personal excellence, but also an imperative of good works. Franklin harped on the necessity of bringing up the young to be "public spirited" and devoted to the common good. As his autobiography advertised to the world, he followed that imperative in his own life. Having made a competence for himself as a bold and talented entrepreneur at the age of forty-two, he retired from private enterprise to devote himself wholly to public service.[69] He already had a long record of spending time and money on the common good of his city and province in war and peace, and his empire-building plans were continuous with the city-building projects of his earlier years.

Nor did the individual and the common good as he conceived them consist merely in material increase and power. Franklin, to be sure, had no patience for the purely inward life, for Aristotelian *theoria,* for contemplation as the ascent of the philosophical or religious mind toward a higher reality. Reflection as a phase of scientific inquiry he understood and boldly practiced. But that was a use of the mind which would have consequences for the external world. His ethic was on the same model, teaching virtue as an inner experience of self-examination, imaginative, critical, and disciplined, but always with a counterpart in behavior. He valued neither the inward nor the outward life by itself but rather their conjunction as virtue-in-action.

He also looked at the economy in this dual light. He preached those virtues which in a free America would lead the individual and the community toward material increase. He also saw this free America as the setting in which those admired traits of character could rise and flourish. While for a time he had some fear of an economy in which commerce overbalanced agriculture, his individual and social ethic presupposed a high degree of commercial freedom and activity. His advice to youth generally, as to young tradesmen in particular, took for granted that they would be free to buy and sell, save and invest, and control the use of their labor and their property. Such a society would give the individual the opportunity to be a self-made man. That meant to achieve "affluence and independence" by his own efforts. It also meant to make his own character by the cultivation of virtue. In this ethic, virtue was a motor of capitalism and capitalism a school of virtue.

Franklin's faith in man's capacity for good works was Arminian, but Calvinism had always harbored that possibility. Milton himself had ridiculed a "fugitive and cloistered virtue" and exhorted republicans to brave "the trial of virtue" and "the exercise of truth." In eighteenth-century America, despite the efforts of Jonathan Edwards in its early years to re-establish a more severe Calvinism, works came to be regarded as less irrelevant to salvation. Even Cotton Mather in his *Bonifacius* (1710)—often reprinted as *Essays to Do Good*—offered "a modest, practical guide to personal and social behavior, every bit as though works mattered and the world would last forever."[70] Democratic man in America, George Armstrong Kelly has observed, needed to be reassured of the value of his visible works, and the Arminian bent of the sects enabled their adherents to look on civil liberty as a field of activity for the mind and so contributed to "the expansion and unification of the country."[71]

Benjamin Franklin's ideas of the commonwealth and of its purpose resembled in many ways what Harrington had conceived. This is not to say that Franklin must have gotten these ideas by reading Harrington's works. What the two men said could also be similar because they both drew on a common background of political thought. Over the following generations in America, spokesmen for the republican cause continued to state and restate that purpose, calling it variously "increase," "expansion," "improvement," "progress," "development," as the circumstances of the country and styles in political language changed, but like their predecessors adapting their ideas of the constitution and of federalism to their changing ideas of what government was for.

The Suffolk Resolves of 1774 called for resistance in the name of "this new world," once a "savage and uncultivated desert" which the colonists had gloriously purchased by "toil and treasure" and which promised an expanding future in "a boundless extent of continent, swarming with millions."[72] In *Common Sense,* Thomas Paine excited his readers with the prospect of the "freedom," "opulence," and "power," of America, if only she had "the legislative powers in her own hands."[73] In the spirit of Franklin, Alexander Hamilton construed the constitution of 1787 in the light of the tasks of nation-building and in his prophetic reports showed how an active central government could lead the way toward making the country rich, powerful, and united. Championed at times by Republicans as well as Federalists and restated by Henry Clay and Daniel Webster, the Hamiltonian program was finally put into effect with new emphasis on its democratic elements by Abraham Lincoln. In later years, although the old external frontier of continental expansion was extinguished, the force of national purpose in our politics did not fail. New frontiers of internal development were discovered and in response new constitutional and federal structures were created.

It is entirely faithful to Franklin's early thought to see it as a first conceptualization of the promise of American life.[74] When he initially seized on these possibilities, he recognized that they might include American independence. But as a passionate imperialist he sought to avert this danger by such proposals as the Albany Plan and colonial representation in parliament. Only reluctantly did he shift the focus of his high hopes from empire to nation. Sharing and often leading the developing thoughts of American whigs, he sought to moderate the stubborn authoritarianism by which Britain maintained its narrow mercantilism. When both objects were frustrated, independence remained the only option. In January 1776 this logical conclusion of Franklin's outlook was published to the world in *Common Sense* by his protégé Thomas Paine. Its grandiose style was not Franklin's but the substance could have been his, and in England some people thought he was the real author.[75]

CHAPTER 5

The Decade
of Agitation

THE BRITISH STARTED the argument by their innovations of the
1760s. These measures, such as the sugar tax and the stamp tax,
were not unduly burdensome and in themselves not sufficient cause
for separation. If the argument had been kept on the plane of how
much and in what ways should and could the colonies contribute to
the costs of empire, perhaps a peaceful solution could have been
found. The Americans, however, not only argued this question of
policy but also even more urgently pressed the question of process.
From the start they did not merely criticize the way parliament was
exercising its powers by levying these taxes; they denied that it had
such powers. Moreover, they framed the question of process not
simply as a matter of prudent housekeeping but rather as an issue of
fundamental constitutional law.

On that high plane the two sides were agreed on the principle of
no taxation without representation. "No subject of England," wrote
Blackstone in 1765, "can be constrained to pay any aids or taxes . . .
but such as are imposed by his own consent or that of his representatives in parliament."[1] In the same year the Stamp Act Congress
resolved "that it is . . . the undoubted right of Englishmen, that no
taxes be imposed on them but with their own consent, given personally or by their representatives."[2] The omission of the last two words
of Blackstone's formulation reveals the question that divided the two
sides: Were the colonists in some form represented in parliament?

Denying that they were, American whigs made two alternative
demands, each being for a form of actual representation. One was
for an American presence in the House of Commons: the parliamen-

tary option. The other was for a constitutionally protected sphere of home rule: the federal option. Rejecting both claims, British administrations and their spokesmen replied that the Americans were already represented—virtually.

None of these responses by itself or in combination could lead to a peaceful solution. For, as controversy drew out their implications, each confronted American republicanism with British elitism. From these confrontations the Americans learned that they had no choice but independence. And in the process of coming to that conclusion, they elaborated the theory of the national and federal republic on which they later built their own new system.

Actual vs. Virtual Representation

The term "virtual" representation came into use at the time of the controversy over the Stamp Act, and the classic exposition of the concept is found in what Burke said and wrote on the topic over the next thirty years or so. For a long time before as well as after, however, the idea was in essentials the orthodox defense against proposals for greater popular influence on the legislature.

One of its main elements was the principle that the MP represented not a particular place but the whole nation. This had come to be generally accepted in England in the seventeenth century. Previously representatives of the shires and boroughs had been regarded as having a more limited role. In Tudor days, they concerned themselves largely with the redress of local and particular grievances in return for the grant of supply to the crown, while questions of the common good—the "matters of state"—were reserved for the initiative of the monarch. During the constitutional struggles that followed, the claim of the House of Commons to take part in discussing and deciding "matters of state" was a central issue. When that claim was made good, the MP *a fortiori* came to be regarded as speaking and voting not merely on behalf of his constituency but on behalf of the whole nation.[3]

That criterion alone, however, is not enough to distinguish virtual from actual representation. This distinction depends on whether one starts from the republican premise that the many can judge the common good or from the hierarchic premise that only the virtuous few can do so. If one presumes that MPs belong to those virtuous few who alone can properly govern, it follows that they should be free of the constraints that actual representation would impose on how they speak and vote in the legislature. Sovereignty belongs to the parliament, not to the people. If, on the other hand, the voter can judge the common good, those constraints are justified and popular sovereignty is affirmed.

No exponent of the republican view of representation had greater influence on American thought than Algernon Sidney, whose *Discourses Concerning Government,* published in 1698 but composed in 1681–83, has been called "more a Bible" to the revolutionaries than any other work except Milton's.[4] In the *Discourses,* Sidney, being both a republican and a nationalist, argued accordingly that the people had the right to choose, instruct, and otherwise control their representative and also that these representatives were sent to the parliament "not for Kent, or Sussex, etc., but for the whole nation." His premise for these conclusions was that "all men are made of the same paste." Kings and parliamentmen alike, therefore, acquire their authority not from superior virtue but from the laws. These laws are made by the people, who may and indeed should frequently change the form of government laid down in them. The legislative power, moreover, being "radically" in the people, the MP must "hearken to the opinions of the electors," so that his judgment may be informed and so that what he says will have more weight when he is known "not to speak his own thoughts only, but those of a great number of men." The electors make sure their representative will listen by means of instructions or by denying him reelection, if they find he has done anything detrimental to the commonwealth.[5]

The retrospective control is preferable, in so far as MPs need to hear the arguments before deciding how to vote. Sidney recognizes the complexity of government by debate and lays the same imperative to listen as well as to speak upon both electors and representatives.[6] The connection of representative and represented, whether mediated by prospective or retrospective controls, remains close and continuous. The MP acts for the national interest. So also does the voter who indeed needs that close and continuous control to ensure corresponding behavior by his MP.

In the early years of the eighteenth century the contrasting doctrine of virtual representation was voiced by the opponents of precisely the procedures of popular influence that Sidney advocated, instruction by voters and shorter parliaments. In 1734, for example, during a debate over whether a new House of Commons should be elected every three rather than every seven years, as then required by the Septennial Act, opponents made much of the principle that MPs represented the whole country, not just their respective constituencies.[7] Against shorter parliaments or instructions from electors, which would increase the "dependance" of MPs on voters, they proclaimed that MPs were, in the words of Sir William Yonge, "the representatives of England" and therefore should be ready to drop their concern for their particular constituencies in favor of "the general interest of the nation."[8]

The crux was the disagreement over the competence of the voters. Winding up against the motion, the prime minister, Sir Robert Walpole, made the orthodox position quite clear. The populace, he argued before an audience few of whom needed convincing, are "wavering in their opinions about affairs of state" and are liable to be misled by "factious and unquiet spirits." More frequent elections would aggravate these weaknesses, communicating to the house of commons the unsteadiness and discontents of the people at large. With longer parliaments, on the other hand, "those at the helm of affairs" have time to show "the justice and wisdom of their measures" and "to set [the people] right before a new election comes." In sum, to shorten parliaments would give too much weight to the "democratical" element in Britain's "mixt" constitution.[9]

The principle that MPs represented the nation as a whole told against popular influence only if one held that the people at large could not grasp the national interest and put it first and therefore would succumb to local and particularistic interests. According to this ancient dogma of the hierarchic tradition, enshrined in Old Whig orthodoxy, the national interest would be better represented by members of parliament who shunned "dependance" on the electors and followed their own judgement of the "the public good in general."[10]

These two ways of looking at representation show the divergent paths of theory and practice taken by Old Whig England and republican America. The theory of actual representation came out of the Commonwealth tradition, which was the common source of radical whig thought in Britain and American in the eighteenth century. In the early 1700s this criticism of state and church was propagated by a group of British writers who were widely read, admired, and copied in the colonies. *Cato's Letters,* for example, one of the more celebrated of these tracts, was excerpted by Benjamin Franklin's brother in Boston shortly after it appeared in London in 1721, and soon thereafter the sixteen-year-old Benjamin himself, in his first excursion into political polemics, used the rhetoric that had been directed against Walpole to denounce the ruling powers in Massachusetts.[11] In this radical whig writing one finds arguments for government by discussion, freedom of the press, manhood suffrage, frequent parliaments, apportionment of seats according to population and property, and instruction of representatives by voters. This was the body of doctrine by which American whigs later defined actual representation and on which they grounded their appeal for American MPs and for a federal division of powers.

What in Britain for long remained only muted protest, in America increasingly became the reality of political life. Already in the colonies in the early eighteenth century, as Pole has shown, representation was "radical" in comparison with British practice. One of the most indicative developments was the rise of instructions, with regard not only to local interests but also to matters of general public concern.[12]

The rise of instructions in the colonies was not a reversion to medievalism but an advance toward republicanism.[13] In the manner advocated by Algernon Sidney the colonists were asserting their right to take part in decisions on the common good. Their control over representatives varied from strict delegation to a trustee relationship subject to frequent accountability.[14] In substance and spirit it differed radically from the thin "substratum" of contact permitted by representation in the Old Whig manner.

Two examples, from the initial and from the final stages of the prerevolutionary resistance, will illustrate how deeply the doctrine of actual representation had penetrated the practice of American dissidence. In May 1764, at the start of the agitation against the Stamp

Act, the town meeting of Boston voted certain "instructions" to their three representatives in the Massachusetts assembly. These instructions had a dual character. In part they urged the local interests of the constituency, "a town that lives by trade." They also and indeed largely were concerned with matters touching the public interest of the whole province: reelection of any legislator accepting an appointive post, the payment of judges, the laws of excise, the reduction of the public debt. Looking beyond Massachusetts, moreover, they directed the representatives from Boston to try to bring other colonies into the united effort against the forthcoming Stamp Act.[15]

Ten years later, during the formation of the Continental Congress, the instructions to delegates from localities and from the provinces displayed the same dual character. Resolutions passed at local meetings, as a historian of the Congress has recently observed, sometimes dealt with matters of essentially local concern. On the whole, however, they did not "resemble the provincial *cahiers* of the Revolutionary France. They were not, that is, a mélange of parochial grievances that had to be converted into a generalized indictment of the existing regime before they justified political upheaval." They already had a general reference, favoring resistance rather than mere protest and militancy rather than concessions, and agreeing in their denial of parliamentary authority and in their support for the resumption of commercial action.[16]

These expressions of public opinion left substantial discretion to the delegates in Philadelphia. They also provided the Congress with a meaningful mandate regarding rights, grievances, and modes of action. No doubt the most notable example of the character and the role of local expressions of opinion on matters of the widest public interest were the Suffolk Resolves. Laying out "a strategy of civil disobedience," these resolutions were drawn up by a convention of delegates from every town in the county and, having been taken to Philadelphia by Paul Revere, they were unanimously adopted as the first resolution of the Continental Congress on September 17, 1774.[17]

The Parliamentary Option

The conflict between the American and the British concepts of representation immediately appeared when James Otis put forward the parliamentary option at the very start of the quarrel. The British administration and its spokesmen promptly saw that to admit this claim would threaten the constitution; after some thought, the Americans realized that to win it would still not give them what they wanted.

Anticipating the passage of the Stamp Act, James Otis, Jr., in July 1764 published a critical pamphlet, *The Rights of the British Colonies Asserted and Proved,* in which he advanced the claim to an American representation in parliament.[18] This pamphlet by the leader of the popular forces in the Massachusetts assembly, who had won renown for his stand against the writs of assistance, was published as a semiofficial document and was "universally approved" throughout the colonies.[19] On first reading, its criticism may seem innocuous. Otis repeatedly granted that parliament was sovereign and specifically that it was "as uncontrollable in the colonies as in England."[20] He conceded, therefore, that although in his view parliament had no right under the fundamental law of the constitution to tax the colonists, it must be obeyed in the confident hope that in due course it would recognize its error and repair its misreading of the constitution.

The correction it should then adopt was evident from the nature of the error. Parliament lacked the right to tax the colonists, because, he said, in words that Blackstone could have used, under the British constitution "the supreme power cannot take from any man any part of his property without his consent in person or by representation." Since the colonists elected not so much as "one member of the House of Commons," Otis went on to infer from his own political philosophy, the way to bring the exercise of this power into conformity with the constitution was to recognize that the Americans had the same rights as their "fellow citizens in Britain" and so should "be represented in some proportion to their number and estates in the grand legislature of the nation."[21]

When one looks more closely at Otis's argument in *The Rights* and his elaboration of it in three other pamphlets published in the following year, its subversive character appears. "Equity," he argued, required that those bearing the burdens of empire should also share in its benefits. "Advantage," he claimed, would redound to both countries from the "knowledge of each other's interests" that would come from participation in a common legislature. What his demand for "actual representation" came to was the familiar republican program of a wider franchise, apportionment of seats according to population and property, and accountability of the elected to the electors. Only by such means could the political system meet the standard of "an equal representation of the whole state," which, according to Otis, was "at least in theory, of the essence of a perfect parliament or supreme legislature." Needless to say, the consequent addition of MPs from burgeoning America would, as he realized, greatly alter the balance of power in the British legislature. If the "theory" were also extended to the whole system of representation in Great Britain itself, it would, as Otis grants, subvert the whole political order.[22]

Otis's willingness to invoke theory led him into even greater depths of opposition. Discussing "the origin of government" in his first pamphlet, Otis began with statements that were unexceptionable in his time: that man by his nature must live in society, that therefore he must have government, and that in this government there must be a sovereign power.[23] When he went on to declare that "this supreme, absolute power is *originally* and *ultimately* in the People," he departed from orthodoxy. Blackstone just might have granted that such a power was in some sense "originally" in the people. He would pull up short at the notion that it is "ultimately" in them. On this point Otis accepted Locke, while Blackstone emphatically rejected him. For Locke "the people" may "remove or alter the legislative" when it violates its trust. For Blackstone such an effort would only plunge society back into the chaos of the state of nature.

Like Locke and unlike Blackstone, therefore, Otis asserts popular sovereignty so far as to make the people the constituent sovereign. Consequences of considerable importance for colonial political thought follow. First, if it is presumed that the people are the constituent sovereign, the way is opened for a theory of limited government, which, nevertheless, recognizes a sovereign power in the state. As that "absolute despotic" power, the people establish the government, giving it by this act a structure of authority, which includes, if so desired, a federal system. That structure of authority is a "fixed constitution"; that is, it is defined, and therefore limited, by law. But the possibility of change is not closed off. The people may intervene to amend the constitution, if the government established by it acts contrary to its trust. Otis makes this trust depend on respect for an original compact, implying thereby that the people can intervene only when the government breaches that compact. In this view, colonial theory had started toward, but had not yet reached, the position that the relation was purely fiduciary, justifying intervention by the people whenever they found it in the public interest.

A second consequence is the suggestion that the people are not only the constituent sovereign but also have the capacity to act as the governmental sovereign. This suggestion can also be found in the Lockean view that when constituting or reconstituting a government, the people act for the common good as a coherent, law-making body. Otis emphasizes this democratic aspect of Lockean theory by speaking of the people, in their constituent capacity, as "a perfect *Democracy,*" the phrase Locke himself used.[24] But if so democratic a government can coherently and justly make and remake the fundamental law of the state, why should it not also under the authority of that grant take on the whole governance of the country?

To be sure, to say that the people are the constituent sovereign does not logically imply that they are also the governmental sovereign. In the hierarchical tradition, the people have often been conceived as consenting to government by the few. In Otis's case, however, his Lockean discussion of "the origin of government" was clearly intended to lend further support to his argument for actual representation. He was making a case not only for limited government but also and especially for self-government. In this view, the consent of the people would not be confined to their occasional action as the constituent sovereign but would also include that continuous supervision and control of elected persons by the voters demanded in the name of actual representation.

The threat to Britain as well as to America was correctly assessed in parliament. "Every objection . . . to the dependency of the colonies upon parliament, which arises to it upon the ground of representation," Lord Mansfield warned the House of Lords in 1766, "goes to the whole present constitution."[25]

Similarly responding to the demand for an American representation in parliament, a Rhode Island tory quickly went to the heart of the matter.[26] Martin Howard, Jr., a leading lawyer of Newport, belonged to a band of fierce critics of the "democratical" constitution of the colony, who premised their opposition on the familiar dogma that "the people in almost every age and country, have been incapable, collectively, of acting with any degree of moderation or wisdom. It was ever impracticable to combine the various passions, humors and interests of a multitude so as to produce harmony, order and subordination in a state." In his *Letter from a Gentleman at Halifax,* published in February 1765, Howard, denying that "the colonies have rights independent of, or not controllable by, the authority of Parliament," laid down the rationale of its sovereign power over the dominions as well as the realm of Great Britain. This rationale could not be that those subject to its authority took part in elections to it, since there were countless persons and many places in the realm itself which had no voice in choosing a member. Nevertheless, "the House of Commons . . . are the representatives of every British subject, wheresoever he be." The truth of the matter, he concluded, "lies here: the freedom and happiness of every British subject depends not upon his share in elections, but upon the sense and virtue of the British Parliament."[27]

In a more considered reply, Thomas Whately, George Grenville's secretary, Howard's correspondent, and chief draftsman of the Stamp Act, conveyed the same message. Echoing recent arguments in parliament and using the term "virtual representation," which had first appeared there,[28] he claimed that "in Fact" the colonists were represented in parliament, although like "Nine Tenths of the people of *Britain*" they chose no members. For, he continued,

> All *British* Subjects are really in the same [situation]; none are actually, all are virtually represented in Parliament; for every Member of Parliament sits in the House, not as Representative of his own Constituents, but as one of the august Assembly by which all the Commons of *Great Britain* are represented.[29]

To the argument that many subjects in the realm itself were not actually represented, the American whig, reasoning from quite different premises, could reply that they ought to be. And so said Otis in a celebrated passage. "To what purpose," he wrote, "is it to ring everlasting changes to the colonists on the cases of Manchester, Birmingham, and Sheffield, who return no members? If those now so considerable places are not represented, they ought to be."[30]

The two sides argued past each other. For the Americans, representation was a means of control of the ruler by the ruled. For the British, representation was a mode of ruling for the common good of the ruled. In this latter sense, the MP and, indeed, as Burke said, all persons in authority, whether elected or not, were representatives of the people—as a parent "represents" his children in a court of law or other transactions with the world outside the family.[31] For one side, to be a representative was to be a person who carried out the wishes of the people. For the other, to be a representative was to be a person who cared for their best interests. For the former, therefore, election as a means of popular control was of the essence of the relationship. For the latter, popular control was undesirable; hence, as Martin Howard said, election was incidental. The conflict was between the old idea of representation from the top down and the new idea of representation from the bottom up.[32]

Nowadays the term representation has been so completely taken over by the whig meaning that we find it hard to keep in mind the premodern meaning attached to the term by the hierarchical tradition. Something of the older distinction, however, does survive in the way we use the terms "responsible" and "accountable" when describing the roles of government officials.[33] When we say that a Congressman is "accountable" to his constituents, we are expressing the whiggish view that he must give an account of his performance in office to the voters who may, if they choose, remove him at the next election.

When we say that he is "responsible" for what he has done or not done, we are judging whether he has discharged the responsibilities of his office. Those duties certainly include showing regard for the common good. This duty attaches to his being a Congressman; and, we might go on to say, it is because Congressmen have this responsibility that we modern-day whigs hold that they should be accountable to the voters. The notion of responsibility echoes the old meaning of virtual representation; the notion of accountability echoes the notion of actual representation. Accountability is the whig way of ensuring that our governors live up to their responsibilities. This distinction and this connection were, I think, what Otis in his confused and verbose way was trying to articulate.[34]

Given his Old Whig political norms, Whately in the passage just quoted could assert, without offending against them, that no British subject was actually represented in parliament. We must dwell on that assertion. What he said was not that some subjects, that is, those with the franchise, were actually represented but rather that "none are actually . . . represented," which would include those with the franchise as well as those without it. The reason he could say this was that on his political premises popular control was not what representation was about.

Starting from quite different premises, Otis could also grant virtual representation yet not surrender the claim for American MPs. For that claim was quite compatible with the contention that MPs represented not merely a set of localities but the nation and empire as a whole. Algernon Sidney had fervently believed both that the MP represented the whole nation and that the franchise should be widely distributed. If one takes the national role of the MP as constituting virtual representation, then it is accurate to say that the colonists were virtually represented in parliament. Otis did at one point say this and thereby brought down on his head much patriotic wrath. On his whig understanding of the matter, however, this did not contradict his demand for actual representation. On the contrary, in his view, this national and imperial responsibility of parliament required actual representation. The body *responsible* for the welfare of the people should be *accountable* to them.

In the true radical whig spirit, Otis extended his attack on the lack of popular control to the electoral system of the British realm itself and so was led to argue not only for American MPs but also for parliamentary reform in the mother country. Taking a quite different view of how the system worked in Britain, some colonial spokesmen held that it did in effect provide for popular control there, although not in America. The course of their analysis led away from the parliamentary and toward the federal option.

Daniel Dulany of Maryland was a leading voice in turning the agitation in this direction. In a closely reasoned and influential pamphlet of August 1765, he held that the house of commons was justified in levying taxes on Britain because of the close connection of MPs and people, electors and nonelectors alike.[35] Because of the propinquity of these persons and the similar incidence on all of taxation, the people were protected against abuses by their representatives.[36]

This justification of virtual representation in Britain *a fortiori* ruled it out as a ground for parliamentary taxation of the colonies, and in so far as it was accepted in Britain, its advocates were opponents, not defenders, of the stamp tax. Rejecting the idea of an American representation in parliament, Dulany found that for reasons similar to those justifying the system in Britain, the proper taxing authority in America was the colonial legislative power. There propinquity and incidence would provide the foundation of knowledge and interest that would justify taking property by the coercive power of government. The colonial charters, Dulany claimed, established this as a right. Parliament remained "superior" in so far as its authority included "such acts as are necessary or proper for preserving or securing the dependence of the colonies." The power to tax for "the sole purpose of revenue," however, belonged exclusively to the colonies, which "by their constitution of government" were "empowered to impose internal taxation." By concluding that "certain powers vested in the inferior limit the superior," Dulany was drawing a line of constitutionally protected federalism.[37]

To the American whigs the federal option seemed to offer a way around the difficulty with which the parliamentary option beset the approach to actual representation. They often described that difficulty as "impracticability." This term does not make clear what they meant. In the years before and after the Stamp Act crisis a good many men of wide practical experience, including Massachusetts governors Shirley, Bernard and, Pownall, spoke for the parliamentary option. Its history runs from 1754, when Franklin included it as a complement to his Albany Plan, until 1778, when the Carlisle Commission, the instrument of Lord North's futile effort for a negotiated peace, proposed that agents "from the different states . . . have the privilege of a seat and voice in the parliament of Great Britain."[38] In between, it found friends and foes on both sides of the Atlantic. As one would expect, there were friends among men of whiggish views, and foes among tory defenders of aristocratic rule. There were also British imperialists who accepted an American representation as strengthening the bonds of empire, and American whigs who rejected it as weakening the reins of self-government. Some found it practicable, although as a second choice. Adam Smith favored independence but thought an American representation was feasible as second best; and John Adams, while arguing for his scheme of "imperial federalism," did not entirely rule out an American representation, although he thought it would be a great "inconvenience."[39]

The weakness of the idea from the point of view of the American whig appears in one of the more specific proposals. In 1770 Francis Maseres, who had been a colonial administrator in America, proposed that "Commissioners," elected from and equitably apportioned among the colonies, be added to parliament, which would consider general matters concerning America, including taxation. The election would be annual, but they could be conducted in the absence of the candidates, who, moreover, Maseres expected, would come from "the English gentry" or from a similar "order" with "liberal education and easy patrimonial fortune" which he saw arising in America.[40] One is reminded of those MPs who in the days of the Septennial Act visited their constitutuencies only once in seven years for the purpose of reelection.[41]

For the same reasons that Otis proposed an American presence at Westminster—to check the power of officeholders and to inform them of the "interests and desires of the people"—other American whigs soon came to reject it. When it took not weeks but months for letters and persons to move back and forth across the Atlantic, what was "impracticable" was the kind of popular control with which Otis and his fellow dissidents had identified actual representation.

In September 1765 the Massachusetts assembly, which up to that point had gone along with the parliamentary option, instructed their delegates to the Stamp Act Congress to oppose it.[42] And in its fourth resolution, drafted by Sam Adams, the Congress unanimously adopted that position on the ground that "the people in these colonies are not and from their local circumstance cannot be represented in the house of commons of Great Britain." Three years later the Massachusetts circular letter against the Townsend duties echoed this objection, asserting that the colonists would be satisfied with no "partial representation" but only with "full and equal representation," which was made impossible by "an ocean of three thousand leagues."[43]

But "theory" as well as "fact" influenced how one judged this question. Whether or not American representation in parliament was "practicable" depended on how highly one valued the electoral connection. From the tory viewpoint, American representation was practicable enough and precisely for that reason was undesirable. In view of what the whig expected from it, American representation, on the other hand, was impracticable and therefore undesirable.

The Federal Option

By the federal option I mean the various proposals put forward by American spokesmen to divide on a constitutional basis the powers of government between Westminster and the colonies. None of these proposals could resolve the conflict. They did, however, launch a debate over the relation of levels of government which in America has lasted for generations—indeed, for some two centuries. And in these first stages of that debate, the main outlines of the national theory of the union were sketched.

Like the parliamentary option, the federal option presupposed that America and Britain were parts of one state. One simple indication of this unitary emphasis is that the term "federal" was not used to characterize these proposals. Given the meaning of the term at the time, its use would have suggested the compact theory of the union. In harmony with their derivation from "foedus," terms such as "federal" and "confederation" were used to refer to political systems established by compact or treaty among separate polities. Americans were acquainted with the general European usage of "federal" to mean a league or alliance of separate, sovereign states, as in the case of the United Netherlands or Switzerland.[44] From 1764 to 1774, the quite different discussion of the federal option presupposed that the problem was how to organize power not among several distinct states but within a single state. On both sides, the colonies and Britain were referred to by such terms as "a Union," not "an Alliance," "one State," not "a Confederacy of many," the colonies being called not "states distinct from the British Empire . . . but parts of a whole."[45] More significant than what was said was what was not said. No more than the British did the colonists in this phase of the controversy seek to derive the division of authority from an agreement between equal and independent powers. They held rather that it was defined by a "fundamental law" superior to the law of any part of the "political whole."[46] Already essential elements of the concept of national rather than compact federalism, which can be found in Harrington and which were adopted by the Constitution of 1787, were being presumed in the discussion of British–American relations.

Needless to say, that fundamental law which, according to colonial views, distinguished between the powers of the British and the colonial legislatures respectively, could not be found in any formal instrument, such as a written constitution, parliamentary statute, explicit convention, authoritative treatise, or judicial decision.[47] Political and legal theory, however, not least in the republican tradition, had dealt with the question of the vertical distribution of authority in states. In their arguments the colonists made use of these ideas from the past, their formulations in turn serving to develop and to pass them on to later thinking about federalism in America.

One line of thought coming down from the Commonwealth was the *argument from liberty*. In a sense, the whole republican case was an argument from liberty, its major premise being that liberty would be better protected by government by the many than by one or a few. The colonial demand for actual representation derived directly from this fundamental republican doctrine and went on to nourish the assertion of popular sovereignty during the making of constitutions that followed the break with Britain.

Recognizing the self-destructive dangers of popular government, republican thinkers like Harrington and Milton had elaborated structures by which those dangers could be avoided and the excellence of self-government realized. One device was a functional separation of powers between central and local governments, as in Harrington's scheme and Milton's modification of it. In both schemes, as in the later American theory of national federalism, liberty was protected by a primary reliance upon "the people," who authorized the constitution and also directed the government established by it. Implicitly in Harrington's scheme and explicitly in Milton's, the sharp constitutional decentralization of powers created the possibility that one level might correct abuses by the other, an opportunity more fully perceived and developed in the thought of American nationalists. Yet both, like the American system, made central, not local, government the seat of primary importance in public affairs.

These considerations relating to federalism, richly developed by Madison and his fellow nationalists, figured in the thinking that led to the Constitution of 1787 and in the later history of American legal and political thought. The argument, as framed by Commonwealth republicans, was concerned with the threat of oppression by central officialdom over the whole country, not by one province or region over another. Precisely that latter danger, however, was the rationale of the American case against London. In the eyes of American whigs, the source of the evil was not just ministers and MPs but the interests they represented and for whom they were seeking to get some advantage over the colonists in matters of taxation or commerce.

As Daniel Dulany framed his indictment, for instance, government by the Westminster parliament was orderly and equitable enough in Britain, where British interests and knowledge determined governmental outcomes. Precisely because those British interests were controlling in parliament, however, they led to disregard of American needs and conditions. What was needed therefore was a sorting out of authority among the legislatures of the various parts of the empire which would give to each control over its own concerns. As we shall have occasion to see in a moment, this is better termed the argument from utility than the argument from liberty.

Another defense of local autonomy can be traced back to the Greek small state theory of community. The conception of the small, close-knit body of people bound together by their own distinctive common life but also embraced in a larger social and political whole, appears in many forms in medieval and early modern thought. The Thomistic polity, like the divine cosmos of which it was a reflection, while monarchic at the center, allowed to its constituent parts the degree of autonomy necessary for the exercise of their distinctive virtues. Among the moderns, both Bodin, the champion of the unitary sovereign state, and Althusius, an early philosopher of federalism, recognized the claims to autonomy of communal bodies such as families, households, and local communities.[48]

The material was there for a powerful *argument from community,* whether in the rhetoric of the monarchic and aristocratic tradition or in the less tainted sources of classical times. It was not, however, deployed by Americans until well after independence, when the Anti-Federalists made the case for the small polity as the forum where republican virtue could best be cultivated. In the prerevolutionary agitation, advocates of the federal option argued for colonial autonomy on quite different grounds. Not virtue but commerce was their main concern. This *argument from utility* enjoyed a long and distinguished future in federal theorizing. Its drift will be suggested by a sampling of the arguments of some of the chief advocates of the federal option during the agitation over the Stamp Act.

In 1765 Stephen Hopkins, the governor of Rhode Island, writing with the endorsement of his colonial assembly, argued that under "the British constitution" parliament had no authority to tax or make laws regarding the "internal government" of a colony, although it was supreme in "general matters." Specifying those "many things of a more general nature" which came under the authority of parliament, he mentioned the "commerce of the whole British empire," keeping the peace among the colonies, and also "perhaps" instruments of commerce, such as money and paper credit. On this reasoning, therefore, as he put it in a later publication, parliament could levy custom duties upon "foreign importations, which is a matter of general commerce." It could not, however, tax the "interior police" of a colony, as had been attempted in the Stamp Act.[49]

As one might expect, this question was lucidly and imaginatively treated by Benjamin Franklin. What he said also strikingly anticipated distinctions of intergovernmental finance made in later times. In his celebrated testimony before the House of Commons in 1766, after a long and penetrating criticism of the Stamp Act as policy, Franklin addressed the constitutional issue. Among Americans, he said, while "a right to lay internal taxes was never supposed to be in Parliament," he had "never heard any objection to the right of laying duties to regulate commerce." Pressed for the criterion by which to distinguish the two sorts of taxation, he replied that in the case of "the external tax" the duty is added to the price of the commodity, which consumers may refuse to pay, if they find it too high. "An internal tax," on the other hand, "is forced from the people without their consent, if not laid by their own representatives."[50]

As the Townshend duties soon made clear, this formal option of nonconsumption was only a limited safeguard against impositions on external commerce becoming in effect compulsory. In his testimony Franklin had moved onto much firmer ground when he observed that the surcharge on imported goods was also justified by "the safety of navigation" secured by the British navy, while the internal tax—which he also referred to as a tax for "local purposes"[51]—was "unconnected with any service" by the imperial power.

In offering this rationale, Franklin anticipated the distinction drawn by Adam Smith a few years later between "general revenue" and "local revenue." "Local or provincial expenses," wrote Smith in *The Wealth of Nations* (1776), "of which the benefit is local or provincial (what is laid out, for example, upon the police of a particular town or district) ought to be defrayed by a local or provincial revenue." Those expenses, such as defense, which are laid out for "the general benefit for the whole society" should, on the other hand, be paid from the general revenue. That would, moreover, be not only more just but also more effective, since local beneficiaries would see to it that a better service was provided.[52]

This principle of "benefit taxation," as it has come to be known in the modern theory of public finance, expresses a more general criterion for dividing powers between levels of government. In recent years, this criterion has been clarified and put to use by advocates of "fiscal federalism."[53] The object is to match public goods with the populations that benefit from them. It follows that while public goods whose benefits are consumed uniformly by the members of a more inclusive community should be provided and paid for by the general government, those public goods whose benefits are confined to subsets of that community should be provided and paid for by the

governments of those smaller communities.[54] If government boundaries at different levels and the distribution of powers among them
are designed according to this criterion, it is said, there will be a gain
in utility, that is, in the satisfaction of these varying preferences for
public goods, and in efficiency, that is, in the use of the resources of
the society as a whole in the provision of public goods. A central
government, according to Wallace Oates, will, however, tend to
make its public goods uniformly available to the members of all
constituent communities, disregarding the possible variations in preferences of their residents. "A decentralized form of government," he
concludes, "therefore offers the promise of increasing economic efficiency by providing a range of outputs of certain public goods that
corresponds more closely to the differing tastes of groups of consumers."[55]

In recent years, echoing the language of Franklin in the 1760s,
Mancur Olson has termed a public good with such a unique boundary an "internality."[56] Where the effects of the public good are so
confined to the local community which benefits from and pays for it,
one may reasonably argue that the community should have the
governmental powers to provide it, free from interference from
higher authority. A public good designed for the benefit of a local
community, however, may have "externalities," that is, effects extending beyond its borders. They may be good, as when the schools
of one community send out educated citizens to the larger world, or
bad, as when efforts to clean up local pollution heighten the sanitary
problems of surrounding areas. Since the local community may not
be willing or able to restrict harmful externalities or to extend beneficial ones, there is need for a more inclusive jurisdiction with appropriate powers which may legitimately regulate the services and distribute the costs among the whole set of affected communities. Also,
like such externalities of the public sector, the external effects of the
private sector of a locality may similarly justify interventions by a
central coordinating and superintending power.

These present-day ways of thinking about intergovernmental finance and intergovernmental relations help clarify the meaning of
those efforts of an earlier generation of Americans to draw a line
between the authority of the British and the colonial legislatures.[57]

Virtually the whole of what Hopkins called the "interior police" of each colony was conducted and paid for by its people, no significant service of this description being provided by Britain.[58] On the other hand, an adequate defense of the sea lanes was not, could not, and would not be provided, if left to the separate action of individual colonies. It made sense therefore, if taxation was to follow benefits, that, as Franklin suggested, the naval protection provided by Britain be supported by each colony in proportion to its external trade, as measured by foreign importations.[59]

These first American efforts to define a federal option were not unpromising. Without exaggerating the clarity of what was said, we may recognize the merit of their intimations of fiscal federalism, namely, that taxation is justified by services and that services should be provided by the jurisdiction benefitting from them. According to this way of thinking, the activities of different levels of government would vary with the interdependence, commercial and other, of the various parts of the country. The rules of constitutional federalism can be so written as to allow for such flexibility. In the American case, surely the leading example is the rule of 1787, which provides that commerce that is local should be regulated by the respective states, while commerce between the states and with foreign countries should be regulated by the general government. The rule is clear, fixed, and even rigid; yet it has permitted the centralization of government required by the tenets of fiscal federalism.

These surely are guides to prudent housekeeping. Prudence, however, was only one of the considerations moving the contestants in the prerevolutionary controversy. They were more concerned with rightful authority. When the British in 1766 prudently decided to repeal the legislation that had caused the uproar of 1764–66, they also most imprudently enacted the Declaratory Act with its inflammatory assertion of the right to bind the colonies "in all cases whatsoever." A little later, again seeking to achieve the original object, they did so by means of the Townshend duties of 1767, which, being in form wholly external, were presumed to meet the objections the Americans had raised against the Stamp Act.

It is hard to say who was the more naive in this matter—the Americans for thinking their initial external/internal distinction was viable, or the British for thinking their subterfuge was viable. The new revenue measures renewed the uproar among the Americans, who now found that the fundamental law of the British constitution forbade parliament to levy any sort of tax, external or internal, upon the colonies, although permitting "impositions" to regulate external commerce.

In the authoritative exposition of the new American position, *Letters from a Pennsylvania Farmer*,[60] which appeared in late 1767 and early 1768, John Dickinson of Philadelphia incidentally revealed the fatal flaw of any federal solution: Who is to judge? Early in 1768, reflecting on what Dickinson was saying, Benjamin Franklin saw the issue:

> I know not . . . what bounds the Farmer sets to the power he acknowl-edges in parliament to "regulate the trade of the colonies," it being difficult to draw lines between duties for regulation and those for revenue; and if the Parliament is to be the judge, it seems to me that establishing such principles of distinction will amount to little.[61]

The problem was not so much that the distinction between external and internal taxation or the distinction between taxation for revenue and regulation was virtually no rule at all. Even if a more substantial criterion, such as the principle of benefit taxation broached by Franklin, had been agreed by both sides, the question would remain: Who is to decide how that principle is to be applied and if it has been applied rightly? Dickinson did not deny that the declared purposes of the Townshend duties—defense, the administration of justice, and civil government—were beneficial. What he affirmed was that what would be done and how it would be done could properly be decided only by a body in which the colonists were represented. How the services were to be provided and paid for, he wrote, "*cannot* possibly be properly *known,* but by the society itself; or if they should be known, *will not* probably be properly considered but by that society." In the same vein as Franklin, he continued:

> If money be raised upon us by *others,* without our consent, for our "defence," those who are the judges in *levying* it, must also be the judges in *applying* it. Of consequence the money *said* to be taken from us for our defence, *may be employed* for our injury. We may be chained

in by a line of fortifications—obliged to pay for the building and maintaining them—and be told, that they are for our defense.[62]

Moreover, according to Dickinson, even if that other governing body acted on sufficient knowledge and good will, the governed would not be a free people. "For WHO ARE A FREE PEOPLE? Not *those*, over whom government is equitably and reasonably exercised, but *those*, who live under a government so constitutionally *checked* and *controlled* [by the power of the purse] that proper provision is made against its being otherwise exercised." That was the crux: good government is no substitute for self-government. "We are taxed without our consent, expressed by ourselves or our representatives. We are therefore—SLAVES."[63]

Who is to judge? For the British, whether like Burke and Chatham, friendly and pursuing conciliation, or like Grenville and Mansfield, hostile and standing on authority, that final judge was the wise and virtuous members of the sovereign parliament. For the American whigs it was "the people." The whig spokesmen had not yet fully worked out the doctrine of popular sovereignty, but as the British had ever more clearly perceived from the start of the quarrel, that was the way the colonial mind was tending. The demand for popular control had destroyed the parliamentary option. It was now destroying the federal option.

Imperial Federalism

In spite of his thundering republican sentiments, Dickinson clung to the old thesis that the colonies and the mother country were "one state." Denying that "these provinces" are "states distinct from the *British Empire*," he wrote: "We are but parts of a *whole* and therefore there must exist a power somewhere to preside, and preserve the connection in due order." This power to act "for the common good of all," "to promote the general welfare," consisted in the power of parliament to regulate trade among parts of the empire and with other nations. Hence, parliament could levy "impositions" which, like fines imposed by a court, incidentally produced revenue but were not designed for that purpose.[64]

Dickinson's effort to stabilize the relationship by means of a federal division of power proved no more lasting than previous American proposals. His distinction between taxation for regulation and taxation for revenue was hopelessly ambiguous—some years later Madison called it "absolutely undefinable."[65] Moreover, as he himself had in effect pointed out, even a reasonably clear and sensible rule could give no security against oppression, if one part of the "political whole" had the final say-so over the extent of its own powers. This inference was incontrovertibly demonstrated by the British reaction to the Boston Tea Party. By the first of the coercive acts of 1774, for example, the port of Boston was closed, ostensibly in order to protect the safety of "the commerce of his Majesty's subjects" and to ensure the collection of customs duties, but actually in order to punish the city and province for the Tea Party.

Confronted by the unlimbering of parliamentary sovereignty in the coercive acts, the Americans made one brief, last stand for a solution. This too could be called federal, not, however, according to the national but according to the compact model. It was premised on a switch from the presupposition generally shared by both sides during the previous decade of controversy that America and Britain were "one state" to the novel assertion that the colonies severally along with the mother country were "distinct states." Its advocates included leading whigs such as James Wilson, Thomas Jefferson, John Adams, and James Iredell who, writing as the crisis deepened in 1774–75, found that parliament had no authority whatsoever over the colonies and that the only bond of union among the parts of the empire was the king.[66]

This view of the British constitution has been called "imperial federalism,"[67] and some writers have praised it as a far-sighted anticipation of the concept of "dominion status" under which the relations of the self-governing parts of the empire were presumably stabilized in later times.[68] A glance at this misleading parallel will show how far out of line the new American position was with British constitutional development and why it could not have been the basis for agreement.

The common thrust of the various versions of "imperial federalism" was to separate the powers of the monarch from those of parliament, rigidly excluding parliament from any authority over the colonies, while admitting the monarch to a substantial governmental role in imperial affairs. That conception of empire and of dominion status was emphatically not, however, the direction actually taken by imperial development in the next two centuries. During that later time, British rule was indeed relaxed; but in so far as Britain did continue to rule, it was by authority of parliament, the monarch's role in government becoming ever less material and more purely symbolic. Early in the present century a number of political leaders from Britain and the self-governing dominions did try to work out a division of authority that was firmly and constitutionally federal. They were unable to do so.[69]

In consequence, when "dominion status" was given formal constitutional definition by the Imperial Conference of 1926, the dominions were declared to be "autonomous communities within the British Empire, equal in status, in no way subordinate to another in any aspect of their domestic or external affairs, though united by a common allegiance to the Crown, and freely associated as members of the British Commonwealth." Five years later the statute of Westminster filled out this definition with legal precision, parliament relinquishing its right to legislate for a dominion, save at the request of the dominion, and the crown being recognized as nothing more than "the symbol of the free association of the members of the British Commonwealth of Nations."[70]

Today the "Commonwealth of Nations" which emerged from these developments, no longer even identified as "British," is referred to as an "association," quite properly not as a "federation," since no formal authority over the dominions remains with the government of the United Kingdom. Its members are united by their symbolic allegiance to the Crown. Although "head of the commonwealth" and, for those members which preferred to be constitutional monarchies rather than republics, "head of state," the British monarch has no governmental power, executive, legislative, or judicial. The members of the Commonwealth are sovereign states in both theory and practice.

The American proposals of the mid-1770s were as out of line with Britain's past as with its future. To suppose that the monarch had a sphere of authority beyond that of parliament—that he could rule where parliament could not—was to overlook the fact that there had

been a seventeenth century. To be sure, there were medieval precedents for royal autonomy unhampered by the Westminster parliament. But by the eighteenth century, prerogative had become only
such part of the ancient discretionary right of the crown as parliament saw fit to leave untouched.[71] Clinching the transition from the
Old Tory to the Old Whig polity, the coronation oath of William and
Mary in 1689 had bound them "to govern the people of this kingdom of England and the dominions thereunto belonging according
to the statutes in Parliament agreed on and the laws and customs of
the same."[72] "Royalty," as Namier observed with regard to the
American proposal of 1774, "was still an active factor in British
politics, and to Eighteenth-century Englishmen any exercise of its
attributes apart from the British Parliament would have seemed a
dangerous reversion to 'prerogative.'"[73]

If the defenders of British orthodoxy could not tolerate such independent authority for the monarch, one is hard put to understand
why American champions of self-government felt compelled to make
such authority the binding power of the political whole of which they
were a part. They did suppose that the monarch would be checked
by the colonial assemblies when acting as king of Massachusetts,
Virginia, and so on, just as he was checked by the House of Commons when acting as king of England.[74] Necessarily, however, his
function as "the superintending power" of the empire would be
independent of the government of any one part of it, entirely at
variance with the passion for self-government of the American
whigs.[75]

The most glaring example of this discrepancy was James Wilson's
*Considerations on the Nature and Extent of the Legislative Author-
ity of the British Parliament,* published in 1774. A recent arrival
from Scotland who had read law with John Dickinson, Wilson had
written the pamphlet in 1768 during the agitation against the Townshend acts. When he had set out on his inquiry, he explains, he fully
expected to be able (like his mentor) "to trace some constitutional
line" defining the power of parliament over the colonies. To his
surprise, he continues, he found himself driven by the force of the
argument to deny the power of the parliament over the colonies "in
every instance."[76]

His premises make that a perfectly logical conclusion. His starting point is the proposition that "all lawful government is founded on the consent of those who are subject to it." By that unexceptionable ambiguity he meant not the presumed consent of some antique contract, nor the present consent of the deferential many to the virtuous few. He meant rather the continuous consent of the bulk of the people, expressed in free and frequent elections, in which they distinguished between those representatives "who have served them well, and those who have neglected or betrayed their interests" and by which they reminded their representatives "whose creatures they are" and held them "accountable for the use of that power which is delegated to them."[77]

The radically republican trend of his thought is further confirmed when he asks: "Upon what principle does the British Parliament found their power?" and makes the astonishing reply that since neither the king nor the lords but only the House of Commons is representative, the authority of parliament resides "in the House of Commons *only*." Moreover, since the authority of the House of Commons comes from its election by the people, this authority ultimately resides in "the collective body of the commons of Great Britain." "For," he continues, "whatever they convey to their representatives must ultimately be in themselves." Wilson agrees with Blackstone that parliament has "uncontrolled authority" in Britain. Sharply contradicting Blackstone, he says that this authority remains dependent upon its source, the people of Great Britain. He is advancing the doctrine of popular sovereignty in all but name.[78]

At this point in the argument, the reader may well conclude that the stage is set for a declaration of the independence of the American colonies. Wilson sharply rejects that implication and instead proceeds to elaborate his theory of imperial federalism. A brief review of the rulings and dicta of certain judicial decisions dating from the fifteenth century and after prepares the way for his contention that "the different members of the British Empire are distinct states . . . but connected together under the same sovereign." American "dependence" is, therefore, acknowledged, but it is a dependence not upon the parliament but solely upon the king. The colonists owe him "allegiance" in exchange for "protection," and it is suggested, although not made explicit, that these mutual obligations arose from compacts between monarch and settlers expressed in "charters or letters patent." While excluding parliament from any authority over the Americans, Wilson enlarges the discretionary prerogative of the monarch in some respects even beyond the sphere allowed to parliament by previous advocates of the federal option. The powers that flow from allegiance, he said, permit the king by his personal authority to regulate foreign commerce, although denying him the right to do so by financial "impositions." The prerogative, moreover, includes powers of making war and peace and alliances, and, in order to prevent interdominion conflicts, an executive power of appointment and management and a legislative veto over acts of the various imperial legislatures.[79]

The discrepancy could hardly be more glaring. Throughout his exposition of the "securities" for liberty of the British constitution, Wilson had recognized the dangers of the monarchy, accepting "the general maxim that the crown will take advantage of every opportunity of extending the prerogative, in opposition to the privileges of the people."[80] Having thrown off the authority of parliament because it was not representative, however, he now acknowledged over a wide sphere of government the intrinsically unrepresentative authority of the king.

Nor was his problem merely that he contradicted his republican principles. It also made no pragmatic sense to pin the hopes of the colonists on such a revival of the personal prerogative. Within six months Wilson acknowledged as much before the provincial convention of Pennsylvania called at the end of January 1775 to approve the work of the Continental Congress. Concluding an oration in which he defended forcible resistance to "ministerial tyranny" as constitutional, Wilson, with only nominal reference to previous episodes in British history, recalled that when the king himself engaged in "such iniquitous conduct . . . the distinction between him and his ministers has been lost: but they have not been raised to his situation: he has sunk to theirs."[81]

Liberty vs. Union

The concept of imperial federalism, far-fetched as it must seem, reflected a grasp of certain harsh realities of the colonial position in the world. As Wilson and others put it, the royal prerogative met the need for "a general superintending power" over this empire of many parts. The sphere of authority he attributed to the monarch was more specific and broader than that conceded by other spokesmen for imperial federalism. Jefferson's version came closest to seeing the king as little more than a symbol, but even he granted the need for "a central link," a "mediatory power."[82]

From the very first the reasoning of the advocates of a federal option had been torn by a conflict between values and necessity. Their argument from utility set forth the case for home rule to meet the internalities of colonial existence but also made imperative a power at the center to cope with its externalities. Stephen Hopkins recognized that there were "many things of a more general nature" over which it was "absolutely necessary" that parliament have the "supreme and overruling authority." Daniel Dulany admitted that "the relation between Great Britain and her colonies might call for an exertion of her superintendence." As the colonial spokesmen shifted their ground, their demand for an ever wider sphere of self-government collided ever more sharply with that obvious necessity for a superintending power at the center. In John Dickinson's thought his exalted republican rhetoric went along with a clear-eyed acknowledgment that the colonies were "but parts of a *whole* and therefore, there must exist a power somewhere to preside, and preserve the connection in due order."[83]

The conflict was sharper still in the case of James Wilson, who advanced a more radical version of republican liberty, while recognizing the need for an even wider sphere of central authority to secure a "union of measures." A few months later a resolve of the Continental Congress drafted by John Adams claimed "the free and exclusive power of legislation" for the colonists, yet expressed, as a purely voluntary concession, their "consent" to parliamentary regulation of external commerce from "the necessity of the case." In his eighth *Novanglus* letter, Adams conceded that "it was necessary there should be some superintending power, to draw together all the wills, and unite all the strength of the subjects in all the dominions," if not in case of war, certainly in the case of trade. The conflict between liberty and union had appeared, and not for the last time in American history.[84]

The theory of imperial federalism did not correspond to the British constitution of the past or of the future, nor to the colonial view of it during most of the prerevolutionary agitation. Yet it can be read into the Declaration of Independence. In 1799 at the height of the controversy over the Kentucky and Virginia Resolutions, James Madison himself, veering sharply from his usual nationalistic stance, came close to accepting that view. "The fundamental principle of the Revolution," he wrote, "was that the colonies were coordinate members with each other, and with Great Britain, of an empire united by a common executive sovereign, but not united by any common legislative sovereign."[85]

In harmony with this view, when the Declaration got to the point of naming the "long train of abuses" which had presumably led the colonists to take up arms, it did not put the blame on parliament, whose assertion of sovereignty had in fact been the main issue between the colonies and the mother country. Instead it directed its fire against "the King of Great Britain," charging him with the "design" of establishing "an absolute Tyranny over these States." The abuses cited in support of this allegation correspond fairly well with the various powers attributed to the king by James Wilson: his executive power in civil and military matters and especially his power of legislative veto. Indeed, the Declaration managed to mention the misdeeds of parliament only in the course of condemning the king's malfeasance in failing to veto these "acts of pretended legislation."

So conceived, the Declaration signifies that these thirteen states have rejected the authority of their common executive because of his breach of contract and now severally assert their right to give their consent to whatever form or forms of government, popular or otherwise, they may prefer. This reading, of course, means the thirteen states would have been left with no way of solving the problem of liberty and union except by erecting a new "superintending power" thanks to compacts with one another.

In some important respects, this reading harks back to 1688, evoking proud memories of the history of English liberty. The Declaration's point by point summary of the abuses of George III resembled in form and in many items of substance the Bill of Rights of 1689, also termed a "declaration," by which the convention parliament had cited the offenses of James II and had given Britain a new executive in William III. The constitutional structure of the two revolutions may also seem to be similar. The Bill of Rights and other formal instruments by which the English sought to legitimate their action avoided any suggestion of an uprising by "the people" and emphasized instead the role of existing institutions, above all the two houses of parliament. In later years, Burke drove home this distinction against the democratic reformers who claimed that by the Glorious Revolution the English people had acquired the right to choose their governors and their form of government. "On the contrary," he declared, " . . . they regenerated the deficient part of the old constitution through the parts that were not impaired . . . They acted by the ancient organized states [estates] in the shape of their old organization, not by the organic moleculae of a disbanded people."[86] Similarly, if the American revolution were the disruption of an imperial federation, the main actors were not "the people" but the "distinct states," which like the English estates of 1688 rejected the old executive for betraying his trust.

This reading of the Declaration supports the compact theory of the founding of the United States. In the days before independence, when proposing ways of concerting their forces against Britain, colonial spokesmen had also at times followed the compact model. In the late summer of 1775, for example, Silas Deane, a delegate from Connecticut, drafted one of the first plans of colonial union. He explicitly modeled it on the New England Confederation of 1643, which had been established by agreement among the legislatures of the four colonies concerned.[87] As this seventeenth-century precedent indicated, such action did not necessarily mean that a new and independent polity was being founded but was compatible with maintaining the imperial connection, which even after the meeting of the Continental Congress in 1774 the colonists professed to honor. In the mid-seventies they were still thinking primarily of constitutional reform within the empire, and until the spring of 1776 plans for confederation intended not "the creation of a nation state, but the continued legitimation of a resistance movement."[88]

After independence, when the Articles of Confederation were being framed, the Continental Congress, although preoccupied with the pressing tasks of revolution and war, could occasionally consider matters of abstract principle.[89] One example was the attack mounted by Thomas Burke of North Carolina in 1777 upon the broad powers allowed to the general government in the draft before Congress. Asserting a form of compact theory so radical as to limit the duration of the confederation to the period of war with Great Britain,[90] Burke, as reported in his letter to the governor of North Carolina, sought to have the proposed agreement among the states say that "all sovereign power was in the states separately and that particular acts of it which should be expressly enumerated, should be exercised in conjunction [that is, by the general government] and not otherwise; but that in all things else each state would exercise all the rights and powers of sovereignty, uncontrolled."[91]

Burke's amendment, which became Article II of the Articles of Confederation, declared that each state would retain "its sovereignty, freedom and independence, and [*read:* as well as][92] every Power, Jurisdiction and right, which is not by this confederation expressly delegated to Congress." While not without ambiguity,[93] this strong assertion of state sovereignty gave comfort to advocates of the compact theory in later years. In any case, the plain words of the Articles clearly implied that the form of government established by them was based on a compact among the several states. The "Confederacy" is termed "a firm league of friendship with each other" of the States, whose "legislatures" "authorize" the "delegates" who "represent" them in Congress to "ratify" the Articles.

CHAPTER 6

The Discovery
of the Nation

THE PROBLEM of liberty and union was being solved, however, not by the negotiation of a compact among the thirteen colonial governments, but by the rise of a national and federal republic among their rebellious inhabitants.

In its very first years, the Continental Congress answered two fundamental questions about the emerging state. The *mode of government* would be republican, drawing its authority from the consent—the active and continuous consent—of the people. The *unit of government* would be continental in scale.

The first, the mode of government question, had been the central question of the long debate over representation in which the colonists had clarified and elaborated their understanding of government by consent, while confirming their commitment to it. In this controversy they had given a great deal of attention to the theoretical aspects of the question, drawing especially upon the intellectual heritage of the Commonwealth writers. The Commonwealth republicans had also pointed to an answer to the second, the national, question. All had advocated the extended republic. Some favored national federalism within the extended republic. All disdained the compact federalism of leagues and confederations.

The colonists could not, of course, put forward the case for the extended republic until they were ready for independence. During most of the prerevolutionary agitation, however, they shared the premise of the Commonwealth writers that the subject under discussion was the government of "one state," "one nation." This was the case whether they were pressing the parliamentary or the federal option, until the concept of imperial federalism was introduced in 1774. Indeed, they showed so little fear of the big state that, not only did they for a time support the parliamentary option, but also, when defending the federal option, they advanced not the argument from liberty which Milton explicitly and Harrington implicitly had accepted but the more pragmatic argument from utility. In this acceptance of an Anglo–American empire, provided its internal arrangements were satisfactory, one may see a precedent for the acceptance of the American republic on a continental scale inaugurated by the Continental Congress.

Despite the compact rhetoric of the Articles, "the idea that the confederation was essentially only a league of sovereign states," as Rakove observes, "was ultimately a fiction. Congress was in fact a national government, burdened with legislative and administrative responsibilities unprecedented in the colonial past."[1] Those colonial precedents embraced a wide degree of self-government at local and provincial levels. Now, however, the colonists were exercising a new power which they had begun to display in the past decade: the capability of governing themselves on a continental scale. Congress, moreover, was acting not only as a government but also as a constituent assembly, which on behalf of the American people authorized the creation of the states and, indeed, by the vote of July 2, 1776, leading to the Declaration of Independence, the creation of the United States. Already, the American people were exercising both constituent and governmental sovereignty. Putting the matter in behavioral terms, we can say that the American people displayed their capacity for unified political action in establishing a system of government, in governing themselves under it, and in creating a federal structure within it.

How the Congress Was Chosen

Unlike the New England Confederation of 1643, the First Continental Congress did not consist of delegates chosen and instructed by colonial governments. Their selection took place after the regular winter meetings of most colonial assemblies; hence, in most cases the colonial legislature could not legally meet or act unless the governor called a special session, and he was a royal appointee. As a result, out of the twelve colonies represented in the Congress, in only Pennsylvania, a proprietary, and Rhode Island, a self-governing colony, did the regular assemblies elect the men who went to Philadelphia.

Elsewhere, they were chosen in a number of extralegal ways: by "revolutionary committees, polling of freeholders, election by illegal assemblies, and revolutionary conventions." In Massachusetts, for instance, although the members of the General Court did meet, select, and instruct their delegates, this was in a locked door session held in defiance of the governor and so contrary to the procedure prescribed by law. In New York there was no single provincial meeting, the delegation being chosen variously by an extralegal election in New York City and county, by the endorsement of a slate by three other counties, and by election of their own delegates by two more. Elections to the Second Continental Congress were hardly less irregular. Called together in 1775 on the instructions of the First Congress, an unofficial body, its members were chosen by the legally constituted assemblies in only five colonies. A constitutional basis for the powers, procedure, and membership of the Congress itself was not established until the ratification of the Articles of Confederation in 1781.[2]

If we are looking for comparisons to help us classify the Continental Congress as a political entity, we will be misled if we think of it as a meeting of governments. A more instructive analogue is the national convention of a political party.[3]

The various mechanisms by which the members of the Congress were chosen and a mandate fashioned for them have several common elements: committees of local activists; local assemblies of adherents; conventions of delegates from these assemblies, which in turn might be represented in a still more comprehensive body. This delegate convention model of political organization has a notable history.[4] Some elements, such as the local committees, go back to the corresponding committees of the Sons of Liberty at the time of the Stamp Act Congress. In the farther past its origins can be traced in forms of organization adopted by Commonwealth republicans and certain Protestant sects. In eighteenth-century Britain, as in America, the system was employed by groups, such as the Yorkshire Association of 1779, which were pressing for more representative government. In the nineteenth century, in both countries, the delegate convention system provided the model followed generally in the organization of political parties.

Like the representative body of a political party, the Continental Congress was founded not upon legally established governments but upon voluntary associations of individuals. It was also partisan in the sense that, as suggested by the qualifying adjective in its claim to speak for "the *good people* of the several colonies,"[5] its cause was owned only by a part, although probably the major part, of the people. That term, "the people," itself was not all-inclusive, embracing in the most liberal understanding of the time no more than the adult white male population. Of "the people," at least a fifth were loyalist, while many others were indifferent. Supporters of the colonial agitation were called "whigs," and it was this partisan political movement, the whig party, which brought into existence and expressed its wishes through the Continental Congress.[6]

This movement was the "constituent power" that created the new state.[7] Where it was able to control or at least resist the agencies of colonial government, its local partisans joined with their fellows in other colonies to send delegates to Philadelphia. There they claimed to speak for their respective provinces, although in all these constituencies they confronted an opposition, great or small, indeed an opposition party, commonly called "tories," who clung to the old loyalties.

At all times the whig movement itself was divided by sharp differences of opinion which historians of a later generation have often quite legitimately characterized as "conservative" and "radical." These differences within the Continental Congress were, however, "relatively narrow," as Rakove observes, in contrast with "the fundamental gap separating the dominant British [and I would add American tory] view of the sources of the Anglo-American crisis from the comparable colonial orthodoxy."[8] They were the sort of differences of opinion which one would expect among political activists committed to government by discussion. And indeed within the Congress they served as a mechanism by which delegates arrived at a balanced and practical consensus on what to do and when to do it.

The ancient political wisdom of the West, which had been ex-emplified in the sad history of the Commonwealth and reiterated by Walpole and other defenders of virtual representation, held that the people at large could not govern because they were "factious" and "unsteady." On the contrary, the whig movement showed strength and cohesion from the days of the Stamp Act Congress, when, although only nine colonies sent delegates, the stamp agents in all thirteen colonies had been forced to resign by the time it met. From then on the movement displayed remarkable consistency of aim and solidarity of support. In the culminating months leading to indepen-dence, the delegates in Philadelphia did not fall victim to internal paralysis, as Old Whig doctrines presumed they must, but showed themselves to be "largely united on goals and tactics alike."[9]

How the Congress Governed

Before the Declaration of Independence, as Rakove writes, "for most intents and purposes the Americans were already acting as if they were an independent nation; waging war, creating new governments, issuing money, and enacting other expedient measures." Its "recom-mendations" were received implicitly as matters requiring obedience. The colonists spoke of them as the "laws" of Congress and expressed their further approval of what their delegates had done by reelecting nearly the whole membership of the first to the second Continental Congress. Unable to prevail upon a single colonial legislature to disavow the Congress, the loyalists were perplexed by its authority, which, lacking a constitutional basis, was "uncommissioned and unauthorized" and so, quite rightly from their viewpoint, could not be "binding even upon [its] constituents."[10]

In its very first days the Congress strikingly displayed its authority when it launched the Continental Association on October 20, 1774. Carrying out the mandate received from their constituents, the dele-gates pledged support for a nonimportation, nonconsumption, and nonexportation agreement against Britain. The pledge expressed a direct relation between the Congress and the people of the whole continent, unmediated by provincial governments. The pledge was taken on behalf not of those governments but of "the inhabitants of the several colonies." The machinery of enforcement likewise was authorized and controlled directly by Congress. Individuals violating the agreement were to be punished by publicity and boycott. Provincial conventions were treated as subordinate agencies of the central government, any province failing to keep the agreement being subject to economic sanctions.[11]

This "astonishing power," this "astounding authority," to use Rakove's characterization, was exercised by the Continental Congress before it acquired a constitutional basis by the ratification of the Articles of Confederation in 1781 and indeed before the Congress had in 1777 agreed on the proposals that were to be submitted for ratification.

How the States Were Created

"The Union," said Abraham Lincoln in his message to Congress of July 4, 1861, "is older than any of the States, and, in fact, it created them as States."[12] At first glance this may seem a puzzling statement. Here along the coast of North America, during the days of British rule, were the thirteen colonies, joined together governmentally only by their common subjection to London. If they were peaceably to become one independent country, as they did, how could that have been brought about except by some form of compact with one another? Was this not what the Articles of Confederation accomplished?

Lincoln, however, was referring to the earlier history which made any such compacts possible. In that time, as the country verged on independence, the colonies had their governing bodies, in most cases extralegal provincial congresses or conventions. Conceivably, the peoples of the respective colonies, acting through these agents of the popular will, could have separately declared their independence and given themselves constitutional governments, which then entered into a continental compact.

But that is not what happened. No colony declared its independence separately or gave itself a constitution before being authorized to do so by the Continental Congress.[13] At first, Congress did this on an *ad hoc* basis. In October 1774, for instance, when Congress refused the request of Massachusetts that it be permitted to resume a system of legal government, of which it had been deprived by one of the coercive acts, the Congress couched its refusal in a resolve which had it "recommend" to the inhabitants of Massachusetts that they continue "to submit to a suspension of the administration of Justice."[14] This resolve, which may seem merely a word of counsel and advice, sufficed to put off the action proposed by Massachusetts for eight months. Then in June 1775, in response to a letter from the provincial convention, the Congress, again by "recommendation," gave the desired authorization which, under the thin pretense of allowing Massachusetts to resume a form of government based on the charter of 1691, stopped short of independence.[15]

New Hampshire was the first to make the transition to statehood. In July 1775 its provincial convention at Exeter instructed its delegates to obtain "the advice and direction of the Congress" with regard to creating a legal government. On November 3, 1775, the Congress gave the desired authorization and, moreover, instructed the New Hampshiremen how to proceed, "recommending" that "a full and free representation of the people be called" which "if they think necessary, shall establish a form of government." One day later Congress granted a similar authorization in response to a similar request from South Carolina.[16] In both cases the Congressional authorization led to the adoption of a constitution, on January 5, 1776, by New Hampshire and on March 23, 1776, by South Carolina.[17] While, as we have seen, Massachusetts had preceded these two states in the attempt to resume legal government, its progress toward statehood was less direct and did not culminate in a constitution until 1780.

On May 10, 1776, the Congress in one of its boldest measures adopted a general resolution, which over the following months ensured that all colonies would acquire state governments.[18] To its author, John Adams, this "recommendation" was "equivalent to a declaration of independence."[19] While the terms of the general authorization of May 10, 1776, were only permissive, its preamble, which was added amid much controversy, made the creation of a republican government in each state mandatory, demanding that "the exercise of every kind of authority . . . under the Crown shall be totally suppressed and all the powers of government exerted under the authority of the people of the colonies."[20] Even for those states, Connecticut and Rhode Island, which retained the forms of their colonial governments, this requirement transformed the foundation on which the authority of their governments was based, changing them from British colonies into American states.

Thus, as Lincoln said, the Union created the thirteen states, and thereafter, under the Constitution, as Lincoln also said, the federal Congress—like the Continental Congress before it—continued to create states out of the vast territory of the American continent.[21]

The Continental Congress also exercised its constituent power when on July 2, 1776, it voted the independence of the whole nation, which it declared to the world two days later. The Declaration proclaimed not that thirteen "distinct nations" but that "one people," in Jefferson's words, had dissolved "the political bands" which had connected them to Britain. "By Authority" of this people "the United Colonies" were declared to be "Free and Independent States" and the new nation-state which they constituted was identified as "the United States of America."

While that new nation-state now had a name, it did not yet have a constitution, except for the states, which the sovereign people had created and whose constitutional status would be presumed and confirmed by the constitution-makers of 1787. In a first effort to establish a constitutional government for the thirteen states as a whole, the Continental Congress in its constituent capacity drafted, approved, and recommended for adoption the Articles of Confederation, which became effective when finally ratified in 1781. According to the explicit terms of the Articles and the mode of ratification, this frame of government was based on a compact among the thirteen states. This compact, however, did not create "The United States of America." That had been done and declared in 1776. No more than an interstate compact today did the Articles of Confederation create a new and independent polity. And when the government designed for this nation by the Articles failed its purposes, the constituent authority of the people was again brought into play to establish and ordain the Constitution of 1787, as we shall have occasion to observe in the next chapter.

We may well ask, why these thirteen? For it was their conjoint boundaries that defined the boundary of the new nation. The old areas of colonial rule established by the British defined the arenas within which whigs and tories contested for power. The continental union of the thirteen, however, owed nothing to previous British administrative definition. The thirteen were only a portion of the two dozen or so British colonies in North America and the West Indies during the period of prerevolutionary agitation. Some of these, especially the older settlements, such as Jamaica, the Bermudas, Bahamas, Barbadoes, and Leward Islands, had much in common with the revolutionary thirteen: a white population of largely British descent, the inheritance of British law, a dominant Protestantism, and a colonial legislature which in some cases had a history of protest going back to the seventeenth century. To these colonies, as to the thirteen, the constraints of the mercantile system as well as parliamentary taxation, such as the stamp tax, also applied.[22]

While these conditions might cause complaint and give rise to whiggish sentiments, the British presence told against any effective agitation, let alone resistance, by such small and scattered populations. Nova Scotia, for example, was included in those "fourteen governments" which, according to Edmund Burke in his last speech on conciliation delivered on March 22, 1775, needed to be reattached to the empire by being given "an interest in the Constitution."[23] Acquired in 1714, Nova Scotia by this date had a population which was not only British but also largely Yankee in origin, thanks in great part to whose efforts the colony had won a legislature in 1758. It had mercantile ties with New England and was contiguous with it in that the territory of Nova Scotia, which included what later became New Brunswick, adjoined Maine, then a part of Massachusetts.

Yet the province gave rise to no militant effort to join the agitation or the ultimate uprising to the south. The Stamp Act elicited only mild protests; the tea which Boston had rejected was shipped to Halifax, where the tax was duly paid. And during the war any whiggish inclinations produced only futile pleas for permission to remain neutral and isolated efforts to aid the revolution across the border. Whatever the wishes of these people, few, poor, and scattered in villages mainly along the coast, they could not make themselves into the "fourteenth colony" in the face of the substantial naval and military forces the British had based at Halifax. John Adams was wrong about their character but right about their motives when he called the Nova Scotians "a set of fugitives and vagabonds who are also kept in fear by a fleet and an army."[24]

South of Nova Scotia a different balance of forces prevailed in the thirteen colonies. It was this continent-wide force, the whig movement, which, driven by the republican idea, defined the boundaries of the new nation-state. That idea, although universal in its claim, by its incidence among these populations answered the national as well as the governmental question, determining not only the mode of government but also the unit of government.

According to Old Whig doctrine, none of this could have happened. The Americans should not have been able to create an effective republican government, certainly not on a continental scale. For the Old Whigs, liberty and union could be joined together only by the rule of the virtuous few. That had been a fundamental issue through the years of agitation before the break, when the colonists were demanding popular government and the British were standing on the wisdom of the ages that government by the many would destroy the social order.

In terms of grand theory, the Americans had vindicated Locke, who believed that "the people" had the capacity to act as the ultimate law-making body. Blackstone had fiercely denied this and so had Burke, both contending that if the people at large were to attempt to set right a wayward government, let alone erect a new and better one, only chaos—a return to the state of nature—could ensue. In Old Whig eyes, the American uprising should have defeated itself. To reject royal authority should have caused disorder within the colonies and among them. But within the colonies, even when royal courts and royal justice were banished, law and order was maintained. Between the colonies, likewise, the opportunity to take advantage of the misfortunes of one another—for instance, to go for the trade that closing the port of Boston had made available to rival ports—was, in Webster's later words, "rejected with scorn."[25]

Burke immediately perceived the American achievement and the failure of the British strategy. He drew no analogy with 1688. Quite the contrary. "We thought," he reminded the House of Commons on the eve of Lexington and Concord, "that the utmost which the discontented colonists could do was to disturb authority; we never dreamt that they could of themselves supply it, knowing in general what an operose business it is to establish a government absolutely new." Overturning that time-honored expectation, "they have," he continued, "formed a new government sufficient for its purposes," a "new government . . . [which] originated directly from the people and was not transmitted through any of the ordinary artificial media of a positive constitution."[26]

In this passage Burke was referring primarily to Massachusetts. The subsequent military action displayed the solidarity of the other colonies with Massachusetts, which Webster celebrated fifty years later as the resistance of "the whole American people" to the strategy of divide and conquer. In 1776, therefore, "the thirteen United States of America" could give a plausible and decisive answer to the national question, when they declared that they were "one people," who found it necessary to assume "among the Powers of the Earth the separate and equal station to which the Laws of Nature and Nature's God entitle them." Around the demand for self-government the nation had coalesced, and during the crucial years of the revolution, through its agent the Continental Congress, the nation acted as that "superintending power" which even advanced whigs during their dalliance with "imperial federalism" had briefly thought only monarchy could provide.

In the transition from colony to state, much remained the same in the boundaries of town, county, and province, the structure and process of law-making bodies, the substance of the law, and the judicial system by which the law was enforced and order maintained. Yet between the "collective legal identity" of a colony and a state a great gap had been opened by the transformation of the moral basis of the polity from royal to republican.[27] Renouncing the old "Allegiance to the British Crown," the Declaration of Independence had asserted the right and ability of the people to overthrow a government and to constitute a new one more to their liking. The old monarchic claim to legitimacy suffered the same sea change at the point where lives and property were most directly touched by the coercive powers of government, namely, in the style of the judicial process.

Massachusetts illustrates the change.[28] When in 1770, for example, certain British soldiers were tried for their part in the Boston Massacre, the indictment followed the traditional form, *"Rex v. Weems. Rex v. Peyton."* The last session of the courts under the royal charter was held in September 1774; the first under the revolutionary regime in June 1776. In the meantime on May 10, 1776, the legislature had passed a bill which, after an indignant preamble denouncing King George for his "unjust War," substituted for any reference to "our Sovereign Lord the King" in the "stile" of the judicial process the phrase "the Government and People of the *Massachusetts-Bay, in New England."* By 1784, following the language of the new constitution of 1780, the indictments were brought, as they still are today, in the name of "The Commonwealth."[29]

"A government absolutely new" had been established, to use Burke's words. There really had been a revolution.

Tom Paine's National and Federal Republic

Compact theory does not fit the facts of the foundation. The national theory, while making a much better fit with that history, was not simply a reflection of it but was also a powerful influence on it. Ideas coming down from the Commonwealth made available the conception of a national and federal republic. Putting that conception fully into words and law was the work of the following years. Yet in the months when independence was being decided, the outlines of the idea were sketched in a pamphlet which was itself a main influence upon that decision. This was Tom Paine's *Common Sense,*[30] which, appearing in January 1776 and being read during the next few months by more than a fifth of the entire colonial population,[31] had a galvanic effect in propelling them to break with Britain.

Common Sense made the case for independence. It also made the case for republicanism. The republic Paine foresaw would be continental in scale, expansive in purpose, and ruled by the sovereign people through a constitutional charter which gave coordinate status to the states and to a strong central government. It may seem odd that this outsider from London who had been in the country just over a year should so perceptively read the mind of the colonists and prophetically foresee their political future. This is not at all odd when one recognizes that Paine, a Quaker and an agitator, came from the same background of Dissent and radical whiggism as most of the American rebels. The republican thrust, which had been moving the colonial agitation, as tories in America and Britain rightly saw from its start, was finally made explicit by this insider from the same tradition.

Paine thought his republicanism, not his advocacy of independence, was the most important message of *Common Sense*. Later generations have agreed by acclaiming his pamphlet for showing how the colonial revolt in America served "the cause of all mankind." In contrast with his later writings at the time of the French Revolution, what he says in *Common Sense* and subsequent writings about American affairs has more in common with the thought of the Commonwealth than with the Enlightenment.

Religious ideas are integral to the argument. The "lost innocence" of mankind is a major premise, introduced in the first lines. Although a glowing optimist, he is not utopian or perfectionist, and for him government, therefore, remains "a necessary evil," even at "the birthday of this new world." While developing his fierce denunciation of monarchy, he, like the Commonwealth writers, feels obliged to take up the problem of Biblical kingship and goes on at great length to show that it was a sinful declination from the older republicanism of Israel. Like John Adams and others of the Puritan persuasion, he explains the rise of free government and the settlement of America as offshoots of the Reformation. Even with regard to political institutions, with whose details he was not greatly concerned, his model of the future American polity owes much to the constitutional republicanism of the Commonwealth.

One of his most perceptive critics saw this clearly and made it a ground for his reply to *Common Sense*. The author, Charles Inglis, a tory pamphleteer, argued that the "republican form" proposed by Paine was unsuitable because "America is too extensive for it," and he went on like Machiavelli and Montesquieu to cite the evidence from Roman history. Claiming that Paine's proposed government "would make *sad work* in America," he found that its "principal outlines" were taken from "Mr. Harrington's *Rota*." The faults of this scheme, he held, were those identified by Montesquieu's criticism of Harrington's *Oceana*, "of which the *Rota* is an abridgment."[32] In those sarcastic comments on *Oceana*, Montesquieu, voicing the usual criticism of republican government, had accused Harrington of advocating such a degree of liberty as could only lead to the same "confusion" that had prevailed in the Commonwealth.[33]

Despite his intellectual debts to the Commonwealth, however, it cannot be shown that Paine brought his message of republicanism with him from England. There the agitation for a more representative government, which had coincided with the American effort and had been greatly stimulated by it, had not become openly republican but remained only a movement for parliamentary reform.[34] The triumph of John Wilkes in 1776 consisted in his presentation to the House of Commons of the first proposal by a prominent politician for comprehensive reform of its method of election.[35] On the fringes of the agitation, the cry of "Wilkes and no king" could sometimes be heard, but the republican movement, such as it was, remained underground, and no evidence connects Paine with the "little knots of republicans and radicals scattered throughout London and its suburbs."[36]

His whiggery is not in doubt. During the years of controversy following the Middlesex election of 1768, Paine, an exciseman in Lewes, Sussex, took a vigorous part in the debates of the local whig society. In 1772 he wrote a pamphlet asking higher wages for his fellow employees. This agitation cost him his job and led to his emigration. But his argument for the excisemen was grounded on their need and service, not political principle. Thanks to his interest in science, he made the acquaintance of Franklin and attended Franklin's "Club of Honest Whigs" in London, which was frequented by theorists and reformers such as James Burgh, Joseph Priestly, and Richard Price, some of whose ideas he used in *Common Sense*. But, although warmly recommended by Franklin, he was still only "an obscure Englishman of whiggish temper" when he emigrated to America in November 1774 at the age of thirty-seven.[37]

According to E. P. Thompson, it was the change in political context that stirred up Paine's latent radicalism.[38] One can easily imagine the heady atmosphere into which this political activist was pitched by his arrival in Philadelphia, where only a few weeks earlier the First Continental Congress had assembled and launched its audacious challenge to the imperial power. The response of the colonists during the next year and a half—"an unexampled concurrence of sentiment," as he termed it in *Common Sense*—visibly contradicted the ancient wisdom that popular government could only destroy order, not create it.

This new environment had a transforming effect on Paine's fortunes and his outlook. Soon becoming an editor of a local periodical, he wrote a great deal in the whig cause, hinting immediately at independence and within a few months turning openly against monarchy. Paine was not the first to come out for popular government. From the early 1770s, colonial spokesmen had been turning against monarchy and hereditary rule in general. It was an advocate—in private—of a republic and of independence, the prominent Philadelphia physician Benjamin Rush, who after being shown Paine's manuscript suggested the title.[39]

Paine, in short, did not import some new "ism" into America but instead caught up with and then gave a lead to the developing thought of colonial whigs. Nor had the American whigs themselves suddenly turned to government by the people. The republican principle was inherent in the demand for actual representation—as understood by them. That understanding had not been immediately put into words but was elicited by events and revealed over time in the shifting positions of the dissidents. The essence was that not king, nor lords, nor parliament was to rule but the colonists themselves.

Paine's contribution to the decision for a republic was to make this premise vividly articulate. The vividness of his rhetoric was important. The vulgar manner of his denunciation of monarchy in the man George III, "the royal brute," and in the institution, "the most prosperous invention the devil ever set on foot for the promotion of idolatry," performed a critical function.[40] Reverence for kingship still could be found in colonial America. In Paine's sarcastic portrayal, writes Stephen Fender, "respect for the traditional iconography of the British monarchy, the lion and the unicorn, is reduced to idolatrous 'worship' of 'the ass and the lion'; William the Conqueror . . . is revealed as nothing more than 'a French bastard landing with an armed banditti.'"[41] Paine's assault, one might say, reenacts verbally the fell deed of the regicides when they cut off the king's head "with the crown upon it."[42]

The symbolism, moreover, drove home substantial truths. The heart of Paine's argument was that kingship failed to perform the function claimed for it, namely, the preservation of order. That, says Paine, is "the most bare-faced falsity ever imposed on mankind." As demonstrated by the history of "that distracted kingdom," England, hereditary monarchy, he continued, "instead of making for peace . . . makes against it, and destroys the very foundation it seems to stand upon."[43]

Here Paine was reiterating themes made familiar by Commonwealth writers. What he said on the point was so much the substance of this argument that one of his critics claimed that *Common Sense* merely plagiarized a Cromwellian pamphlet purporting to show that monarchy had brought not order but disorder to Scotland.[44] Henry Parker, also a seventeenth-century republican, had said the same about kingship in England and Harrington about kingship in ancient Judah and Israel.[45] In the spirit of the same authors Paine struck at the root of the hierarchic tradition, declaring that "all men being originally equal," there is no "natural or religious reason" why kings should be distinguished from subjects "like some new species."[46]

The union necessary for liberty and security could be achieved only under republican government. Paine did not use the term "popular sovereignty," but in his scheme, according to "nature and reason" the people would rule, exercising both constituent and governmental sovereignty. In the rise of government, he supposed, representation had been introduced, but only as a matter of "convenience" because of the increase in "number" and "distance." The relation between voters and representatives was close and continuous. Representatives were chosen not because of their superiority in virtue and wisdom but because they were persons "who are supposed to have the same concerns at stake which those have who appointed them, and who will act in the same manner as the whole body would act were they present." Thanks to frequent elections, they would establish a "common interest with every part of the community." Upon this common interest and "not upon the unmeaning name of king" would depend "the strength of government and the happiness of the governed." Paine put into words what had been on the tip of the tongue of colonial spokesmen such as James Wilson, Thomas Jefferson, and John Adams before they recoiled briefly into the fantasy of imperial federalism. Indeed, Adams said that there was nothing original in *Common Sense* since he had said it all before![47]

Great as was Paine's preference for government by the people, he did not therefore think them any less in need of governance. As keenly as any tory he recognized their fallibility and found in government the corrective. This perception informed not only his general outlook but especially his immediate fears. His anxiety over the weakness of government continually appears. Much as he admired the "unexampled concurrence of sentiment" that united the colonists and "their spirit of good order and obedience to continental government," he found "truly alarming" "a visible feebleness in our affairs." "The continental belt," he said, "is too loosely buckled." Apprehending the typical failure of republican government, factious dissension, he also feared the consequent danger of a demagogue and would-be king who "laying hold of popular disquietudes" might "sweep away the liberties of the continent like a deluge."[48]

The remedy was "a Constitution of our own" which would inform the world "that in America the law is king." That need was "the most powerful of all arguments" for independence, for only such a form of government could "keep the peace of the continent and preserve it inviolate from civil wars."[49]

Paine's constitutionalism was as fundamental to his thought as his republicanism, and indeed is inseparable from it. It is constitutionalism in the American, not the British, mode: the charter he proposes is authorized by the people, but it lays down the law by which the people must govern themselves. While he confined his specific suggestions to "hints," his pervasive concern with the nature of a future American polity initiated, as Pauline Maier has pointed out, "a new controversy over the internal structure of republican government."[50]

According to his brief sketch, a "charter of the United Colonies" would be drawn up and authorized, not by a compact among the several colonies, nor even with ratification by them, but by a "continental conference." This body would include fifty-two members drawn from the Continental Congress and from the colonial assemblies. A majority, sixty-five in the total of one hundred and seventeen, however, would be "representatives of the people at large," five being elected by direct vote in each colony. Thanks to the experience of the officeholders, this body would have "knowledge." Thanks to "being empowered by the people," it would have "a truly legal authority." In this "intermediate body between the governors and governed," the people appear in their constituent capacity, a majority being chosen directly and a minority indirectly by them.[51]

The structure of government it would establish, while not confederate, would neither be unitary. The conference would prescribe the organization of both the central and the provincial governments. Each colony would have an annually elected assembly. It would also send delegates to the central Congress, chosen not by the assembly but directly by the people in districts. The basis of representation, it appears, would be population, not population and property, let alone superiority in virtue and wisdom. The charter would contain something in the nature of a bill of rights, since it would secure "freedom and property to all men, and above all things, the free exercise of religion, according to the dictates of conscience." It would not provide for a separation of powers, the Congress being a unicameral body with a President whose choice would rotate among the colonies and whose powers would presumably be only those of a presiding officer.[52]

Paine does, however, provide for a division of power between levels of government. The charter, he says, would draw "the line of business and jurisdiction" between the Congress and the provincial assemblies. Since this allocation was made by the constituent sovereign, it would give coordinate legal status to each level of government, as in the Commonwealth models of national federalism. Paine did not specify the powers to be given to each level. His general rule for the division of power, however, was: "Always remembering that our strength is continental, not provincial." In this rule as in the repeated admonitions of his writings in *The Crisis* during the war,

Paine appears as an advocate of strong central government, justifying his claim in later years that he "ought to stand first on the list of Federalists." This radical democrat was also an ardent centralizer.[53]

He was also an ardent nationalist. He harped continually on the obvious fact that the strength of the colonists depended upon maintaining their unity. He perceived that they had proved that unity by their behavior in protest and in battle. He was confident that they could produce a government which would draw the "continental belt" tighter for the sake of victory against their enemies and peace among themselves. The government that would achieve these ends would not be imposed upon the people but would emerge from them. Representation, as he conceived it, would ensure that elected persons could never become "an interest separate from the electors." A "common interest," moreover, "with every part of the community" would arise from the close and continuous relation of electors and elected.[54]

Paine's nationalism was expansionist. Like Franklin, he foresaw an America that would become ever more wealthy and populous. "Our plan is commerce," he declared. Thanks to commerce, our material progress "stands unparalleled in the history of other nations," and upon that foundation colonial military and naval power could more than match the British. But, he continued, looking still farther into the future, "America does not yet know what opulence is" in comparison with what it would achieve once her commerce was freed of British fetters and "the legislative powers" were in her own hands. What was at stake, he admonished his readers, was "not the affair of a city, a county, a province, or a kingdom; but a continent—of at least one eighth part of the habitable globe."[55]

Here, he declared, heralding the advent of independence, "the birthday of a new world is at hand, and a race of men, perhaps as numerous as all Europe contains, are to receive their portion of freedom from the events of a few months." If other American whigs were content—or ever had been content—to vegetate in their little republics along the North American coast, happy with the status allowed them by the imperial power during the century of benign and salutary neglect, Paine surely was not one of them. He perceived as clearly and was as strongly drawn to the prospect of a great and growing empire of freedom as James Harrington, Benjamin Franklin, or Alexander Hamilton.[56]

His proposed constitution with its guarantees of individual and political liberty was an instrument for realizing this expansive national purpose. Not least, its provisions for federalism, like those of the Articles and the Constitution, opened the way to an expansion which, like Franklin's plan of 1754, would maintain republican equality and exclude any new colonialism.

In the long run he was prescient. His synthesis of democracy and nationalism under a strong central government in a federal system foretold the actual future of America with remarkable accuracy. In the immediate future, his call for independence was also echoed by an enormous response. Its declaration was pronounced in Jefferson's exordium on behalf of "one people" and on the grounds of a democratic political philosophy. His fear that without constitutional government for the whole continent the states would fall into self-destroying conflict was only too richly verified by their behavior under the Articles of Confederation. His call for a continental conference to offset these dangers was not heeded for more than a decade, although he claimed to have been the first to renew the appeal in 1780.[57] A full statement of the national theory of how the union and American federalism had come into existence and its embodiment in fundamental law would have to wait on the debates and decisions of that later time.

PART THREE

THE NATIONAL AND REPUBLICAN CONSTITUTION

"Sᴛᴢᴇ ᴡᴀꜱ ᴛʜᴇ ᴋᴇʏ," writes Edmund Morgan. The problem confronting the framers of the Constitution was how to establish a government which was at once national in its vision and popular in its foundation. On one hand, a government continental in scope was necessary for domestic tranquility and national defense. On the other hand, the weakness of the federal authority under the Articles of Confederation enabled the forces of localism to dominate the center as well as the periphery. How to overcome localism, according to Morgan, was "the central problem" blocking the way to successful self-government.[1]

"The problem presented itself initially and forcefully in the formation of governments for several states," writes Morgan. Typically, the new state constitutions provided for an upper house which, it was hoped, would moderate the more parochial lower house. Defeating these hopes, both branches of the respective state legislatures tended to divide on particular issues in much the same way. Representatives with a broader outlook did appear, but, being few in number and scattered through the two houses, "they were frequently overpowered by the localists." As a result, the state legislatures passed laws "violating the treaty with Great Britain, issuing paper money as legal tenure, refusing to pay their states' quotas of national expenses, raising their own salaries and lowering those of other government officers." The state governments, as James Madison concluded, were "failing to fulfill the functions of government, failing to protect property rights and the other rights of individuals and minorities."

Reflecting on the failures of his home state, Virginia, Madison identified the source of the trouble as the "spirit of *locality.*"[2]

A conception of popular government that was emphatically national in its focus was at hand. Descending from the republican thought of the Commonwealth, its principles had been gradually reformulated by the American whigs during the controversy with Britain leading to independence. The claim of actual representation was informed by an ever more evident demand for popular sovereignty, which, whether it was to be exercised by way of the parliamentary option or the federal option, agreed with and reflected the Commonwealth tradition. As exemplified by Harrington and others, this tradition also showed how such a regime could be federal. In 1776 Tom Paine had summarized these trends in *Common Sense* where he sketched the outlines of a national and federal republic for the United States. A "continental conference," such as he repeatedly proposed, to tighten "the Continental belt" did not meet until 1787.[3] In that year at the constitutional convention in Philadelphia, the national outlook prevailed and "the Continental belt" was tightened. In theory and in law, intergovernmental relations in the United States were firmly based on national federalism.

National federalism did not win its victory easily and without compromise. On the plane of theory, it faced a formidable enemy. Critics of the Constitution drew support from the powerful case for compact federalism advanced by what one historian has called "the best political science of the century."[4] This was the theory of the "confederate republic" elaborated by Montesquieu in *The Spirit of the Laws,* first published in France in 1748 and translated into English in 1750.[5] It was in reply to this theory that James Madison framed the main lines of the national case in his argument for the "compound republic." In order to bring out the basic theoretical differences between the Federalist advocates and the Anti-Federalist opponents of the Constitution and the national theory, Chapter 7 will examine the grounding of the Anti-Federalist case in the political science of Montesquieu.

From the viewpoint of national federalism, the Constitution derived legitimacy from two sources: a conception of authority, setting out how "the people of the United States" would govern themselves, and a conception of purpose, indicating what this authority would be used for. As the constituent sovereign, "the people" would "ordain" the Constitution, converting the 4,543 words proposed by the Philadelphia convention into a fundamental law binding on both federal and state governments and dividing authority between them. As the governmental sovereign, the people would also be the active political force which, under the authority of the Constitution, directed the nation toward the fulfillment of its "great objects." In their most important capacity the American people were the American nation, whose liberty, peace, welfare, justice, and more perfect union were those "great objects" which the federal and state governments would serve.

The national theory will be taken up under two main headings: the conception of authority, dealing with the people as the sovereign, both governmental and constituent (Chapters 8, 9, and 10); and the conception of purpose, identifying the people as the nation created, maintained, and developed by the sovereign (Chapter 11).

CHAPTER 7

Montesquieu's
Confederate Republic

THE FEDERALIST CASE, as stated in the famous papers of 1787–88, was framed as a reply to the opponents of ratification. It will help clarify what the advocates of the Constitution were saying if we first look at the theoretical underpinning of the arguments they were trying to refute. These arguments, put forward by writers of newspaper articles and pamphlets and by speakers at the state conventions and other public gatherings, reflected a miscellany of interests and styles. Yet for such a fragmented body of utterance they displayed a remarkably high degree of theoretical coherence. This was owing in no small degree to the pervasive influence of Montesquieu. The Anti-federalists, as Cecilia Kenyon has remarked, were his "staunch disciples."[1] Montesquieu's model of the confederate republic, having been a major source of Anti-Federalist thought, is an indispensable guide to the theoretical underpinning of the case for compact federalism advanced by the Anti-Federalists and by their successors of the states' rights school of constitutional interpretation.

Montesquieu restated the dilemma of scale in much the same manner as Machiavelli, but without attribution. "If a republic be small," he concluded, "it is destroyed by a foreign force; if it be large, it is ruined by an internal imperfection." In contrast with Machiavelli's despair, however, Montesquieu purported to find a solution in a certain type of federalism. If, he reasoned, a number of small republics would join together by "a convention" or "agreement" to form a "confederate republic" on the lines of the United Netherlands or the Swiss cantons, they could amass defensive power without exposing themselves to the "internal imperfection" that threatened a unitary regime in a large republic.[2] In offering this solution to the dilemma of scale, Patrick Riley has observed, Montesquieu was the first theorist to suggest a connection between federalism and popular government.[3]

The Structure

Montesquieu's model of the confederate republic had two elements. The first, and most important, was an elaboration of Machiavelli's small republic theory; the second, Montesquieu's principal contribution to the model, was his solution of the dilemma of scale by means of compact federalism.

Like Machiavelli, Montesquieu held that the large republic, in contrast to the small republic, is subject to self-destructive tumult and disorder. "In an extensive republic," he wrote, "the public good is sacrificed to a thousand private views. In a small one, the interest of the public is more obvious, better understood, and more within the reach of every citizen." Moreover, he thought, scale not only produces the excessive pluralism that impedes self-government. It also brings into existence aggregates of economic and political power—"men of large fortunes" and "trusts too considerable to be placed in any single subject"—which under conditions of disorder threaten the republican regime.[4]

When Montesquieu refers to the "smallness" or "largeness"—that is, the scale—of a state, he sometimes means area, sometimes number, and often both. Sheer distance, he finds, can independently have an effect, requiring, for instance, the quickness of decision and execution of which despotic rather than monarchic or republican governments are capable.[5] But, as in Machiavelli's analysis, the cutting edge of Montesquieu's argument is his perception of the effect of numbers. As with Machiavelli, it is the increase in military manpower brought by confederation which enables the many small, weak states to defend themselves. Similarly, with regard to the internal governance of republics, it is not the extent of territory that undermines the populous, unitary regime but the disruptive effect of the "thousand private views."

In Montesquieu's scheme, as numbers grow, differences multiply;

so also as numbers diminish, diversity declines, homogeneity is approached, and the prospects of self-government are enhanced. In some conceptions of society, diversity is seen as consisting of interdependent and complementary and therefore harmonious elements.[6] That is not Montesquieu's view. For him, as for Machiavelli, diversity leads to conflict, and so disrupts government by the many, while similarity leads to harmony, thereby providing a basis for popular government. Such, with this stress on number, is the way Montesquieu was read by his disciples among the Anti-Federalists and also by his great critic James Madison.[7]

The reduction in scale, according to Montesquieu, will also reduce the aggregations of power that threaten the big republic. A smaller government will mean less danger from over-powerful administrators wielding authority commensurate with their great "trusts." A smaller territory will make it harder for large properties to be accumulated distant from governmental control. In a small republic, in contrast with a large, if an oppressor did appear from such a source, "the people might any instant unite and rise against him."[8]

Montesquieu's emphasis on scale is so great as to lead him sometimes to speak of it as not only a necessary but indeed a sufficient condition for the variation in the forms of government. Smallness, he seems to say, will not simply favor republican government but will by itself produce such a regime, as moderate extent will produce monarchy and great size despotism. Evoking the central theme of his great work, he can say flatly that "the spirit of [a] state will alter in proportion as it contracts or extends its limits."[9]

It would be untrue to Montesquieu's method to conclude that he offered such a single-cause analysis. In his scheme, the republican spirit is created and sustained by other forces as well as the powerful influence of scale. The motivating value of the republican spirit is virtue. "Virtue," he declares, at the very start of his treatise, is "the spring which sets republican government in motion, as honor is the spring that gives motion to monarchy." In this usage, virtue has a special character. It is "not a moral, nor a Christian, but a political virtue." It is appropriate for, indeed peculiar to, republics. When characterizing this human capacity, Montesquieu does not follow Aristotle or Aquinas. Unlike the "virtue" of their schemes—which, as "wisdom," qualified and entitled a small minority to rule—the "political virtue" of Montesquieu's scheme is not a kind of "being" but a kind of "sensation," and indeed "a sensation that may be felt by the meanest as well as the highest person in the state."[10]

The rationale of this "sensation" is "the love of one's country and its laws."[11] Unlike Christian virtue, this "political virtue" is not a love of all mankind; although general, it is not universal.[12] Yet its moral demand is severe. "Virtue," writes Montesquieu, "is a self-renunciation, which is ever arduous and painful" and "requires a constant preference of public to private interest."[13] The laws and the conditions they foster, however, can make it easier for republican virtue to achieve the painful self-sacrifice required by the public interest. The laws of the republic express the twofold norm of republican virtue, the love of equality and the love of frugality. Equality is promoted by laws which lessen differences in wealth and property; frugality, by laws against great accumulations. These laws and the conditions they create presumably reduce the influence of the two great social vices, ambition (the vice of the few) and avarice (the vice of the many). In contrast with the extended republic, these laws work in the same direction as the reduction in scale to create greater homogeneity. In such a small community of small and equal proprietors, private interests are more alike, the diversity of the "thousand private views" of the extensive republic is reduced, and the gap between them and the public interest is narrowed.[14]

Montesquieu does not neglect the need for the direct inculcation of virtue. Republican government, he thought, must call upon "the whole power of education," whether exercised through the example of parents or the care of other members of the community. Yet here also smallness is a help, since education means "training up the whole body of the people like a single family."[15] If virtue means self-sacrifice, then realistically speaking, the circle which it embraces must be small, both for the sake of homogeneity and for the sake of the closeness which as in a family enable individuals to identify with one another.

Leagues of small states which created a central government for certain purposes go back to classical antiquity.[16] By the time Montesquieu used the term *fédérative*—in English "foederal"—to refer to

political systems of this kind, however, the new theory of international relations that had emerged in the sixteenth and seventeenth
centuries had given the term a quite distinctive meaning.[17] The main
premise of this theory was the concept of sovereignty. Taking its
modern form in that period, sovereignty was conceived as the legal
authority of a government which was unlimited over persons within
its jurisdiction and which in its relations with other governments was
limited only by restraints, such as treaties, which it might impose on
itself and so of which it could judge infractions by its sole authority.[18]
Lawyers and political theorists came more and more to agree that it
was typical and proper for governments to have this power, which
made them in law internally supreme and externally independent. In
1765, for example, Blackstone stated this doctrine for Britain in his
Commentaries, where he elaborated in a classic formulation the
proposition that the King-in-Parliament has "that absolute despotic
power, which must in all governments reside somewhere."[19]

Into a political world so conceived, Riley has observed, it was hard
to fit such regimes as the Swiss Confederation, the United Provinces,
or the Holy Roman Empire. The commonly accepted solution to this
problem of classification was to assimilate these exceptions to the
model of international relations which emerged from the doctrine of
sovereignty. Accordingly, these regimes were treated not as themselves sovereign but as leagues or alliances formed by treaty among
sovereign powers.[20] The central government so created, if indeed it
could be termed a government (*pace* Blackstone), was called "foederal," from *foedus,* meaning treaty or compact. This term, coming
from *fidere,* meaning to trust, indicated the fragility of the authority
of such a government.[21]

"Federal government," writes Riley, "thanks to its status as a mere
contract was reduced—by writers like Pufendorf—to a kind of agreement in private law; it was no longer even a public form of order,
and so became subject to all the vicissitudes of ordinary agreements."
As in private contracts, bad faith by one party freed the others of
their contractual obligation and, since no sovereign judge could exist
between member states, each was the judge of such infractions.
Among the consequences of thinking of federal government as based
on a contract was the idea of secession, "the idea of simply breaking

a disagreeable contract whenever any pretext of bad faith on the part of any other party arose." In the nineteenth century, as Riley goes on to observe, this view of federalism as a mere contract was fundamental to John C. Calhoun's constitutional theory, justifying secession from the Union and nullification of its laws.[22] Montesquieu's confederate republic, being based on a "convention" or agreement, had similar properties. Indeed, such was the flexibility of this regime that "the confederacy," according to Montesquieu, "may be dissolved and the confederates preserve their sovereignty."[23] Secession was a fully acknowledged right.

This derivation from the theory of international relations does more than indicate how legitimate authority will be distributed in Montesquieu's confederate republic. To make these small republics the basic constitutional units of the polity also shapes the political process of its central government. The representatives of the member states at the center will be like ambassadors of independent nations, and their discussion and decision-making will have the nature of diplomatic bargaining and balancing among the interests of their constituencies. An ambassador is a delegate: his task is to take the national interest of his country as given and to promote this end by the most effective means at his disposal. Similarly, in a republic on the confederate model, the various members would have their several internally determined interests which the general framework of government would defend, but not invade, regulate, or modify. The members of the confederation could bargain over the exchange of benefits that would be useful to their respective purposes. This exchange of benefits, however, would be instrumental to, not constitutive of, the interests being served. In this process, as in rational choice theory, the preferences of the parties would remain unchanged.[24] The bargaining by which it was conducted, moreover, would presumably not lead to overreaching by any party, but would rather keep these small "commonwealths for preservation" in balance with one another.

The Mechanics

As compared with national federalism, the idea of compact federalism which informs Montesquieu's model of the confederate republic leads to quite different views of sovereignty, liberty, democracy, community, and political development. The grounds and consequences of these differences will be made clearer if we look further into some of the general principles of Montesquieu's political science. Our object is not a comprehensive account of Montesquieu's whole system of thought based on a consideration of all the works and writing of this sophisticated and many-sided mind as it evolved over half a century. Our concern is to cast light on the thinking of his Anti-Federalist disciples by looking at *The Spirit of the Laws,* which was far and away the best known of his works among eighteenth-century Americans.

That scholars such as Gordon Wood may today term this work "political science" reflects the modernity of Montesquieu's approach.[25] In method he cut himself off from the teleology of ancient and medieval political thought. He referred rarely and then only disdainfully to Aristotle, and to Aquinas not at all; and while presumably a Christian and a Catholic, he was unable to prevent *The Spirit of the Laws* from being condemned by the theology faculty of the Sorbonne and placed on the Index by Rome.[26] In that work he sought in a thoroughly modern spirit to classify the principal forms of government known to man and to explain the general causes that sustained them and that brought about their decline and fall.

He was, however, no clinically objective positivist. In championing what he called liberty against absolutism, he put himself clearly in opposition to the current advocates of centralized government, rational administration, uniformity of the laws, and the rest of the program of "enlightened despotism." Yet he believed that constitutions could be reformed by human thought and choice; hence, his book. He defended freedom of expression and condemned cruel punishments. He favored the development of commerce, but thought of it as an activity conducted "with a view to the advantage of the state" and, rejecting the laissez-faire ideas of the physiocrats, believed that government could and should interfere to secure those advantages.[27]

In method and values he was modern, but for his preferred form of government he looked back to the Middle Ages. Harrington, we will recall, detested the mixed government of that period with its "wrestling match" between king and barons.[28] In Montesquieu's eyes, on the contrary, "the best species of constitution that could possibly be imagined by man" was the "Gothic government" of feudal Europe and, while recognizing that its time had passed, he found many of its features in contemporary monarchies.[29] In this conservative, not to say reactionary, spirit he upheld the *thèse nobiliaire* against the *thèse royale* of the early philosophers, such as Voltaire, Helvétius, and the physiocrats. In seeking to advance that cause he used his new political science to defend the old hierarchical, corporatist society which, although deeply challenged, was still very much alive. As Nannerl Keohane has observed, this conservative spirit was particularly marked in *The Spirit of the Laws*.[30]

Typically, in his analysis in this work of a properly constituted government, its components were several bodies, ranks, and orders, each exercising such power as to keep it in a balance with the others that would maintain the liberties of all. The analogy with mechanics was explicit. When showing how "the laws" and "the springs of government" interact, mutually strengthening one another, he concludes by quoting Newton's third law of motion: "And thus it is in mechanics, that action is always followed by reaction." The mechanical analogy informs his statement of the notion of political balance as a general law: "To form a moderate government," he wrote, "it is necessary to combine the several powers; to regulate, temper and set them in motion; to give, as it were, ballast to one, in order to counterpoise the other." Discussing monarchy, he writes: "It is with this kind of government as with the system of the universe, in which there is a power that constantly repels all bodies from the centre, and a power of gravitation that attracts them to it." Whether or not the analogy is anything more than a metaphor, it does throw light on how he conceives the basic entities of the system and their relations with one another. When we reflect on his famous aphorism, "power should be a check to power," we are not far wrong if we call to mind an image of solid spheres hovering in constant interactions that maintain a changeless equilibrium.[31]

Balance in a political system is maintained by the isolation of its constituent bodies from one another. Within each such constituent body the individual members are motivated by its distinctive values, which thereby give its members a strong common interest against other bodies. Thus, in a monarchic regime, each noble aspires to rank and preferment for himself, but in consequence also defends that system of honor against encroachment by any outside force. In this manner each body is isolated from the others but appropriately empowered by the constitution to maintain its interest against the others. In the aristocratic republic, for example, "the nobles form a body, who by their prerogative, and for their own particular interest restrain the people." In the scheme that Montesquieu sees as best for his times, descending from the Gothic constitution and resembling the English system, the legislature consists of two houses, one of the nobles, the other of representatives of the people, "each having their assemblies and deliberations apart, each their separate views and interests."[32]

While Montesquieu favored a wide franchise for the lower house, he severely separated voters from representatives. In his eyes, the discussion of public affairs is a task for which "the people collectively are extremely unfit." In consequence, any sort of law-making—"a right to active resolutions"—such as instructions or referenda, would be excluded from the role of the people, as "a thing of which they are absolutely incapable." "They ought to have no share of government," he writes, "but for the choosing of representatives, which is within their reach." In sentiments such as these one finds no encouragement for the doctrine of popular sovereignty, which gave American republican theory its unique form, or for its expression in that close and continuous supervision of representatives by voters which arose in American practice.[33]

In his monarchic system, the role of the people is modest; so also is that of the monarch. Although the laws are enacted by authority of the monarch, his function is only that of an executive in domestic and foreign affairs. He "can have no share in the public debates," nor is it necessary that he make proposals to the legislature, his business "consisting more in action than in deliberation." He has a power of veto, but presumably only in order to protect his constitutional position.[34] The monarch is by no means a leader, such as the American president became. The charm of the system is that no person, no single part, no general will or consensus, but the system itself, its balance of powers, preserves the rule of law, peace, and liberty.

This balance does not depend solely upon the distribution of legal powers. Constitutional powers are distributed to those distinct corporate bodies which are the fundamental components of the system and which also have other sources of influence. The nobles, for instance, are also "distinguished by birth, riches, or honors," and indeed the reason why, unlike the common people, they should have a direct and not merely an indirect representation is precisely that they also have these "other advantages in the state." One of these, the "patrimonial jurisdiction" of the nobility, like similar privileges of the clergy and the cities, is a force which has both supported and checked monarchic governments.[35] Clearly, while Montesquieu does not confine the relevant sources of power to the law of the constitution, neither does he reduce them to the "social substructure."[36]

Liberty is the security of living under a rule of law. That rule of law does not mean, as in some conceptions, the maintenance of the same basic rights for everyone everywhere in the realm. It does not entail uniformity among the authoritative rules by which the realm is governed. On the contrary, as in France of the *ancien régime,* the hierarchic structure of society requires the diversity of the particular laws applicable to the various strata, since the "difference in rank, birth, and condition . . . is frequently attended with distinctions in the nature of property." Likewise, the territorial corporate communities, such as the provinces, will also have "different laws" and "different customs."[37] As the interests common to the various bodies and orders are diverse, so also, said Montesquieu in an echo of the Middle Ages, liberty is plural. The separation of powers enables the various components to maintain their distinctive liberties against encroachment by others.

Thus, by the strategy of isolation, diverse liberties are preserved. "Preserved" is the right expression. For the system is profoundly conservative in the generic sense of that word. Summarizing the effect of the separation of the legislative, executive, and judicial powers, Montesquieu sets forth this fundamental principle of his whole science of politics, its tendency to changeless equilibrium: "These three powers," he writes, "should naturally form a state of repose or inaction. But as there is a necessity for movement in the course of human affairs, they are forced to move, but still in concert." He fully recognizes that human affairs do suffer change. An improperly constituted government will be transformed—for worse, as when a too extensive republic collapses into despotism, or for better, as when the prince of a petty state is tempted to tyrannize by the very smallness of scale that then produces the reaction setting up a republic. Material development can undermine the values that have supported a regime, as when commerce weans the nobility away from the ethos of honor supportive of monarchy. Even in a properly constituted government the parts are in constant agitation, naturally and indeed continuously seeking to encroach on one another.[38]

Their respective powers, constitutional and other, however, enable each to fend off these efforts and maintain the equilibrium. Power is a check upon power. The essential work of the constitution is to restrain such efforts. And the negative concept of constitutionalism that derives from this vision of politics makes the prime function of the constitution the restraint of the exercise of power rather than the direction and utilization of power for national purposes. As Melvin Ritcher writes in a summary statement of Montesquieu's "single most important doctrine," the "intermediary bodies, such as the nobility, the parliaments, the local courts of seigniorial justice, and the church" as well as "other constituted bodies, provinces, towns, guilds, professional associations," all have the "present function . . . to balance one another and to serve as a barrier to despotism."[39]

The principles of Montesquieu's political science which inform his analysis of monarchic government also appear in his analysis of the confederate republic and illuminate how it functions. In both we see a balance of power among separate political bodies, each united by an exclusive common interest, and all maintaining by constant external interactions the equilibrium of the whole. In each case diversity is dealt with by a strategy of isolation.

Montesquieu's confederate republic and Harrington's commonwealth have much in common. Both are republican in that each is a model of government by the many. Both are federal in that each divides authority between levels of government by exceptional legal means. The authors of both recognize a conflict between the public interest and private interests and make it a major task of the republican order to overcome this conflict. To this end, both find it necessary to reduce great accumulations of power and to provide for education in civic virtue. Both agree that a commitment to the public interest must motivate citizens and their representatives. Both also propose further constitutional structures and make them the main topic of their writing.

The structures they propose, however, express radically different conceptions of the political process. These differences follow from different conceptions of republican virtue, the capacity that enables men to govern themselves. For Montesquieu, republican virtue is a commitment to the common good which subdues and overrides private interests; for Harrington, virtue is the power of reason to discover by discussion a common interest that embraces and reconciles private interests.

Starting from this conception of political virtue, Harrington seeks to bring the many private and particular interests of the state together in a process of central deliberation so constructed and motivated as to elicit from them the commonalities of the public interest. A wide range of private interests is admitted, indeed welcomed, into the central legislature, where they are not overridden or rejected but utilized and united, thanks to government by discussion.

For Montesquieu, while legal and social conditioning can reduce diversity, the political process cannot. If lawmaking is to approach agreement, it must therefore start as nearly as possible from homogeneity. Within the member republics, their small scale will foster homogeneity. In the central government, agreement is favored by the narrow scope of policy, which is limited mainly to defense. Central policy is so limited because assistance with defense is all that the members of the confederation need from one another. Security is the rationale of their *foedus*. Otherwise they are politically and morally self-sufficient. Defense, moreover, is a matter on which the members can fairly easily agree, since it involves no internal regulation of the diverse interests of the confederacy but only the external protection of the territories within which they flourish. Such deliberation as occurs in the central government deals not with the adaptation of ends but the adoption of means to an agreed end. Preferences among the several members are fixed.

In the confederate republic, the political process of the central government is a matter of balancing and bargaining among the respective interests of the member republics; in the extended republic, the political process seeks reconciliation of the diverse interests of the subnational constituents in an inclusive view of the national interest. As commonwealths for preservation, the members of the confederate republic are committed to interests that are constant; as a commonwealth for increase, the extended republic welcomes diversity of interests and the prospect of expansion. One polity consists of small, isolated, homogeneous, and static units; the other of a large heterogeneous, integrated, and dynamic whole.

Starting from these opposing views of virtue and the political process, the two philosophers move toward different solutions to the problem of scale. For Montesquieu, the separateness of individuals can be overcome only in small groups sternly committed to self-denying altruism; for Harrington, even populations on the scale of the nation-state can be brought by discussion under constitutional government to a common understanding of and a commitment to the national interest. Montesquieu's confederate republic copes with diversity by isolating differences in small states related to one another by only a few external needs, such as defense. The extended republic of Harrington would integrate diverse interests in one great republic with a wide scope of central responsibilities.

On the nature of sovereignty, the constitution, and federalism, the two models of republican government differ accordingly. In both, sovereignty is popular. In Oceana, however, it is the people at large of the whole nation who ratify the "orders," making them law, indeed law "unalterable" by any organ of government, while the fundamental law of the confederate republic is nothing more than the "convention" agreed by the governing bodies of the member republics. For Montesquieu, it is right that power should remain largely within these constitutent bodies, since they are the true political communities. For Harrington, these governments serve local needs and guard against the possible abuse of power by the center; yet even in this role, they act as subdivisions of one nation.

The Confederate Republic in America

Madison's theory of the extended republic, set out in *Federalist* 10 and in other writings before and after the composition of that classic statement, was framed in reaction to the theory of the confederate republic.[40] As Douglas Adair has observed, Madison stood Montesquieu's theory on its head.[41] That Madison took the confederate model so seriously might lead one to think that Montesquieu's exposition had been known for a long time and had come to be widely accepted among American whigs, and, moreover, that American ideas about the intergovernmental aspects of the new regime came explicitly from this source. Some students of the period have said as much. For instance, when giving an account of the adoption of the compact model in the Articles of Confederation, Gordon Wood declares that the whig leaders consciously followed Montesquieu, "the best political science of the century," in their perception of the problem of scale and its solution.[42]

When assessing Montesquieu's influence on American political institutions at the time of the founding, one must distinguish between the use made of his ideas on federalism and the use made of his ideas on other topics, particularly separation of powers. From mid-century, *The Spirit of the Laws* was widely known and often quoted on such broad topics as liberty, commerce, taxation, representation, and corruption. During constitutional controversies in particular colonies, its authority was also called on to support colonial views of the separation of powers.[43] At the Constitutional convention in 1787 and during the debates on ratification, Montesquieu's authority on this topic was frequently invoked and his rationale for these provisions was accepted by both Federalists and Anti-Federalists.

Montesquieu's model of the confederate republic with its unique fusion of republic and federal ideas, however, does not appear in colonial thought until the mid-seventies; and even then and during the years leading to the calling of the Constitutional Convention, references to his ideas on federalism are few and indecisive. These ideas do come to the fore of political controversy during the debates at the convention and especially during ratification. They were used not by Federalist defenders of the Constitution but by its opponents. It was Montesquieu's model of the confederate republic, set in its larger intellectual context, that gave coherence to the arguments of the Anti-Federalists. When one looks into the source of American political thought in the eighteenth century, not compact federalism but national federalism proves to be the more deeply rooted. If we must cite one single thinker as the main source of the structure and theory of American federalism, it is Harrington, not Montesquieu.

The two main elements of Montesquieu's model, the small republic theory and the compact solution, could, of course, have had separate histories. The small republic theory could have come down from an earlier source, such as Machiavelli, as some historians suggest when they speak of it as "traditional."[44] If so, Americans could have come to know it quite independently of the writings of Montesquieu. In this earlier period, however, evidence for colonial use of the small republic theory separately is as scarce as for the use of it in the Montesquieuian fusion with the idea of a compact.

When we look at the arguments against the Constitution put forward by the Anti-Federalists in the 1780s, we do find ideas descending from the radical whig opposition to Walpole, which had been echoed by some Americans in the early eighteenth century: the stress on civic virtue, the fear of commerce, the suspicion of corruption and conspiracy at the highest levels of government.[45] But this Opposition ideology had nothing to say about the question of fundamental importance to the confederate model, namely, the problem of scale, and specifically the small republic theory. Nor indeed could the opponents of Walpole have plausibly proclaimed the democratic virtues of the small communities of England of the Augustan age, when the great whig notables dominated the periphery no less coercively than the center. The rotten borough system, which was viewed as beneficent "influence" and as nefarious "corruption" by adherents respectively of virtual and actual representation, was admitted by both sides to be a pillar of aristocratic power. To be sure, government in that time was markedly localized in comparison with what the Stuarts had attempted. This was not, however, the localism to which the seventeenth-century republicans had aspired, but rather a rule by territorial magnates which Namier later termed "civilian feudalism."[46]

Like the Anti-Federalists, the radical whigs of the Augustan age opposed what they called "consolidated" government. Unlike the Anti-Federalists, however, they did not mean by this an imbalance between central and local government. They meant rather an imbalance at the center within the "mixed constitution" brought about by excessive royal and ministerial power. It was "corruption" of this sort that led reformers like those with whom Benjamin Franklin associated to side with parliament against king and court in the years before the decade of resistance to parliamentary power inaugurated by the Stamp Act. In the rhetoric of the Opposition whigs, "consolidated" government did not mean overcentralized government.

Colonial experience included one significant experiment in voluntary intergovernmental cooperation. This was the New England Confederation of 1643, which Donald Lutz has termed "the first major attempt at federalism in America."[47] Based on an agreement among the four governments in what later became the two colonies of Massachusetts and Connecticut, its purpose was primarily "offense and defense." The scheme ceased to function shortly after the Restoration, which brought back that "protection" whose removal by the "sad distractions" of the civil war had been given as the main reason for its founding. Its rationale did not include that distinctive element of the compact theory, the small republic thesis. Moreover, the next major effort at federation, Benjamin Franklin's Albany Plan of 1754, rejected the compact model. As we have seen, Franklin thought a voluntary compact neither feasible nor desirable and proposed that the union be based on enactment by a superior authority, the British parliament.

During most of the period of prerevolutionary agitation, the American whigs had made no use of the small republic theory, either as a "traditional" belief or as an argument based on Montesquieu, in their defense of the powers of the colonial legislatures against the British parliament. When they argued the "parliamentary option," they presupposed a single state to whose central legislature the colonies, like its constituencies in Great Britain, would send representatives. When they argued the "federal option," they did not premise their reasoning on the problem of scale or the small state theory of republicanism. Basing their case not on the "argument from liberty" or on the "argument from community" but on the "argument from utility," they presupposed not a confederation of sovereign states but a single state in which authority was divided between levels of government.

In the very last stages of the agitation, however, one can perhaps find some trace of the Montesquieuian fusion of republican and federal theory in colonial thought, when a number of leading whigs switched to the argument for what has been called "imperial federalism."[48] In this view, as we have seen in Chapter 5, the several colonies along with England were conceived as "distinct nations," linked only by separate compacts with the king. During the controversy over independence, its leading advocate, however, was by no means committed to a Montesquieuian confederate republic. Thomas Paine's conception of an independent America was democratic and federal, but also strongly national, in the Harringtonian tradition, as his tory critic Charles Inglis sharply emphasized. While obviously well aware of Montesquieu's analysis of the problem of scale, Inglis confined his criticism to Harrington's national model and made no mention of the confederate republic as a solution to the problem of popular government in a big country. He would surely have been obliged to deal with that subject if the compact model had figured materially in the intentions of American whigs. Doubt of Montesquieu's influence on the American idea of union is increased by the failure of Thomas Burke, that ardent champion of state sovereigny, to call on his authority. Although well-read in political theory, the author of the amendment that became Article II of the Articles of Confederation did not cite Montesquieu, nor did he develop the small republic thesis in support of his cause.[49]

Conceivably Montesquieu's thinking about federalism also had some influence on Jefferson at this time. As the notes in his Commonplace Book show, during the years 1774–1776 he was making a study of *The Spirit of the Laws* (in French), including the idea of the confederate republic. During this same time he also advanced an argument for American rights based on a version of "imperial federalism" which in a rough and ready way could be fitted into the Montesquieuian model.[50]

In the Declaration of Independence, this view of the empire, which made the king the only link among the colonies and with Britain, was implied by the focus on George III, not the parliament, as the source of the evils leading to the break. Needless to say, this view of the role of parliament and the king, like the idea of imperial federalism in general, does not fit the historical facts. Moreover, we must note, although it was one step in the argument later advanced by the Anti-Federalists during the debate over the Constitution, it does not controvert the fundamental nationalist view. That view, as we shall have occasion to see in more detail later on, centers on how independence was achieved. When the issue was raised at the Constitutional Convention in 1787, the Federalists asserted that it was the American people, acting through the Continental Congress, who authorized the peoples of the colonies to form state governments, and then, again acting as "one people," to use Jefferson's words, declared their independence. When the Anti-Federalists denied this version of events and said on the contrary that "the separation from G.B. placed the 13 States in a state of nature towards one another," James Wilson, in a hot reply, "read the declaration of Independence," which, we may recall, asserts that it was "by the Authority of the good People of these Colonies," that "these United Colonies" had been declared "free and independent states." "The United Colonies," concluded Wilson, were declared independent of Britain "not individually, but Unitedly."[51]

In the early 1780s one might feel justified in tracing the Montesquieuian fusion of federal and republican theory in the views of David Howell, a delegate to Congress from Rhode Island. In the name of "the Sovereignty and Independence" of the states, Howell, "a localist politician from a small New England State," conducted a campaign against the proposed federal duty on imports. Declaring that only in "New England," and especially Rhode Island, could one find "pure and unmixed Democracy," he hoped that "our little state" might be able to defeat the proposed impost. Reflecting sentiments which, according to Rakove, would grow in future years, he took the strong states' rights position that "the Articles . . . [were] a constitution framed with the primary purpose of securing the liberties of the states."[52]

Looking back over political thinking in America during the generation before the convention of 1787, one finds very little use of the idea of compact federalism, whether one looks for explicit reference to Montesquieu's model, or, regardless of attribution, for its crucial element, the small republic theory. In contrast, the coming of the

Constitution in the late 1780s brings these Montesquieuian ideas into prominence with a rush.[53] Paradoxically, the first emphatic evidence of this connection is James Madison's critique of the confederate model in his argument for the extended republic, initially set out on the eve of the Convention and then developed during the debates over the framing and the ratification of the Constitution. At no point does Madison openly disagree with Montesquieu. Indeed, on such questions as the separation of powers he pays abundant tribute to him.[54] For, although favoring a strongly centralized government, Madison clung to the old whig opposition to consolidation within it. Yet Madison unquestionably made the Montesquieuian argument the principal theoretical target of his criticism when he developed his own ideas on intergovernmental relations. And well he might, since in the debates during the framing and ratification the Montesquieuian model was by far his most formidable foe on the plane of theory.[55]

The Anti-Federalist Case

While the Anti-Federalists had no single spokesman comparable to Madison and made no single statement of their ideas comparable to *The Federalist,* their arguments at the convention and during the ratification make a coherent case for compact federalism, often with a clear reference to Montesquieu. Like the nationalists, they sought to defend republican liberty. Contradicting the arguments of national federalism, however, they held that homogeneity, not diversity, was the better ground for popular government, and that the small rather than the large republic was more likely to be homogeneous. Luther Martin of Maryland, a leading critic of the nationalist proposals at the convention and an ardent opponent of ratification of the Constitution, summarized this fundamental opposition between the two viewpoints, in terms echoing Montesquieu's reasons for preferring the confederate republic. In a report of January 27, 1788, to the Maryland legislature, he wrote:

the members of a state government, the district of which is not very large, have generally such a common interest, that laws can scarcely be made by one part oppressive to the others, without their suffering in common; but the different states composing an extensive federal empire, widely distant one from the other, may have interests so totally distinct, that the one part might be benefited by what would be destructive to the other.[56]

Within each state, according to the Anti-Federalists, liberty would be protected by the same body of individual and political rights, and, broadly speaking, these rights were used for the same purpose. Only within such a small consensual polity could that "love of one's country and its laws" flourish which Montesquieu had termed "political virtue" and which he found indispensable to popular government. Ideally, like the devoted citizens celebrated in Book 4, chapter 5 of *The Spirit of the Laws,* the members of these small republics would put the public interest ahead of their private interests. Terming the cultivation and exercise of virtue "happiness," they found in it the purpose of the common life of each state.[57]

The language recalls the eudaemonism of Aristotle, but no more than Montesquieu's was the substance of their thought on virtue and government classical. Strenuously asserting that every person has a right to an equal vote, Luther Martin declared that no man should have more votes than another because he was "more strong," "more wealthy," or "more wise."[58] On the merits of commerce they were ambiguous, and able scholars have differed over whether they were for it or against it.[59] They surely did not aspire to the poverty of tiny and uncommercial San Marino, which the Federalists taunted them with cherishing as their ideal. Fearing the corrupting influence of luxury, one of their better known spokesman, "Cato," called commerce "the foe of virtue."[60] While not voicing outright opposition to commerce, some recoiled from the "too vigorous commercial policies" championed by the Federalists. Explicitly, Anti-Federalists rejected the "dazzling ideas of glory, wealth and power" which they imputed to the Federalists. They were not attracted by "the dignity and splendor of the American empire" acclaimed by Gouverneur Morris.[61]

Although the exercise of liberty would give rise to homogeneity within each state, among the states the outcome was diversity. According to Roger Sherman of Connecticut, author of the Connecticut

Compromise and a leading Anti-Federalist, each state "like an individual" had its "peculiar habits, usages and manners."[62] Viewing diversity as a source only of conflict, the champions of the small republic would avoid conflict by isolating diverse interests from one another under separate governments. By contrast, the big republic would bring conflicting interests and opinions together in the same forum and seek through rational deliberation to reconcile them in generally acceptable conclusions.

Yet the terms "diversity" and "interest" do not adequately convey the distinctive character and moral standing claimed for the states by the defenders of the compact approach. "Individuality," a term often used, comes closer to their meaning. Speaking in favor of equal representation in the Senate, the learned Dr. Johnson of Connecticut used the term to distinguish the two sides in the prolonged debate over this question. One side, according to Dr. Johnson, thought of the states as "so many political societies," each with its "individuality," while the other side considered the states as merely "districts of people composing one political Society." Comparing the Virginia with the New Jersey Plan, he said that, while "the latter was . . . calculated to preserve the individuality of the States," the Virginia plan was charged with a tendency "to destroy this individuality." He feared that "the general sovereignty and jurisdiction" of "the national Government" would endanger "the individuality of the States" and therefore argued that they should have "a distinct and equal vote for the purpose of defending themselves in the general councils."[63]

Some years earlier during the debate in the Continental Congress on the proper basis of representation, Dr. John Witherspoon, a member of the faculty of the College of New Jersey (later Princeton), had spoken of the states as "moral persons," and, according to Donald S. Lutz, had "laid out most clearly the compact view which underlay opposition to proportional representation," viewing "each state as equivalent to an individual, and thus the national government as a compact between individual states, each considered as a self-sufficient community."[64]

At the Philadelphia convention, taking this analogy as his premise and coming to similar conclusions, Luther Martin of Maryland advanced a view of the origin of the republic which had far-reaching and destructive implications for the nature and purpose of the union. "When a number of states unite themselves under a federal government," he said, "the same principles apply to them as when a number of men unite themselves under a state government." Quoting Locke and other social contract theorists, he argued that "the States like individuals were in a State of nature equally sovereign and free" and that the Declaration of Independence had returned them to that condition. For, he claimed, the Declaration not only separated the colonies from Great Britain but also from one another. Being "sovereign and free," each state therefore could form a union with other states only by an agreement "in the same manner as treaties and alliances are formed." For historical parallels supporting his case, Martin harked back to the Amphictyonic confederation, which Madison found to be one of the sorrier examples of failed federalism, and to the United Netherlands, which Madison judged with almost equal scorn.[65]

In Luther Martin's mind it followed that since individuality, which begot sovereignty, was a property of each particular state, the purpose of the general government was "merely to preserve the State Governments; not to govern individuals." These critics of the nationalists' proposals admitted that some strengthening of the general government was needed. But its powers should be as few as possible and should be narrowly, not broadly, construed.[66] In their opinion the supremacy clause of Article VI and the necessary and proper clause of Article I went too far.[67] Certainly, there was no need for a central power which would intervene in state government ostensibly against faction and for liberty. The dangers of oppression, as Montesquieu had shown, came from usurpers of "the supreme power" of the extensive republic.[68] Although the union was necessary for security, internal and external, the states were the guardians of liberty. "At the separation from the British Empire," declared Martin, "the people of America preferred the establishment of themselves into thirteen separate sovereignties instead of incorporating themselves into one: to these they look up for the security of their lives, liberties & properties; to these they must look up."[69]

Not all the reasons given and certainly not all the motives felt by

critics of the movement for constitutional reform fit the Montesquieuian model. Yet even those criticisms which seem idiosyncratic
sometimes make sense if the reader will put himself into the critics'
frame of mind. Consider, for instance, the implausible argument that
the Constitution would enable the few big states to overpower and
oppress the many small states. This was the main charge of the
opponents of proportionate representation in the Senate. It was
the rationale that Luther Martin found in the division generally of
the delegates to the Philadelphia convention and indeed, to his way
of thinking, the motivation of the two sides. And to be sure, in so
far as proportionate representation was adopted, a few more populous states would have a majority in the legislature. But, as the
reformers correctly replied, and as our later history abundantly
showed, those big states—Massachusetts, Pennsylvania, and Virginia—had no interest in common which would lead them to unite
against the small states. As Madison presciently observed, if in the
future any alignments divided state from state in our politics, they
were far more likely to reflect interstate sectional interests, such as
slavery, rather than issues related to relative size.[70]

In this reply as in the composition of *Federalist* 10 Madison was
employing a type of analysis which led him to conclude that our
political alignments would coincide with the lines of nationwide
interest groups. If one will, however, look at the political world
through Anti-Federalist eyes, these prospective alignments appear in
an entirely different light. From that point of view, the basic behavioral units of American politics are not functional interest groups,
cutting across state lines, but separate polities, the states, each with
its unique and cohesive individuality. Having a common life valued
for its own sake, each state would be morally and politically self-
sufficient. As Ellsworth expressed it in a heart-felt phrase: "I depend
for domestic happiness as much on my state government as a new-
born infant depends upon its mother."[71] The states, as such free and
independent political persons, might have hostile designs on others,
especially if tempted by the opportunity for self-aggrandizement presented by proportionate representation. For that system would enable a minority of the states which happened to be exceptionally
populous to use their specious majority in the federal legislature to

indulge their ambitions. Equal representation, on the other hand, would protect all states, and especially the less populous, by obliging the federal government to make decisions by a sound application of majority rule which counted each state as one and no more than one.

This line of reasoning, which followed logically from the premises of compact federalism as set forth by Montesquieu, informed the bulk of the criticism of proportionate representation during the fierce and prolonged controversy over the composition of the Senate in the Convention of 1787. Given those premises, it was far from unreasonable—with due allowance for the normal hyperbole of American political rhetoric—to conclude in the words of Luther Martin that "the system proposed [by the Constitution]" was "the most complete, most abject system of slavery that the wit of man ever devised, under the pretence of forming a government for free states."[72]

The same arguments supported the objection, as voiced by Patrick Henry, that the phrases in the Preamble of the Constitution dealing with the source of its authority should read "We, the States," rather than "We, the People." In the same vein, Anti-Federalists favored ratification of the Constitution by each state legislature, which the people of each state had established as their representative in all external relations, rather than by a convention of the people, which suggested that a new authority superior to those state governments was being created.[73]

The Anti-Federalist case is the "argument from community" which was latent in the existence of thirteen separate and long-settled colonies and which could find support not only in Montesquieu but also in some of the weightiest contributions to Western political thought going back to the Greeks. There was a high intellectual and moral appeal in their portraits of the civilizing effect of the common life of those close-knit bodies of people. In comparison with the extended republic, a polity of this sort could also be considered more democratic in the sense that its smaller area and greater homogeneity of interest made it "closer to the people."

The very qualities that heightened its solidarity, its political and moral self-sufficiency, however, severely curbed its capacity to form a union with other societies. Potential externalities, material and ideal, might suggest the possibility of closer relations. But if they threatened to conflict with the existing order, the demands of the common life would have priority. Externalities harmful to other states could easily be justified by communal values. Since politically a government was justified only if socially it was a community, it would be hard to find a rationale for self-government in the newly settled territories of the West. The Anti-Federalist vision of a series of small communities of altruistic virtue hugging the Atlantic seaboard could not realize the promise of the expanding empire of liberty foreseen by Benjamin Franklin. Anti-Federalist America would be modeled on Harrington's "commonwealth for preservation" not his "commonwealth for increase."

CHAPTER 8

Madison's
Compound Republic

TO SAY THAT MADISON was concerned with matters of theory is not to say that the ideas of political philosophers were the main influence on his proposals for constitutional reform. He was not primarily a man of thought but a man of action. What set him thinking about constitutional reform were the dreadful failures of the Confederation: the weakness of the new republic abroad, the conflicts among its member states, and, above all, the worst vice of "the spirit of locality," the invasion of liberty by factious majorities within the states. In identifying these failures, uncovering their causes, and prescribing reforms of governmental structure to remedy them, he made use of wide reading in the history of republics and federal government. In 1784 he began building up his library on federalism. At his request Jefferson sent him from Paris some two hundred volumes on these subjects, and in what he later said and wrote, as one sees in *The Federalist,* he made abundant use of such scholarly references. This is not to say that historical research did much to change his ideas. It is more likely that, as Marvin Meyers concludes, the lessons he drew from his studies simply confirmed his harsh and hard-earned judgments on the Confederation.[1]

Set forth in his writings and speeches before and during the convention and in *The Federalist,* especially the classic exposition of numbers ten and fifty-one, Madison's theory of the compound republic fits logically with his fierce criticism of the "vices" of the regime established by the Articles of Confederation. That criticism falls under two main headings: first, the external and internal weaknesses of a government based on a compact among a number of small sovereign republics; and, second, the heart of his case, the danger of majority tyranny within such small states. These two lines of argument controvert the two elements in Montesquieu's model of the confederate republic: the compact solution and the small republic theory. The remedy for both failings Madison finds in the sovereignty of the people at large in the compound republic. Governing themselves under the conditions, such as federalism, imposed by the law of the Constitution, the people are the sovereign power which concerts the action of the government at home and abroad and ensures a superior justice within the states and the nation. In this capacity we may refer to them as the governmental sovereign. The people are also the constituent sovereign which, conditioned by no positive law, ordains those conditions under which it governs itself.

Critique of Compact Federalism

Nationalist critics of the Confederacy found that it suffered from the same failings in foreign and domestic affairs for which Milton and Harrington had condemned the compact federalism of their day. These failings, which had impaired the war effort against Britain, became more pronounced after victory had relaxed the pressure of a common enemy for cooperation. The government of the United States could not make the British turn over the Western forts as they had promised in the Treaty of Paris, nor could it retaliate against them when they discriminated against American shipping. It could not prevent the states from endangering national security by independently and separately making war on the Indians and violating treaties with foreign states.[2] In short, as Governor Randolph complained when introducing the Virginia Plan at Philadelphia, Congress could neither prevent a war nor support one by its own authority.[3] In domestic affairs, the same "imbecility" was displayed. The Congress could not prevent the states from transgressing on one another's rights, as, for instance, when they disrupted the economic life of the union by discriminating in favor of foreign and against interstate trade. Nor, as Madison observed, could it concert action for "national purposes," such as "national seminaries," "canals," and "other works of general utility."[4]

The Federalists held that one reason for the external and internal weakness of the Confederation was the general government's lack of adequate authority, especially in matters of finance, defense, and commerce. Ultimately the requisite shift of authority from periphery to center was accomplished by the Constitution, principally by sections 8 and 10 of Article I, which added to and clarified the authority of the federal government and laid down specific limits on the powers of the states. Yet in the eyes of the Federalists a formal reallocation of authority would not bring about a real centralization of power unless it also dealt with another and no less fundamental problem. This was the inability of the federal government under the Articles to regulate directly the action of individuals.

In *Federalist* 15, Hamilton, who had long criticized this lack of direct federal administration, summarized the case against it. Government, he wrote, implies the power to make laws, and laws, if they are to control behavior, must be backed by a sanction. In so far as a law applies to individuals, it can be enforced by the courts and police. If, however, it is to be applied to governments, as was the case with most federal powers under the Articles, it can be enforced only by military action. Such a condition, he concluded, is not government but a state of war. In any case, since the Congress could not and indeed would not resort to this mode of enforcement, its "requisitions" on the states were reduced to mere "recommendations."[5]

This failing was particularly serious with regard to the financial and military needs of the Union. In these fields, according to Hamilton, the Articles gave the federal government a quite wide field of action. The United States, he wrote, have nearly "an indefinite discretion to make requisitions of men and money; but they have no authority to raise either by regulations extending to the individual citizens of America." Article VIII, for instance, authorized the Congress to raise revenue, declaring that "expenses that shall be incurred for the common defence or general welfare, and allowed by the United States in Congress assembled, shall be defrayed out of a common treasury, which shall be supplied by the several States." Only the states, however, had the authority to tax, that is, to take money from individuals, in order to meet these requisitions. "The consequence of this," observed Hamilton, "is, that though in theory their resolutions concerning these objects are laws, constitutionally binding on the members of the Union, yet in practice they are mere recommendations which the States observe or disregard at their option."[6]

Putting his analysis in more general terms, Hamilton asserted that "the great and radical vice" was "the principle of legislation for states or governments, in their corporate or collective capacities, and as contradistinguished from the individuals of which they consist." If such a "government over governments" (Madison's phrase) were to secure compliance with its laws, it would have to back them with the threat of military action. Otherwise, like the Confederation, it would suffer from the "imbecility" of having those laws flouted by its member states.[7]

According to this analysis, the underlying problem was not authority but structure; not too narrow a statement of the authority of the Congress but a flaw in the procedure by which it would be exercised and applied. The Articles gave the Congress the authority to make "determinations" binding on the states (Article XIII) over a wide range of policy. Since, however, the Congress could not mount a credible threat of enforcing these demands on the states, their compliance was in effect voluntary, thereby raising the typical difficulties of uncoerced burden-bearing among a largish number of independent actors.

Madison and Hamilton were acutely aware of these difficulties. Self-interest, they realized, might lead a state to refuse compliance because it exaggerated the "inequality" of the burdens imposed on it. But even when a state recognized the benefit to itself from general compliance, its "distrust of the voluntary compliance" of the others might well induce it to reject a burden which it feared the others might not assume.[8]

Madison lucidly described this problem when later in life he wrote, "The radical infirmity of the Articles of Confederation was the dependence of Congress on the voluntary and simultaneous compliance with its Requisitions, by so many independent communities, each consulting more or less its particular interests and convenience and distrusting the compliance of others."[9] Even in the case of laws recognized to be beneficial to all, as Madison observed, the separate sovereign states, unsure of one another's compliance, would flout demands with which they, nonetheless, had a "latent disposition" to comply.[10]

The extension of federal authority would seem to solve the problem stated by Hamilton in *Federalist* 15. If laws are effectively to control behavior, as Hamilton said in that paper, they must be backed by a credible sanction. Against a recalcitrant state, the federal government under the Articles could not mount such a threat. Recognizing this fact, as Madison recalled, the states generally felt free—and, one might add, were virtually compelled by self-interest—to pick and choose what laws they would obey. If, however, the general government were given the legislative and executive power to act directly against individuals, then surely it could muster sufficient coercive power to enforce its "determinations" and so to create among citizens generally a readiness to comply and an expectation of compliance. The free rider problem would be solved.

The framers of the Constitution did indeed follow this clear implication of rational choice theory. The very first of the powers the Constitution gave to the federal government was the power "to lay and collect taxes . . . for the common defence and general welfare." Yet the men of the nationalist persuasion did not find this change in the structure of power sufficient to solve the problem of "imbecility." They did enlarge the power of the federal government and make it directly applicable to individuals. They also found, however, that these changes in the law of the Constitution required a more commanding theory of the authority of the Constitution. This need was supplied by the idea of national sovereignty.

From the Federalist viewpoint, as most cogently expressed by James Madison, the fundamental "vice" of the Confederation was the idea of confederation itself: that is, compact federalism. Although the Articles have "the form of a constitution," endowing the Congress with powers of "Government," concluded Madison in his analysis of April 1787, "the federal system . . . is in fact nothing more than a treaty of amity of commerce and of alliance, between independent and Sovereign States," lacking "legal and coercive powers" and depending upon "voluntary compliance."[11]

Thanks to this "independent authority" of the states, he observed, even when the federal government made "constitutional requisitions" entirely within the formal authority conferred on it by the Articles, the states often failed to comply. Indeed, since the Union was not "a political Constitution" but only "a league of sovereign states," "the doctrine of compacts" gave to the states the right to dissolve the Union—"if they chuse"—on the ground that some state or states had breached the agreement.[12] The terms of such an agreement, therefore, whether a specific grant of power to the federal government or the broad assertion of "perpetual union" affirmed in the Articles, could not stand against the right of the sovereign state to secede, or, *a fortiori*, to exercise the lesser rights of nullification or interposition, or simply to delay in complying with the presumed imperatives of the federal government. Nor would the extension of federal administration to the individual citizens of the several states extinguish these implications of compact theory, as shown by the logic of the nullifiers and secessionists of the next century.

The New Legitimacy

It followed that the reallocation of authority set out in Article I of the Constitution could not accomplish its purpose of bringing about a shift of actual power unless that grant of authority was given a new and stronger basis of legitimacy. Madison's theory of the extended republic provided this new legitimacy. In its terms, "the union of the States," as he had prescribed in his critique of the vices, was conceived not as "a league of sovereign states" but as "a political constitution by virtue of which they are become one sovereign power."[13]

Madison, needless to say, did not locate this "one sovereign power" in a monarch or aristocratic few who, thanks to their superior virtue, had the divine and/or natural right to rule the many. Nor could he ascribe it to an institution which, over and apart from the people, like the British king-in-parliament, had the final say in lawmaking for the whole country. As heirs of the struggle for actual and against virtual representation, American whigs could not place this ultimate authority anywhere but in the people. Repeatedly this commonplace of whig rhetoric was asserted by the successful revolutionaries. "The genius of republican liberty," wrote Madison in a characteristic formulation in *Federalist* 37, demands "not only that all power should be derived from the people, but that those intrusted with it should be kept in dependence on the people."[14]

Anti-Federalists, as whigs of the compact school, could take that to mean the separate sovereign peoples of the thirteen states. As the fierce critic of the compact solution and of its governmental offspring, the Confederation, Madison could not accept that attribution. Instead, the sovereign power to which he appealed was "We, the people of the United States," who in the words of the Preamble "do ordain and establish" the Constitution. Madison elaborated this fundamental of nationalist theory in *Federalist* 46, where he replied to the charge that the Constitution so divided sovereignty between the two levels of government as to create the dread problem of *imperium in imperio*. Accusing these "adversaries of the Constitution" of having "lost sight of the people altogether in their reasonings on this subject," Madison pointed out that both federal and state governments are "substantially dependent upon the great body of the citizens of the United States" and "are in fact but different agents and trustees of the people, constituted with different powers, and designed for different purposes." Therefore, he said, "the ultimate authority, wherever the derivative may be found, resides in the people alone." They are, he declared, echoing Locke's words, the "common superior" of all government, federal or state.[15]

This appeal to national sovereignty gave to the authority of the federal government a kind of legitimacy which it had lacked before. In the light of Madison's theory, the Constitution not only enlarged the powers of the federal government; it also made the exercise of these powers the acts of a body with the right not merely to recommend but rather to command in the name of the sovereign which authorized it.

The authors of *The Federalist* did grant that the Articles of Confederation gave the federal government the "authority" to make laws which "in theory" were "constitutionally binding." The principles of the confederate republic on which such theory was based, however, nullified the normative force of these attributes. Its resolutions were, in Madison's phrase, only "nominally" authoritative. As a mere "league" based on a "treaty" which left sovereignty to the states, the Confederacy lacked authority to impose sanctions not only on individuals but also on governments. To be sure, it also lacked the actual military force to coerce a recalcitrant state. But this was because it lacked the authority to command the collective action of the governments which did command men and money. If the Congress had had even a modest degree of such authority, it would not have found it hard to coerce so small a polity as the continually recalcitrant Rhode Island. But, as Hamilton pointed out, because of "the nature of the social compact among the States," there was "no express delegation of authority [to the Congress] to use force against delinquent members."[16]

Until the "government of the United States" was given a new normative foundation, its attempts at collective action would continue to be attended by "imbecility." Madison's theory of the extended republic embodying the concept of national sovereignty met that normative necessity. "Ordained" by "the people of the United States," the federal government under the Constitution made laws which were commands authorized by the sovereign power. They imposed penalties backed by the threat of coercion. Moreover, under these laws, constitutional and statutory, federal authority extended to individuals. It also extended to states, which it could lawfully command and forcibly constrain when they interfered with the execution of its constitutional powers. On the compact theory, legitimating the Articles, the federal government had neither sort of power; on the national theory of the Constitution it had both.

The assertion of national sovereignty by the theory of the extended republic gave a new normative status to the exercise of the powers of the federal government, freeing these powers from any state veto and making them superior to any contravention by state action. National sovereignty also legitimated the exercise of these powers directly over individuals. The problem of a "government over governments" under the Articles, therefore, was not that the federal government was obliged to govern through the state governments. This structure of administration can be effective in a federal or in a unitary state. Today in Germany, for instance, under what has been called "horizontal federalism," the federal government has only a small bureaucracy directly in its employ, most of its programs depending for their administration upon state and local governments. If these state or local officials fail to act, however, the federal government has procedures for intervening and directly executing the laws, which in their terms apply to individuals.

In America, state government has often relied upon local governments to carry out its laws. At the time the Constitution was being framed, for instance, Massachusetts had virtually no administrative apparatus of its own but used the towns for such purposes as tax-gathering. In the 1830s Tocqueville observed this feature of government in New England and praised it for its ideal combination of centralized legislation and decentralized administration. In Massachusetts, which he chose for the purpose of illustrating the system, the towns were charged with appointing assessors who would levy the tax specified by the state legislature. If they failed to act, the state could intervene by means of the county court of sessions and the county sheriff to impose and collect a heavy fine from the inhabitants of the recalcitrant town. Even though they were enforced by local governments, state laws applied in terms to individuals—for instance, the restrictions on travel on Sunday.[17]

Madison himself expected the new federal government to govern through the state governments, rather in the manner of the New England states in relation to their local governments. In *Federalist* 45, while trying to reassure those who feared for the power of the states, Madison remarked that in the matter of internal taxation by the federal government, "the eventual collection, under the immediate authority of the Union, will generally be made by the officers, and according to the rules, appointed by the several States." He even thought it "extremely probable that in other instances, particularly in the organization of the judicial power, the officers of the States will be clothed with the correspondent authority of the Union." This expectation, one may add, was wholly in accord with the administrative structure proposed for Oceana. In that system, the central government would have had virtually no bureaucracy and would have depended almost entirely upon the shires and other local governments for execution of its laws. At the present time, the huge expansion of conditional grants in aid by the federal government to state and local governments has made them the administrative agents of a vast array of national programs. This introduction of "horizontal federalism," which breaks with the sharp separation of the spheres of activity of the different levels of government sometimes thought to be the norm of our system, actually is not out of line with the thoughts of some of the earliest advocates of national federalism.[18]

In *Federalist* 20 Madison summarized his criticism of the Articles by terming "a sovereignty over sovereigns," "a government over governments," a "solecism."[19] The impropriety, however, is better identified in the former than in the latter expression. According to compact theory, as restated by Montesquieu and enshrined in the orthodoxies of international law, sovereignty remained with the states. No matter what powers, such as taxation, might nominally be given to the federal government, it could not make this power effective since each state would remain the final judge of the propriety of its use. Whether the compact limited the reach of the general government to the states or extended it to individuals made no difference to that ultimate sovereign power and responsibility. In order to make the centralization of power proposed by the Constitution effective, therefore, its advocates were obliged to advance the new view that the sovereignty of the people at large was the sole source of authority in the polity.

National sovereignty was asserted implicitly and explicitly from time to time in the debates at Philadelphia and in speeches and writing during the period of ratification. The principle was implied by the nationalists' analysis of the reasons for indirect administration under the Articles. If, as they thought, indirect administration rested on the reservation of sovereignty to the states, it followed that in order to remedy this vice, sovereignty could no longer be attributed to the states but would have to be found in the whole nation. The same reasoning that deduced indirect administration from state sovereignty also validated the inference that national sovereignty was the necessary premise of direct administration. And since these men were republicans, national sovereignty meant popular sovereignty; that is, the sovereignty of the people of the whole nation.

Explicitly, the most lucid and succinct assertion of national sovereignty comes in the concluding words of the Preamble of the Constitution, stating that it is "We, the People of the United States" who "do ordain and establish this Constitution." That these words unmistakably referred to the people at large of the nation was evident from the immediate reaction of the Anti-Federalists, who in the words of Patrick Henry objected that this attribution of constituent sovereignty should read "We, the states" not "We, the People."[20]

In *The Federalist*, national sovereignty appears as the alternative to the sovereignty of the states in the critique of the Articles in the earlier papers, especially numbers 15–22 by Madison and Hamilton. Hamilton's summary in numbers 21–22 brings out the connection of ideas relating direct administration to national sovereignty. He begins by discussing indirect administration at some length as "the most important defect" of the Confederation and then goes on to examine illustrations of this and related failings. Denouncing "the existing federal system" because it rests on "no better foundation than the consent of the several legislatures," he proclaims "the necessity of laying the foundation of our national government deeper than in the mere sanction of delegated authority." Identifying that "deeper foundation," he concludes: "The fabric of American empire ought to rest on the solid basis of THE CONSENT OF THE PEOPLE. The streams of national power ought to flow immediately from that pure, original fountain of all legitimate authority." It is clear that he is referring not to thirteen separate peoples but, as he wrote a few pages earlier, to "the people of America."[21] For him as for Madison, the action of this "one sovereign power" made "government" possible.

A recent study of nationalist thought describes the origin and consequences of this idea. Edmund Morgan attributes the "invention" of national sovereignty to James Madison who, he writes, envisioned a national government resting for its authority not on the states, and not even on the people of the several states considered separately, but on "an American people, a people who constituted a separate and superior entity, capable of conveying to a national government an authority that would necessarily impinge on the authority of the states." Madison, he continues, appealed to the "popular sovereignty" of "the people of the United States as a whole," who "alone could be thought to stand superior to the people of any single state."[22]

Despite the sharp divisions in public opinion at the time of ratification, the wide acceptance of national sovereignty, as Morgan has observed, was demonstrated by the general compliance by states and people with the demands of the new federal government. This new level of compliance was even more notable because under the guidance of Alexander Hamilton during the presidency of George Washington, these demands were far greater than the most ambitious efforts of central control under the Articles. Moreover, compliance, no doubt, engendered compliance. As the new level of compliance appeared, the free-rider temptations of the old voluntary system would be reduced and further compliance would be encouraged. Not only would acceptance of the new normative status of federal authority influence individual behavior, but the higher expectation of compliance by others would make it less imprudent to comply with federal demands which the citizen and his state governments already had a "latent disposition" to accept.

That latent disposition became patent not only in the behavior of individuals but also and especially in the behavior of state governments, whose cross-grained action had been a principal problem requiring radical constitutional reform. The states had ample opportunity to block the change: they could have refused to send delegates to Philadelphia; they could have refused to call ratifying conventions; they could have refused to recommend ratification to their voters; they could have sabotaged the new scheme by refusing to send senators or take part in presidential elections. Instead, state governments called on the nation to remedy their own deficiencies and heartily supported their self-administered corrective.[23]

Critique of the Small Republic Theory

To say that "the people of the United States" ordain the Constitution raises two questions: the question of unity and the question of legitimacy. First, how did these many and diverse individuals comprising the people achieve sufficient unity to issue a command, speaking with one voice and not the usual cacophony of the mob? Second, why should that imperative have greater legitimacy, making it more deserving of obedience than the commands of the peoples of the several states within their respective spheres of self-government? In his theory of the extended republic, Madison addresses the second question, in the course of answering which he also answers the first.

The "vices" which Madison had identified under the first heading of his critique of the Confederation, the attack on compact federalism, were failures of power: the inability to cope with foreign dangers and to control internal conflict. To say that the assertion of national sovereignty remedies these failures of power, however, begs a crucial question. For if "the people of the United States" are to serve as that "one sovereign power" without which, according to Madison, there can be no true government, they must be and act as "one." This question of unity raises an ancient objection to popular government: the denial that, whatever may be their right, the people simply do not have the capacity to govern themselves. Any such attempt is bound to be brought down by their self-destructive pluralism.

To say that the many can found a state as well as govern themselves as a state merely presents the problem in a more acute form. The old denial controverts their capacity to act as constituent sovereign as well as governmental sovereign. In the republican manner, Locke had claimed that the people, having made themselves one community by the original social contract, could constitute and reconstitute governments, of which they were the "common superior." In response, defenders of government by the few, such as Blackstone and Burke, had contemptuously asserted that if the many tried to act on this principle by withdrawing consent from a government, they could only plunge themselves back into the anarchy of the state of nature. Like Machiavelli, Montesquieu had limited this criticism to the extended republic, which, in his opinion, being distracted by "a thousand private views," would be incapable of giving rise to a coherent governing power.

The heart of Madison's case against the Confederation was the failure of justice in the small republic: its tendency to tyranny of the majority. On the capacity of the extended republic to offset this danger rested the greater legitimacy of national over state sovereignty. The process, moreover, that remedied this failure of justice also gave rise to a coherent governing power that would remedy the failures of power.

Like Machiavelli and Montesquieu, Madison held that as numbers grow, differences multiply, and that as numbers diminish, diversity declines. "The smaller the society," he wrote in *Federalist* 10, "the fewer probably will be the distinct parties and interests composing it."[24] Far from then inferring that as homogeneity is approached the prospects of republican liberty improve, Madison comes to the opposite conclusion. To be sure, it follows that if perfect homogeneity were established, diversity as an impediment to self-government would be removed. In real life, however, as Madison pointed out in a letter to Jefferson, perfect homogeneity is never achieved; hence, no polity will lack a minority whose different ideas and interests make it vulnerable to oppression by the majority.[25]

In Madison's analysis, therefore, the diminution of diversity resulting from small scale produces a growing danger to republican liberty. For, he continued, "the fewer the distinct parties and interests, the more frequently will a majority be found of the same party; and the smaller the number of individuals composing a majority, and the smaller the compass within which they are placed, the more easily will they concert and execute their plans of oppression."[26]

Such majorities he terms "factions." They occur when human nature is exposed to the conditions of republican liberty, individual and political. Reason, self-love, and a diversity and inequality of "faculties" are inherent in human nature. Under republican liberty, these differences in faculties give rise to ideal and material differences among the members of society. Those differences relate to beliefs, occupations, persons, and things. Politically, the most important are "the different degrees and kinds of property," which Madison termed "the most common and durable source of faction."[27] The passion of self-love attaches individuals to these varieties of property and biases in their favor the capacity of reason for impartial judgment.

The attachment of individuals to these material things, as well as the things themselves, are termed their "interests." Interests vary with different degrees and kinds of property, the persons entertaining them forming different groups in society: those with and those without property; creditors and debtors, landowners, craftsmen, merchants, and bankers and "many lesser interests." When taking part in politics, each of these interest groups is a "faction." Given the distortions of self-love, the pursuit of its particular interest by such a group is likely to be, as Madison said in his culminating definition, "adverse to the rights of other citizens, or to the permanent and aggregate interests of the community."[28] In so far as a polity is governed by the republican principle of majority rule, a faction embracing a majority will be able to express these adverse tendencies in deeds of injustice which may well be as oppressive as the tyranny of one or a few. Tyranny of the majority, therefore, is a vice peculiar to small republics.

Madison's use of the term "interest" has at least three meanings. It sometimes refers to the outcome or product of the individual's distinctive faculty—for instance, a material thing, such as a farmer's property, that is, his land along with his use of it. In this sense of product, interest also may refer to ideal possessions, such as religious and political beliefs and the practices associated with them. He therefore included among interests "a zeal for different opinions concerning religion, concerning government, and many other points, as well of speculation as of practice."[29]

Madison also uses the term "interest" to refer to a subjective feeling, the passion of attachment to such material and ideal products of individual activity. In this sense, a person may be said to have an interest (feeling of attachment) in his interests (his property, material or ideal). Also we may say that a person does not understand his "true interest," meaning that however attached he may be to his material or ideal possessions, he is not following the line of conduct or thought that would best protect or promote them. While, therefore each person knows best what he thinks and has, a ground for argument may arise over what his true interests are. Hence, people's opinions about their interests as individuals or groups may be changed by rational discussion.

Finally, Madison also takes the term interest *tout court* to mean interest group. In this sense he uses the term synonymously with not only faction but also "party." This meaning of party is contrary to present-day usage, which allows for interest groups with a broader base and focus than Madison specifies and which takes a more favorable view of political parties as not only inevitable but also desirable in systems of self-government. Madison's pejorative view of party accords with the received opinion of his time. Harrington and Hume had written critically of party and warned of its dangers. Edmund Burke's conception of party as "a body of men united for promoting by their joint endeavors the national interest upon some particular principle in which they are all agreed," from which our present more favorable view descends, would presumably have escaped Madison's strictures.[30] That view, however, had been advanced only in 1770 and had not yet been generally accepted in Britain and America. Jefferson's celebrated case for party government was, of course, still in the future.[31]

When Madison criticized the compact solution, he found its principal vice to be the typical difficulty of collective action by purely voluntary cooperation among a largish number of independent actors. Although later in life he termed this "the radical infirmity" of the Confederation, actually during the years of constitution-making he and his fellow nationalists held that by far the greatest danger confronting republican liberty was the threat of faction, the danger of tyranny of the single-interest majority inherent in the small republic. The threat was twofold. Individual liberty was threatened by the prospect of direct attacks on individual rights. The threat to popular government came from the danger to the freedom of opinion necessary for self-government.[32] In his analysis of this double threat to justice under the Confederation Madison focused his attention on a source of republican disorder inherent in human nature: self-love. Previously he had shown how interest groups came into conflict even when their interests were intrinsically compatible. Now he was concerned to show what sometimes made their interests incompatible.

In Madison's analysis of faction, the diversity and inequality of faculties also figure along with self-love as a source of interest-group conflict. The examples he mentions are group conflicts produced by the division of labor. He holds that diversity will vary with scale, as in the dependence of specialization upon the size of the market. His denial of the small republic supposition that perfect homogeneity of interests can be reached, however, is an empirical, not theoretical, inference. His conception of self-love strikes more deeply at that supposition. Even if *ex hypothesi,* a society small enough to be composed only of persons with identical and equal interests could be found or created, self-love would still persist. Conflict would be ruled out only if we also supposed that its members had vanquished self-love and lived wholly according to the dictates of self-sacrificing virtue.

Rejecting this improbable speculation of small republic theory that self-love can be totally subjected to altruism, Madison looks for a remedy primarily in the structure of society. From his analysis of scale and diversity, it follows that the way to prevent factions from becoming majorities is to "extend the sphere" of the society so as to "take in a greater variety of parties and interests" and thereby "make it less probable that a majority of the whole" will have the motive or the opportunity to invade "the rights of other citizens." Departing radically from Montesquieu's hypotheses, Madison welcomed to his republic the diversity of faculties.

Although aware of the dangers to freedom and order flowing from the projection of these capacities upon the social and political world, he nevertheless makes their protection "the first object of government."[33] Indeed, he thinks of these diversities less as a problem than as an opportunity. He finds in their multiplication in the extended republic the primary condition enabling the regime to realize its superior potentialities and to overcome the weakness and disorder to which popular government is otherwise prone. While recognizing the danger of faction from the interplay of self-love and diversity, he seeks not to extinguish the sources of this interplay but so to utilize its effects as to enhance liberty and power. It is sometimes asked whether Madison favors pluralism. Certainly, he did not look to eliminating interest groups, as did the champions of the small republic. He welcomed pluralistic diversity as a primary condition of government in the public interest.

Increase in the variety of interests can have this elevating influence because not only does self-love condition reason but reason also conditions self-love. When discussing the sources of faction, Madison does not say that self-love is the only motive. He grants, for instance, that men are also moved by "moral" and "religious" motives, even while he asserts that these alone and unaided are inadequate to control the effects of self-love.[34] Reason inclines men in some degree toward "impartiality" when judging the relation of their interests to the interests of others. The main variable governing the balance between self-love and reason is pluralism, functioning, as we shall have occasion to observe, within a constitutional structure. Reduction in the number of interests puts it more within the reach of any single interest to dominate the political arena. Conversely, as interests multiply, this prospect, along with the antagonism arising from the fears and hopes it engenders, is diminished. As increasing diversity breaks down parochialism, the opportunity is widened for rational deliberation to perceive common problems and to discover common solutions to them. In sum, as a decline in pluralism diminishes the influence of reason, an increase heightens it and raises the prospect of agreement on the public interest.

Justice and the Public Interest

Madison takes seriously the notion that there is such a thing as the public interest, constituting a standard by which the action of governments and citizens can be judged. He refers to this standard by various terms: "public interest," "common interest," "common good," "public good," "general good," "the good of the whole," "the permanent and aggregate interests of the community," and so on. In a particular strong statement, Madison remarked, while discussing the purpose of the Constitution, that "the public good, the real welfare of the great body of the people, is the supreme object to be pursued."[35]

That he believes that such a standard exists is implied by his definition of faction in which the meaning of that term is clarified by the contrast with "the rights of other citizens, or the permanent and aggregate interests of the community." In that definition, to be sure, the term "common interest" is used pejoratively when he observes that the members of a faction are moved by "some common impulse of passion, or interest." Normally, his use of this term is broader. At times it seems to mean "enlightened self-interest," as when he criticizes action based on "the immediate interest" of "one party," which fails to take "into view indirect and remote considerations." But the context in which he makes this reference shows that the norm transcends such fragile and volatile calculations. The contrast with "immediate interest" is with "the rights of another, or the good of the whole."[36]

This same disjunction is used when the interest of a faction is said to be "adverse to the rights of other citizens, or to the permanent and aggregate and permanent interests of the community."[37] This disjunctive phrase is not to be taken to mean that there are two standards, the rights of citizens and the public interest. Yet neither are the two identical. The rights of the citizens, like republican liberty, are individual and political. The individual rights, deriving from "the first object of government," the protection of the inherent faculties of man, are the traditional Anglo–American legal rights of person and property. The political rights are the guarantees of freedom of expression and participation making self-government possible. Madison's comprehensive term for the enforcement of these rights, individual and political, is justice.[38]

Justice is not identical with the public interest, but it is a necessary condition for its realization. Individual rights enable citizens to express their faculties in the cultivation of their interests, material and ideal. The enforcement of the obligation of contract, for instance, protects the faculty of acquiring property. If, therefore, a majority of a state legislature, acting on behalf of debtors, were to relieve them of this obligation, it would be acting as a factious majority. Such, according to *Federalist* 10, were the dangers against which the extended republic would defend the individual.[39]

Through their political rights citizens would have the opportunity to govern themselves in the public interest. The protection of political rights was necessary if republican government was to realize Madison's hope for its "more enlarged plan of policy" under the Constitution.[40] This plan, embracing in Madison's thought such enterprises as canals, seminaries of learning, and "other works of general utility," required legislation going beyond the mere protection of rights, but such policies could not achieve their goals without that protection. Justice does not imply any specific conception of the public interest, but the public interest presumes justice.

How did Madison conceive that the danger of faction was to be averted and the conditions for realizing justice and the public interest ensured? The main safeguard was the extended republic. As we have seen, largeness of scale would give rise to a diversity of interests which *a fortiori* would avert the dangers of homogeneity. That much follows by simple logic from his critique of the small republic. But how would diversity accomplish more than this negation? What could it do to promote the positive ends of government?

In some passages of Madison's exposition the negative meaning predominated. In the paragraph in *Federalist* 10 in which he identified the dangers of the small republic, Madison immediately inferred that the remedy is to extend the "sphere" of the society. By taking in "a greater variety of parties and interests," he wrote, this enlargement of scale will "make it less probable that a majority of the majority of the whole will have a common motive to invade the rights of other citizens." "Or if such a common motive exists," he continued, presumably thinking of the influence of area as well as number, "it will be more difficult for all who feel it to discover their own strength, and to act in unison with each other."[41]

Under these conditions, government by a factious majority would surely be avoided. But would government by any kind of majority be possible? The goal of this aggregate of single interest groups, it may seem, would be so diverse and/or conflicting that no majority could be got together in support of a coherent line of action. The scene is that envisioned by Montesquieu when he foresaw the extended republic being reduced to anarchy by "a thousand private views." This would be "limited government" with a vengeance.

Without suggesting that Madison favored such an extreme of negative constitutionalism, some scholars have concluded that he did plan for a passive general government held in deadlock by social and economic pluralism.[42] That conclusion does not fit with the governmental activism which Madison shared with his co-author, the great nation-builder, Alexander Hamilton. Hamilton fully expected that in the extended republic majority coalitions would form which would be less prone to injustice and confusion than the state governments and which would use the new powers of the federal government to advance "liberal and enlarged plans for the public good."[43] In his critique of the Confederation, Madison expressed similar sentiments when, lamenting the "want of concert in matters where common interest requires it," he hoped for a power at the center that could provide "for national seminaries, for grants of incorporation for national purposes, for canals and other works of general utility."[44] In *Federalist* 46, looking forward to a "more enlarged plan of policy" under the Constitution, Madison foresaw the need for government intervention to promote national prosperity.[45]

Winding up one of his most notable papers, *Federalist* 51, Madison made clear his support of positive government by multi-interest majorities. "In the extended republic of the United States, and among the great variety of interests, parties, and sects which it embraces," he wrote, "a coalition of a majority of the whole society could seldom take place on any other principles than those of justice and the general good."[46] As in Hamilton's formulation, such a majority would preserve republican rights and liberties while pursuing policies in the public interest. Such a majority would be a coalition of many interests; it would, however, be not a factious but what we may call a civic majority.

Government by Discussion: Hume

By what process would such a majority be brought into existence? One way of grasping Madison's model is by contrast with the process of "balancing" in Montesquieu's political mechanics. This process is exemplified in the relations of the members of his confederate republic. We can readily conceive of the delegates of its member states forming coalitions with majority, even unanimous, support regarding a few severely limited matters, such as defense. These small states avoid conflict by isolation from one another. *A fortiori* they do not enact laws which invade, modify, or regulate their distinctive interests. And the process by which they come to agreement is a process of bargaining limited to mutual concessions which, involving no change in the preferences of the bargaining agents, do not trench upon these interests.

This radical limitation of the scope and activity of the general government is necessary if decision-making is to be confined largely to the member states, where, according to Montesquieu's doctrine, smallness of scale enables the regime to remain republican. It follows that the interests represented in the coalitions by which the whole confederation will act will be few. On the basis of Montesquieu's political science, it is inconceivable that a state should successfully govern itself by coalitions constituted from "the great variety of interests" embraced in the Madisonian republic. An attempt to do so would lead to that internal anarchy which Montesquieu, like Machiavelli, thought would surely destroy any attempt at self-government on a large scale.

In constructing his alternative to the confederate republic, Madison conceived of civic majorities which were formed by a radically different process and which led to a radically different outcome in law and governance. The best guide to understanding the process is not Montesquieu but Harrington. His work had been known in the colonies from very early days and belonged to the canon repeatedly cited by American revolutionists and reformers. *Oceana* came to be so highly regarded in Massachusetts that at independence John Harrington's words were echoed in the aphorism Adams included in his draft of a constitution for Massachusetts: "In the government of the Commonwealth of Massachusetts, the legislative, executive, and judicial power shall be placed in separate compartments, to the end and that it might be a government of laws, and not of men." Adams took from Harrington the notion of a second chamber modeled on the senate of Oceana, which he thought would provide an "aristocratic" element in the new state governments. This proposal, put forward in his *Thoughts on Government* (1776), was adopted with variations by many of the new constitutions and in some minds justified the inclusion of a senate in the federal Constitution of 1787.[47]

This pervasive influence of Harrington is reflected in a long letter on the need for a new constitution which, appearing in the Boston *Herald American* of June 11, 1787, was signed "Harrington." Citing the dangers of "Caesars and Cromwells" brought on by the "anarchy" of the Articles of Confederation, the writer attacked "the narrow scale of state government" and called for a more centralized regime under "one supreme legislature" which would ensure peace and prosperity as well as liberty. As Rakove has observed, "Harrington's" letter strongly resembles James Madison's emerging theory of the compound republic.[48]

A more direct and specific influence transmitted Harrington's thought to the great debate of the 1780s. This was David Hume's modified version of *Oceana* presented in his essay, "Idea of a Perfect Commonwealth."[49] First published in his *Political Discourses* of 1752, four years after the publication of *The Spirit of the Laws,* Hume's essay pointedly, although not explicitly, took issue with Montesquieu's small republic thesis. Denouncing "the falsehood of the common opinion that no large state, such as France or Great Britain, could ever be modelled into a commonwealth," he argued that, on the contrary, "a republican government" could more easily be preserved "steady and uniform without tumult and faction," in "a more extensive country than in a city." Smallness of area as well as number was the source of these defects which in "a large government" were remedied because "the parts" were "so distant and remote." The extended republic—offsetting the oppressiveness of aristocratic rule, because it was republican, and the pressures of popular passions, because it was large—held the promise of government in the "public interest."[50]

Emphasizing the role of number and the pluralism of parties and interests, as well as "parts," Madison restated and elaborated Hume's revision of Harrington's model. Along with this stress on popular government and scale, he echoed other themes of Hume's account.

Whatever may have been Hume's ultimate preference among political systems, he attempted in this exercise, starting from the premise of government by the many, to design a system of institutions which would show among that class of governments "what is the most perfect in the kind."[51] He rejected as impractical the drastic reform of the economic base of the state proposed in Harrington's agrarian law. The franchise in his model—although, like Harrington's, extended to small proprietors—was rather more limited. He narrowed the participation of voters and bestowed on them no extravagant praise.

No more than Harrington or Madison, however, was he attempting in the Aristotelian or Thomistic manner to impose on his commonwealth the reign of the virtuous few. Like Harrington, who abhorred oligarchy, he excluded rule by the "grandees." Faithful to the Commonwealth tradition, he sought to design a structure of government by discussion, embracing a large electorate which would produce outcomes that were both coherent and relevant. Elections were annual, and the electorate was apportioned equally throughout the commonwealth. His system was representative, but on crucial questions decisions of the higher magistrates were referred to the large directly elected local assemblies, which Hume termed "the people." This was actual, not virtual, representation. He termed his system "a well-tempered democracy."[52]

The system was so tempered as to combine the order of aristocracies with the good will of democracies without succumbing to aristocratic self-love or to democratic turbulence. This fusion of coherence and relevance was not accomplished by the rule of one man, or a few men, of supreme virtue. Like Milton before him and Madison after him, Hume used the term "refine" when he described the process of representation. This refining of the opinion of the voters did indeed depend in part upon the better judgment of the men they chose as their representatives. Hume held that the voters, although too "ignorant" to hold office themselves, were capable of choosing representatives of "middling sense," who in turn would choose senators who in the limited Harringtonian meaning would have "wisdom."[53]

Specifying no property qualification, Hume did not identify this senatorial elite with a distinct social order or economic class. For refinement of the voters opinion, moreover, he trusted mainly to the structure rather than the personnel of the representative system. The process induced by this structure was not a balancing of classes, social orders, or interest groups but an interplay of opinion within and among the various institutions of government. What he sought in the legislative process was the kind of debate which in the British parliament "brought [a bill] to maturity, all its conveniences and inconveniences weighted and balanced." Valuing this process for its redress of grievances and reform of abuses, he criticized Harrington's scheme because it confined the power to propose bills solely to the senate, a defect he remedied by extending the legislative initiative to the lower levels of government.

In a further democratic revision of Harrington's scheme, he did not forbid but facilitated debate in the local assemblies and provided that when proposed laws were submitted to their members a copy with the reasons for it should be given to each member "in order to deliberate concerning it." Hume admired the adversarial proceedings of the British parliament, and, following Harrington, he institutionalized the opportunity for criticism. A body of defeated candidates were charged with reviewing the public accounts, with no right to control but only "the power of accusing and appealing to the people."[54]

Thanks to this constitutionally structured government by discussion, Hume sought to avoid the weaknesses and elicit the strengths of the big republic. This restatement of a familiar theme of republican thought in America and Britain anticipated Madison's conception of the political process in the extended republic. One aspect of the structure was the federal character of its territorial division of powers. While Hume did not fully clarify the status of the rules laying down the frame of government of his model, he did suggest that they might be established by "a combination of men" in an enactment preceding and distinct from the laws made under the authority of these rules.[55] In this sense the division of powers between the central and local authorities was constitutional as in a system of national federalism. Clearly Hume rejected compact federalism, as appears in his sharp criticism of the Dutch example. Moreover, although he said that each of the counties was "a kind of republic in itself" and made the national law-makers selected by them also the law-makers for their respective counties, he did not give these local assemblies individually the power of veto over central legislation which each province in the Dutch republic possessed.[56] There was no suggestion that they were separate, autonomous, sovereign bodies.

The federalism reflected in the distribution of powers was a federalism of interaction, not separation, and like the other features of the constitutional structure, served the purpose of rationalizing government by discussion. As in Harrington's model, the most prominent expression of this effort in Hume's revision was its special kind of bicameralism. The national legislature consisted of a smaller, indirectly elected senate and a larger directly elected branch. While the senate remained at the center, exercising executive as well as legislative functions, the more popular branch met in separate assemblies in the counties from which they had been elected. The reason, as for Harrington, was the danger of disorder in a very large assembly. So, while permitting debate among these law-makers, Hume sought to ensure rational deliberation by forming them into small bodies of one hundred members each, rather as in Milton's proposal of 1660. Given this decentralization of the national legislative function, according to Hume, "though every member be only of middling sense, it is not probable that any thing but reason can prevail over the whole. Influence and example being removed, good sense will always get the better of bad among a number of people."[57] Hume trusted that this dependence of national legislation upon these small representative assemblies, which he termed "the people," would protect the public interest against faction.

While the two branches of the national legislature were institutionally separate, in the exercise of their powers they were interdependent. Proposals of legislation moved from the senate to the more popular assemblies, which had the final say. Their decision was made by a majority of the counties, but this seemingly confederal feature was illusory since the equal apportionment of voters to legislators and the equal electorates of each county meant that a vote by a majority of counties also embraced a majority of legislators representing a numerical majority of the national electorate. The interaction was shifted in the other direction by the power of the senate to veto legislation by the county assemblies when they were making by-laws for their local jurisdictions. This invention of Hume's would have lent support to the veto over state legislation which Madison found so important and which he doggedly tried to have assigned to Congress in the Constitution.

It seems almost certain that Madison read and was influenced by Hume's famous essay. The similarity of their arguments—the premise of the big republic, the breadth of the franchise, the commitment to government by discussion, the presumption of a strong, active central government, the central legislative veto over local laws, the federal character of the institutions—would support this inference. Yet the influence which Hume may have had on Madison is not the main point of this comparison. What the similarity shows, above all, is the continuing power of the common source of their ideas, the thought of Commonwealth republicans, especially Harrington. Given this common heritage of politically active people in Britain and America, it is entirely conceivable that Hume and Madison followed their similar trains of thought quite independently of each other. The point of comparing the various steps in their reflections is to use what each has said most clearly to clarify and explain the line of analysis of the other. In this respect, Hume's exposition is particularly helpful by bringing out the conception of government by discussion as the rationale of Madison's vision of pluralistic integration in the compound republic and, more specifically, by suggesting that a structure of national federalism in which the levels of government are not isolated, but interacting, could serve this rationale.

Government by Discussion: Madison

In *Federalist* 51, by means of an illuminating comparison, Madison indicated how diversity can instigate this process of rationalization. He wrote:

> In a free government the security for civil rights must be the same as that for religious rights. It consists in the one case in the multiplicity of sects. The degree of security in both cases will depend on the number of interests and sects; and this may be presumed to depend on the extent of the country and number of people comprehended under the same government.[58]

At first glance Madison may seem simply to be making the obvious point, which I have mentioned, that where there are many factions, no one of them, for lack of a majority, will be able to rule. In this light, the safeguard of our liberties would be such a mutual blocking and checking among a number of groups with differing objectives as would prevent government action in favor of any one group. That reading would fall in with the view that Madison advocated a negative constitutionalism consisting in a balance among groups that would produce "limited" government. This meaning, however, fits poorly with the logic of the argument in which Madison, after again taking note of the dangers of majority tyranny in a small state, goes on to reaffirm the promise of positive government on "principles . . . of justice and the general good" in the extended republic. Moreover, if he intended merely to restate the theory of balanced pluralism, there would have been no point in his mentioning the parallel with religious liberty and, indeed, in claiming that it took this comparison to reveal the true ground of our rights. If one is to understand what it was in Madison's thought that led him to give such emphasis to this comparison, it is necessary to look at what he says when writing directly and at length on religious liberty and on how freedom of expression is connected with the protection of other rights.

In 1784 Madison elaborated his ideas on religious liberty in a paper entitled *Memorial and Remonstrance,* its purpose being to support Jefferson's proposal to disestablish the episcopal church in Virginia.[59] One argument was pragmatic, the other normative, the first fitting the balancing model and the second the discussion model of political process. The long history of attempts to impose religious belief by government coercion, as Madison pointed out, fully supported by the history of religious conflict since the Reformation, had caused "torrents of bloodshed," but had failed. Toleration, the withdrawal of government from such "vain attempts," was therefore necessary for "social peace." No one sect could win; so freedom of conscience should be conceded by all to all. That conclusion depends on there being a multiplicity of sects, as Voltaire observed in a passage that Madison was fond of quoting. "If one religion only were allowed in England," he wrote, "the government would possibly become arbitrary; if there were but two, the people would cut each others' throats; but as there are such a multitude, they all live happy and in peace."[60]

This pragmatic admonition, however, had a severe weakness. For such a stalemate alone would produce only an uneasy armistice, continually in danger of being breached as the shifting social balance tempted militants to try for monopoly. Nor did Madison find it a sufficient ground of freedom of conscience. He also championed a new norm guaranteeing freedom of conscience justified on natural rights theory. Religious belief, he claimed, very much in the Miltonian vein, could be, and could only be, directed by reason and not just the reason of a priestly few but the "conviction and conscience of every man." This common human capacity made freedom of conscience an "unalienable" natural right. This equal right of "every man," to choose which religion he would practice, was held "on the same tenure as all other rights" as "a gift of nature."[61]

For people who were deeply serious about religion, it was not easy to move from mere toleration to admitting—and understanding— that other faiths than their own represented not simply sin and finitude but spiritual efforts worthy of respect. The appreciation of this new norm came from many sources, not least from liberal Protestantism itself. Yet the multiplicity of sects engendered by the Reformation surely facilitated this perception by making it ever harder to ignore the common human capacity that was being expressed in the variegated world of heterodoxy. The long controversy, scholarly and popular, over the rising individualist theory of natural rights gave form to this new view, as set out by Madison in his systematic defense of a uniform and general right of freedom of conscience.

Madison's theory of the rights of property was similarly grounded. As he said in *Federalist* 10, the principal task of "modern legislation" is to regulate the "various and interfering interests" of "the different degrees and kinds of property."[62] For some times and in some places such differences in proprietorship have conveyed to owners great differences in social standing and economic and political power. Medieval thought discriminated severely between different types of property—land, for instance, holding pride of place above commercial capital. The various components of ownership were distributed up and down the feudal hierarchy, and the economic activity of agriculture was integrated with the governmental activity of lordship. Material gain from the cultivation of land was held to be legitimate, as the "natural" fruit of planting seed or breeding animals. Material gain from commerce, on the other hand, was illegitimate, since money was sterile; hence, profit could arise from trade only by unfair dealing.[63] In a culture dominated by such norms, a free market in goods was as abhorrent as a free market in ideas, and an economy such as that fostered by the American republic was inconceivable.

A necessary condition for the emergence of such an economy was a conception of property justifying all types of private ownership.

Some of the medieval bias was removed by advances in economic and legal theory, such as the new views of "usury" justifying gain from commerce. Locke's treatment of property in the *Second Treatise* similarly tended toward reconciliation. Rather than basing ownership upon social and political function, Locke took an individualist approach, justifying property in general by a labor theory of value. Then rather than contrasting the claims of a natural and a money economy, he concluded that as the latter superseded the former, the old legitimation held, with the result that virtually all types of private property were equally justified.[64]

Like Locke, thinking along individualist lines, Madison found a common ground for private ownership in the inherent "faculties" of each person, which, however, being diverse and unequal, justified the various degrees and kinds of property. Like the equal right of every man to determine his own religious belief, each person also enjoyed as "a gift of nature" the right so to employ his faculties as to acquire, use, and dispose of property. In attitudes toward private property as toward religious liberty a similar transformation had taken place. From a situation of pluralistic conflict new norms in philosophy and law had emerged, in each case taking the form of a general rule applying uniformly to all members of the society. In both cases the original conflicting interests/opinions were not overridden but rather were included in a reconciling formula. Yet in each case also a new norm had come into existence, recognizing the value and legitimacy of a certain human capacity. Fundamental preferences had changed, and as the new norms were accepted in the political culture, behavior and government action had been altered.

In each case it had been the multiplicity of the initial conflicting forces which instigated the transformation and which continued to sustain it. Moreover, the greater the multiplicity, the greater the impulse to change, since an increase in the number of instances of the underlying capacity widened the field of observation and therefore enhanced the incentive to perceive the principle being illustrated. In short, as Madison asserted in the passage quoted from *Federalist* 10, the security of civil rights, such as property, was the same as that for religious rights, the security of each resting on a rationalization of diverse and conflicting motivations.

The way Madison framed the comparison, however, shows that

there is more to the relationship than this parallel. It makes sense to single out the ground of religious liberty as the basis to which the ground of other rights is to be compared because religious liberty enjoys a certain priority in both origin and value. It was on behalf of religious liberty that Milton wrote *Aereopagitica*. In the course of his argument, he showed that the rational powers of the individual enable him not only to decide what he will believe but also, by discussion with others, to criticize, correct, and amplify his religious beliefs. This same capacity, as Milton also concluded, enables the collectivity to heighten the rationality of its thought in secular as well as in sacred matters, and in later years defenders of freedom of speech and the press, whose concerns were wholly secular, adopted the Miltonian reasoning.[65] These political freedoms, therefore appear not only as rights of the individual but also as necessities of the republic, constituting the means by which government by discussion defends all rights. Resting on the same logical base as freedom of conscience, the political freedoms become, in Madison's words, "the only effectual guardian of every other right."[66]

With the whig mind of his day Madison shared this faith in the rights and powers of freedom of expression. Neither in law nor in opinion were the freedoms of conscience and of speech and the press as amply protected in that time as they are today.[67] Yet as Stephen Holmes has remarked, the belief in "the truth-generating capacity of uncensored debate" had come to be widely accepted by the eighteenth century.[68] After Milton, among the more eminent advocates of this position one can name Harrington, Sidney, Locke, and Franklin. The idea was presumed by John Adams's attack on the Stamp Act in 1765; and in Thomas Jefferson later times found one of its most eloquent champions.[69]

Nor was the faith in political free speech confined only to the leading minds. In the 1720s Trenchard and Gordon, the popular whig pampleteers, affirmed it in *Cato's Letters*.[70] So also did the unknown author of a pamphlet issued in 1776 relating to the controversy over a constitution for the new state of Pennsylvania. Rejecting the argument of the old regime that heredity justified a second legislative chamber, the author defended a unicameral legislature which allows all parties to voice their positions in the same forum, carrying the possibility of compromise and reconciliation. Different parties, "blended together, would hear each other's arguments."[71] The more parties and interests in society, the greater the need for mutual engagement in a common forum.

By occasional comments and the implications of what he said and wrote, Madison showed his sympathy with government by discussion. His full statement of the case comes in his report explaining and defending the famous resolutions of the Virginia legislature which declared the Alien and Sedition Acts of 1798 unconstitutional. In identifying the legal premises of his argument, Madison linked the two great freedoms of expression as jointly protected by the first amendment,[72] saying in the words of the protest itself that by the Constitution "liberty of conscience and freedom of the press are equally and completely exempt from all authority whatever of the United States." In the body of his argument he again appeals to consequences—not to the balancing effect of toleration but to the informing and rationalizing effect of public discussion. Asserting that "the right of electing the members of the Government constitutes . . . the essence of a free and responsible government," he concludes: "The value and efficacy of this right depends on the knowledge of the comparative merits and demerits of the candidates for the public trust." The unconstitutional violations of the Sedition Act were therefore especially alarming since they attacked the right of free discussion "which has ever been justly deemed to be the only effectual guardian of every other right."[73]

Madison would not deny that a pluralistic balance could help protect both religious and civil rights. In his thought, however, their security has sounder and more far-reaching foundations. For Madison, freedom of expression is the first right of the citizen of the new republic, and for him, as for Justice Holmes rather more than a century later, according to "the theory of our Constitution . . . the best test of truth is the power of the thought to get itself accepted in the competition of the market."[74]

Toward Power and Justice

For Madison as for Hume the statement of the problem of faction points to the solution. For both, a faction is a group based on a "separate interest" (Hume). For both, likewise, this implies that there is something more inclusive, the public interest. Problem and solution are indicated by a set of contrasting terms, such as private and public, local and general, partial and impartial. The task of government in each commonwealth is to enact into law and embody in governance what is public, general, impartial.[75] For both, such outcomes are in themselves more "rational" since reason as a norm points toward the universal. Hume trusts that "reason can prevail over the whole." Madison similarly holds that "it is the reason alone, of the public, that ought to control and regulate the government."[76]

Madison had quite extraordinary hopes for the outcome of this process of rational deliberation. In his view, the widening of the variety of interest on which majorities are based will do more than merely reflect the discrete interests of their members. The generality of majority opinions will be elevated to a level extending beyond its immediate constituency. In any republic, large or small, majority rule in the sense of rule in the exclusive interest of the majority is oppressive.[77] In the extended republic, committed to government by discussion, the wide variety of interests that must be included in any majority will force its outlook on policy to embrace the interests of a still wider public. The judgments of the extended republic will be more just because they are more general, and they will be more general because, perforce, they must include a greater variety of interests. So much so indeed that Madison can expect that in the United States, "a coalition of a majority" will normally take place only on "principles . . . of justice and the general good."[78] In short, universal standards supported by consensus will be approached.[79] Government would still be majoritarian, but the governing majorities would be not factious but civic majorities which uphold unbiased justice and express the public interest. As in Harrington's ideal commonwealth, the rule of reason in the governing of the republic would comprehend "the interest of the whole people."[80]

Such a degree of agreement among the people would, in effect, make them that "one sovereign power," possessing the unity necessary to be the imperative authority which ordains the Constitution and to be the political body which governs itself by means of that Constitution. The crucial question of how this degree of coherence was achieved and expressed arose from Madison's critique of small republic theory, demonstrating the greater legitimacy of the extended over the small republic. That analysis showed how the big republic achieved greater coherence when it provided a firmer protection of republican liberty and a more inclusive view of the public interest. Rooted in the concept of national sovereignty, Madison's analysis answered both the question of unity and the question of legitimacy, remedying both the failures of power and the failures of justice that plagued compact federalism.

According to Madisonian theory, the extended republic gives rise to a coherent governing power which also protects republican rights and promotes the public interest. This claim has commonly been made by the friends of popular government, who have held that the many have not only the right but also the capacity to govern themselves. Their opponents on the hierarchical side have denied this claim, reasoning in the spirit of the Thomistic axiom that "a social life can not exist among a number of people unless under the governance of one to look after the common good; for many, as such, seek many things, whereas one attends only to one."

Controverting Aquinas and most of the leading minds of Western political thought, Madison concluded that the many could look after the common good as justly and effectively as had been claimed for the few. Like the traditionalists, he recognized the problem confronting any polity of how to reconcile the inevitable diversity of society with the necessary unity of government. Similarly, his analysis of faction started from the premise of pluralism in its recognition that society is divided into many different and conflicting groups. Differing from his fellow republicans of the compact school, he denied that this diversity could be eliminated by a reduction in the scale of the polity. On the contrary, he found a solution in the very multiplication of faction. Differing from both traditional and compact theorists, he saw in the enhanced pluralism of the extended republic the prospect not of anarchy leading to caesarism but of coalitions aiming at justice and the general good.

Madison feared tyranny of the majority. That fear, however, was focused on the states, not the nation.[81] The danger spots were those small republics where the homogeneity of the people exposed them to domination by a faction. To the nation, on the other hand, he looked for salvation of the republican cause. In the states both the people and their representatives might be drawn into a factious majority. If office-holders at the federal level embarked on "ambitious encroachments," however, they would be opposed by "the people themselves," the whole constituency of the extended republic. From them would come that "one spirit," that "national will" which would mobilize the resources of the states to restore the constitutional equilibrium and to protect republican liberty.[82]

CHAPTER 9

Auxiliary Precautions

HIGHLY AS HE THOUGHT of the rationalized and civilized majorities of the extended republic, Madison did not believe that their rule alone would suffice to ensure the success of government by the people. Like the "orders" of Oceana, the Constitution of the United States was indispensable if the excellences of popular government were to be fully realized. "A dependence on the people is, no doubt, the primary control on government," he wrote in his great summarizing essay, *Federalist* 51, "but experience has taught mankind the necessity of auxiliary precautions." In contrast with a unitary regime, he continued, "the compound republic of America" divided the powers of government by two sorts of "auxiliary precaution": not only the separation of powers but also federalism.[1] Another institution included in the Constitution also supplemented that primary dependence on the people, namely, representation. Although in another place Madison also referred to representation as an "auxiliary desideratum,"[2] it was a more basic institution than federalism or separation of powers, since those institutions presupposed bodies chosen by the voters directly or indirectly. The Presidency, the Congress, and the Supreme Court represented the people of the United States as did the state as well as the federal level of government.

In the Madisonian scheme, representation and the extended republic are complementary. On the one hand, representation made popular government on a large scale possible. Modern Europe had discovered this device by which "the will of the largest possible political body can be concentered, and its force directed to any object which the public good requires." The achievement of America had been to make this discovery "the basis of unmixed and extensive republics," thereby proving false the opinion, based on the experience of the "turbulent democracies" of the past, that popular government "can never be established but among a small number of people, living within a small compass of territory."[3]

Conversely, the extended republic made representation possible. "It cannot be believed," wrote Madison, "that any form of representative government could have succeeded within the narrow limits occupied by the democracies of Greece."[4] Even if a small republic were nominally to adopt representative institutions, its small scale would make it so subject to popular passions that it would in effect be a "democracy" in the pejorative sense. Representation, which necessitates the big constituencies of the big republic, would presumably restrain passion and enhance reason in the deliberative process of popular government.

In contrast, therefore, with the direct democracy of ancient practice, American governments, as Madison saw and wished to see them, provided for "total exclusion of the people, in their collective capacity." This startling phrase did not mean that Madison was taking sides with aristocracy or the rule of the virtuous few.[5] Quite the contrary. Representation, he emphasized, was the agency by which the "will" of the people was "concentered" and "directed" toward the public good. In the Madisonian model, as in Harrington's, that "will" entered the deliberative process in the form of the various interests asserted by the electorate of the extended republic and emerged in the government's determinations of the public interest. While direct democracy was excluded, the process of deliberation included the represented as well as the representatives.[6]

Representation

No question, Madison's analysis of representation contains an elitist strain, although it is more in the form of hope than expectation. One reason why the extended republic can overcome faction, he wrote, is that it will "refine and enlarge the public views by passing them through the medium of a chosen body of citizens." Adopting Milton's and Hume's use of the term "refine," Madison sought representatives with personal qualities that would "enlighten" the process of deliberation. He hoped for men "whose wisdom may best discern the true interest of their country, and whose patriotism and love of justice will be least likely to sacrifice it to temporary or partial considerations."[7]

He did not think of this elite as a social order or economic class and specified no qualifications of birth, property, or social standing for membership in it. It was identified by no other external criterion than the choice of the people. In the hope of increasing the chances that this choice would fall on "proper guardians of the public weal," he looked to the big constituency which was logically entailed by the big republic.[8] As an elite which would "enlarge" and "enlighten" the views of their constituents, rising above local prejudices and looking beyond short-run considerations, these representatives, like the senatorial generalists of Oceana, would enhance the role of reason in the deliberations of the commonwealth. Even more widely than Harrington's gentry, Madison's representative elite was distanced from the governing class of Old Whig politics, which in Burke's classic portrait disciplined and directed the populace for their own good and whose authority depended only in small part upon election. Madison did not favor the corporate representation of class and community which Burke eulogized, preferring rather the "arithmetical" scheme proportioning representation to the enfranchised population which Burke scorned.

In Madison's theory of representative government, this modest elite would do far less to refine and enlarge the public views than would the institutions of constitutional government. Like Harrington, he looked far more to "good orders" than to "good men" to advance the republican cause. In his view, representatives were better qualified to make the laws than were the voters, not because of their superior virtue but because of their position in the structure of deliberation, which enabled them to be better informed of the conditions of their constituents than did the constituents themselves.[9] How little he expected from "the body of chosen citizens" is revealed by how much he trusted to the institutions within which they operated. He spent virtually no time on the education, selection, and operations of an elite in comparison with the overwhelming attention he devoted to the structures and processes of representation, separation of powers, and federalism.[10]

In the passages of *The Federalist* in which he was concerned with the elite, Madison severely qualified its role by making clear that the feature of the big republic upon which he "principally" relied for avoiding faction and its evil effects was not the big constituency, which it might possibly be hoped would produce superior candidates, but the variety of interests into which the people at large were divided. In his broader survey in *Federalist* 51, after similarly pointing out that "the primary control" on government is "dependence on the people," he turned immediately to the further protection afforded by federalism and the separation of powers, saying nothing about men of superior wisdom or more ardent patriotism, concluding his essay rather with a succinct statement of how "the multiplicity of interests" makes the extended republic "more duly capable . . . of self-government."[11]

In his view of the role of the people in republican government, Madison renewed the central thrust of the idea of actual representation which the American whigs had advanced against the British orthodoxy of virtual representation. This tradition of government by consent did not mean the deferential consent of the represented to the rule of the virtuous few but the participatory consent of the represented, who chose, watched, and judged their representatives. The people at large, the electorate, asserted the interests from which the deliberations of their representatives started and, while, as Algernon Sidney had said, they learned from what their representatives said, they also had, thanks to the power of election and reelection, the final say over what their representatives did.[12]

In the light of these ideas, which Madison shared with his whig predecessors, the people appeared in both a constitutional and an autonomous capacity. Representation, along with the "auxiliary precautions," would further rationalize and civilize the civic majorities of the extended republic. Governing themselves through these institutions, the people appear as the constitutional people. Yet in deciding how to use these constitutional agencies, the people acted independently of them. They chose their representatives according to the rules, but that choice itself was not dictated by the rules but was made freely by the voters. Ideally, in the Miltonian manner, each voter, after taking part in public discussion, made up his own mind, deciding what he would demand, what he would accept and whom he would support for office.

Fully to realize the excellences of popular government, this autonomous people needed a constitution. And they knew it. They were, therefore, the political force which established that frame of government. Confounding the champions of hierarchy, such as Blackstone and Burke, they confirmed the old republican faith that the people at large have not only the right but also the capacity to overthrow an oppressive government and (to echo Burke's astonished phrase) "to establish a government absolutely new." Nor did that capacity for free and orderly self-direction lapse after these institutions had been established but continued to inform the people's use of them in order to clarify their common interests and find the means of their satisfaction. To create the institutions of self-government is a recognition of the people's need for these institutions. It is also a supreme display of the people's capacity for self-government.

Separation of Powers

The two auxiliary precautions, federalism and separation of powers, had a common rationale: the principle of dividing power in order to protect republican liberty and to promote the excellence of popular government. This did not mean creating "separate centers of power" by cutting up government in any way that would hamper its operations for the sake of "limitation."[13] The proposed divisions of power had certain purposes which required not an arbitrary dismantling of the governmental machine but a careful differentiation of its parts according to function, leading to a corresponding reassembly of the whole by a system of constitutional controls. Since Madison gave more attention to theory in his discussion of the separation of powers, as one might expect from its long history in political thought as an institution of free government, it will be useful to summarize his ideas on that topic and then see what light they throw on how he expected the federal division to work. In each instance, an institutional structure of representative government enhances rational deliberation, while allowing for the dominant influence of the people at large.

In the development of their new science of politics, as Gordon Wood has observed, the Americans elevated the doctrine of the separation of powers into what Madison called "a first principle of free government."[14] The doctrine distinguished between two sorts of controls. One was the control which kept the powers separated; the other was the control exercised by the powers so separated. Writing about the separation of powers in *Federalist* 48, Madison pointed out how it was maintained by giving each branch "a constitutional controul"[15] over the others. This control consisted in a "partial agency in the acts of the others," for instance, the President's qualified veto over measures passed by the two houses, or the Senate's power of refusing consent to certain of the President's appointments. The legislative and executive powers so differentiated also acted as controls on the governing process. For instance, the President would presumably use his veto, a control of the first type, to prevent the Congress from encroaching on the executive's quite proper sphere of concern with particular persons, events, and objects. So confined, the legislature would be obliged to exercise its legislative power not by arbitrary *ad hoc* commands but by general rules, a control of the second type and an essential of free government.

The controls, whether by partial agency or by differentiation, would be effective because they were designed to take advantage of "the personal motives" of office-holders. As Madison never tired of saying one way or another: "Ambition must be made to counter ambition. The interest of the man must be connected with the constitutional rights of the place."[16] To be sure, the law of the constitution formally assigned to different sets of officers the functions to be performed, executive, legislative, and judicial. But Madison put little trust in such "parchment barriers."[17] Disinclined to seek constitutional ends by legal imperatives requiring conformity with these ends, he preferred to use law to create situations which would incite office-holders incidentally, but voluntarily, to conform to the norms of their office. The members of each branch, jealous of power, would be vigilant to use their controls by partial agency to counteract encroachments by members of the other branch, the effect of these mutual "checks" being to maintain the constitutional "balance." In methodology it was surely social science. Predicable motivations intrinsically unconnected with constitutional norms were so manipulated as to produce behavior conforming to those norms.

Both the theory of separation of powers and the theory of mixed government share the idea of using different branches of government to check and balance one another. The end served by these controls, however, is quite differently conceived by the two approaches. For the theory of mixed government, the division of power among branches of governments was designed to balance different social bodies represented in those branches. In the early eighteenth century, for instance, British writers spoke of their "balanced constitution" consisting of the "three estates of Kings, Lords and Commons," all of which shared in "the Supreme Legislative Power." "Balance" resulted since the consent of each was equally necessary to the exercise of that power. Each was also said to be a "check" upon the others since it could withhold that consent. This check, however, unlike the control by partial agency of Madison's scheme, was not intended to confine each to a certain function but to prevent any of the social bodies represented by them from becoming dominant.[18]

The two theories were sometimes combined. In keeping with the notion of mixed government, Montesquieu held that the aristocracy and the common people should be given coordinate authority in law-making in order to allow each to protect itself against the other.[19] John Adams envisaged some such balance between classes in his futile proposals for a bicameral legislature. For the authors of *The Federalist*, Montesquieu's principal contributions were his functional distinction between the "three sorts of power," legislative, executive, and judicial, which, he claimed, are found in every government, and his explanation of why their separation was a necessary condition of liberty.[20] Elaborating on suggestive remarks by Montesquieu, Madison greatly clarified the importance of controls by partial agency.[21]

In Madison's scheme, the purpose of the controls by differentiation was not the balance of social classes but governmental efficiency and republican liberty. If each function were to be effectively performed, the agency charged with it would need to be differently appointed, composed, qualified, and empowered. As Gwyn observes, the idea goes back to the seventeenth century, when Commonwealth thinkers "argued that those activities called legislative can best be performed by one kind of institution, while those called executive can best be performed by another."[22] Harrington's separation of powers, for example, was not an attempt to balance social classes but a functional differentiation to promote rational deliberation.[23]

In America, not only Madison but also other leading thinkers, including John Adams, Thomas Jefferson, John Jay, and James Wilson, stressed the efficiency rationale. Hamilton brilliantly exemplified this approach in *Federalist* 70, where he argued that in contrast with the law-making agency, which was necessarily plural, the executive should be unitary for the sake of "decision, activity, secrecy, and despatch." Similarly, the judiciary was seen to have duties which required that its members be specially qualified in the law and exceptionally protected in their independence.[24]

This functional view of the separation of powers makes a good deal of sense as political science. Some 179 years after Madison and Hamilton explained and defended it in *The Federalist,* two American political scientists found themselves reformulating it as a conclusion of their discipline. They had set themselves the task of framing a model of the political system that could be used generally in the comparative study of government. Taking a structural–functional approach, they identified five functions, which included, along with interest articulation and interest aggregation, the three functions of rule making, rule application, and rule adjudication.[25]

The implication of these conclusions is that if a system of authoritative command is to be effective, it must differentiate among the structures performing these functions. The use of general rules is economical of time and effort and more coherent in outcomes than dependence on a series of *ad hoc* decisions. The environment which the system seeks to control has uniformities, similar economic and social conditions, which call for similar treatment. To work out anew for each such situation the proper action to be taken leads to duplication of effort and inconsistency in outcomes. Government by a body of general law administered by skilled executives monitored by an independent judiciary makes for a more effective system of control—in short, for a more powerful state. Even in a system in which one body, such as the British cabinet, includes persons charged with executive duties and also in effect controls law-making, the two functions are kept separate. Normally, the executives act only after getting authorization for their action by general legislation to which they are strictly held accountable by an independent judiciary.

For a government which attempts to coordinate the interests of the many, a separation of powers, each of which represents the same social body, the people at large of the nation, heightens the probability that discussion and decision will realize these economies of generalization by focusing on common interests requiring similar treatment. Such a structure contributes to that Madisonian "refinement" of the interests which the voters communicate to their representatives. If the functions are not differentiated, there will be muddle, inconsistency, incoherence, and in general a failure of the system of public choice to aggregate and effectuate the preferences of the members of the polity. As Stephen Holmes has remarked, "Specialization improves everyone's performance."[26]

The laws, constitutional and statutory, which provide for these controls by partial agency and by differentiation do indeed apply restraints. To think of them solely as "checks" to ensure that the government is "limited," however, is a distortion. Their purpose is not simply to limit the power of government but rather to make its exercise more effective. The object of the control on the Congress is not to prevent law-making but to ensure that it will be by general rule. The object of the check on the President is not to hamper his activity but to enhance the "energy" of his execution. The controls are not disabling but enabling, not limiting but empowering; and in Madison's as in Harrington's thought, the theory of the separation of powers which justifies them reflects not a constitutionalism of restraints but a constitutionalism of incentives.[27]

While the authors of *The Federalist* regarded efficiency as a major criterion of what they called "good government," as attested by the first sentence of their first paper, their main object was the protection of those indispensable conditions for the realization of the public interest, the individual and political rights of republican liberty. The controls institutionalized in the separation of powers according to the findings of their new science of politics served not only efficiency but also this great and primary purpose.

The principal exhibit was the separation of the legislative and executive powers. The advocates of this "auxiliary precaution" echoed familiar arguments. They feared, quite reasonably, that if the authority charged with enforcing the law also made that law *ad lib*, he might well be tempted in the absence of a general rule controlling his actions to adapt his choice of objects to his personal ambition and interests. They also hoped, again plausibly, that if the legislative power were entrusted to a "numerous" body, that the laws would have a better chance of being general than if they were made by one person or a few.[28] And general laws favored liberty by giving the individual security against arbitrary compulsions by government, a necessary condition if he was to develop and exercise his faculties. This same argument for the separation of the legislative and executive branches in the interest of the rule of law was also held to justify a further separation of both of them from a qualified and independent judiciary.

Needless to say, the rule of law alone was not a sufficient condition for the protection of liberty. The separation of powers which secured the rule of law was only an "auxiliary precaution." The primary dependence of the republican regime upon the will of the people meant that the law-making body needed to be not only numerous but also representative, and, according to Madisonian theory, representative of a large and diverse people.

Moreover, the successful operation of the separation of powers itself depended upon the intervention of this political force. In the Madisonian model of republican government, all branches were directly or indirectly chosen by, representative of, and therefore accountable to the people at large.[29] The controls of the separation of powers were not operated solely by the personal interest and ambition of office-holders but ultimately under the influence of their constituents.

The executive, for instance, was felt to be especially in need of protection against the legislature. His principal control was the veto. Ambition would lead him to use this control to protect his constitutional position. Since he was ultimately accountable to the people, however, his personal motivation was also informed by "public opinion," the President's "fortitude" in protecting "the public good," as Hamilton remarked, being "stimulated by the probability of the sanction of his constituents."[30]

The legislature also needed countervailing power against the executive, the principal danger being the use of patronage, as practiced by the Crown to control parliament and by certain colonial governors to control their assemblies. Against this danger, the Congress had a control by partial agency in the Senate's power of consent to certain executive appointments. This control would be effective, however, not only because the Senate was jealous of its power but also because the "notoriety" of the process of consent "by an entire branch of the legislature" would mean that "the public would be at no loss to determine" who was responsible for making bad appointments or rejecting good ones. As in the other instances of checks and balances, the influence of the people was indispensable to maintaining the constitutional equilibrium and realizing the public interest. For the protection of liberty, as Marvin Meyers has observed, Madison trusted not to legal imperatives but to institutional checks and balances and, "finally, to an enlightened public opinion under a system of popular government."[31]

Why Have States?

The controlling influence of the people is even more marked in Madison's federal design. Unless this influence is recognized, the vertical division of power between levels of government makes little sense in terms of Madisonian theory. Having shown so convincingly the grave dangers of independent state power to republican liberty, how could Madison justify the existence of the states with their strongly protected, even though limited, powers? Does it not seem that the real reason for keeping the states was simply that they were there, too powerful politically in the country to be absorbed into a fully unitary regime and strong enough at the Philadelphia convention, despite the many friends of central government, to force deep compromises on the nationalist agenda? That pressure for compromise was indeed effective. But national theory, properly understood, and as its spokesmen repeatedly asserted, does not collide with the existence of the states. On the contrary, once the role of the people in the process framed by the federal division of power is appreciated, federalism becomes no longer a menace to republican liberty but, on thoroughly national grounds, a means of protecting it.

According to Madisonian theory, the basic guarantee of republican liberty was the national will engendered by rational deliberation in the compound republic. Under the Constitution, the national will would be directly and proportionately represented in one house of the legislature of the federal government, and indirectly in its other elements. The federal division of powers, however, would exclude that beneficent influence from the sphere of legislative powers reserved to the states. Even though "local" and "internal" in their purview, those powers were in that day wide indeed, including, in Madison's words, "all the objects which, in the ordinary course of affairs, concern the lives, liberties, and properties of the people, and the internal order, improvement, and prosperity of the State."[32] With the ability of the national will to break the violence of faction excluded from this sphere, it followed, according to Madisonian theory, that throughout the nation within the jurisdiction of state government, the constitutional guarantees of federalism would allow free rein to tyranny of the majority.

Fully aware of this danger, Madison included in the Virginia Plan, which introduced into the Philadelphia convention the Federalists' proposals for a new frame of government, a series of provisions to strengthen the influence of the national will. As compared with their status under the Articles, the powers of Congress were enlarged and made directly applicable to individuals, not indirectly through the states. National influence would also have been enhanced by a broad unspecified grant of authority to Congress, but this central control was weakened when the convention insisted on an enumeration of Congressional powers. Madison also proposed that representation in both houses of the federal legislature be direct and proportionate. That much was readily granted for the lower house, but a similar proposal for the other branch of the federal legislature was defeated, after the most prolonged controversy of the convention, when the states were given equal and indirect representation in the Senate.

In the most radical of its nationalizing proposals, the Virginia Plan directly attacked the danger of faction in state government by including a veto for Congress over state legislation. The scope of this veto was variously conceived, but if Madison had had his way it would have extended not only to the constitutionality of state laws, but also to their policy in "all cases whatsoever." "He could not but regard an indefinite power to negative legislative acts of the States," he told the Convention, "as absolutely necessary for a perfect system."[33] This proposal was defeated, although Madison fought for it stubbornly, arguing even after the Convention had adjourned in a famous letter to Jefferson that the general government must have a veto on state laws in order not only to defeat encroachments on its constitutional powers but also to protect the rights of individuals against factious majorities in the states.[34]

At the federal convention opponents of the veto, while developing their argument, suggested that the courts could be counted on to perform the same function, thereby directing attention to the possibilities of judicial review.[35] Both Madison and Hamilton, as *The Federalist* makes quite clear, expected that the federal judiciary would enforce upon both the federal and the state governments the constitutional division of powers between them.[36] Against the states the Constitution also protected a few individual rights, particularly by its prohibitions, in Article I, section 10, of bills of attainder, *ex post facto* laws, and laws impairing the obligation of contracts.

When in 1789 the amendments which would constitute the Bill of Rights were being framed in Congress, Madison attempted to have their principal guarantees apply to the states as well as the federal government. He failed, and his purpose was realized only in this century when, thanks to a new reading of the Fourteenth Amendment, the Supreme Court concluded that those great individual and political rights of the republican canon also bound the states. A long series of decisions dating largely from 1937 and reflecting the views of justices appointed by Franklin Roosevelt finally accomplished in many respects a main purpose of the Congressional veto over state legislation.[37] But at the time of the ratification of the Constitution, whose rationale Madison sought to discern and defend, judicial review gave republican liberty only slender protection against infringement by the states. In this institutional framework, it would seem, federalism would blight the best hopes of Madisonian theory by its protection of the wide sphere of power reserved to the states.

Madisonian theory made a persuasive case for popular government on a continental scale. The enlarged and more commanding authority of the federal government promised to cope with the problem of power, the conventional internal and external weaknesses of compact federalism inherent in the Confederation. Without the safeguards proposed by the Virginia Plan, especially the Congressional veto, however, federalism would seem to bar a solution to the problem of justice by giving constitutional protection to jurisdictions prone to majority tyranny. Much as he regretted the absence of these further safeguards, however, Madison clearly believed that the Constitution did in other ways provide controls that would protect republican liberty from invasion by factious majorities in the states. And not only did he believe that these dangers of federalism could be offset; he also held that federalism would work positively to protect republican liberty, classifying it along with the separation of powers as one of the main institutions of the Constitution by which "the rights of the people" would be protected.[38]

What functions does federalism perform? How can the performance of these functions promote efficiency and protect liberty? Very simply put: Why have states? The Madisonian answers contrast sharply with the "argument from community" advanced by the Anti-Federalists.

The Constitution does not answer these questions in theoretical terms. The Virginia Plan had suggested criteria with broad connotations, proposing that "the National Legislature" have the power "to legislate in all cases to which the separate States are incompetent, or in which the harmony of the United States may be interrupted by the exercise of individual legislation."[39] This proposal was defeated, and in its stead the final draft enumerated the powers of Congress, amplified them by the necessary and proper clause, laid down a series of mandates, positive and negative, largely on the states, and by implication defined the powers of that level of government as the residuum.

Madison gave this miscellany of imperatives a rationale by a differentiation of the functions of the two levels of governments. Observing that the Constitution "referred" "the great and aggregate interests" to one level and "the local and particular" to the other, Madison justified the existence of the states by the danger that the latter interests might be neglected if no separate agency was charged with their "superintending care." He made the same distinction by other pairs of terms, such as "the great and national objects" of the general government in contrast with the "local circumstances and lesser interests" assigned to the states.[40]

This differentiation of function reflected distinctions which had surfaced during the prerevolutionary debate with Britain over the federal option—the question of how and why divide power between Westminster and the colonies.[41] The "argument from utility" expressed in Benjamin Franklin's external/internal criterion, relating powers to services, which he had developed during that controversy, prefigured the general/local rationale advanced by Madison, who in fact often used the terms "external" and "internal" when spelling out what he meant by that rationale.

Present-day advocates of fiscal federalism give the terms "internality" and "externality" a similar meaning when they distinguish between functions appropriately assigned to a local government and those justifying a more inclusive jurisdiction. Thinking along these lines, Wallace Oates concludes that since a central government will tend to make its public goods uniformly available to members of all constituent communities, a "decentralized form of government therefore offers the promise of increased economic efficiency providing a range of outputs of certain public goods that corresponds more closely to the differing tastes of consumers."[42] This argument for a local level of government is quite in the spirit of Madison's reasoning that without a jurisdiction the interests of the locality will be neglected. Nor is it anachronistic to impute such a degree of rational choice thinking to men who read Adam Smith and David Hume and who were so acutely aware of the "free rider" problem of compact federalism.[43]

In this sense, there were for Madison certain purely local interests which were regulated more efficiently by state governments than by the general government. Since these interests were internal, so also should the effects of a state's action regarding them be confined to its boundaries. One "vice" from which the Union suffered under the Articles had been state favor toward local interest groups by action which had harmful effects on interest groups outside the state: for instance, state regulations burdening interstate commerce. In the eyes of the nationalists, negative externalities such as this justified adding to the powers of the general government the regulation of commerce between the states.

Following the same logic of self-interest and distrust, states also had often failed to produce those positive externalities benefitting the Union as a whole: as when, for instance, they refused to provide men or money for the federal military force. "The spirit of *locality*," which so deeply troubled and incensed Madison, supported these misdeeds of commission and omission by the states. They displayed the "imbecility" of compact federalism and gave substance to the new definition of the functions of the two levels of government according to the general/local criterion of national federalism.

Like the separation of powers, the division of power according to the general/local criterion under federalism, however, had as its object more than efficiency. Indeed, the legal basis of federalism, its constitutional status, makes an uneasy fit with that criterion. If the boundaries of state government, in accord with the external/internal rationale, are to remain congruent with the pattern of local interests, they must be continually adapted to the changing contours of economic and social development. Look at a map of the United States. Those symmetrical quadrilaterals which occupy so much of its space were not drawn to harmonize with clusters of economic, social or cultural coherence. When from time to time geographers propose new boundaries for regional government which would fit them to such clusters, centering, for instance, on the vast metropolitan areas that have grown up in the past generation or two, the profiles bear no resemblance to existing state lines. Yet these present state boundaries are immobilized by constitutional guarantees which put them beyond alteration even by the difficult procedures of constitutional amendment, thanks to Article IV, section 3, which provides in effect that the boundaries of no state shall be changed without its consent.

The further purpose of federalism, which Madison chose to emphasize and which does necessitate a constitutional status for the states, is his version of the "argument from liberty." In *Federalist* 51 he notes that federalism is one of the "auxiliary precautions" that provide the "double security" to "the rights of the people." The succeeding paragraph once again rehearses the theory of the extended republic as the source of the political force that protects "justice and the general good."[44] Two earlier *Federalist* papers, numbers 28 and 46, which deal with the federal division of powers, bring out in more detail how that political force accomplishes this end, as we will see in the next section of this chapter.

The People as Common Superior

In *Federalist* 28, while discussing the problem of national defense, Hamilton examines the possibility of a military confrontation between the two levels of government. On one plane of analysis, his solution is an instance of the familiar mechanism of checks and balances. Under the federal division of power ordained by the Constitution, he argued, conflict would be avoided because the coercive power possessed by each level of government—the standing army of the general government, on the one hand, and the militia of the states, on the other—would enable each to resist any "usurpation" attempted by the other. "Power being almost always the rival of power," he wrote, "the General Government will at all times stand ready to check the usurpations of the state governments, and these will have the same disposition towards the General Government."[45]

This safeguard, however, did not consist of a mere mechanical stand-off. It averted conflict only because an overall controlling political force limited and directed the interaction of levels of government. Only up to a point was this balancing done by "a machine that runs of itself." Hamilton's next sentence reveals the engineer in the machine. "The people," he continued, "by throwing themselves into either scale, will infallibly preponderate. If their rights are invaded by either, they can make use of the other as an instrument of redress." Thanks to their control of coercive power on both levels, "the people . . . are entirely masters of their own fate."[46]

Since Montesquieu was a leading advocate of checks and balances, we may be inclined to look to his account to clarify the operation of this scheme. The process that Hamilton foresees, however, resembles only superficially the political mechanics of Montesquieu's confederate republic. In that system the several petty states, like the various orders of his monarchic regime, kept one another within their appointed spheres without the intervention of an outside force, by exertions of power by each on all just sufficient to maintain the equilibrium. In Hamilton's scheme, however, the balance is not maintained because the military checks on each side are equal in coercive power and therefore so evidently ensure an immediate stand-off if either tried to usurp the authority of the other that neither will make the attempt. The balance is maintained rather by a balancer, the people at large of the whole nation, performing as a coherent political actor. This political actor will judge intergovernmental disputes that threaten military action and by its prospective intervention and certain victory forestall armed conflict. Confrontation is averted by anticipation.

It is a strikingly original and emphatically nationalist analysis of how the federal division of authority is to be maintained. The subject of the analysis, an imaginary military conflict between the general and the state governments, while hardly irrelevant to our history, is of no practical interest today. The exercise, nevertheless, brings out principles of nationalist theory which still help explain how our constitutional system operates. First, ambition checks ambition, since the legal structures on each side of the federal division create offices which their holders, impelled by personal interest in power, will attempt to defend and extend. These checks, in Hamilton's example consisting of the military power of the nation shared by the two levels of government, are controls "by partial agency," not like the mutual controls of two differentiated branches but like the controls of two houses of a bicameral legislature.

Second, as in the case of the separation of powers, the political force that uses these controls to prevent usurpation is a coherent political actor and *a fortiori* not the separate peoples of the several states but the people of the whole nation. In so far as they are acting on the institutions of government, namely, the organized coercive power at each level, they are the autonomous people acting independently of these institutions. Moreover, this national and autonomous political force is ready to act not only through the federal government to control state governments but also, as Hamilton emphasizes in this paper, through state governments to check the federal government. Depending on circumstances, the states may be the objects of the national will, or may serve as agents of it. In this latter capacity, the states illustrate how the state as well as the federal level of government is representative of the people at large of the United States.

Finally, the example also makes clear how far-fetched it would be to suppose that fine-tuning the powers of different agencies of government could through its effects alone maintain the constitutional balance. In that day, the military force available to the states would overwhelm any force that could conceivably be mustered by the federal government—in Madison's assessment, a half a million men against only twenty or thirty thousand. If the protection against usurpation depended solely upon the interaction of these controls, independent of any further action by the people, the states would triumph in any test of force, offensive or defensive, justified or unjustified, against the federal government.

Since this exercise of political imagination supposes that at least one of the parties to the confrontation threatens to exercise powers not granted to it by the Constitution, it takes us beyond the realm of constitutional politics and into the realm of revolutionary politics. Nevertheless, because the possibilities it supposes condition the intentions of potential transgressors, these possibilities, although not realized, help maintain the regime of constitutional politics.

Within that regime, how do the controls institutionalized by federalism operate? Madison's discussion of intergovernmental conflict in *Federalist* 46 adapts the logic of the military paradigm to constitutional politics. In this paper Madison seeks to reassure those critics who fear that the powerful new general government will endanger the states. His immediate answer is to draw attention to that political force to which the general government, as well as the states, will be subject. This is the people at large of the extended republic, on whom, according to the argument in *Federalist* 10, the nation will primarily depend for the protection of its liberties. The error of critics, therefore, is to assume that the general and the state governments "in their efforts to usurp the authorities of each" will be "uncontrolled by any common superior." Accusing these "adversaries of the Constitution" of having "lost sight of the people," he writes:

> Notwithstanding the different modes in which [the federal and state governments] are appointed, we must consider them as substantially dependent on the great body of the citizens of the United States . . . The federal and State governments are in fact but different agents and trustees of the people constituted with different powers, and designed for different purposes . . . The ultimate authority wherever the derivative may be found, resides in the people alone.[47]

In no way contradicting his often asserted proposition that the checking process depends in the first instance upon the rivalry of the two sets of office-holders, Madison does not make this competition the conclusive control on who will come out on top. Explicitly, he declares that "whether either, or which of them, will be able to enlarge its sphere of jurisdiction at the expense of the other . . . will not depend merely on the comparative ambition or address of the different governments." Rather the outcome *"in every case"* (my emphasis) will "depend on the sentiments and sanction of their common constituents."[48]

At one stage in his argument Madison supposes for purposes of analysis that the conflict has reached the point of military conflict. The reason, he hypothesizes, is "ambitious encroachments" by the federal government. Even more than Hamilton, he emphasizes the national character of the political force that will lead the state governments to their inevitable victory. "Every [state] government would espouse the common cause. A correspondence would be opened. Plans of resistance would be concerted. One spirit would animate and conduct the whole." A "national will," making use of "the national force" consisting of the several militias of the states, would surely defeat such mad "enterprises of ambition" on the part of federal office-holders.[49]

As in Hamilton's paradigm, the saving political force is the people at large of the nation, the common constituents of the federal and the state governments. In this instance the common constituents use the state governments to set right the federal government. "A few representatives of the people," writes Madison, "would be opposed to the people themselves; or rather one set of representatives would be contending against thirteen sets of representatives, with the whole body of their common constituents on the side of the latter."[50] The encroaching power is federal officialdom. It is not, and in Madisonian theory cannot be, the national people. A faction may dominate the voters of the small polity of a state. But the national people are the "common superior" which remains faithful to the Constitution and in its behalf intervenes against encroachment at whichever level it may occur. These "common constituents" are not state governments, not state peoples acting as units, but the individual citizens comprising the American nation.

Madison sets his military paradigm in a larger context. The accusation to which he is replying and the frame of reference of his reply show that he is mainly concerned with constitutional politics. He starts from a familiar feature of everyday political behavior, the effort of one or the other level of government "to enlarge its sphere of jurisdiction," and grants that an equally familiar force, consisting of "the comparative ambition or address" of each government will have a bearing on the outcome. This mutual watchfulness was deliberately established by the Constitution and is one means by which federalism serves to protect liberty. The defeat of encroachment, however, will not be accomplished by a stand-off between two bodies of ambitious office-holders but by the commitment of one body, the people of the United States, to the Constitution and to republican liberty. The people can enforce these "sentiments" because of the "sanction" they possess as the "common constituents," who as the individual citizens who vote in state and in federal elections can call office-holders at both levels to account.

Their control was the vote, which enabled them to defeat encroachment by whichever level it was attempted. Thanks to that power they could affirm constitutional and republican values by political rewards and punishments as they would by victory and defeat in the emergencies of revolutionary politics.[51]

From his specific concern with the federal system in *Federalist 46,*

Madison turned a few days later in *Federalist* 51 to a summary of how he expected the new system would operate as a whole to protect "the rights of the people." The two parts of his summary, whose connection he emphasized by an italicized designation as *"First"* and *"Second,"* dealt respectively with institutional and with political aspects. Taking up the institutional division of powers, he observed that in "the compound republic of America," these powers are divided intergovernmentally by the federal structure and interdepartmentally by the separation of powers and bicameralism. In each case the rivalry of office-holders would serve as a control, which in intergovernmental relations as in the separation of powers is exerted not in one direction only but is mutual, as Madison said when he concluded: "Hence, a double security arises to the rights of the people. The different governments will control one another, at the same time that each will be controlled by itself."[52]

Madison then summed up what he had said about the body that would exercise political control over these institutional checks—the national electorate of the extended republic. Restating the main arguments of *Federalist* 10, he concluded with regard to this body that "a coalition of a majority of the whole society can seldom take place on any other principles than those of justice and the general good." It was through such a civic majority that the "whole body of . . . common constituents" of both state and federal governments would act politically as the "ultimate authority," "the common superior," within the federal system.[53]

As this summary indicated, the purposes to be served were the protection of the "constitutional equilibrium" and the promotion of "justice and the general good." The means for achieving these ends were both institutional and political.

According to national theory, the federal division of authority established two sets of governments which would watch and control one another. The guarantee of constitutional status was necessary if they were to perform this function. Neither a wholly unitary government nor a mere alliance could meet this need. For if the central government could rule the states without limitation, as in a unitary republic, the states would be gravely weakened in their efforts to stand up to encroachment or usurpation from the center. Nor, if the states had such unlimited authority over their relations with the central government as to be able to secede from or nullify its authority, could the central government act to protect the constitutional equilibrium or to control faction within the states. These constitutional guarantees were not mere "parchment barriers" but created institutional structures and called up political forces which would give effect to the verbal formulations of the Constitution.

Madison granted that federal officialdom could become corrupt, and in state governments he saw a means of guarding against this danger. His faith in the constituency of the federal government, the people at large of the extended republic, however, moderated his fears of any great threat to the republican cause from the new federal government.[54] His principal concern was the threat of faction within the states, for faction threatened not only interests with external effects and therefore within the sphere of federal responsibility. Local majorities could also oppress groups whose interests according to the constitution were subject to the exclusive authority of the state as matters relating to a state's "internal order, prosperity and improvement."[55]

The Control of Faction

The theory of the compound republic required that some way be found to get over this constitutional hurdle so that the national will might be brought to bear upon local faction. Otherwise, a wide sphere of local life and state government would be open to tyranny of the majority. The Congressional veto over state legislation would have done the job. A specific governmental control exercised by the federal government, it would have bridged the division of powers between the two levels so substantially that Madison could tell the Convention that "the negative proposed on the State laws will make it [the Congress] an essential branch of the State Legislatures."[56] A control by partial agency, its scope would have included more than maintaining the constitutional equilibrium. As Madison strongly insisted in a letter of April 16, 1787, to George Washington, its function would also have been to protect local minorities threatened by factious majorities in "all cases whatsoever."[57]

If the veto had been accepted, controls by partial agency would have bridged the federal division of powers symmetrically, although not equally, in favor of both levels. The state legislatures would choose members of the federal senate; the Congress would have a negative on state legislation. Even after the defeat of the Congressional veto, there remained some institutional means by which the broader perspective of the national legislature might be brought to bear on factious abuse within the states. For example, in Madison's opinion the power of Congress to override state regulation of elections to the House of Representatives would serve as protection against what "a strong faction" within a state might attempt if the state had exclusive control.[58]

Today we think of judicial review by the federal courts as the principal institutional means by which legally binding decisions may conclude intergovernmental conflicts and protect individual rights against government interference. At the Philadelphia convention the defeat of the Congressional veto led to discussion of further measures, from which in the minds of some delegates at any rate the idea of judicial review took shape. Madison and Hamilton expected the Supreme Court to umpire the "constitutional balance."[59] At the time of the adoption of the Constitution, however, its role in protecting the rights of the individual was limited to the few, although important, safeguards set forth in Article I, section 10. Later, when the Bill of Rights was adopted, its guarantees were directed only against action by the federal government, not the states. Moreover, as Madison fully realized—and this is the important point—if the federal courts, "the weakest of the three departments of power,"[60] were effectively to enforce these "parchment barriers," they would need the support of a political force that could stand up to popularly elected legislatures, federal and state. In Madison's mind that controlling political force would be, as in the case of separation of powers, the people at large of the extended republic. The national will would achieve its objects not by means of the Congressional veto but through the participation of the people at large in state and federal elections.

In *Federalist* 46, after stating in general terms that the people at large, the common superior of both levels of government, would maintain the constitutional balance, Madison went on to show how, and why, the people would do this by shifting their support from one level to another. In remarks that would reassure critics who feared for the states, he began by granting that at the time of writing the people felt a greater attachment to their respective state governments. He also inserted into these remarks the observation that sometimes, although only "rarely," "the members of state government" carry into their deliberations "a bias in favor of the general government." This bias, he believed, might well increase as the general government gave proof of "better administration."[61]

By that innocuous phrase, he did not mean only more effective government. In an earlier paper, *Federalist* 27, Hamilton had expanded on its significance. Embracing in this reference to "better administration" the main values of the theory of the extended republic, Hamilton asserted that "the general government will be better administered than the particular governments" because its councils would be better informed but especially because they would be "less apt to be tainted by the spirit of faction . . . which, in smaller societies, frequently contaminate[s] the public councils." This advantage on the side of the general government, moreover, would be strengthened by the "extension" of its activity into "what are called matters of internal concern."[62]

The controlling force in this nationalist shift was the common constituents, whose concern for the interests constitutionally assigned to one level was carried over and imparted to the other level. As their attachment to state government imparted "a local spirit" to federal deliberations, so also their shift in attachment to the federal government would heighten "the national spirit" in state deliberations.[63] This interaction of levels of government by way of their common electorate served as an incentive to mutual recognition of the interests of each.

Such intervention by the common constituents could also serve as at once a restraint and an incentive. In *Federalist* 30 and 31 Hamilton gives an example. He was defending the absence of an explicit constitutional rule defining how the power of taxation should be shared by the two levels of government. In reaction to the broad grant of power to Congress in Article I, section 8, of the Constitution "to lay and collect taxes, duties, imposts and excises," the not unreasonable criticism had been urged that such an "unconfined" power in the hands of the government which has the authority to lay down "the supreme law of the land" could be used to extinguish the taxing power of the states "upon the pretence of an interference with its own."[64]

Hamilton granted that the two levels of government would be inclined to "encroach" on one another in the field of taxation as in other fields. Observing that the Constitution assigned certain specific powers to the federal government, he concluded his defense by saying that "everything beyond this must be left to the prudence and firmness of the people; who, as they will hold the scales in their own hands, it is to be hoped, will always take care to preserve the constitutional equilibrium between the general and the State governments."[65]

This example from *Federalist* 30 and 31 illustrates the general proposition laid down in *Federalist* 46 that "the people" would control the constitutional balance in their capacity as the "common constituents" of the two levels of government. As in the military paradigm set out by Hamilton, they "hold the scales in their own hands," because they are the electorate that chooses both state and federal officials.[66] The rationale of their choice would derive from the Constitution, not directly in obedience to an explicit rule but indirectly in response to the implied need of each level of government for sufficient taxing power to exercise its constitutionally based nontaxing powers. Following this implication, the electorate would act through state elections to restrain state governments and through federal elections to restrain the federal government.

In a similar manner, the dual electoral process would bring the liberal sentiments engendered by the extended republic to bear as a restraint upon the two levels of government in defense of republican liberty. This consequence of the national will for the federal government was a fundamental thesis of the whole Federalist case for the Constitution. The intrusion of the national will upon state government would also impose its standards upon that level of government. Against tyranny of the majority in the states, the political process would give republican liberty further protection beyond the then limited scope of judicial review. This nationalization of state politics would perform the function for which the congressional veto had been designed, the protection not only of the federal division of power but also the rights of individuals within purely local spheres of action. As in the military paradigm, the people at large would support that side which was protecting their rights and oppose the side that was invading them.

This political interaction between levels of government would very considerably modify the general/local rationale for the states based on efficiency. In that new light the federal division appears less as separate governments with different powers than as separate governments with shared powers.[67] Despite the constitutional division of authority, the national will could influence the substance and spirit of internal state action. The states, likewise, were not expected to remain ensconced behind their constitutional barriers, occupying themselves solely with the limited topics of local governance. The reason for the states was not solely or even primarily what they did to promote efficiency by caring for local interests, while leaving general interests to the federal government. The states were also expected to be a means by which the people could influence the federal government. As Madison wrote in the immediate sequel to *Federalist* 51, "the federal legislature will not only be restrained by its dependence on the people, as other legislative bodies are, but . . . it will be, moreover, watched and controlled by the several collateral legislatures."[68] In Madison's eyes, the institutional means available to states for influencing the use of federal power were considerable. The principal form was the voice and vote of the two members that each state legislature appointed to the U.S. Senate. Madison also listed in *Federalist* 46 a number of other devices, legislative and administrative and just short of interposition, by which state governments could resist federal initiatives.[69] He recognized that these controls could be used for parochial as well as national interests, but hoped, somewhat in the spirit of John Adams, that the method of choice and conditions of office of Senators would enhance their wisdom and broaden their understanding.

The states, in short, opened to the people of the nation a second avenue, so to speak, by which to control and direct the federal government. These institutional channels would have good effects, however, providing they were used by the right political force. Illustrating how the constitutional limit on appropriations to two years would be made effective against a Congress that attempted to circumvent it, Hamilton wrote: "the State legislatures . . . will be ready enough, if anything improper appears, to sound the alarm to the people and not only to be the VOICE, but, if necessary, the ARM of their discontent."[70]

"Checking," as a restraint on federal government action, was one rationale of these controls by state government. Yet, as an activist and nation-builder, like other Federalists advocating a strong and effective government at the center, Madison also perceived how these intergovernmental controls could be used not only to restrict but also to shape and direct federal action. One of his most imaginative examples was his prognosis in *Federalist 56* of how state laws could come to serve as models for federal legislation. He premised his analysis on the assumption that the members of the House of Representatives would have "due knowledge" of the "interests and circumstances" of their constituencies, thanks largely to their familiarity with the laws of their respective states. Taking taxation and the militia as probably the most important objects of federal legislation, he foresaw legislators from across the country pooling their knowledge of their home state laws when drafting federal laws. Indeed, he painted a scene of "the skilful individual in his closet, with all the state codes before him," compiling "a law on some subject of taxation for the whole Union."[71]

In his *American Commonwealth*, first published in 1888, James Bryce made a similar point when he observed that "federalism enables a people to try experiments which could not safely be tried in a large centralized country."[72] Bryce was thinking about imitation among the states, but as federal regulatory legislation grew, state experience also often served as a model for Congressional action. This capacity was characterized in the concept of "laboratories for experimentation," given wide circulation by Justices Holmes and Brandeis in later years.[73] This positive, national function of the states, as Madison's perceptive speculation indicated, was a possibility inherent in the structure of American federalism on the Federalist plan.

"*Divide et impera,* the reprobated axiom of tyranny," wrote Madison, "is under certain qualifications, the only policy, by which a republic can be administered."[74] National federalism makes that principle serve the cause of popular government by reversing the roles of governors and governed. Now the governed divide their governors for the sake of the people's interests. The object of the controls of the federal system is not merely to preserve the "constitutional equilibrium" between the federal and state governments. It is primarily to enable the common superior of both, the people at large of the nation, to intervene at either level in order to promote justice and the general good. This division of power makes the governed the arbiter between the two sets of governors and the champion of the people's rights within each.

CHAPTER 10

Sovereignty and
Ratification

THIS WHOLE SPLENDID EDIFICE of incentives and restraints would collapse in the absence of the new normative basis of the Constitution. The theory of the compound republic, developed by the critiques of the compact solution and of the small republic idea, provided this normative basis, legitimating the action of the people when, as the constituent sovereign, they ordained the fundamental law. But how were the people to exercise their sovereignty? By what procedures, by what institutional means, could this vast and vaguely defined aggregate, the people at large of the United States, exercise their undoubted theoretical authority to convert the 4,523 words of the Philadelphia draft into positive law binding on states and individuals? How was the Constitution "ordained"?

Two models drawn from recent experience gave specific but contrasting illustration of how republican principles might be put into practice in the founding or reform of a state. One, the confederate model, derived from compact federalism, had been followed in the adoption of the Articles of Confederation. As an example of how a new polity (if not a new state) might be created, this model had precedents in the common view of the United Netherlands and Switzerland as alliances or leagues based on a treaty *(foedus)* among several separate, sovereign states. Although the New England Confederation of 1643 did not create a new and independent regime, the manner of its formation filled out the idea of how popular approval might be given to a central coordinating body. The defining characteristic of the confederate model was that the confederation was not established directly by the people at large but by popularly elected governments, the assent of each of which, regardless of size, was equally necessary to conclude or to amend the agreement on which the new polity was based.

Another model, which was also exemplified by and which indeed had originated in American experience, gave the people at large a more direct part in the process of authorization. This was the constitutional convention, a body elected specially, and in some cases solely, for the purpose of establishing or altering the fundamental law of one of the states, an innovation which R. R. Palmer has called "the most distinctive institutional contribution of the American revolutionaries to Western politics."[1]

How the Constitution Was Ordained

The necessity which prompted this invention arose when the colonies, on the eve of independence, sought to establish properly authorized governments in the place of the informal and extra-institutional bodies by which they had been carrying on their agitation and resistance. To entrust this task to a legislature which performed the work of day-to-day governance would not satisfy the American demand for a fundamental law binding the legislature itself. Thanks to its manner of election, a constitutional convention in comparison with a legislature was felt to be more closely representative of the ultimate source of power in a republic, the people at large, and therefore competent to set conditions upon the organs of daily governance to which in the name of the people it delegated a prescribed authority. Authorized by their election both to frame and to adopt a fundamental law, such constituent assemblies came to be widely used in the later history of democratic constitutionalism. Only three years after the adoption of the U.S. Constitution, the first constitution of the French Revolution was framed and adopted in this manner by a body terming itself "l'assemblée constituante."

A procedure extending popular participation even further was added when in 1780 Massachusetts subjected the draft framed by its constitutional convention to ratification by a popular vote. A specially elected convention drafted, but did not adopt, the state constitution, that act being performed directly by the voters, under a franchise which for this constituent purpose relaxed the usual property qualification by giving the vote to all males over age twenty-one. Although the people cast their votes in their respective town meetings, the majority required for ratification was not a majority of the towns but a majority of all individuals taking part in the statewide vote.[2]

The whole process of drafting and ratification was conducted amidst ardent and prolonged public debate, and although the procedure laid down by the legislature for ratification made no formal provision permitting voters to propose and adopt amendments, it was provided that if necessary the constitution would be so altered as to be agreeable to "the sentiments of two-thirds of the voters throughout the state."[3] In 1780 no such action was felt to be necessary, but a precedent of sorts had been set. And in this spirit in 1787 the members of the Massachusetts convention that had been convoked to ratify the U.S. Constitution expressed so much support for the addition of a bill of rights that Governor Hancock, a leading Federalist and the mover of the resolution of ratification, added to his motion a recommendation that such amendments be adopted. Previous to this action by Massachusetts, five states had ratified the Constitution without conditions. Thereafter all states but one suggested similar amendments. In consequence, one of the first acts of the First Congress was to draft and submit for ratification twelve amendments to the Constitution, of which ten became the Bill of Rights.[4]

Although in the United States the practice of ratification originated in Massachusetts, the idea was not without precedent in the earlier history of republicanism. During the Puritan revolution, the radical republicans who in 1649 presented *The Agreement of the People* to parliament as the fundamental law of a new regime asked not that it be imposed by law but that it be submitted for popular approval. Although the Agreement provided for quite substantial measures of decentralization, protected by constitutional sanction, the Agreement itself was based not upon a compact among local governments or communities but upon direct assent by individuals. Indeed, the method of ratification proposed by the Agreement provided that all adherents indicate their assent by personal signature. If most of the supporters of the parliamentary cause approved, steps would be taken by parliament to put the Agreement into effect.[5]

Harrington likewise supposed that the "orders" of Oceana had been "ratified and established by the whole body of the people."[6] This approval had presumably been given in the small local assemblies of the parishes. His method of apportionment presumes arithmetical representation, not the old corporate system of the medieval parliament, under which constituencies had equal representation regardless of size. He does not say, however, whether the yeas and nays were taken by a count of individuals or of parishes. A preference for arithmetical representation did not necessarily exclude a count based on the number of parishes rather than individuals. In Milton's remodeling of Oceana of 1660, the county assemblies, when serving as the popular branch of the national legislature, made their decisions by a vote of a majority of counties, not a majority of all assemblymen. Similarly, Hume, who in his reconstruction of Oceana, also proposed a decentralized legislature, would have its decisions made by a majority of local assemblies. These seemingly confederate features of the Miltonian and Humean schemes, however, did not imply any favor toward compact federalism, which both authors explicitly and sharply condemned.[7] If we can assume that small assemblies and their constituencies will be homogeneous and that they are the same size, it makes sense even on an arithmetical basis to take the count by local body, not individual legislators or voters.

In Oceana, as in the later American procedure, ratification was only one element in the process of constitution-making. While Harrington, like other champions of popular government of his time, held that a republican regime ought to be legitimated by a vote of the people, he did not suppose that the business of drafting the constitution could be performed by the same bodies and procedures that accomplished its ratification. The task of framing the document he gave to two central bodies whose composition and appointment attracted most of his attention when he was setting out the machinery of constitution-making and whose discussions he used as the vehicle for describing the institutional structure of the Commonwealth and explaining how it would work. In this scheme the "council of prytans," a small committee of experts, which received and reviewed suggestions from the public and passed them on to its parent body, the "council of legislators," which debated and decided on the text. A decisive leadership in these bodies was exercised by the Legislator who, legitimated in his role by "the universal suffrage" of the republican army, appointed the committees.[8]

Later American practice roughly paralleled the two-step procedure of Harrington. In contrast with constitutional authorizations by a legislature, or indeed by a constituent assembly, the separation of drafting from ratification provided for a greater assertion of popular sovereignty. At the same time, this procedure was adapted to the fact that drawing up a constitution would be better done not by the people at large but by a small representative body capable of informed and orderly deliberation and decision. In conformity with this model, the U.S. Constitution was debated and drafted by a small body of delegates—almost exactly the same size as Harrington's council of legislators—and was then submitted for ratification by local assemblies. Since this procedure sought to reconcile wide popular approval with rational deliberation, its adoption as a method of constitutional reform is what one might well expect from men with the Federalist bias of the Philadelphia delegates and the leaders who instigated their meeting.

Within that general framework of action, however, they did not find it easy to work out the institutional details that would fit their nationalist and republican premises. Although the gathering at Philadelphia was called a "convention," its authority was distinctly modest in comparison with the role recently acquired by convocations of that name. Its members were chosen not directly by the people but by the state legislatures. Its powers were, as Madison said, "merely advisory and recommendatory." Even within that narrow limit, it may have exceeded the strict legal limits of its charge, confirmed by the instructions of several states to their delegates, merely to recommend revisions of the Articles of Confederation.[9] To be sure, Congress approved of the convention's draft, and the state legislatures arranged for ratification. Yet Madison's anxiety was evident in his long and involved apology for what the convention had done, culminating in the argument that the "approbation" of the "supreme authority" of *the people themselves* would "blot out antecedent errors and irregularities."[10] Clearly, the modesty of the convention's powers and the irregularity of its actions made ratification indispensable; and, moreover, for the Federalists such a method of ratification was necessary as would convey the legitimacy demanded by nationalist theory.

Madison's Gap

Nationalist theory required that ratification be both popular and national, a procedure which expressed the will of individuals, the ultimate authority in a republic, and which embraced a single nationwide constituency, acting on behalf of the people at large of the United States. The procedure actually followed had three elements. The vote would be taken in delegate conventions specially called by the legislatures in each of the states for the purpose of ratification. In the computation of the majority necessary for ratification, the count would be by states, not individual voters or delegates. Ratification by nine states would suffice to establish the Constitution between these states.[11]

Does this procedure satisfy the demands of nationalist theory for a method of approval that is both national and popular? Nationalists have thought so. But states' rightists have also found confirmation of the compact theory in it, drawing from their interpretation support for a narrow rather than a broad construction of federal power, for rejection of judicial review by the federal judiciary, and for nullification, interposition, and even secession—and, beyond these vital differences over the law of federalism, for a fundamentally different conception of what the United States is and can be, including a denial that it is one nation and one people.

James Madison clearly believed that the method of ratification met the demands of nationalist theory. Yet the difficulties into which his own thoughts on this matter lead show how important it is to get the answer straight. Madison's principal contribution was his insistence that ratification be by conventions. As experience under the Articles demonstrated and nationalist theory postulated, the first necessity was to avoid ratification by legislatures. For that procedure would put the law of the Constitution on the same legal footing as other laws of those bodies. A state which had ratified by an act of its legislature could therefore by a similar instrument legally override provisions of the constitution or laws made under its authority, or indeed revoke its original assent and withdraw from the Union entirely. Even if the state had not taken the trouble to back up its recalcitrance with legislation, it could safely ignore the presumed imperatives of the federal government under the Constitution, for like treaties, the Articles and the laws made under them carried no coercive penalty administered by an authoritative agency.[12]

On the other hand, a convention of delegates elected specifically for the purpose of ratification would bypass the state government, with its institutionalized jealousy of federal power and its responsiveness to "local demagogues," and would control state legislation and state constitutions by acting in the name of the ultimate authority, the people at large. "A system founded on the Legislatures only, and one founded on the people," observed Madison, was "the true difference between a league or treaty, and a Constitution."[13]

Ratification by this procedure, according to Madison, would be not only popular but also national: the act of a single sovereign power, "the great body of citizens of the United States." Madison made that point clear in *Federalist* 46, where he discussed how the people function in their two capacities, as the common source of the authority of all governments, state and federal, and as the common control on their behavior. While he was mainly concerned in this paper with the latter role of the people as governmental sovereign, at its start he emphasized their constituent sovereignty. Invoking an analogy not with the law of contract but with the law of agency, he observed that "the federal and State governments are in fact but different agents and trustees of the people, constituted with different powers, and designed for different purposes." Hence, he concluded, "the authority, wherever the derivative may be found [that is, in the state or in the federal government], resides in the people alone." And by "the people" he meant not the separate peoples of the several states but, in his words "the great body of citizens of the United States." It was this body of individuals which was the constituent sovereign, the source of authority of both levels of government. Hamilton had made the same point in *Federalist* 22 when he concluded that "the streams of national power ought to flow immediately from that pure, original fountain of all legitimate authority, THE CONSENT OF THE PEOPLE."[14]

Only a few weeks before setting down this nationalist version of constituent sovereignty, Madison offered what surely seems to be a quite incompatible view. In *Federalist 39*, replying to a charge of Brutus, a noted Anti-Federalist writer usually thought to have been Robert Yates, a delegate from New York to the Philadelphia convention, that the Constitution would establish a unitary republic based on a "consolidation of the States,"[15] Madison took up among various topics the method of ratification. When he called this method *foederal*, his meaning in the context can only be understood in the then conventional sense of *foedus*, or treaty, given it by the concept of compact federalism. "The Constitution," he said, will be "founded on the assent and ratification . . . by the people not as individuals composing one entire nation, but as composing the distinct and independent States to which they respectively belong. It is to be the assent and ratification of the several States, derived from the supreme authority in each State—the authority of the people themselves."[16]

That the process is "federal," he went on to argue, appeared in the fact that popular assent is given not by "a *majority* of the people of the Union," nor by "a *majority* of the States," but by "the *unanimous* assent of the several States that are parties to it, differing no otherwise from their ordinary assent than in its being expressed, not by the legislative authority, but by that of the people themselves." Continuing the emphasis on the process as compact, he declared: "Each state, in ratifying the Constitution, is considered as a sovereign body, independent of all others, and only to be bound by its own voluntary act."[17]

On this understanding of the method of ratification Madison's device of depending upon state conventions rather than state legislatures did eliminate one weakness of the old procedure. State law could not stand against federal law made under the Constitution, nor could a state legislature revoke the assent of the state, since the Constitution had been agreed by the constituent authority of the people of the state. Moreover, since the people of the state had the authority to change their constitution, their assent to the U.S. Constitution could authorize federal powers contravening provisions of the then existing state constitution.

Yet the fundamental flaw of compact federalism remained. What a constituent sovereign gives it can also take away. If the people of a state, acting as "a sovereign body," had ratified the Constitution, they could in the same capacity intervene as the final judge of infractions of the instrument so ratified, and act accordingly.

In a later generation when southern states' rightists sought to nullify acts of Congress and ultimately to take their states out of the Union, they took advantage of this fatal gap in Madison's reasoning by acting not through their state legislatures but through state conventions. In 1832 the state of South Carolina, carrying its opposition to the federal tariffs of 1828 and 1832 to the point of resistance, called a state convention, which, declaring the relevant acts of Congress unconstitutional and therefore null and void as law, forbade the federal collection of custom duties in the state. During the ensuing debate in the U.S. Senate, John C. Calhoun cogently stated the case for nullification in what may well seem an echo of Madison's reasoning in *Federalist* 39. "The people of the several states," he argued, ". . . are united as parties to a constitutional compact, to which the people of each state acceded as a separate sovereign community, each binding itself by its own particular ratification." By this compact "the people of the several states" delegated to the general government "certain definite powers." The general government—of which the federal judiciary headed by its Supreme Court is only a branch—cannot be "the final judge" of these delegated powers. On the contrary, "as in all other cases of compact among sovereign parties, without any common judge, each [state] has an equal right to judge for itself, as well of the infraction as of the mode and measure of redress."[18]

The argument fits what Madison said in *Federalist* 39. It also directly contradicts what he said in *Federalist* 46. According to *Federalist* 39, the Constitution derives its authority from "the people . . . as composing the distinct and independent States," but according to *Federalist* 46, from "the great body of citizens of the United States"—that is, from "the people . . . as individuals composing one entire nation," precisely the body which Madison in *Federalist* 39 had in these words denied would perform this office.

The problem is not merely one of textual criticism: that is, of identifying an apparent contradiction between two statements by Madison in the highly authoritative *Federalist* and seeing whether or not they can be reconciled. The conflict goes to the heart of the nationalist doctrine. As Calhoun's argument makes clear, the states' rights view of ratification powerfully supports the logic of nullification and secession, which on nationalist grounds are ruled out, except as a revolutionary last resort. A more important consequence of this conflict of ideas of ratification, however, is their opposing conceptions of the political body which takes part in and results from this process. If the Constitution is a compact among the states, then the Madisonian theory of the compound republic is ruled out. The nationalist view that the diversity of interests and ideas in the big republic can produce a public opinion which supports just and orderly government is denied, and along with it the belief that the individuals comprising "the great body of citizens of the United States" are "one people" capable of ordaining a constitution and of governing themselves under it.

If we go along with the states' rights view of ratification, we will conclude that the states and their respective peoples are the fundamental governmental and political units of the country; that is, the states are the communities within which our political values are principally determined and lived out and which therefore constitute the principal behavioral units of the politics of the nation as a whole. In comparison, any common life we have as a nation and as one people is thin and circumscribed. As Calhoun said, "The very idea of an *American People*, as constituting a single community, is a mere chimera."[19]

The National Solution

The conflict over the significance of ratification reflects this conflict over American political reality. The apparent contradiction between *Federalist* 39 and *Federalist* 46 powerfully focuses this deeply rooted conflict over what the United States is and continues to be. Nationalist theory has advanced three ways of coping with the apparent contradiction.

One was put forward by Madison himself in his later years when, confronted by the challenge of nullification explicitly and of secession implicitly, he strenuously sought to bar the way to disunion. His task was made more difficult by his authorship of the Virginia Resolutions of 1798 which the nullifiers, not without reason, cited in support of their cause.[20] While primarily concerned with distancing himself from this construction of his views, Madison also harked back to his thoughts in Federalist 39.[21] In various forms during the 1830s, he set out his view of ratification and its significance for the Union.[22] Putting himself in the nationalist camp, he firmly asserted that no single state had the power of nullification and rather less firmly denied that right to any number of states less than all. How he reached these conclusions is obscure. Repeatedly terming the Constitution "a compact," he seemed to say that at the time of the founding, constituent sovereignty was possessed, and had continued to be possessed thereafter, by the people of each state, but that it could be exercised only by the peoples of all the states acting together. "The sovereignty which makes . . . a Constitution," he wrote, " . . . resides not in a single state, but in the people of each of the several states, uniting with those of the others in the express and solemn compact which forms the Constitution." This constituent sovereign, consisting of all the separate state peoples, not the Supreme Court of the federal government, was, moreover, the final judge of infractions of "the constitutional compact." Similarly, while no single state, or number of states less than all, could nullify or secede, all the states by votes of their respective peoples could dissolve the Union, leaving the individual states intact as sovereign and independent polities.[23]

This line of theory does produce a kind of constituent sovereign consisting of a conglomerate of all the states acting as separate peoples. It does not reconcile Federalist 39 with Federalist 46, which found constituent sovereignty in "the great body of citizens of the United States." Indeed, by a further modification Madison seems to desert that fundamental position of nationalist theory brought forward by him at the start of Federalist 46, where he had contended that the problem of divided sovereignty was solved by the action of the people as "the common superior" of both levels of government. Taking an opposite tack in his final observations in 1835-36, Madison wrote that "the people of the several States must be a sovereign as they are a united people," but this was only "to the extent of that compact or Constitution." Expanding on that qualification, he said that the states are "sovereign" with regard to their "attributes," as the United States is "sovereign" with regard to its "attributes."[24]

Madison had made much the same point in a letter of March 16, 1833, to Daniel Webster, while commenting on Webster's reply to Hayne. There he stated his agreement with Webster's view of nullification and his disagreement with Webster's nationalist view of constituent sovereignty. Elaborating on his contrary conception that "the Constitution was made by the people, but as embodied in the several States that were parties to it," Madison concluded that this compact made the people of the several states "one people, nation, or sovereignty for certain purposes" but "not so for others."[25] Sovereignty, in short, was radically and ultimately divided between the federal government on one hand and the states on the other, certain powers going to one level, other powers to the other, with no "common superior," no "one people," which authorized each or which could judge and control them. In the light of this argument, in sum, there is no constituent sovereign even in the conglomerate sense. The citizen confronted by conflicting imperatives arising from different readings of the Constitution by the two "sovereign" governments could not know where to look for legitimacy. Terming this conclusion Madison's "straddle," Professor Amar observes that it had no followers.[26]

A second nationalist view copes with the apparent contradiction by reading the two conflicting descriptions in Madison's account as referring to two stages or aspects of a single process. In this view of ratification, the peoples of the several states first formed themselves into one American people, who thereupon, acting as the constituent sovereign, ordained the Constitution. Madison does suggest such a twofold process by his continual use of two terms, "assent and ratification," meaning quite conceivably "to consent and to confirm," when saying how the new frame of government would be constituted.[27]

It is worth considering how the two-stage model might find support in a theory of state-founding that was familiar to the framers. For John Locke also there are two stages in the origin of government. First a number of individuals consent to form one people, one political society or community, which then establishes a form of government with certain delegated powers and which under certain circumstances can intervene to reform or reconstitute that government.[28] By analogy one could think of the formation of the Constitution as a two-stage process in which the individual states, like the individual persons of Locke's account, first formed one body which then established the frame of government. During the controversy over the Constitution spokesmen on both sides often thought in terms of social contract theory. While defending the supremacy clause in *Federalist* 33, Hamilton attempted to bolster his argument by arguing that just as individuals who enter into a society must submit to the laws of that society as the supreme regulator of their conduct, so also when a number of political societies form a larger political society, the laws of the latter must be supreme over those societies and their members. From this account, however, one cannot tell how, or whether, he would fit the analogy to his nationalist premises. To reason by analogy in this manner between states and individuals makes more sense for the Anti-Federalists since they did attribute "individuality" to the states. When elaborating his Anti-Federalist argument, Luther Martin asserted that independence put the former states into a state of nature with one another which they remedied by a social compact creating an "alliance," not a "consolidated republic."[29]

Madison's references to ratification as both a compact among state peoples and an ordinance of one American people, appearing respectively in *Federalist* 39 and *Federalist* 46, are made so confidently and come so close to one another in point of time that one finds it hard not to feel that somehow, with or without help of the Lockean analogy, Madison reconciled the seeming conflict in his thought. Attributing such a reconciliation to Madison, Professor A. R. Amar has recently presented a two-stage view of ratification as a meta-legal theory justifying the constituent sovereignty of a unitary American people. Acting in the conventions of the several states, he writes, the previously sovereign peoples agreed to reconstitute themselves into one common sovereign, the unitary national people. Only then, he continues, did the United States become a nation. And it was this nation, this people, who also in the process of ratification ordained the Constitution. The most important thing accomplished by the Constitution, he concludes, was to bring into existence this one, sovereign national people.[30] "It was by these very acts," he writes, "that previously separate state Peoples agreed to 'consolidate' themselves into a single continental people . . . The ratifications themselves . . . formed the basic social compact by which formerly distinct sovereign Peoples, each acting in convention, agreed to reconstitute themselves into one common sovereignty."[31]

This two-stage version of ratification has merits. Its conclusion confirms the central claim of national theory that one sovereign power, the people of the extended republic, ordained the Constitution. It bridges the gap in Madison's exposition in *Federalist* 39 and 46 and gives a more plausible account of his thought at the time of the founding than do his own attempts two generations later. Yet it has grave failings as theory and as history. Its weakness as theory is that it concedes Calhoun's major premise that the Constitution was an agreement among several sovereign communities. It therefore invites the inferences drawn from this premise by nullifiers and secessionists.

This weakness as theory depends on the two-stage version's weakness as history. As a report of a series of events that occurred in the real world of the American 1770s and 1780s, it is unconvincing. The two-stage account of ratification requires us to believe that the great body of citizens who took part in that process had theretofore remained dispersed in thirteen separate political communities during their agitation against British rule, their declaration of independence, their long war effort, and their years of self-government after victory, but now in the brief period of a few months in 1787–88 transformed themselves into "the American people." One can conceive this, but one cannot imagine it. The two-stage description may satisfy the logical requirements of the meta-legal theory necessary to give legitimacy to the law of the Constitution, but it jars with one's knowledge of how a people, a nation, actually comes into existence and with the record of how that happened in America.

In this instance, as generally, contract theory is a poor guide to history. We do better to disregard its appealing speculations and found our theory on the more empirical basis of history, in the manner of Harrington, who based his utopian sketch on what he took to be the real possibilities revealed by the behavior of a particular society in a recent recorded past.

History and theory, common sense and political science, are better served by a third nationalist view. The core of the idea is that the sovereign American people, who did ordain the Constitution, far from having been constituted by the various state peoples at the time of ratification, had already existed for a generation and indeed was the sovereign power which had created the states in the first place and which had given them such authority as they did or ever would possess.

Rooted in Commonwealth thought, confirmed by the events of the agitation and the revolution, expressed by Federalist spokesmen during the debates in Philadelphia and ratification, developed by jurists and statesmen during the early nineteenth century, and summarized in the classic language of Lincoln's reply to secession, this one-stage unitary nationalist view of the Constitution and its ratification was given its first comprehensive formulation by James Wilson of Pennsylvania. After Madison the leading mind at the Philadelphia convention, Wilson advanced his view at the very start of the ratifying process in several speeches at the Pennsylvania state convention late in 1787. His ideas were promptly taken up by advocates of the Constitution in other states and became, as Gordon Wood has said, "the basis of all Federalist thinking."[32]

The timing was fortunate. In the debate over the Constitution, as Wood tells the story, sovereignty had quickly become the central issue. The Anti-Federalists in their defense of the existing Confederation claimed that the Constitution would create a "divided sovereignty" which could not last and, if adopted, would lead to a consolidated regime. "The problem of sovereignty," declares Wood, "was the most powerful obstacle to the acceptance of the new Constitution the opponents could have erected." Madison's initial attempt at rebuttal, echoing *Federalist* 39, that the Constitution was "not completely consolidated, nor . . . entirely federal," could not cope with the Anti-Federalist attack, which was grounded in the near universal belief of the time in a sovereignty that was supreme and indivisible.[33]

By contrast, Wilson, in his defense of the Constitution, argued that sovereignty was unconditional, popular, constituent, and national. Like his opponents, accepting the Blackstonian position, he agreed that "in all governments, whatever their form, however they may be constituted, there must be established a power from which there is no appeal, and which is therefore called absolute, supreme, and uncontrollable." Unlike Blackstone, however, he located this power of the American system not in any government, federal or state. "It resides in THE PEOPLE, as the fountain of government," he declared, using the same metaphor as Hamilton in *Federalist* 22. This sovereignty of the people was constituent in that it could delegate authority and also modify or take back what it had delegated. Hence, a federal system was possible, as was a reform of that federal system. "The power both of the general government and the State governments, under this system," he said, "are acknowledged to be so many emanations of power from the people." The people, therefore, "can distribute one portion of power to the more contracted circle called State governments; they can also furnish another proportion to the government of the United States." This power, he asserted, is superior to any and every constitution, state or federal.[34]

A crucial focus of the Pennsylvania debate was the phrase characterizing "We, the People of the United States" as the authority which ordained the Constitution. This meant, declared Wilson, that the Constitution was not "a compact" but "an ordinance of the people." His Anti-Federalist opponents, we must note, granted this meaning of the Constitution and precisely for that reason urged its rejection on the grounds that, so understood, it would destroy "the old foundation of the Union" by excluding "the principle of confederation."[35] That principle, which conceived the Constitution as a compact, left constituent sovereignty with the several states. By contrast, as an ordinance, the Constitution expressed the command of the one sovereign power, the people at large of the United States.

In making these assertions Wilson was in effect restating with some elaboration the argument of *Federalist* 46 where Madison refuted the charge of divided sovereignty and asserted the doctrine of national sovereignty and national federalism. Wilson, however moved beyond Madison's two-stage version of the founding when he presented the historical ground of his theory of sovereignty. In his speech of November 26, 1787, having asserted the claims of national sovereignty, he continued marking out the un-Madisonian direction of his thought:

> When the principle is once settled that the people are the source of authority, the consequence is that they may take from the subordinate governments powers with which they have hitherto trusted them, and place those powers in the general government, if it is thought that they will be productive of more good.[36]

This sentence, hinging on "hitherto," expresses the nationalist view of our constitutional history that the reallocation of power by the Constitution from state to federal government was simply a further exercise of the constituent sovereignty which the American people had exercised in the past, as when they brought the states themselves into existence.

At issue with the two-stage version as well as the states' rights position of the Anti-Federalists, was the question of precedence: which came first, the American people or the peoples of the several states? At the constitutional convention a few months earlier, Wilson had taken the lead in arguing for national precedence. In a thumbnail sketch of constitutional history supporting his argument, he observed that among "the first sentiments" expressed by the Continental Congress of 1774–75 was the opinion that Virginia, Massachusetts, and other colonies were "no more." The general sense was: "We are now one nation of brethren. We must bury all local interests and distinctions." Then came the formation of the States, which were "trusted" with certain powers by the sovereign people. Now "the tables at length began to turn. No sooner were the State Governments formed than their jealousy and ambition began to display themselves." "Each," he went on, in a metaphor reminiscent of Harrington's fable of the two girls cutting the cake, "endeavoured to cut a slice from the common loaf, to add to its own morsel, till at length the confederation became frittered down to the impotent condition in which it now stands." As evidence of this decline he invited the delegates to "review the progress of the Articles of Confederation thro Congress," leading to the present "want of an effectual control in the whole over its parts."[37]

Crucial to the nationalist view was the significance of the Declaration of Independence. Presenting a typical Anti-Federalist opinion, Luther Martin declared that "the separation from G.B. placed the thirteen States in a state of nature towards each other." Hotly denying that "when the colonies became independent of G. Britain, they became independent also of each other," Wilson then "read the Declaration of Independence," which states that it was "by the Authority of the good people of these colonies" that "these United Colonies, had been declared free and independent states." "The United Colonies," asserted Wilson, were declared independent of Britain "not individually, but Unitedly."[38]

On more than one occasion, Wilson and his nationalist allies at the federal convention asserted that the states had never been sovereign at any time before or after independence. Rufus King emphasized the inferior position in international relations. The States, he said, "did not possess the peculiar features of sovereignty, they could not make war, nor peace, nor alliances nor treaties." Even under the Articles, "a Union of the States is a Union of the men composing them, from whence a national character results to the whole." With regard to domestic matters, Madison emphasized the limitations on the authority of the states, saying, not without some exaggeration, that the laws of the states "in relation to the paramount law of the Confederacy were analogous to that of bye laws to the supreme law within a State." Although something of an Anti-Federalist, Elbridge Gerry, reminding delegates that he had been a member of the Continental Congress at the time the Articles were framed, "urged that we never were independent States, were not such now, and never could be on the principles of the Confederation."[39] As Professor Richard Morris has concluded, "the overwhelming number of Founding Fathers supported the view that the United States in Congress Assembled acted in the capacity of an independent sovereign state."[40]

Joseph Story's Classic Exposition

The propositions, historical and theoretical, advanced by James Wilson at the federal convention and during ratification embrace the main points of what has been termed the classic exposition of the unitary nationalist theory of sovereignty set down by Joseph Story in his *Commentaries on the Constitution of the United States* (1833).[41] Story, a Jeffersonian Republican from Massachusetts, appointed to the Supreme Court in 1811 by Madison, and from 1829 Dane Professor of Law at Harvard, prefaced his commentaries with a constitutional history of the colonies before the adoption of the Constitution. A summary of his more formal exposition will bring out the coherence of Wilson's various statements of the nationalist point of view.

Story's main historical thesis was that the Continental Congress, which he termed "the first general or national government," was organized not by the colonies or states but "with the consent of the people acting directly in their primary sovereign capacity, and without the intervention of the functionaries, to which the ordinary powers of government were delegated in the colonies." Illustrating the extra-constitutional origin of the Continental Congress, he notes that initially its members were chosen not by colonial governments but by the popular branch of colonial legislatures or by conventions. The lack of constitutional continuity with the previous regime made this body "a revolutionary government," which lasted until the adoption of the Articles of Confederation in 1781. Emphasizing its direct connection with the people, he commented: "The Congress, then assembled, exercised *de facto* and *de jure* sovereign authority; not as the delegated agents of the governments *de facto* of the colonies [that is, the British regime], but in virtue of original powers derived from the people."[42]

As in Story's treatise, the Continental Congress may properly be termed a "government," occupied as it was for most of its fourteen years with such duties as fighting a war, raising an army, borrowing money, making alliances, and regulating trade with other countries.[43] It may also be seen as an early and major example of that great American invention, the constitutional convention embodying the constituent sovereignty of the people. Its three principal acts in this latter capacity appear in Story's account: its declaration of independence, its authorization of state governments, and its role in drafting and recommending for adoption the Articles of Confederation.

Taking up the question of independence, Story observed that at the time of their separation from Britain, the colonies were already under the "dominion of a superior controlling national government whose powers were vested in the general Congress with the consent of the people of all the states." At the moment of independence, therefore, the colonies "did not severally act for themselves, and proclaim their independence." The Declaration was "the united act of all." This "united act," moreover, was not the act of state governments or of people who had been chosen by such governments but was "implicitly the act of the whole people of the united colonies."[44]

The transition from colonies to states, moreover, had taken place before independence when the Continental Congress had "authorized the formation of new governments in the states." To its rebellious constituencies, the Congress had "recommended" that they adopt new governments, which they did, according to Story, "in compliance" with those recommendations. It followed that none of the states so formed were or pretended to be sovereign in the Blackstonian sense of having "supreme, absolute and uncontrollable power." For, declared Story, "in our republican form of government, the absolute sovereignty of the nation is in the people of the nation." Distinguishing between two sorts of sovereignty, one "absolute," the other "subordinate," he explained that although the states were sometimes called sovereign, as, for instance, in the letter of Congress to the states in 1777 recommending ratification of the Articles, this meant sovereign in the "subordinate" sense of "exercising within a limited extent certain usual powers of sovereignty." Neither before nor after the independence were the states sovereign "in any absolute sense," as they would have been if they had declared their independence separately and then had sent delegates to form a league or alliance.[45]

As for the Articles of Confederation, since the sovereign people did not ratify them, the Confederation rested on "no better foundation than the consent of the state legislatures." By contrast, the Constitution was not made or ratified by the states as sovereignties or political communities but was rather adopted in state conventions, by "the immediate representatives of the people." Repeatedly, Story denied that the Constitution was a compact. It is rather, he said, a fundamental ordinance or law. In this respect the U.S. Constitution is like the state constitutions, which are not compacts in the sense of being merely contracts but are fundamental laws prescribed by the sovereign power in the state, the majority of its people. With approval he quoted James Wilson's assertion that the Constitution is not a compact but a government founded on the power of the people, since, as Wilson concluded with a flourish, "there can be no compact unless there are more parties than one." While rejecting the idea of a compact, however, Story heartily approved Madison's statement in *Federalist* 39 that the frame of government is "partly national and partly federal," his meaning of federal, being, of course, national federalism. The reason for the federal division of authority, he said, was to protect liberty, since each state moved "by love of its government and of the Union" would act to check the federal government and "to enlighten public opinion."[46]

James Wilson was prescient in his anticipation of the theory of national federalism which came to dominate political discourse on the nature of the Union. His brief reconstruction of the constitutional history on which he based this theory was also, as far as it goes, faithful to the facts, when compared with the more scholarly account of Story and with the history summarized in the present chapter and in chapters 6 and 10. The fundamental fact was the demonstration by a large part of the inhabitants of the thirteen colonies that they could act as a unified political body: that they could so act in criticizing and resisting British colonial rule and in establishing in its place a government under their control, and, when that government failed, in constituting a new and more effective system.

This body of persons shared a common political ideology largely shaped by the republican tradition of the Commonwealth, which set them apart as the whig party. They are properly called a party. They did not include all "the people," if you mean by that everyone living in those colonies. Far from it. The larger part—perhaps fifty to seventy per cent[47]—of adult white males had the franchise. But even among the politically active part of this number, the whigs confronted a substantial opposition, the tory party. Although, however, in this sense limited, the whig party was a continent-wide movement, which, sharing common political values and demands and linked by a network of communication and action, competed for power with the tories in all the colonies. In other parts of the British empire in

America whigs were also active, but only in the thirteen contiguous colonies along the coast did they succeed in defeating the colonial regime, thereby determining the boundaries of the new nation. Within those boundaries, the whigs were the incipient nation[48] sufficiently numerous to claim that they spoke for "the people," or as (perhaps recognizing their partiality) they sometimes called themselves, "the *good people*" (their emphasis) of these colonies.

The jurisdictions of colonial rule established by the British were the arenas within which this contest took place. The units of political behavior, however, were not these separate colonies, as political or as governmental units. The whig party was a coalition, but not a coalition of whig colonies in combat with a coalition of tory colonies. No colony was wholly whig or wholly tory. The whigs were a continental coalition of various interests and several shades of republican ideology, exemplifying the pluralism of the extended republic perceived by Madison. Yet this coalition held together for more than a generation, directing the agitation and conducting the war, thereby astonishing our enemies and even some of our friends, such as Edmund Burke, by vindicating the republican faith that the many have the capacity to govern themselves. As such a behavioral unit, the whig coalition may properly be regarded as "one people," the political force that brought the new system into existence, and solid factual ground for James Wilson's meta-legal theory, identifying "the people" as the sovereign power of the new republic.

As Wilson perceived, the establishment of the states did introduce an organizational base for the disruption of the original unity. During the struggle over constitutional reform, the whig coalition was divided by deeply rooted differences over practical and normative questions. Both Federalists and Anti-Federalists, however, were republicans, in great part the same people who had fought the good fight against British colonialism. Sharp as the Anti-Federalist criticism of the Constitution had been, the divisions arising during the controversy quickly dissolved. The very state legislatures that had blocked reform facilitated the adoption of the new frame of government. While ratification of the Articles of Confederation had taken four years, within a little more than a year of the conclusion of the federal convention, a national election was held under the provisions of the Constitution. Compliance with the demands of the new government by individuals and states was more prompt and complete than it had been with the lesser demands of the Confederation. By the time of election of 1792, the issues of the debate over ratification had subsided.

Critique of Article VII

Both the Wilsonian and the Madisonian view of ratification controvert the states' rights thesis that the Constitution is a compact agreed by the several states exercising their authority as the ultimate constituent sovereignties. By contrast, both nationalist views share the postulate that the people of the United States ratified the Constitution as the sole and unitary sovereign. The Wilsonian interpretation makes a stronger case in theory for that postulate by avoiding the tortured history of the Madisonian two-stage version. If the nation was sovereign enough to authorize the creation of the states and to declare and to secure their independence, it was surely also the power called into action to reform the defective government erected by the Articles. The Madisonian concession that the states were sovereign until ratification opens the way to the extrapolation that these bodies politic continued, even after the new delegation of power to the Constitution, to retain the sovereignty they had enjoyed for more than a decade, which capacity arguably was further displayed in ratification by state action.

Theoretically the Wilsonian view is tighter and historically it is more faithful to the facts. It is clearly the superior adversary of the states' rights view. But the question remains: can it best the opposition? Which makes the better fit with the facts of ratification, the Wilsonian nationalist view or the states' right view? It will facilitate the comparison to look at the three elements of the process—the vote by convention, the count by states, and ratification by nine.

We may first look at the rule of nine, since in the final analysis that is the key to the answer. This succinct provision of Article VII that "the ratification of the conventions of nine States shall be sufficient for the establishment of this Constitution between the States so ratifying the same" may seem to be a requirement of unanimity, comparable to Article XIII of the charter of the Confederation, which required the assent of "every State" of the thirteen for amendment of that charter, as in the original ratification of the charter itself. So Madison regarded it when he argued in *Federalist* 39 that "the act establishing the Constitution would be the act of the people, as forming so many independent States, not as forming one aggregate nation," and cited in support of this view that it would "result from the unanimous assent of the several states that are parties to it."[49]

If we look at the legislative history of this provision and at its effect on the process of ratification, its meaning, however, is quite different. When the delegates at Philadelphia took up this question on August 30, 1787, after having already decided on a vote by state conventions, they were much concerned with finding a decision rule for counting ratifications that would bind all thirteen states by a less than unanimous count. The draft Article before them read simply, "The ratifications of (blank) States shall be sufficient for organizing this Constitution." The numbers suggested ranged from seven to thirteen, reflecting sentiments running from the more to the less nationalist.[50]

So long as the delegates tried to answer the question within this framework, however, they faced a dilemma. If the old rule of the Confederation requiring the assent of all thirteen were adopted, the door would be opened for one or a few states to use their veto in order to exact special privileges or indeed in order to block the whole enterprise, a possibility exemplified by experience under the Confederation. If the decision rule were less than all, on the other hand, dissenting states might well refuse to be bound, thereby choosing to stay out of the Union. The "republican principle," to be sure, was majority rule, but no such procedure had been adopted by some preceding Lockean agreement of all with all. Despite Wilson's appeal along these lines to "go to the original powers of Society," even so ardent and sensible a nationalist as Rufus King felt obliged to say at the end of the day's session that the old rule of thirteen was necessary, "otherwise as the Constitution now stands it will operate on the whole though ratified by a part only."[51]

Reflecting an overnight change of mind, King opened the next day's session with a proposal that broke through this restrictive framework of decision-making. His amendment confined "the operation of the Government to the States ratifying it," the number nine thereupon being fairly easily agreed.[52] The intended effect was made clear during the course of ratification when the rule of nine led to the assent of all thirteen, but without giving any a veto. A case in point was New York. There the revenue from an impost on merchandise flowing through the state had created a powerful interest opposed to the commerce clause of the Constitution. Despite the brilliant argumentation of Publius in the newspapers of the state, the Anti-Federalists had won a solid majority in the ratifying convention. Obliged, however, by the news of ratification by nine other states to consider a future outside the Union, the convention changed its mind and gave its assent.[53]

The new procedure did not impose the rule of a majority, not even an extraordinary majority, nor did it require unanimity. Yet it resulted in the assent of all the states. This way of coping with the dilemma of ratification had already been intimated by James Wilson during a brief discussion on June 5th. Expressing the fear that the requirement of unanimity would enable "a few States" to defeat the scheme, Wilson proposed that a smaller number—Charles Coatesworth Pinckney immediately suggested nine—be adopted, "with a door left open for the accession of the rest."[54]

The change in the decision rule on August 31st, which brought about this result, was a clever device conceived by men not unaccustomed to rational choice thinking. Its effect was not a crude exercise of majority power which forced New York to join the Union against its wishes. On the contrary, the new rule simply gave each state an incentive to consider its long-run as well as its short-run interests. In this respect, the revised rule exemplified a familiar feature of other provisions of the Constitution, which typically sought so to structure decision-making as to heighten the rationality of government by discussion.

We may now turn to the nationalist case for the vote by conventions and the count by states. The first of these rules was a central issue dividing fairly neatly Federalists from Anti-Federalists. Pronounced Anti-Federalists, such as Luther Martin, Roger Sherman, and Oliver Ellsworth, clung to ratification by the state legislatures.

Delegates who felt that the federal government must have a new normative basis for its powers, however, insisted on vote by convention. Rufus King, an ardent nationalist, although not denying that the state legislatures were "competent" to ratify, thought that "a reference to the authority of the people expressly delegated to Conventions" was "the most certain means of obviating all disputes and doubts concerning the legitimacy of the new Constitution." George Mason, who was something of an Anti-Federalist on the question of centralization, came to the same conclusion for much the same reason, the need for "a reference of the plan to the authority of the people."[55]

Thinking of the experience of states such as Massachusetts, where the constitutional convention had been developed, however, one may wonder why such approval could not have been given by one general convention, chosen by the voters of a nationwide constituency and acting for the whole country by a majority or greater vote of its delegates. What could be more national, more popular? The possibility had been suggested in the original Virginia Plan, which in its fifteenth Resolution provided that the proposals of the Philadelphia convention be "submitted to an assembly or assemblies of Representatives, recommended by the several Legislatures to be expressly chosen by the people, to consider and decide thereon." And during a discussion of ratification on July 23rd, Gouverneur Morris put the idea to the delegates. Having declared that "the people of the U.S., the supreme authority," could alter the fundamental law "by a majority of them; in like manner as the Constitution of a particular State may be altered by a majority of the people of the States," he proposed that the Constitution be presented to "one general Convention, chosen and authorized to consider, *amend,* and establish the same."[56]

This seemingly sensible proposal found no support. A procedure to get ratification which could reasonably be perceived as rendered by "a majority of the people" was not unfeasible within the understanding of that term, "the people," among delegates. If there could be a national House of Representatives which, in the words of Article I of the Constitution, represented "the people of the United States," there could also be a national convention, larger in membership if judged necessary, but similarly representative of the people and capable of making decisions on their behalf. According to Article I, the members of the House would be chosen in each state by electors qualifying under the state electoral laws and would be allotted to each state so that there would be one member for no less than thirty thousand members of the "population," calculated as the total number of free people, excluding Indians not taxed, and including three fifths of "all other persons," that is, slaves. On this understanding, thirty-three members of the House, its total having been temporarily set at sixty-five, would represent a majority of "the people." Madison similarly used the number of members from each state as an index of its "people." On the basis of such an index the Constitution could have provided for a procedure of ratification by a general convention comprised of a comparable number of delegates to be elected in each state, according to its procedures and franchise.

The plan was conceivable, but the drawbacks were considerable. Two stand out. One was that such a gathering would in effect redo what the delegates at Philadelphia had already done. This had been suggested in the Virginia Plan when it said that a ratifying assembly would "consider" as well as "decide" on the proposals, a point made quite specific in Gouverneur Morris's motion emphasizing the word "amend." When explaining their reasons for not signing the completed draft, Governor Edmund Randolph and George Mason, champions respectively of a more and a less "vigorous" federal government, also expressed their desire for "another general Convention," thereby revealing the conflicts which would again divide such an assembly.[57]

Nor, to come to the second flaw in this proposal, can one imagine that such a general convention could have acted as a constituent assembly, as required by Morris's provision that it "establish" a new constitution. Ratification would still have been necessary. By this time public opinion required such a further indication of popular approval, as provided in the two-step model of Oceana, recently developed in the states and ultimately embodied in the amendment procedure of Article V of the Constitution.

The republican demand for approval by "a majority of the people," which Morris's plan had sought to satisfy, still remains to be considered. During the final discussion of ratification on August 30th and 31st, which centered on the question of "how many states?" this further question of "how many people?" was a closely related concern. Madison voiced it specifically when suggesting that the rule for ratification call for approval of at least a majority of the states, which would be seven, and at least a majority of the people, which would mean approval by states entitled to at least 33 members of the House. The rule of nine met the second as well as the first requirement, but without saying so. Calculated according to the index of representation in the House, as proposed by Madison, any nine states would have had not only a majority of the states but also a majority of the population. According to Article I of the Constitution, representatives would be allotted to the states as follows: Rhode Island, 1; Delaware, 1; New Hampshire, 3; Georgia, 3; New Jersey, 4; Connecticut, 5; North Carolina, 5; South Carolina, 5; Maryland, 6; New York, 6; Massachusetts, 8; Pennsylvania, 8; Virginia, 10. Ordering the states from smallest to largest and counting upward from the smallest, one reaches 33 members as soon as nine states are counted. The eight smallest states, which are reached with the Carolinas, total 27; the next smallest, which could be New York or Maryland, would make a total of 33.[58]

That nationalists were thinking along these lines is indicated by Madison's interventions.[59] The object of his more complicated procedure requiring two sorts of counting was achieved by the simple rule of nine. That rule not only solved the problem of maximizing consent by states without courting a veto but also more than met the nationalist need for popular ratification by securing approval by an overwhelming majority of the people of the extended republic. In essentials, this procedure rejected the Anti-Federalists' position. The rejection of ratification by state legislatures was their most signal defeat. Concession on that point would have clearly preserved state sovereignty and, more important, the vision of the small republic as the primary political community of the country. Hardly less significant and for the same reason was the defeat of the old rule of unanimous ratification which had been followed in the adoption of the Articles of Constitution and required for constitutional amendment by that document. Concessions to Anti-Federalist sentiments can be found in the wording of the procedure adopted and certainly in the rhetoric of its defense by nationalist spokesmen during the ratification debates. On balance, however, the assertion of the Preamble that it was "We, the People of the United States" who "do ordain and establish this constitution" was a fair and faithful summary of the facts of ratification.

Sovereignty, the Constitution, and Democracy

In their struggle to limit the exercise of parliamentary sovereignty, the dissident colonists had at times denied the doctrine of sovereignty itself. "Supreme or unlimited authority," replied the Massachusetts counselors to Governor Hutchinson in 1769, "can with fitness belong only to the sovereign of the universe."[60] Yet as resistance blossomed into revolution, the rebels were obliged to appeal precisely to such a power, which could withdraw law-making power from one government and vest it in another and which, therefore, being the body that authorized certain human agencies to make law, could not itself be limited by that law. It would seem that the Americans were positing an authority that was at once unlimited by positive human law and yet limited by it.

The confusion, not to say self-contradiction, was cleared up by the distinction between two sorts of sovereignty. One sort of sovereignty, consisting of the power to overthrow and to reconstitute governments, was necessarily unlimited by the law made by such governments. Another sort of sovereignty, consisting of the powers vested in governments by the law of the constituent power, was supreme in the sphere given it by that human law, but also *a fortiori* limited by it. These two sorts of sovereignty were exercised by the same human agency, the people of the United States, who, exercising their constituent sovereignty, declared their independence and in due course ratified the Constitution, and, thereafter, exercising their governmental sovereignty, governed themselves under its law.[61]

So the Americans made their point against the British by establishing a government limited by positive man-made law. But they had also conceded the British point by granting the existence of a human law-making power unlimited by man-made law. The sphere of law in which such sovereignty was supreme and unlimited was the sphere of man-made law, the law made by human agencies, enforceable in courts and backed by governmental force. This authority which British jurisprudence ascribed to parliament and American jurisprudence to the American people, was not thought to free these agencies from divine or natural or moral law. Quite the contrary. Indeed, governments were established precisely in order to protect the rights of subjects/citizens prescribed by such norms and set forth in the theory that defined and justified sovereignty of one kind or the other.

For in both the American and the British cases, sovereignty in the sense of the ultimate authority in the state was founded not on a man-made law but on a theory. There could be no man-made law vesting sovereignty in parliament, since parliament was the ultimate author of such law. Its sovereignty, as conceived in the eighteenth century, was a conclusion of the theory of the balanced constitution. As expounded by Blackstone, that theory showed why parliament must have this "absolute despotic" power, if the rights of the subject were to be protected. No individual or body of persons within the British dominions, he pointed out, could be exempt from the law-making power of parliament, otherwise that exempt person or body of persons would be legally free to do whatever it pleased to any others, thereby depriving subjects generally of the protection of the law of parliament.[62]

That law offered that protection because of the composition of parliament. Thanks to virtual representation, parliament brought the wisdom of the realm to bear on its deliberations on the manifold interests of the empire. Thanks to the requirement that law be made by agreement among the king, lords, and commons, parliament balanced the participation of social classes in such a way that no class could disrupt the rule of law with regard to personal security and private property. Parliament in short was self-limiting in fact though not in law and therefore could be trusted with the legally unlimited authority indispensable to sustaining a social order in which the rights of the subject were protected. Because of this intrinsic self-limitation of parliament, it made no sense to add further checks, such as judicial review, as some American whigs suggested,[63] for that would only upset the judicious balance already achieved by the existing constitution.

According to nationalist theory, the American people in their constituent capacity were also such a legally unlimited power. "Confrontation with the Blackstonian concept of legal sovereignty," Gordon Wood has observed, "had forced American theorists to relocate it in the people-at-large."[64] As in Blackstone's jurisprudence, the nature of this agency imposed limits upon its activity. The limit emphasized by the nationalist idea of constituent sovereignty was not an arrangement of social classes or institutions but the scale and diversity of the extended republic. Thanks to their pluralism, the American people would display that tendency toward coalitions aiming at "justice and the general good." Self-limiting and self-directing, as set forth in Madisonian theory, the American people, in their constituent capacity, could be prudently considered, as James Wilson asserted, the "absolute, supreme, and uncontrollable" power above all law in the American polity.[65]

This constituent sovereign, one must emphasize, was not limited by positive law, not even by the law of the Constitution defining how the Constitution was to be amended, since that law too had been made by the constituent sovereign and so presumably could be overruled by it. As E. S. Corwin has remarked, the amending power, like all other powers organized in the Constitution, is "a delegated, and hence a limited power." "The one power known to the Constitution which clearly is not limited by it is that which ordains it—in other words, the original, inalienable power of the people of the United States to determine their own political institutions."[66]

This power to make and remake the constitutional framework, whether exercised as the original unlimited power of the people or as the amending power, was not the agent of normal, day-to-day governance. To say that there was a sovereignty which was constituent, that is, constitution-making, was to say that the government of the country would be conducted not directly by this unlimited power but under the limits of the Constitution established by it. In American constitutional thought of the nationalist persuasion sovereignty of both sorts, constituent and governmental, was exercised by the American people. In the latter capacity they were sovereign but, like "the people" in Harrington's Commonwealth, "upon conditions." Those conditions, laid down in the law of the Constitution, were sometimes restraints, such as those imposed mainly on the states in the body of the Constitution and those imposed on the Congress in the Bill of Rights. In general, however, the conditions were not so much limits for the sake of more restrained government as incentives for the sake of more rational government. The nationalists thought of the Constitution in this positive sense. Thomas McKean, an ally of James Wilson and chief justice of Pennsylvania, for instance, described it not as a set of restraints on government but as "a declaration of the people in what manner they choose to be governed."[67] Constitutionalism is sometimes thought of as hostile to democracy. In our beginning the leading spirits thought of the Constitution not as an impediment to self-government but as an instrument of it.

In nationalist theory, the constituent sovereign was "one people," acquiring both unity and legitimacy from its characteristics as the free and diverse population of the extended republic. This constituent power divided the attributes of sovereignty, that is, the various powers of governing, between the federal and the state governments. The American people, who governed themselves through these institutions, using them to make and to enforce laws in their respective spheres, were unitary. They were the political force which held to account the separated branches of the general government and the divided levels of the federal system. In that latter capacity they were the "common constituents" of both federal and state governments who, shifting their support from one level to another, used these institutions to maintain the constitutional equilibrium and to protect republican liberty and promote the public interest.

Similar as British constitutional doctrine was to American, it could not provide the grounds for a constitution on the American model. Both schools of thought posited an ultimate unlimited legal authority in the state. Both trusted to the balancing of institutions and blending of ideas to make government self-limiting and self-directing. In British thought the main block to constitutionalism in the American sense was the premise of virtual representation. On that premise the British might conceivably locate the foundation of parliamentary sovereignty in the deferential consent of the people at large to the rule of the wise (and the holy) at some time in the distant past. This deference and the implicit incapacity of the people, however, would permanently bar them from acting as the power which could legitimately overthrow and reconstitute government.

In the British view, therefore, the people at large could not ordain and establish a constitution stating in law the conditions under which parliament and other organs would govern. British government could be self-limiting in accordance with its inner mechanisms. It could not be limited or conditioned by a superior man-made law setting out the organs and procedures of government and the purposes, such as the protection of individual rights and the promotion of the public interest, which this government was to serve. Only the American commitment to popular sovereignty made possible the American idea of a government bound by the man-made law of a constitution. Our man-made constitution, to put the point a little differently, necessarily implies a constituent sovereignty exercised by the people at large. That constitution and the government it ordains acquires legitimacy and therefore can command the allegiance of its citizens because of the authority of the power ordaining it. That constituent power can claim legitimate authority because of its grounding in the democratic theory of the compound republic. Constitutionalism in America, in short, is not a barrier to, but an instrument of, democracy.

CHAPTER 11

James Wilson's
Social Union

IN THE CONSTITUTION, the American people declared "in what manner they choose to be governed." Legitimacy was also claimed for the Constitution for another hardly less powerful reason. The Constitution established government not only by the people but also for the people. It had a claim on their loyalty and obedience not only because of its republican structure of government but also because of its national vision of purpose; not only by reason of its statement of how power would be exercised but also by reason of its view of what that power would be used for.

Schumpeter suggested this further basis of constitutional legitimacy when, ridiculing the reasons the Americans gave for their revolution, he found that their great attachment to the new regime flowed not from its provisions for self-government but rather from the "prodigious development" following upon its creation. That development, with its veritable prodigies, was, however, by no means unforeseen or unintended by the authors of the Constitution. The Preamble recognizes a twofold basis of legitimacy. While concluding with its assertion of the popular foundation of the authority of the Constitution, the Preamble, as E. S. Corwin emphasized, also prefaces that assertion with a list of the "great objects"[1] which the new frame of government will serve: "a more perfect Union . . . Justice . . . domestic Tranquility . . . Defence . . . the general Welfare . . . and the Blessings of Liberty." Judging by what the framers said at the convention and during the ratification, the last of these was their primary object. But in their eyes republican liberty itself had a dual character, including not only the political rights intrinsic to self-gov-

341

ernment but also the rights of individual liberty, which such a government would presumably maintain. "Justice" would embrace the protection of these individual rights, while the promotion of "the general Welfare" looked to more contingent concerns of the common good. Order at home and peace abroad were instrumental to securing these ends, but also as security, an end in itself. "A more perfect Union" meant at least that stronger central government which was the immediate consequence to be hoped for from the Constitution.

The Federalists had sought this strengthening of central power as their principal reform, in order to make liberty more secure than it had been under the weak and illiberal governments of the Articles of Confederation. With equal zeal the reformers had also aimed to make the new republic not only a more free but also a more secure, a more prosperous, and a more virtuous nation, using the term "virtuous" in a modern, not a medieval or classical, sense of the word. In their vision the United States would be not a set of small, static, like-minded communities quietly hugging the Atlantic coast but a rich, powerful, diversified, and expanding nation, popular in its foundation and continental in its aspirations. In short, the Federalists framed the structure of authority of the new republic in the light of the purposes of national development they expected it to serve. The "more perfect Union" to which they aspired meant not only a less imperfect government but also a less imperfect nation.

One cannot doubt that for the people who made the Constitution, as for those who made the Revolution, self-government was a good in itself and a distinct ground of legitimacy. The advocates of the Constitution necessarily, therefore, were much concerned to show how the processes of the new regime would conform to this standard: how "the people of the United States" would ratify the Constitution and would then govern themselves under it by means of representative institutions which would, in Madison's words, "concenter" and "direct" the "will" of the people toward "the public good."[2] Their case for this authority structure, however, could not readily be separated from consideration of its consequences. The republican allocation of power was regarded not only as good in itself but also as a means to certain ends. The authors of The Federalist, as we have seen, continually extended their advocacy from demonstrations of the popular character of the new regime to confident calculations of the greater security, prosperity, and liberty it would bring to the nation. This is what one would expect from thoughtful people. "All political institutions and processes," Martin Diamond has said, "are intelligible only in the light of the purposes or ends for which men devise them or which, unintentionally, they come to serve."[3]

Purpose, Medieval and Modern

It will clarify the role of purpose in Madisonian constitutionalism if we look at it in a larger context of comparison and contrast. A glance back at the political tradition from which and against which, as we have seen in Chapter 1, republican ideas emerged will make the point. For what Thomistic and Madisonian constitutionalism have in common—and it is a great deal—will highlight their profound differences regarding the main questions of constitutional theory: legitimacy, consent, representation, rule of law, and, above all, the ends of government by which political institutions, such as federalism, are justified and made intelligible.[4]

Among the identities are those features which entitle both systems to be called "constitutional." The term "constitution" in its broad modern sense of the whole body of rules by which a country is governed, did not come into use until the seventeenth century and the term "constitutionalism" itself not until 1832.[5] Yet the features of political systems which those terms denote also appear in Thomistic theory. For one thing, both medieval and modern constitutionalism are not only descriptive but also normative. Both advance titles to "legitimacy," to use the term by which the framers of the American Constitution characterized the claim of a government to the obedience and loyalty of their citizens/subjects.[6]

In elaborating a claim to legitimacy, both Thomistic and Madisonian constitutionalism accepted its twofold basis. Both grounded their normative claims on a theory of proper means and proper ends, describing, explaining, and justifying the structure of authority and purposes it ought to serve. From that point of agreement, their trains of thought radically diverged.

For Aquinas the structure of authority was implicit in the differentiation of virtue. The rule of the wise and the holy was laid down in the eternal law which distinguished the few who ruled from the many who were ruled and which ranked the rulers themselves from higher to lower in a hierarchy under a single head. Although unambiguously hierarchic, government in the Thomistic conception was by consent, not by coercion. For Aquinas, however, this consent was the consent of deference, not participation. Subjects of lesser degree could not grasp the idea of the common good, let alone contribute to its formulation. Nor could they, apart from the guidance of their rulers, ascertain their individual good. They could, however, be brought to recognize and accept the legitimacy of the regime by the symbolism and myth surrounding their rulers. Coercion was necessary only for the wicked, who, unlike the good, refused to accept willingly the rule of the wise and the holy.

In accord with this flow of authority from above, representation likewise was from the top down. Its rationale was not delegation but personation, by which the ruler represented his people not because they chose him or imparted their wishes to him but because he embraced the whole panoply of virtues which any one of the ruled could possess only in part. Representation was of the virtues descending from above, rather than of the actual wishes arising from below. Appropriately, this conception gave rise to the theory of "virtual representation."

For Madison, on the other hand, consent meant government in which the many took part in deciding what was the common good. They did this not by direct democracy, as in the popular assemblies of ancient republics or in the referenda and plebiscites of modern times, but by a system of election and office-holding which subjected the representative to close and continuous supervision by the represented. It was hoped that the voters would choose as their representatives people of superior knowledge and good will. Primarily, however, the representatives rather than the represented were qualified to make the laws not because of their superior virtue but because their special position in the structure of deliberation. Yet it was the conditions and the interests of the represented which were the materials on which decisions were based. It was the represented who decided who would make those decisions and whether the decisions they made were satisfactory.

In comparison with the old system of elite rule, republican government by discussion would claim to be superior on two counts: it was open to the whole sweep of ideas and information in the society, and it was responsive to its whole array of interests. Under a properly designed constitution, therefore, republican government could be expected to excel, as Harrington claimed, in both understanding and will. Not the differentiation of virtue but the superior wisdom of the multitude elicited by the structure of the constitution was the ground of the authority of the law.

Both systems limited and directed the exercise of authority by defining the purposes for which it might be used. One such limitation was imposed by the "rule of law."[7] This means that any act of government must be authorized by a rule that is general, prospective, and limited in the scope of power it confers. Acts lacking that authorization are "arbitrary," as in the case of rewards and punishments administered according to the mere personal will or interest of the ruler or rulers and intended solely as benefits or burdens for one part of the society. This does not mean that the governmental act may not refer to one part of the society, but rather that it must have a rationale connecting it with the good of the society as a whole. To abide by the rule of law, therefore, implies that the government will be conducted for the common good, another aspect of constitutionalism shared by both medieval and modern embodiments.

The rule of law pervades Thomistic thought. For Aquinas, God Himself was subject to the eternal law in that it was impossible for Him, even in the exercise of His omnipotence, to deviate from that law, which was His essential being. When issuing His commandments He could no more violate the ultimate rules of right and wrong than He could alter the principles of logic and arithmetic. *A fortiori,* the governors of mankind, secular and ecclesiastical, as faint images of divine rule, were bound to follow that portion of the eternal law which had become known to them as the natural and the divine law. Any governmental imperative contrary to these general norms was no law but "a perversion of law."[8] Strictly, these rulers could not make law; they could only "declare" it.

When in this sense legislating, the will of the ruler was supreme in so far as there was no higher human authority that could overrule him. He was "sovereign." Yet this sovereignty attached to his will only because his wisdom, reflecting the eternal law, gave him a superior understanding of what was right and good and directed him to use his law-making power to forward those purposes. Although his authority as the sovereign who made such law was absolute— *legibus solutus*—since no one could overrule him, it could not be arbitrary because he was bound by the very law that gave him sovereignty.

American constitutionalism was not without parallels. In the Madisonian system also, the powers of federal and state governments were bound by a body of law with superior authority, namely, the law of the Constitution. Since this law authorized their existence and activity, legislation by them contrary to its imperatives was no law. In this constitutional theory, the People, as the sovereign power which established the fundamental law, were absolute because, being the source of the authority to make laws, no human agency had the legal authority to overrule it. Did this fundamental man-made law have a transcendental character like the higher law—eternal, divine, natural—of Thomistic theory? Clearly, in Madisonian as in Thomistic theory, the law of the Constitution did not acquire its normative character, its legitimacy, from the mere will of the sovereign. Indeed, the people were trusted with this ultimate authority because it was inferred that the scale and diversity of the extended republic would direct its will toward "justice and the general good." Recognizing a higher law in this sense, the People of Madisonian theory, like the virtuous ruler of Thomistic theory, could be absolute, because they would not be arbitrary.

The theoretical abyss between Thomistic and Madisonian constitutionalism appears not only in the different means by which the higher law was put into effect but also and indeed even more strikingly in the radically different way this higher law conceived the ends that government would serve. For Aquinas these ends, like the purposes of every kind of being in the divinely ordered cosmos, were fixed by the eternal law. This law, proceeding from the essences of the divine mind, embraced all possibility. Accordingly, the cosmos created in its image was perfect; that is, it lacked nothing, containing every possible kind of being. Created all at once, as it had to be, else the Perfect Being would have created something imperfect, this cosmos was unchanging in its completeness. To be sure, various kinds of being suffered recurring cycles of birth, growth, decay, and death. Man's sinfulness had set in motion a great drama of his fall and redemption, culminating in the last judgment. In this perfect cosmos, however, there could be no evolution, no development, no progress in kinds of being, or in their ends and ordering. In the economy, for instance, specialization, while making social life more productive, could not develop over time, since it was fixed in types and inherent in men's natures.

The fixity of the cosmic order was necessarily reflected in the fixity of the social order. The array of virtues was constant in number and type, consisting of the four classical and the three Christian virtues. Interdependent in operation, these virtues constituted a community of ends maintained by human law. Government served this community not by creating opportunities or incentives but directly by imposing on its subjects by positive law the imperatives of natural and divine law. Law maintained rights, but these were rights to do what was right as laid down by secular and ecclesiastical authority. Liberty was not to do what the individual thought was right but to do what was known to be right as taught and enforced by rightful rulers.

In this closed society one narrow avenue of change was open. Since, as Aquinas grants, human reason has been able to advance in its knowledge of the eternal law as embodied in the natural law, it is possible for the wise ruler in some degree to make new law reflecting such deeper comprehension. The truths of the faith expressed in the divine law, however, do not change, and this law, known to and declared by the priestly hierarchy, always controls the less authoritative truths of reason. Human reason, as Aquinas emphasizes, will err unless it is guided by faith.[9]

In sum, the purpose of government was to assist all men, rulers and ruled alike, toward the perfection of virtue and the achievement of their highest end, a saving vision of God. In the state this left little room for innovation and in the church none.

The paradox of Thomistic constitutionalism was severely to limit innovation by government, while calling for the widest intervention with individual thought and behavior. American constitutionalism reversed these priorities, as the culmination of the centuries-long effort of republican thought to cope with its rupture with medievalism. In contrast with the Thomistic model, Madisonian theory sharply restricted the power of government to intervene in individual action, but vastly widened the possibilities of innovation by collective action. The hinge on which this reversal turned was freedom of conscience. In the exercise of this freedom, citizens and their representatives, when taking part in self-government, were at liberty to look for guidance to a higher law. Being very largely disciples of the Reformation and in some degree pupils of the Enlightenment, Americans of that time agreed fairly widely on certain precepts of divine and natural law.[10] They did not, however, as required by Thomistic theory, share a uniform religious faith whose maintenance and enforcement was the first duty of secular as well as ecclesiastical government. On the contrary, in Madison's conception of the new republic, as in Milton's ideal, freedom of conscience was the individual's first right, from which was derived that "only effectual guardian of every other right," freedom of speech and the press.[11] The worst of all offenses in the Thomistic vision had become the first right of the individual in the Madisonian vision.

As in Milton's exposition, the case for religious freedom inevitably embraced freedom of thought in all matters, sacred and secular, political and nonpolitical. The same principle that restricted government intervention with individual thought and expression also opened the way for new ideas of how to achieve old ends individual and social, and indeed for new conceptions of those ends themselves. Change was built into the ideal basis of the society.

The federal element in republican and in Thomistic thought reflects these contrasting principles. In the Mosaic model sketched by Aquinas, the subordinate ruler and the community he ruled had a sphere of autonomy. His presence limited the "full power" of the "kingly authority" at the center. Rules with recognized authority limited the rule-making power of the center. There was in short a true federal government.[12]

The basis of this federal division was the cosmic principle which endowed each of the various components of the whole with a distinctive kind of being. A similar conception of community appears in the theory of compact federalism, which bases the rights of the member state upon its distinctive "individuality." These communities of the confederate republic, however, are self-sufficient, except for a few external requirements, otherwise neither needing nor contributing to a larger whole. In the Thomistic polity, on the other hand, local jurisdictions are integrated parts of a larger community of ends, from serving which they derive their rights. With this Thomistic recognition of the interdependence of parts and whole, national federalism has more in common in so far as in its view local variation contributes to the diversity from which the nation emerges.

In its structure of authority the national republic, in contrast with the confederate republic, resembles the Thomistic monarchy by locating sovereign power in a single authority. For Aquinas "every natural governance is the governance of one," a regime which is a necessity for "the common good of the many."[13] The theory of the compound republic does not deny this principle but seeks rather to show how the rule of the many can achieve an appropriate unity. By contrast, compact theory posits the rule not of one, but of several, namely, the plurality of sovereign states united only by a treaty. In the national republic, the People, as the unitary sovereign, like the "chief judge" in the Mosaic regime, endows the subordinate governments with their limited authority and then governs subject to those self-administered limits.

Such resemblances between medieval and modern constitutionalism are helpful mainly because they bring out the differences. In both compact and national federalism, the similarities with the Thomistic model are profoundly qualified by the fact that authority, instead of descending from above, rises from below. The republican and Thomistic models are distinguished even more sharply by the conceptions of purpose by which their respective federal systems are given direction. This is especially true of national federalism, which sets itself ends that impel it on a course of continual change.

The Four Great Objects

The one legally unlimited power known to the Constitution, the power of the American people to determine their political institutions,[14] does limit itself by its allocation of authority. This definition of what means are proper, and so implicitly a definition of what means are improper, limits government. That is, however, only such limitation as is inherent in the positive intention to pursue a goal.[15] The positive goals of the Preamble, moreover, are not fixed once and for all. Like the Constitution as a whole they express the will of the constituent sovereign and can be legitimately changed by it. The existence of the amending clause expresses this expectation that even in matters of fundamental law change is inherent in our political order.

Although the Preamble is the controlling statement of purpose, its meaning needs to be clarified from other sources: the text of the Constitution, authoritative commentary such as *The Federalist,* and not least the history of republican thought in Britain and America. Read in this context, the "great objects" of the Constitution can be summarized as liberty, prosperity, security, and, implicitly, the cultivation of republican virtue, all of which were conceived not as static attributes but as dynamic and interdependent components of a commonwealth for increase.

Self-government was an end in itself, but it was also a means to an end, the protection of individual rights. The long struggle for individual liberty in thought and in action presumed that government by the people would be the principal guarantee. A free government would create and sustain a free society. That was no doubt its primary purpose. But was it the sole purpose? The primacy of individual liberty in the republican conception of ends has made this an easy and familiar inference. Friedrich's definition of constitutionalism as a system of effective, regularized restraints on government, for instance, makes the preservation of liberty its sole and sufficient justification.[16]

Yet when we look at what was said and done during the generation of the founding, we also see great concern with other objects. As Millican has recently observed, the authors of *The Federalist,* while obviously committed to individual rights, did not bother to define them and indeed paid little explicit attention to the question, except to argue that no enumeration in a bill of rights was needed.[17] In their minds the Constitution, founded upon the extended republic, would protect "justice," their summary term for maintenance of individual rights. Their exposition of the merits of the Constitution, however, gave no less attention to how it would promote "the general good." In this emphasis their exposition was at one with the main text of the Constitution, which devoted only a few lines to the explicit protection of individual rights, elaborating rather the powers of the federal government, which were directed mainly at two other great national objects, prosperity and security.

The allocations of power in Article I, sections 8, 9, and 10, show an overwhelming concern with these two objects. Of the eighteen subparagraphs in section 8, over two thirds, some fourteen, are concerned with internal and external security and with economic matters, seven being devoted to each of these topics. The two following sections, 9 and 10, which limit federal and state action respectively, are similarly focused. Throughout these allocations of powers, means are fitted to ends. Usually the connection is implicit. Sometimes it is quite explicit, as when the "common defence" is named as a purpose for which tax revenues may be used. Nor in that case is the authorization merely permissive. A positive duty of national defence is also imposed on Congress and the President, any doubt being removed by the legislative and executive oaths of office.

The other main category of grants of power also has a national purpose. These grants—to coin and to borrow money, to impose tariffs and to regulate commerce, to tax and to spend, to regulate bankruptcies, to protect patents, and so on—were not a miscellany but a coherent system of rules with a purpose. That purpose included protection of the private economic rights of individuals, but it did more than that. These rules defined and protected these rights not only as norms of some conception of natural law and abstract justice but also and especially as the legal framework of a free capitalistic economy.

Needless to say, the establishment of a free economy was not accomplished by laissez faire, but took a great deal of government intervention, constitutional and statutory.[18] That free economy was also a national economy, subject to government restraints and incentives, externally in relation to other countries and internally in relation to its own development. These purposes and the vision of the American future which they informed occupied much of the attention of *The Federalist*. The restraints on economic welfare imposed by state barriers to interstate trade had been in Madison's eyes one of the principal "vices" of the Confederation.[19] Accordingly, the commerce power was granted to the federal government so that it might promote "unrestrained intercourse between the States."[20] That meant not only restraints on state action but also incentives to such intercourse, as Madison had foreseen when on the eve of the convention he took note of the need for federal power to act positively for the "common interest" in such matters as grants of "incorporation for national purposes, for canals and other works of general utility."[21]

The scope of the powers granted in the Constitution cannot be understood apart from the purposes which they were intended to serve. One of the more striking illustrations of purpose as a determinant of authority in Federalist constitutional thought comes in Hamilton's defense, in no less than seven papers (numbers 30–36), of the "general" and "indefinite" power of taxation given to the federal government. Rejecting the proposal of a rule defining how this vital power of government was to be shared by federal and state levels, he concluded, as we have seen, that the task of maintaining the "constitutional equilibrium" in this respect could and should be left to "the people." The only standard he offered for judging the extent of this power of the federal government was "the purposes of its institution." He identified these as the "security," "prosperity," and "reputation of the commonwealth."[22]

The "prosperity" which according to Federalist doctrine the Constitution was designed to serve was not a static condition defined by some traditional or Aristotelian standard of adequacy or sufficiency but a future of continual material increase. The substance of this future and the role of the federal government in realizing it was spelled out over the following years in Hamilton's great papers on fiscal and economic policy. But the theme was powerfully sounded in the early *Federalist* papers, 1 to 38, where the authors argued the main case for the shift of power from the states to the federal government under the Constitution. In *Federalist* 11, for instance, Hamilton sketched these expectations of economic growth in the context of the new centralization. Thanks to the new powers of the federal government, he observed, American trade would expand abroad and at home, private enterprise and public purpose working together for the same end. Externally, federal power would act to release "that unequalled spirit of enterprise, which signalizes the genius of the American Merchants and Navigators, and which is in itself an inexhaustible mine of national wealth." "Under a vigorous national government the natural strength and resources of the country, directed to a common interest, would baffle all the combinations of European jealousy to restrain our growth." At home, the creation of a national market by the new central powers, would enable "an unrestrained intercourse between the States themselves [to] advance the trade of each by an interchange of their respective productions."[23]

In view of the differences that later arose between Hamilton and Madison, one would expect Hamilton to be the more ardent champion of economic growth. And in the choice of topics which they developed in favor of the new centralization, Madison did show more concern for liberty and Hamilton for prosperity. Yet neither rejected and each often used the arguments of the other. Hamilton made use of Madison's theory of faction to support his case for federal power.[24] In *Federalist* 14 Madison, echoing the line of reasoning set out by Hamilton in previous papers, termed the Constitution the "guardian of our commerce" and the ground of "greater intercourse" throughout the Union facilitated by "new improvements" in the form of "roads," "canals" "accommodations," and "interior navigation." The parallels of their thought were reflected in the similarities of their rhetoric. Hamilton spoke for "liberal or enlarged plans of public good," Madison foresaw a "more enlarged plan of policy."[25]

That other "great object," security, also had individual and social aspects. It embraced the right of the individual to be protected from harm by other persons thanks to the traditional safeguards of the civil and criminal law and from harm by the federal government thanks to such guarantees as *habeas corpus* and the ban on bills of attainder and *ex post facto* laws. Security also referred to the preservation of the general social condition of peace in the form of "domestic tranquility" and defense against foreign foes. Both authors lent their argumentative talents to making the case for security in this latter social sense. Hamilton's papers dealt especially with the military side, showing the need for a standing army and for "unconfined" access to tax revenues for purposes of defense.[26] Madison was more concerned with the political side, his demonstration of national sovereignty providing the basis of a coherent and effective mobilization of resources for security at home and abroad.[27]

Peace was not only an end in itself but also a necessary condition of the achievement of other national purposes. Concern for the national power to provide for security was inseparable from concern for economic strength. Hamilton pointed out how a richer economy would provide more abundant revenues, which in turn would enable the United States to maintain a strong navy, that indispensable instrument for protecting and expanding our foreign trade. Winding up his assessment of "the importance of the Union, in a commercial light," he found it natural to suggest how "greatness" in economic matters could give us a dominant position in the Western Hemisphere. Virtually anticipating the Monroe doctrine, he foresaw "one great American system, superior to the control of all transatlantic force or influence, and so able to dictate the connection between the old and the new world."[28]

Although overseas trade was a main focus of Federalist aspiration, the prospect of westward expansion also excited their nation-building imagination. Madison vividly articulated this continental vision of material increase. Thinking of the public lands being surrendered by the states to the federal government, he termed "the Western territory" "a mine of vast wealth to the United States" and, in view of future acquisitions, concluded that "we may calculate, therefore, that a rich and fertile country, of an area equal to the inhabited extent of the United States, will soon become a national stock." Moreover, the Constitution, which, in contrast with the Articles, welcomed expansion, would give the authority to form this territory into "new States" to Congress, which was already doing that without authorization, in response to what Madison termed "the public interest, the necessity of the case."[29] Already some 200,000 Americans out of a total population of less than 4 million were beyond the Appalachians, pressing westward toward the Mississippi. That "great country, populous and mighty" imagined by Benjamin Franklin nearly half a century earlier, was being realized on the American continent.[30] In Federalist eyes, the constitution was designed to protect and to promote this commonwealth for increase.

Like Benjamin Franklin, the authors of *The Federalist* valued economic growth and national power. Franklin also looked forward to a nation which was not only rich and powerful but also virtuous. These Franklinian virtues were twofold, individual and social. As all the world knows, the individual virtues were the disciplines of bourgeois excellence preached by Poor Richard. In Franklin's ethical system, the individualist virtues were the motor of capitalism, and capitalism was the school of these virtues. The creation of a free and growing economy required these norms as its cultural base, along with its political base in the institutional and legal framework of republican government.

Federalist thought reflected a similar ethic when its spokesmen referred to property as "the primary object of society"—to use the words of Rufus King at the federal convention.[31] This did not mean that these champions of property rights were crass materialists, who thought of the new regime as merely an instrument for amassing personal wealth. They assuredly did not disdain material possessions. As Appleby has observed in a vivid clarification, the ideology of the American whigs conceived of the new system of individual rights as "the democratization of material well-being."[32] They also, however, regarded property as an index of personal character and its acquisition as a sphere of character formation. This term "property" did not and does not mean merely possessions but the right to possessions acquired and held under certain conditions.[33] If obtained by force or fraud, possessions are not property. The idea of a right to private property is that there is an ethical justification for individuals getting, keeping, and using certain things in certain ways. This premise was asserted during a debate at the federal convention when Charles Cotesworth Pinckney argued for a property qualification for those holding office because ownership of property was a sign they were "independent and respectable."[34] Yet delegates were unwilling to apportion representation in the House among the states according to wealth as well as number of inhabitants, voting down such a proposal "by so general a no, that the states were not called."[35]

For Federalists, private property was an "interest" of first importance. But the modern republican conception of interest, which goes back to the seventeenth century, does not exclude, but indeed entails, an ethical foundation. One sees this in Madison's analysis of the basis of individual rights in general. In the realm of politics, he said the most important interests were those relating to "the different degrees and kinds of property." But for Madison the normative character of the general right which protected private property equally in all its varieties came from its grounding in the "faculties" of individuals. Ethically and economically, Madison's "faculties" performed the same function as Franklin's "virtues." They were the capacities of the individual which enabled and moved him in the pursuit of his interests, including material well-being. "The protection of these faculties," wrote Madison accordingly in *Federalist* 10, "is the first object of government." Nor did he contradict this statement when in *Federalist* 51 he said that "justice is the end of government." That later phrasing served rather to emphasize the premise of his jurisprudence which made justice the equal protection of these different and unequal faculties by a system of legal rights.[36]

Franklin's table of virtues included not only a discipline of personal excellence but also an imperative to do good works. He continually harped on the need to bring up the young to be "public spirited" and devoted to the common good. As exemplified in his own life, these social virtues were to a great extent exercised by participation in politics and government. Madison, likewise, while rejecting the unreal supposition that men can act solely out of self-denying altruism, held that they do have a capacity of reason inclining them toward "impartiality." Conditioned by the extended republic and the auxiliary precautions of the Constitution, reason, he believed, will lead the people to seek and quite possibly to agree on the "public interest." Where there is government by discussion, the clash and contrast of diverse interests and ideas will raise public opinion out of parochial and toward wider and more inclusive perspectives. It is entirely faithful to Madison's thought to see the "great objects" of constitutional government as including the cultivation of republican virtue, in both its individual and social aspects. As the free economy was a school of individual virtue, the free polity was a school of social virtue.

Not that the Constitution in so many words connects public policy with republican virtue. The inference follows only when the constitutional prescriptions are looked at in the light of Madison's theory of "faculties." In the past, republican thinkers had taken a similar view. We have briefly recalled what Franklin said. Harrington and Milton, as we have seen, also were profoundly concerned with the bearing of free government on the character and culture of citizens. Similarly inspired, Hamilton had suggested in the first lines of the first *Federalist* how exemplary the self-governing American people would prove to be when in a famous passage he challenged them "by their conduct and example" to decide "whether societies of men are really capable or not of establishing good government from reflection and choice, or whether they are forever destined to depend for their political constitutions on accident and force." He was making an appeal to what he called "patriotism," a social virtue of self-made men which moved them to create a self-made nation.[37]

The Fragility of Reason

The theory of national federalism makes sense, as far as it goes. Intellectually and morally it is coherent and convincing. It appeals to both the norms of republican ideology and the calculations of interest. But something is missing. One cannot fail to see the fragility of an order based only on a commitment to impersonal ideals and the utilitarian satisfactions. This failing was widely perceived at the time. Thoughtful people recognized that the young republic would have to enlist in its support the affections of its citizens as well as their prudent idealism. Vaguely but earnestly they spoke of the need for "attachment" to its institutions and "affection" among its people, for "veneration" and for "sympathy."[38]

These doubts about the new regime did not arise from some circumstance, material or ideal, peculiar to America. In the West generally the great liberating movement of the age put the sovereign, rational individual at the center of its theorizing. To see in this premise a prescription for pluralistic disorder was a reasonable fear. In 1790, although the effort to liberalize the French state was still in its moderate phase, Edmund Burke exposed its self-destructive potential in a fierce but prescient polemic against the rationalism of the *philosophes*. He wrote:

> On the scheme of this barbarous philosophy . . . laws are to be supported only by their own terrors, and by the concern which each individual may find in them from his own private speculations, or can spare them from his own private interests. . . . Nothing is left which engages the affections of the commonwealth. On the principles of this mechanic philosophy our institutions can never be embodied, if I may use the expression, in persons; so as to create in us love, veneration, admiration or attachment. But that sort of reason which banishes the affections is incapable of filling their place. These public affections, combined with manners, are required sometimes as supplements, sometimes as correctives, always as aids to law.[39]

The leading advocate and principal author of the national theory of American federalism himself shared these fears. Indeed, according to Herbert Storing, this question of public affections was examined "most profoundly" by Madison in *Federalist* 49.[40] In that paper Madison considered Jefferson's proposal that breaches of the Constitution be corrected by appeals to "the people" acting directly through conventions.[41] According to Madison, although such an exercise of constituent sovereignty was appropriate on "certain great and extraordinary occasions," frequent popular interventions to alter the frame of government were dangerous. Among these dangers was the threat to "that veneration which time bestows on every thing, and without which perhaps the wisest and freest governments would not possess the requisite stability." Reason must rule, but rationality was not enough to secure that result. No matter how "rational" the design and operation of a government might be, he wrote, it would "not find it a superfluous advantage to have the prejudice of the community on its side."[42]

A devoted, although not an uncritical, Virginian, Madison recognized that the main weight of "prejudice" would be on the side of localism, not nationalism. In *Federalist* 46, when taking up the question whether the federal or the state governments would enjoy the greater support of the people, he started from the acknowledgment that "the first and most natural attachment of the people will be to the governments of their respective States." These bonds, as he saw them, were a mix of the rational and the nonrational, of interest and of affection. The states, he observed, would have "the superintending care" of "all the more domestic and personal interests." With their affairs, "the people will be more familiarly and minutely conversant." And with the members of their governments, "a greater proportion of the people [will] have the ties of personal acquaintance and friendship, and of family and party attachments." The resulting imbalance, Madison feared, meant that members of the national legislature, being chosen locally, would be moved by "a local spirit" to judge measures "according to their probable effect, not on the national prosperity and happiness, but on the prejudices, interests and pursuits of the governments and people of the individual States."[43]

Hamilton was no less exercised by the danger to the Union arising from local attachments. The "propensity of the human heart" to be attached to what is less distant and diffusive, he thought, would be strengthened by the objects of state government. Since state governments would regulate "all the personal interests and familiar concerns to which the sensibility of individuals is more immediately awake," they would win the "affection, esteem and reverence"— "the great cement of society"—of the people of the states, making these governments, "not infrequently, dangerous rivals to the power of the Union."[44]

Madison and Hamilton were not without hope that this imbalance would be corrected. The cause would be that "better administration" afforded by the federal government. This term embraced the whole broad case for the extended republic as the vehicle of greater liberty, security, and prosperity which had been summarized by Hamilton in *Federalist* 27 and which was included by reference in Madison's analysis in *Federalist* 46.[45] That appeal, however, was to the reflections and calculations of reason. It was an appeal to the principles of a great cause and to the fine-tuned advantages of the marketplace. What it lacked was a voice that spoke to the heart as well as the head, which called up images of home and hearth, of known persons and named places.

This appeal of the personal and the familiar has a grip on the affections which the universals of reason cannot match. In the annals of American federalism, the classic example of its power is the fateful choice made by Robert E. Lee when on the eve of the Civil War he rejected the offer of command of the Union armies. Lee granted that the rational arguments were on the side of the Union: he thought secession was unconstitutional, regarded the dissolution of the Union as a calamity, and would give up all the slaves for its preservation. On the other hand, he simply could not raise his hand against "my relatives, my children, my home" and therefore would not draw his sword "save in defence of my native State."[46] Three quarters of a century earlier, Federalists were right to wonder how the argument for "better administration," even in all its amplitude, could compete with the appeal of "the spirit of locality."

To these doubts James Wilson addressed a robust and persuasive reply. His theory of social union claimed to show how the extended republic could deeply engage the affections as well as the reason of the citizen. Wilson's ideas were fundamentally at one with the thinking of Madison and Hamilton, although those of Wilson's ideas that differed from their approach also significantly improved on it. At the federal convention, for example, in opposition to Madison's proposal in the Virginia Plan to make the federal executive a committee, as under the Articles, Wilson was the first delegate to move that it "consist of a single person."[47] Moreover, as we have seen, Wilson's ideas about sovereignty, while in the same mold as Madison's nationalism, more fully satisfied the demands of history and theory. Similarly his theory of how public affection arises in the great republic supplements, but does not contradict, the Madisonian theory.

Participation and Public Affection

Wilson's role at the federal convention, which makes him hardly inferior to Madison and Hamilton among the architects and spokesmen of the new regime, entitles this supplement to be considered a reasonable extrapolation of the theory of national federalism. Its claim to consideration is strengthened by the shape actually taken in the future by American government and politics. "The ideas of James Wilson," wrote the most recent editor of his works, Robert G. McCloskey, "more nearly foreshadowed the national future than those of any of his well-remembered contemporaries. Not one of them—not Hamilton or Jefferson or Madison or Adams or Marshall—came so close to representing in his views what the United States was to become."[48] One major aspect of Wilson's achievement, as McCloskey brings out in his brilliant introduction, was to reconcile the opposing positions of Jeffersonian democracy and Hamiltonian nationalism, showing that "democracy and national union," far from being opposed, are "natural partners."[49] Both an ardent democrat and a centralizer, Wilson characterized the connection at the federal convention in a vivid metaphor, repeated in his writings, declaring that "he was for raising the federal pyramid to a considerable altitude, and for that reason wished to give it as broad a base as possible."[50] Making good on his rhetoric, Wilson favored direct election of not only the House but also the Senate and the President. According to McCloskey, he was "the *only* important founding father who expressed himself unequivocally" in favor of "one man, one vote." I shall argue for the philosophical superiority of his ideas not only on democracy and nationalism but also on the role of the states in "a federal republick," to use a term of his coinage.[51]

Born in Scotland in 1742, he was educated at St. Andrews at the height of the Scottish Enlightenment, where he imbibed the ideas of the "common sense" school of philosophy from its then leading proponent, Thomas Reid. This system of thought, advanced in opposition to the skepticism and conservatism of David Hume yet bearing the unmistakable marks of that great mind, continued to influence Wilson, who framed his own ideas as a "deeply-thought-out restatement of the common sense philosophy." Emigrating to America in 1765, he read law with John Dickinson in Philadelphia and took a leading part in the movement of resistance, rebellion, and post-revolutionary constitutional reform in Pennsylvania. He was one of only six men who signed both the Declaration of Independence and the Constitution. A Federalist leader at the constitutional convention, he was the principal figure in the struggle for ratification in Pennsylvania. He was very largely the author of that state's constitution of 1790 and was appointed by Washington as one of the original justices of the U.S. Supreme Court.[52]

While many of the things that Wilson said and wrote helped to develop and to defend the idea of national federalism, his principal contribution was his theory of social union set forth in his lectures on law delivered in Philadelphia in 1790–91. The preeminent legal scholar of his generation, he wrote these lectures as part of a plan, never completed, to explain and justify the American Constitution in the light of a general theory of government and politics grounded on theology and psychology.[53]

In these lectures in a long passage on elections to the legislature in state and nation, Wilson carefully spelled out how social union was consummated. A primary consideration was the structure of the situation with which a republican constitution confronted the citizen exercising his right of suffrage. Referring to Pennsylvania by way of example, Wilson recalled that before the Revolution, the suffrage, being limited to elections to the lower house, could be frustrated by the unelected executive and upper house. After the Revolution, by contrast, the suffrage, having been broadened to embrace "all the legislative, and many of the executive officers of government," gave voters the opportunity and the incentive to act through their representatives for "the noblest interests of the commonwealth, without the apprehension of disappointment or control." Surely, he inferred, that "must have a powerful tendency to open, to enlighten, to enlarge and to exalt the mind."[54]

The key to the transformation of preferences was the widening of the scale of choice. Being exercised on this "extensive scale," wrote Wilson, the right to vote would turn the attention of the voter away from "private industry" to "the contemplation of public men and public measures." The Constitution carried further this work of enlightenment and elevation by conferring on the electorate new rights in the choice of a federal government possessing greatly enlarged powers and scope.[55] Agreeing with Wilson that "the dimensions of the human mind are apt to be regulated by the extent and objects of the government under which it is formed," his close friend, Benjamin Rush, similarly conceived the consequence. "Think then," he wrote, "of the expansion and dignity the American mind will acquire by having its powers transferred from the contracted objects of a state to the more unbounded objects of a national government!—A citizen and a legislator of the free and united states of America will be one of the first characters of the world!"[56]

The right to vote was the incentive to this wider focus of the mind. But the exercise of that right was only "the business of a day." The "benign influences" of the suffrage on the electorate preceded and succeeded this act. In preparation for it, the voter would employ himself "making researches," "acquiring information," and "discussing [candidates] with his neighbours and fellow citizens." This phase of understanding would be followed by action when the voter made his choice, an act of will which was inseparable from the preparations for which it had been the instigation and the purpose.[57]

The consequence of this composite act of understanding and will was the generation of public affection. "A habit of conversing and reflecting on these subjects, and of governing his actions by the result of his deliberations," wrote Wilson in summary, "will form, in the mind of the citizen, a uniform, strong, and lively sensibility to the interests of his country." Moreover, this habitual sequence of understanding, will and affection individually in each voter will create collectively "the most endearing connection among the citizens" and "the most powerful, and, at the same time, a most pleasing bond of union between the citizens, and those whom they select for the different offices and departments of government."[58]

As a theory of public affections, Wilson's view differed from that of *The Federalist* primarily by holding that the social bond in a republic came not so much from the benefits of self-government as from the very process of self-government; not from utility but from participation. The national republic would therefore have a stronger hold on the emotions of its citizens than would state governments not only because of the results of "better administration" but also and chiefly because of the wider focus of participation.

For Madison and Hamilton, "better administration"—utility in the broadest sense—would draw the attachment of citizens away from the states and to the federal government. "Time," in the form of precedents that were "ancient as well as numerous," would then add to the support of the regime and its laws the emotional force of "veneration," "reverence," "prejudice."[59] In view of the role of utility, one may call this an economic theory of public affection. The citizen realizes greater utility from the central institutions of the big republic because of their greater satisfaction of his views of his individual interests and of the public interest. They make him and the country freer, more secure, and more prosperous. In the course of time, these habitual satisfactions shift his emotional attachment to the central government. Once they have been formed, these sentiments have great force, but utility has guided their cathexis, their selection of objects.[60] Patriotism arises from the utility of the *patria*.

By contrast, Wilson's theory of the increase of public affections is radically political. The fundamental emotional thrust is toward wider social association. The means by which this expansion of emotional attachment has taken place, however, is the process of self-government. Citizens take to loving the country which they are creating, as Wilson suggests in his analysis of voting. In this same vein he remarked at the federal convention, "the People" will shift their attachment to the new central institutions because they will view the national government "as more important in itself, and more flattering to their pride."[61] As a generalization from recent American political action, the assertion was accurate. Much as the rebellious whigs had sought to promote their interests by means of actual representation, they no less had sought these wider rights of self-government for its own sake. They were patriots before they had a *patria*. As Robert Frost, reversing his celebrated line, once remarked, "we were the land's before the land was ours."

If people act in accord with the Madisonian view of motivation, the voter's paradox will arise when the voter, as a rational man, weighs the trouble of voting against the fact that this single act, in the context of the vast number of people voting, will have only a negligible effect in bringing about the result he seeks.[62] Wilson gives three reasons which meet this problem. One, which he gave in a 1788 oration celebrating the Constitution, is that "one ticket may turn the election," meaning presumably that it might break a tie. This condition satisfies the logic of rational choice theory but is no more convincing than its probability. In the same oration, he also urged voting as "the duty of every citizen," his presumption being that a big turnout was necessary to assure the election of "representatives that are wise and good."[63] In a speech given the next year at a state constitutional convention, he offered a reason far more consistent with his own theory of the moral sense which is moved not only by intellectual and moral reason but also by the social passion.

Expressing his fears of low turn-out, which he implied was observable during Pennsylvania's colonial days, he attributed this behavior to the inadequacy of opportunity and incentive to engage the moral sense in its social aspect. Reversing these disincentives, the democratization of the franchise after the Revolution, however, would assure a good turn-out by bringing into play the social passion which makes voting an end in itself as an expression of the capacity and impulse to act in association with others.[64]

The Social Passion

In Wilson's psychology of politics, this passion for self-government is a fundamental "faculty" of human nature, an "innate moral sense," leading us to seek the society of others.[65] Wilson emphasized that this impulse is not a derivative but an independent force moving the individual toward further association, speaking of it variously as "the social passion," "the social aim," "social virtue," "our social affection."[66] Society, Wilson readily granted, is enormously useful to the individual, making available to him the services of others necessary for survival and for the better satisfaction of his wants. But the social passion does not depend on or arise out of utility; on the contrary, it creates the social conditions that make possible works of utility, such as stable systems of exchange and mutual assistance.[67] Here is the great contrast with the Madisonian approach, which, as we have seen, makes the utility of mutual assistance the ground of public affection. For Wilson utility accompanies, but only by following, sociability.

Ancient and medieval thought also gave a primary role to the social impulse, holding that if it were to be properly expressed, its embodiment in action must be directed by the ruling few. As republicans, Wilson and Madison denied any such radical inequality of virtue among men and premised their theories on the proposition that human beings in general possessed the inherent capacity to govern themselves, individually and collectively. For Madison, although men differed greatly in their "faculties," they all had "reason" sufficient to enable and to entitle them to live a free, republican life. For Wilson similarly this capacity, which he termed "the moral sense," was common to all men despite their great inequalities of "talent," and therefore imperatively justified the denial that any were created with natural authority over others.[68]

For both thinkers this first premise of republican thought, its faith in such a common human capacity, reconciled their belief in a higher law with their commitment to popular sovereignty.[69] Both termed this higher law "the law of nature." Wilson explicitly said that it had been laid down by the will of God, who had endowed his human creatures, even those who were "savage and brutish," with a "guide" in the form of "an innate moral sense" which enabled them "to perceive the qualities of right and wrong, and other moral qualities in action."[70] But who on earth was to have the ultimate coercive power to declare what that law is and how it shall be applied in human affairs? For Wilson as for Madison, the people—and only the people—could be trusted with this ultimate human authority. That exclusive right came from their grasp of the higher law, most reliably expressed by the national and constitutional republic.

The philosophical focus of Wilson's lectures gave him the opportunity and the incentive to elaborate the psychological grounds for this conclusion more fully than Madison could do in *The Federalist*, preoccupied as it was with the task of political persuasion. Wilson, therefore, took great care to demonstrate how the dual moral and intellectual capacity of the moral sense meant that every act of will was also an act of understanding. From this conclusion it followed that the will of the individual, being informed by both the norms of the higher law and by knowledge of the objective situation, was by nature not arbitrary. For the same reasons the will of the people, expressed under the proper social and political conditions, was legitimately sovereign. When the people of the United States "ordained" the Constitution, this command was authoritative, therefore, not because the will of the people could legitimize any command no matter how arbitrary but rather because it was the conclusion of the rational deliberation of the members of the extended republic. And their conclusions, while by no means infallible, were more likely to be in accord with what the higher law required of government than those of any other human collectivity.

Wilson's closer examination of how the will is related to the

understanding also leads to his more ample theory of public affections. For Madison the will is divided. There are two sources of
conation, the normative and the impulsive, reason and the passions.
Thanks to reason in its normative aspect, according to Madison, the
individual recognizes and feels obliged by the higher law. Self-love,
however, often moves his will in an opposite direction. Under the
favorable conditions of the national and constitutional republic, reason will control, leading the individual to seek solutions which reconcile the conflicts of self-love in society.

For Wilson, as for Reid, by contrast, the will is unified; there is but
one source of conation, the social passion.[71] So conceived, the will is
not mere gregariousness, mere unthinking fellow-feeling.[72] The conception of social association to which it aspires is already informed
by the higher law. "Society," writes Wilson, "is necessary as well as
natural to us." But since "man is made for society," it is natural
before it is necessary.[73] Consider, for instance, the norm underlying
the obligation of contracts typically enforced by municipal law. That
norm, according to Wilson, proceeds from our inherent intellectual
capacity to make promises and our inherent moral perception that
promises should be kept. Promise making and keeping are necessary
if we are to enjoy the benefits of association with others in society.
But it is not the need for these benefits that sets this capacity in
motion. On the contrary, the association with others entailed by
promise making and keeping is an object of the social passion and
enjoyable in itself. Similarly, according to Wilson the social passion
leads us to seek an association with others in which the innocent are
not harmed and private property is respected.[74]

The rights of man in Wilson's scheme are the conventional canon
of republican thought. They are not derivative from the necessities
of a social existence but are inherent in human nature. Nor are they
inherent in the sense of being the coercive voice of reason or conscience which imposes its imperatives on the natural passions of
mankind. The rights of man rather are implanted in the ruling
passion which makes men naturally citizens of the republic.

The danger of perfectionism lurks in Wilson's exalted view of the
social passion. When reading some of the grandiloquent passages of
his lectures on this subject, one may well long for not only the

astringency of Madison's style but also the skepticism of his psychology. Although Wilson recognizes our "fallen state" in words, he is less willing than Madison to admit that self-love as well as circumstance is a source of conflict.[75] Yet in a larger sense when one compares the two theories of public affections with the actual record of modern national feeling, Wilson surely can make the greater claim to realism. Even such ardent patriots as Madison and Hamilton showed a certain intellectual timidity when it came to recognizing the powerful attachment that the modern nation, and not least the American nation, could arouse among its citizens. More perceptive in his nationalism as in his democracy, Wilson gave us in both respects a more faithful portrait of the American future. And not only that, but also a more faithful portrait of the motivation and behavior of his contemporaries among the American whigs. Madison's analysis of the affections of citizens inching forward under the attractions of "better administration" is a caricature of the bold and generous hearts who conceived and championed the Constitution. These leaders, moreover, were not merely exemplary but also typical of the whigs, who as individuals and as a movement displayed a formidable integrity over two generations of resistance, revolution, and state-building.

Wilson foresees an attachment of the people to the new republic comparable to that attributed to the citizens of the small state by classical writers. What he says, however, is not an echo of ancient philosophy but an anticipation of modern democratic nationalism. He is too egalitarian to be a follower of Aristotle or Plato. Man in society, he said, partakes of its "sympathetick pleasures" as well as its "mutual services" only "when he is united with his equals."[76] More to the point, the social passion as conceived by Wilson does not limit our participation to the small state of classical republicanism but on the contrary urges the citizen toward the ever more extended republic. Wilson accepts Madison's theory of faction as a vice inherent in the small republic. With greater emphasis than Madison, however, he attributes this exhibition of "human imperfection" not to self-love but to circumstance. The fundamental motive is the same social passion which in the extended republic can be "raised to the greatest height" and "enlarged to the greatest extent." Where

smallness of scale restricts its operation "within a narrow and contracted sphere," however, its force may be directed to supporting the
interests of a part rather than the interests of a larger whole.[77]

The application to the politics of the federal republic in America
is explicit. In this "confederated government," Wilson finds, some
people will support "the government of their state, as a rival, for
social and benevolent affection, to the government of the United
States" despite the fact that in cases of conflict "justice and general
utility" will be found on the side of "the national government." He
does not fear for the outcome of such a contest for the attachment
of the people. "Expanded patriotism," he writes, "is a cardinal virtue
in the United States." And that "virtue," that "passion for the commonwealth," that "devotion to the publick," transcending "contracted motives or views," will "preserve inviolate . . . the connexion
of affection as well as interest between all the parts."[78]

Like other Federalist thinkers, Wilson looked forward to a future
of continual increase, material and ideal, under the Constitution. "It
is the glorious destiny of man," he wrote, "to be always progressive.
Forgetting those things that are behind, it is his duty, and it is his
happiness, to press on towards those that are before." No more than
his Federalist colleagues did he disdain prosperity for individuals and
the nation. Material progress went hand in hand with the expansion
of society. He paid little attention to the mechanisms of economic
growth. While recognizing the effect of the division of labor on
productivity, he did not identify increasing specialization as a motor
of material progress. He did, however, stress the importance of
technology. As social association is enlarged, he wrote, "knowledge
is increased: inventions are discovered: experience improves them:
and the inventions with their improvements, are spread over the
whole community. Designs of durable and extensive advantage are
boldly formed, and vigorously carried into effect."[79]

The ultimate justification of material progress in his eyes was the
intellectual and moral improvement that accompanied it. As he admonished the delegates at the convention in one of his most quoted
remarks, "he could not agree that property was the sole or the
primary object of Government & society. The cultivation and improvement of the human mind was the most noble object."[80] As one

would expect from his view of the intimate connection between understanding and will, this cultivation of the mind was twofold, including both "the arts and sciences" and "political and moral improvements." "Our progress in virtue," he continued, "should certainly bear a just proportion to our progress in knowledge." "Where good government prevails, there is the country of science and virtue. Under a good government, therefore, we must look for the accomplished man."[81]

In this broad sense, the cultivation of virtue was the supreme purpose of constitutional government. To Wilson's way of thinking as to Benjamin Franklin's way, however, virtue was not a mere ascent to higher levels of contemplation but rather a broader understanding of society expressed in policies promoting the "public interest." For Wilson the republic was concerned with character formation—the cultivation of "the accomplished man"—but republican virtue in his conception, as in Franklin's, was virtue in action.[82] The perfecting of the Union went along with the perfecting of its citizens. He wrote:

> A nation should aim at its perfection. The advantage and improvement of the citizens are the ends proposed by the social union. Whatever will render that union more perfect will promote those ends. The same principles, therefore, which show that a man ought to pursue the perfection of his nature, will show likewise that the citizens ought to contribute everything in their power towards the perfection of the state.[83]

As explained in his analysis of voting, the heart of the process was individual reflection and collective deliberation—in short, government by discussion. The model, one authority on Wilson has observed, was "conversation," as "exemplified in Wilson's native Scotland, especially by the current rage for 'discussion' clubs and 'philosophical' societies" and which he claimed to find among the citizens of Philadelphia. Both "useful and entertaining," "conversation" had remarkable capabilities for "improving individuals and their relations in nearly every sphere of social life."[84] In his examination of the politics of republican government, Wilson called this process "moral abstraction."

Moral abstraction is analogous to intellectual abstraction, the capacity of the mind to perceive "resemblances" and to classify them in ever more inclusive categories. It expresses will as well as understanding, however, being "a principle of good will as well as knowledge," since its judgments move the individual to act with benevolence toward an ever wider sphere of humanity. "By this power," wrote Wilson, "a number of individuals, who, considered separately, may be so minute, so unknown, or so distant, as to elude the operations of our benevolence, yet, comprehended under one important and distinguished aspect, may become a general and complex object, which will warm and dilate the soul."[85]

In calling attention to this capacity for public affection on so large a scale, Wilson identifies the remarkable power of modern nationalism which, as Hans Kohn has emphasized, enables millions of individuals who have no direct connection with one another to feel powerfully at one.[86] The nation as a social entity, however, sets limits to the political institutionalization of benevolence. On the one hand, the social passion which rises from friendship among individuals to "patriotism," "a circle of benevolence limited by the state," ultimately as "philanthropy" embraces "the whole human race."[87] On the other hand, in this latter form, "between all nations," it does not create "a social union" comparable to "a civil society." "The connexion is merely notional," writes Wilson, "and is only made by the mind, for its own convenience."[88] Madison, we may recall, also said in his advocacy of the extended republic that its scale must be "within a practical sphere."[89] Wilson is more specific, finding that limit in the nature and boundaries of the nation-state.

This extension of affection to a wider public can take place in the absence of the institutions of government. Civil society, or "the state," as Wilson also calls it, can deliberate, decide, and act—for instance, when ordaining a government.[90] Yet the process of moral abstraction is facilitated by political institutions, legislative, executive, and judicial, which exercise the coercive power delegated to them by the society.[91] Wilson's defense of bicameralism illustrates the point. He favored two houses of the legislature at both levels of federal government not because, as John Adams hoped and believed, an upper house would put men of greater wisdom in a position of power[92] but rather because two houses would improve the process of deliberation. On this topic Wilson followed not the theory of mixed government but the theory of separation of powers. The two houses, he granted, would represent the same democratic electorate but, differing in number of members, length of terms, and size of constituencies, would therefore take different views of public problems and what should be done about them. Competition, generated by their duality, would incite them to be severely critical of one another. "Rivals in duty," the two houses would thus be "a double source of information, precision, and sagacity in planning, digesting, composing, comparing and finishing the laws, both in form and in substance." No more than for Madison would the office-holders of a representative government merely reflect the immediate wishes of their constituents, but rather because of their position in the structure of deliberation they would enable popular government to produce its superior outcomes.[93]

Public Affection and Federalism

The social union to whose perfection moral abstraction tends is a whole, consisting, however, of distinct parts. How Wilson conceives this reconciliation illuminates his conception of federalism. For Wilson as for Madison, the people, as the sovereign power which ordains the frame of government, are a body politic capable of coherent action. In both accounts, the moral and intellectual grounds for its coherence are similar. Madison infers that the majority coalitions of the extended republic are more likely to be just because they are more general and that they are more general because they must embrace a wider variety of interests. The conditions that establish the legitimacy of the republic also promote its unity. With some similarity of reasoning, such as the stress on diversity and generality, Wilson justifies majority rule in the pregovernmental civil society, holding that it is "not so probable" that the majority, as compared with the minority, will be mistaken in the manner in which it effects the "purpose" for which the society was constituted. By no means a crude majoritarian, Wilson immediately qualifies this conclusion by adding that "by positive institution," meaning presumably something in the nature of a constitutional law, this rule may be modified

by the requirement of "the consent of a number larger than a majority . . . even unanimity."[94]

So far, the Madisonian and Wilsonian accounts agree fairly well.
Thanks to his more ample theory of public affections, however,
Wilson adds something that is missing in Madison's account. The
processes of moral abstraction which have led to the formation of
"the state" will also have brought into existence ties of public affection among the participants. Here is a further bond of union which
adds to the intellectual and moral bonds considered by Madison.
These sentiments therefore work to maintain the unity of the state
and nation even when disagreement arises. In the light of the intellectual and moral bonds of social union, one can argue that when
disagreements arise on some issues, as they must in a free society, the
dissident minority submits to the will of the majority because of
countervailing expectations of agreement on other matters. Without
rejecting this reasonable inference, the Wilsonian view identifies
bonds of national unity other and no less strong than those of
intellectual and moral assent. Needless to say, dissent over grand
issues of public policy can weaken and ultimately break the bonds
of public affection. But history and common sense testify that modern nations are held together by much more than the rational forces
of intellectual and moral conviction. As an observer of nations and
as a member of a nation, one must recognize the empirical soundness
of Wilson's concept of social passion.

In this respect, Wilson's way of looking at things makes him a
more thorough-going nationalist than Madison. It also makes him a
more thorough-going federalist by pointing the way toward a more
persuasive rationale for the states in a federal system. Madison's
classic defense of the states as agencies by which the people of the
nation can restrain or instruct the federal government is not pre-
cluded by Wilson's analysis. Indeed, Wilson's case for bicameralism
as a means of heightening the rationality of the deliberations of a
political body resembles in its focus on institutional structure Madison's defense of the federal division of authority. In contrast with
Madison's view, however, Wilson sees localism in a light that makes
it much more amenable to a system of national federalism. In the
course of saying why the national will has a superior normative

claim, Madison draws a contrast between state and nation that leaves the political system subject to a tension between the personal attachments that flourish within a state and the impersonal authority of the federal government. For Madison the national perspective reconciles conflicts of interest by eliciting their common and complementary properties. Expressing the imperatives of impersonal justice, such a reconciling formula *a fortiori* excludes what is personal and so what is affectual in the interests reconciled.

Such a reconciling formula illuminates a solution by "the dry light of reason," to use a term coined by Francis Bacon when setting forth his idea of rationality.[95] In this conception, reason prevails when people, even if strongly committed to certain ends, nevertheless assess reality, choose their means, and express their positions in a way that is not swayed by passion. Madison takes this view. He holds that, although people are often moved by passion, which is bad, they can to some extent overcome it and follow the "impartiality" demanded by reason. Much more in accord with common experience, Wilson says that emotion accompanies all processes of the mind, the good as well as the bad. Taking pains to emphasize this point, he declares that the operations of the mind are not confined to "reason" but embrace all elements of the moral sense, inseparably including emotion.[96]

It follows that the expansion of the mind which goes with the extension of the republic will continue to have an affectual quality. Here Wilson departs from the view of public affections which would confine them to the face-to-face relations of small numbers of persons and would oppose the motivations of this "sense of community" to the demands of justice. Wilson's conception of the moral sense implies, however, that these affectual bonds extend also to the great associations of the nation-state. That greater breadth moves the national will closer to the demands of justice, yet also lends to these bonds of nationality the emotional strength of small societies. In Wilson's theory of social union, the nation as well as the smaller societies which it includes can have a common life. Community and justice are not opposed but are two aspects, the affectual and the intellectual-moral, of the American nation-state.

The contrast that Wilson draws between the nation and the states within the nation is not the contrast marked out by Madison between a larger society ruled by the imperatives of impersonal justice and smaller societies which give a home to "all the more domestic and personal interests of the people."[97] At all levels, the bonds of social union, says Wilson, are of "the same nature."[98] The difference therefore is not between the impersonal and the personal but between the more and the less inclusive.

Both Madison and Wilson presented strategies of nation-building. Madison, the more cautious and exact thinker, appealed to the citizen as political consumer. He expected and surely hoped that "better administration" would turn the people toward the new nation and away from their too great attachment to the states. In his scheme, however, there was an ineradicable tension between the nation and the states, deriving from his dualistic conception of the mind which sharply opposed the impersonal demands of reason to the particularistic focus of the passions. Although initially stronger in their appeal to the people, the parochial states remained morally and culturally inferior to the cosmopolitan nation.

Wilson appealed to the citizen as political producer. Less exact in thought and expression but bolder by far in imagination, he grasped the promise of democratic participation as an instrument for making the nation more of a nation, and perceived the powerful passions which it could summon to the support of the compound republic. As he foresaw, the American people became a symbol of legitimacy attracting feelings of loyalty and allegiance which were no less potent than those enjoyed by the personalized regime celebrated by Burke's praise of monarchy and which lent a hardly less comparable stability to the risky experiment in individual freedom under popular government.

At the same time, Wilson's unitary conception of the mind, transcending Madisonian dualism, reduced the moral gap between the nation and the states. Although more contracted in their scope, the bonds of social union were of "the same nature" in the states as in the nation. Wilson clearly takes a more generous view of the states than does Madison. Even while pointing out the danger of faction, he observes that "faction itself is frequently nothing else than a warm but inconsiderate ebullition of our social propensities"—those "noblest propensities of our nature."[99] Referring to faction as "esprit du corps,"[100] in accord with the usage of his time, he says that the effects of such an attachment to a smaller society are not intrinsically and always bad, but can be "beneficial or pernicious." As in Wilson's model of the bicameral legislature, beneficial effects flow from competition, but not competition for an advantage harmful to others but competition to excel in the achievement of some larger purpose. This may be a generally valued accomplishment, as when schools compete in their studies or sports, or rival towns in their "manly exercises." Or it may be a direct contribution to a purpose of a larger society, as when a regiment contributes to victory in battle. On this model, the states, while serving local interests, will not harm one another but will conform to the demands of the national interest and, conceivably, may contribute directly to its realization.[101]

As examples of social union, the states have value in themselves. They therefore merit the degree of autonomy conferred by constitutional status because a governmental framework, such as that provided them by authority of the nation, is necessary for democratic participation. Wilson vividly revealed this necessity in his comparison of Pennsylvania as a colony and as a state. As a colony it was subject to a higher authority that could strike at the heart of the exercise of the moral sense by arbitrarily interfering with self-government. Thanks to the democratization of government after the Revolution, voters now could act through their representatives for "the noblest interests of the commonwealth, without the apprehension of disappointment or control."[102] No less than before, that opportunity and incentive, however, required constitutional protection. Within their sphere, these lesser communities also gave expression to the moral sense.

In this respect, Wilson was a more through-going federalist than Madison. As a nationalist, however, he explicitly made the states "subordinate" to the nation.[103] In words virtually echoing Madison's notable phrase in *Federalist* 51, he said that in cases of conflict between the two levels of government, "justice and general utility" would be found on the side of "the national government." Accepting Madison's theory of faction, he agreed that the imperatives of the federal government would more closely approximate the universals of reason. Unlike Madison, however, he did not confine its greater normative standing to this claim to rationality in contrast with the attachments arising from passion embodied in the states. Wilson perceived that the more inclusive populations of the modern democratic nation-state could generate even more powerful public affections. In his view, the great authority of the new national and federal republic was grounded in both reason and passion.

That made all the difference. Some years after the Civil War, Walt Whitman reflected on the test to which its outbreak had put the Union. In his eyes the victory had been won by "the People, of their own choice, fighting, dying for their own idea . . . Down in the abysms of New World humanity there had form'd and harden'd a primal hard-pan of Union will, determined and in the majority, refusing to be tamper'd with or argued against, confronting all emergencies, and capable at any time of bursting all surface bonds, and breaking out like an earthquake."[104]

Conclusion:
Liberty and Union

THIS BOOK STARTED with the way certain ideas about federalism are used in present-day controversies over public policy. President Reagan, for instance, seeking to narrow the sphere of federal social and economic programs, proposed that governmental responsibilities be shifted from Washington to the states. When in defense of this line of policy, echoing the compact theory of our constitutional origins, he claimed that the states had created the federal government, champions of federal activism attacked him, citing in opposition the national theory.

The President, like his critics, used a conception of the proper allocation of authority in the federal system to support the purposes he wanted the system to serve. Nothing unusual in that. Conceptions of authority and of purpose have been interconnected in American thinking about government from our early days. The idea that the United States is one nation, to be maintained and developed under the special responsibility of the federal government, is a dominant, although not an uncriticized or unrivaled, theme of our political culture. With an eye to its earliest formulations, this idea has been called Hamiltonian, and the Introduction sketched how this purpose of consolidating the union has been tested in the three great trials of sectional, economic, and racial conflict. Similarly, we may term Madisonian the coordinate conception of how the American people, the ultimate political force of our governmental system, authorized and directed it toward achieving this purpose and coping with such trials.

Together these two conceptions make up the national theory of the Constitution and of the federal system it establishes. As the references to Hamilton and Madison suggest, this theory can be found in ideas widely shared among the men who took the lead in framing and advocating the Constitution. These ideas are a theory in the sense that they form a coherent body of thought describing and justifying the institutions established by the Constitution. Part Three has been devoted to its general principles, their embodiment in institutions, and the hoped-for consequences in processes and policies. Parts One and Two were necessary in order to bring out more fully the significance of the national theory. They present the formidable political philosophy, entrenched in centuries of Western tradition, against which the idea of the national republic arose and defined itself. They show how this radically new viewpoint, advanced by Commonwealthmen of the English seventeenth century, was taken up by the American rebels as the rationale of their resistance and of the revolution which led to the Constitution.

Strong Democracy

The framers and advocates of the Constitution—whom it is both fair and convenient to call Federalist—were not trying to weaken government but to strengthen it. They were centralizers. Reacting to the sorry record of weak and illiberal government under the Articles of Confederation, they sought as their principal reform to strengthen the federal government. They did this by adding to its formal powers, by making these powers directly applicable to individuals, and, above all, by enhancing the normative force of these powers by basing them on the sovereignty of the people at large of the whole nation. The Articles also had been based on the principle of popular sovereignty, but the background of ideas of that frame of government implied legitimacy not for one but for thirteen sovereignties. The Constitution acquired a greater normative force because, as Morgan says, the attribution of sovereignty to the people of the United States as a whole alone could be thought to stand superior to any single state.[1]

One way to strengthen government is to impose the rule of a central elite. That option, although fearfully anticipated by "the men of little faith," was barred to the framers. The ideal base for aristocracy, let alone monarchy, in any serious sense could not be found among the "good people" who had risen against British rule, as even those who saw some merit in these traditional options fully acknowledged.[2] If the normative claim of the federal government was to be strengthened, its rationale would have to be grounded in the republican principles of the uprising against the virtuous few at Westminster. That task was accomplished by James Madison's theory of the national and federal republic.

It was a seemingly self-contradictory effort, since, as Madison recognized, those whose behavior had to be regulated were themselves the regulators.[3] In Madison's view, the regulated would recognize the greater normative claim of their will as a nation than as the members of any single state, not simply because, as Morgan suggests, the nation was the larger body, but because the national will was closer to "the principles of justice and the general good." The enhanced legitimacy of government under the Constitution rested on two principles: democracy and nationality. As republicans, the people of the United States were committed to self-government by rational deliberation; as a nation, while united by their whig premises, they were divided by interests and opinions sufficiently diverse to force their deliberations to rise above parochial attachments and toward decisions worthy of general assent. The pluralism which the philosophers of the old regime had perceived as the root of republican self-destruction was transformed into the source of strong democracy.

This paradox of how under the right conditions diversity can lead to unity is the heart of Madisonian theory. The conditions are set by constitutional government in the compound republic. The process is rational deliberation in which the initial preferences of participants are changed, as their diversities are reconciled with one another. The product is a civic majority informed by a more comprehensive view of the public interest. In this way the new republic would acquire the capacity to do what the confederation had been unable to do: to safeguard and advance our interests abroad, to control conflict among the states at home, and, above all, to protect liberty against that radical vice of compact federalism, tyranny of the majority within the individual states. Thanks to the Madisonian design, the weak and illiberal government under the Articles would give way to strong, liberal government under the Constitution. Liberty and union, far from being antagonistic to one another, would flourish together.

We admire the bold advances of the Federalists toward self-government. But the way they seized on the potentialities of the nation was a no less necessary step in their escape from the old regime of the authoritarian few. They grasped and acted on the meaning of "nation" and "nationalism" before the terms came into common use. They saw the American nation as a body whose basic unit was not kindred, clan, or corporate community but the individual. This nation of individuals, nonetheless, was united by bonds as strong as those constituting the old organic order. In America as in Europe, nationalism immensely strengthened the modern state, increasing its control at home and its impact abroad.

The bonds of nationality performed the function of drawing boundaries, identifying the social aggregate within which republican government would operate. Nationality made these individuals "one people," imparting to them the common principles and public affections necessary for self-government. The nation, moreover, was not only in these ways essential to the new authority structure; it was also the object of its governance, constituting the people whose greater liberty, power, opulence, and virtue were what government by the people was for.

The authors of this new and radical regime were also practical men. To be sure, in what they proposed, as in what they rejected, they were moved by general ideas drawn from European political thought. They were also acutely aware of the connection of the particular and the general and of the crucial importance in politics of knowing how to get from here to there. They were superb political engineers, James Madison being the exemplar. When making a case for the Constitution during its ratification, therefore, as when working out its provisions at Philadelphia, they were centrally concerned with the specific and detailed means of achieving their purposes. Part Three of this book, in consequence, has devoted far more of its pages to the Madisonian mechanism than to the Hamiltonian goal.

Constitutionalism for Self-Government

This concern with the institutions of authority has continued to characterize American constitutionalism. That is not incidental, but follows from the primary commitment to self-government by the many.

If the "confusion" and "tumult" which have traditionally been perceived as the self-destructive vice of government by the many are to be averted, there must be order in the participation of the many. The recognition of this necessity in the compound republic appears in the "auxiliary precautions" of the Madisonian scheme. These were the institutions of representation, separation of powers (including bicameralism), and federalism. This institutional ordering, however, was not simply restrictive, a set of restraints designed merely to prevent disorder. For Madisonian nationalists, as for Harrington, they were primarily incentives, a mechanism for eliciting the superiority of popular government. This superiority consisted in greater understanding of the public interest, thanks to the capacity of these institutions, drawing on the diverse interests and opinions of the people at large, to acquire and to assimilate a wider knowledge than would be available to government by the few. Also, in the Madisonian, as in the Harringtonian scheme, these institutions would avert the danger of aristocratic self-love, thereby imparting to republican government a superiority in good will.

To achieve these appealing possibilities, government by the people would have to be conducted according to a system of explicit rules setting out how power would be distributed and exercised. To design such a system would be complex and difficult. Harrington's labored exposition reflects the difficulties. Hume said it would take "a constitution designed with masterly skill." An audience of aspiring republicans would perhaps have preferred a portrait of the society that was to be created. And certainly a vision of the freedom, power, wealth, and virtue of the future nation did inspire the Federalists. Their first and greatest concern, however, was to work out the rules of how to get there from here—the design of the institutions of authority, the Madisonian mechanism.

The commitment to popular government, in short, makes the American Constitution not only explicit but also facilitative, rather than restrictive: not a system of regularized restraints for the protection of individual liberty against government by the many, but a system of regularized incentives for the protection and promotion of rational deliberation by government by the many. The law of the Constitution does impose restraints on government action. These are mainly concerned not with the powers of government but with the purposes for which those powers may be used, as exemplified by the protection of the great freedoms of religion, speech, press, and assembly by the Bill of Rights. Few positive services are mandated, although one might think of some obligations of the judicial system, such as trial by jury and the issuance of writs of *habeas corpus,* under this heading. Otherwise, powerful as the "great objects" of the new regime were in motivating the framers and in setting goals that would legitimate the use of constitutional powers, the overwhelming concern of the document is with the structure of authority. In the American scheme, constitutionalism is not a barrier to, but an avenue of, self-government.

Although its emphasis is on institutions, the national theory justifies them morally and personally by general principles. Important as motivation and justification, these principles can be inferred from what was said about institutions. The point is illustrated by the major defeat of the nationalist cause at Philadelphia, the compromise which resulted in equal representation of the states in the Senate. From the viewpoint of those Anti-Federalists who thought of each state as having "individuality," this provision could be considered a victory for the principle of corporate representation. On that principle in its medieval form, the constituencies of the House of Commons, the ancient communities of shire and borough, were each given the same number of representatives regardless of wealth or population. In contrast with this medieval practice, the Commonwealth republicans displayed their radical individualism by their adoption of proportionate representation when they assigned different numbers of representatives to the constituencies of their proposed new legislature. Madison showed that he shared this radical individualism when, rejecting any appearance of corporate representation, he fought stubbornly for proportionate representation in the Senate as well as the House of Representatives.

This same principle was expressed in Madison's thinking about interests and interest groups. In his view the group resulted from the capacities and choices of individuals. The interest groups which he identified as the primary motors in politics and the main source of faction—the landed, the commercial, the banking, and other occupational and proprietary groups—were not the fixed groups of ancient organic communities, but the shifting interest groups of a developing market economy. At a later date in Britain during its great age of reform, similar economic conditions under the auspices of liberal political ideas finally broke the system of representation out of the remnants of the medieval mold and based it on constituencies of individuals rather than corporate bodies.[4] Although James Wilson more clearly perceived how participation would create the social bonds of new communities, these communities likewise were groups whose boundaries were not fixed but fluid, as the democratic and social impulse led to more inclusive bodies.

The same radical individualism underlies the nationalist theory of rights. The foundation of rights, according to Madison, is the diverse and unequal "faculties" of individuals. The protection of these faculties, according to Madison constitutes "justice" and is "the first object of government." One particular right holds pride of place as "the only effectual guardian of every other right." This is the right of freedom of expression, for political as well as for personal purposes.

The faculty so exercised is "reason" which, for Madison as for Milton, renders the individual capable not only of following a moral criterion but also of deciding what that criterion ought to be. Madison takes a balanced view of reason, seeing it as a normative as well as an instrumental power, which under the right circumstances is capable of controlling individual action. These circumstances include the characteristics of nationality in the extended republic as well as the "auxiliary precautions" of the Constitution. Under such circumstances, government by discussion, starting from the diverse interests and opinions of the people at large, will tend toward decisions protecting justice and promoting the public interest.

The Constitution whose institutions facilitate these outcomes in not a mechanism of mere majority rule. That is "the republican principle," but the national theory also depends on other rules for its success. The stipulation that the republic be large and diverse is such a rule and in Madison's exposition is a prime reason why coalitions of majorities will be civic majorities and not factious majorities. At certain points in the representative process, majority rule must be invoked if there is to be any government at all. But other characteristics of these institutions are in no sense a mere projection of majority rule. The separation of powers, for instance, is a device of political engineering to promote the rule of law in legislation and an energetic focus on the particular in execution. While these other rules do have the effect of limiting majority rule at some points, that is only an incidental result of their rationale, which is to facilitate rational deliberation. American constitutionalism is not primarily restrictive, but facilitative. Its aim is not to put a brake on popular government but to make it work.

Federalism and Liberty

What then in the theory of this system of strong, popular, national, and deliberative government is the reason for having states? In the debates over central–local relations from colonial days to the adoption of the Constitution, three main arguments had been advanced for local governments with the Constitutional protection of states: the arguments from community, utility, and liberty. The argument from community, which descended from the political philosophy of ancient Greece through medieval conceptions of the organic, corporate society, had been reformulated by continental thinkers such as Althusis and Bodin. This idealization of the small community had played no part in the thought of the American rebels, but in Montesquieu's powerful exposition had contributed to the advocacy of the small republic by the Anti-Federalist opponents of the Constitution.

The argument from utility had provided a rationale for the division of authority between the colonies and Westminster when the prerevolutionary debate turned to the federal option. Reflecting the way economists think, as one sees in Adam Smith's treatment, it was and has continued to be a sensible and practical premise for deciding what functions should be assigned respectively to central and to local governments. Madisonian nationalists by implication invoked utility when they distinguished the proper functions of the two levels as "local" and "general," giving these terms much the same meaning economists intend with the terms "internal" and "external." So also did nationalists at a later date, as when Daniel Webster in effect called on the economists' conception of collective goods to defend the policy of internal improvements.

Strong as a definition of the respective functions on grounds of efficiency and effectiveness, utility is weak as a standard for dividing powers with constitutional protection which *a fortiori* can be adapted to the demands of a developing economy only with great difficulty. Present-day federalism can to some extent cope with these rigidities as to boundaries and powers by the liberal use of the congressional spending power to win state consent to changes that might otherwise be opposed on constitutional grounds. But that is to use the argument from utility to bypass federalism, not to implement it.

The argument which was foremost in the minds of the framers and which still holds greatest promise as a rationale for states is the argument from liberty. That was the reasoning of the Commonwealthmen, Harrington, Milton, and the Levellers, in their anticipations of national federalism. The protection of liberty was also the ground of Montesquieu's defense of the kind of federalism embodied in his confederate model. Contrary to the thinking of the Commonwealthmen and the American nationalists, however, the main danger to popular government, according to Montesquieu, came from the central authority of a wide jurisdiction. Conversely, the principle safeguard was the peripheral governments.

While holding that the people at large in the larger jurisdiction were the best guardians of liberty, the nationalists also perceived that central office-holders could become corrupt and oppressive. In this light, they too considered the states to be institutions for correcting the deviations of the center. Madison emphatically sees the states performing this function as agents of the national will. That perception is clearest in his version of *divide et impera,* the tactic of the people at large using the states to mobilize national action against central misconduct. Each state has its separate task of governing "the local and personal interests" of its citizens, in contrast with "the great and general interests" primarily entrusted to the federal government. It also has the crucial task of serving as the "agent and trustee" of the people at large of the nation. The national will, as the constituent sovereign, created the states and, as the governmental sovereign, uses them to protect the fundamental liberties of the individual. Reflecting this same principle of *divide et impera,* the federal government, moved by the national will, protects the minorities of the states against the danger of factious state majorities. The federal system is interactive. While it separates the governing processes of the two levels on the principle of utility, it also integrates them politically for the protection of liberty.

Nor, as members of this interactive system, are the states confined to the negative function of restraint. They also perform a positive function when, as "well-springs for reform," they show how government can enlarge opportunity and incite one another and the federal government to follow their successful experimentation.[5] In performing this positive function, as in performing the negative function of restraint, states serve the fundamental liberty of republican man to make something of himself and of his nation.

Originally, the states set the example when the Constitution was brought into existence. Although that effort was directed toward shifting power to the center, the states did not prevent, but rather facilitated, the adoption of the new political order. At various stages of the business of launching the convention, securing ratification of its proposals, and manning the institutions it established, they could have brought the whole enterprise to a halt. Instead, in the spirit of their function as characterized by Madison in *Federalist* 46, they were the agents which "the national movement" utilized to bring about the great transformation. And similarly in later years again and again the Union renewed and reformed itself through the initiative of the states.

Radicalism and Prudence

The existence of the states makes the United States a compound republic. But while the republic is compound, the nation is unitary. The nation is that "one people" who bring the republic into existence and who govern themselves by means of its institutions for the sake of their "increase" as a nation. These "auxiliary precautions" of the Constitution are notable for their prudence, as exhibited in the provision of two levels of government, each safeguarded by the separation of powers and together giving American liberty its "double security." The good sense of these institutions, however, must not blind us to the radicalism of their design. They are not half-measures. In the nationalist view, they serve not to hamper government by the people but to make it effective.

The nationalists were under no illusions that they could somehow find a governing class in American society which they could slyly insert between the people and power. Nor did they suffer from the opposite illusion that the immediate wishes of the multitude expressed a general will indicating without further refinement the common good. They recognized as fully as any Machiavelli or Montesquieu the self-destructive danger of government by the many which, when overwhelmed by "confusion" and "tumult," gives rise to demagogues and tyrants. No more than an individual could the people rely on first impulse to identify what was rational and right. As in the Miltonian scheme, the high value of an individual's thought required each to listen to and learn from others. As in the Harringtonian model, that process of listening, learning, and deciding required "good orders" if paralysis was to be avoided and the "excellence" of government by the people was to be realized.

The design of the system was radical in that its moving political force, its "primary control," in Madison's words, was the people. To say that the people could perform this task is to say that they could act as one. In the nationalist conception, accordingly, the nation was unitary in origin, operation, and outcome. It was one as the people who constitute the republic, as the people who govern it under the Constitution, and as the people whose union the constitutional order seeks to perfect. In the way they thought of national unity, the nationalists again displayed their prudence as well as their radicalism. They did not mean by national unity something rigid, static, and therefore, in the real political world, quite impossible. As they saw it, the United States as a commonwealth for increase would be constantly on the move. The model is not the changeless equilibrium of Montesquieuian political science in which a balance of power between separate and only externally related bodies maintains diversity by a mechanism of isolation. The model is Miltonian, the interaction of individuals with one another leading toward agreement, which, as it is achieved, provokes a new and fruitful diversity.

The radicalism of this point of view appears sharply if we review the role of the people in the whole system, as sketched in three of Madison's more remarkable papers, *Federalist* numbers 10, 46, and 51. Throughout, the analysis presumes that the people are one. *Federalist* 10 focuses on "the Union," whose members, thanks to the diversity consequent on largeness of scale, are prepared for the process of rational deliberation which broadens the horizons of public policy and protects it against domination by faction. This same premise continues to figure in *Federalist* 46 and 51. Concerned with institutions, the first with federalism and the second with separation of powers, these papers examine the interaction of the people and these institutions. The role of the people is particularly marked in *Federalist* 46. There, setting forth the republican version of *divide et impera,* Madison gives "the great body of the common constituents" of the two levels of government the decisive part in determining the outcome of the inevitable rivalry between state and federal government. In *Federalist* 51, after examining how he expects the separation of powers to work, Madison reviews the institutional basis of the "double security" which protects "the rights of the people." He then returns to *Federalist* 10, summing up what he had said there about the political body that would exercise political control over these institutional checks, the people at large of the extended republic. Restating the argument of *Federalist* 10, he concludes with regard to this body that "a coalition of a majority of the whole society can seldom take place on any other principles than those of justice and the general good."

Such a conception of popular government is not utopian. In contrast with the authoritarian doctrine that had dominated Western political thought, however, this view of the American people, of what they are, what they can do, and what they can make of themselves, is profoundly radical. And today its radicalism—not diminished but enhanced by prudence—speaks as clearly to us as it did to the Americans of that time.

The genius of the nationalists was seeing what could be done with diversity. They not only tolerated diversity, they welcomed it, making its dynamic influence the ground of liberty and progress. They saw that by rational discourse different opinions could be brought into agreement and diverse interests fitted together in the public interest.

This affirmation of pluralism had a no less important converse. It meant the rejection of the claim to certainty. The rules of this political process treated no opinion as having a monopoly on truth and no interest as embracing all that was right and good. Spokesmen could and did make these claims, but if they were to win power, it had to be by an open and uncoerced competition. And if they did win, their views were subject to criticism, amendment, and rejection by the same process that had brought them to power.

That was a great change from the received opinion and practice of previous ages, when the few were exalted above the many because it was believed that they had such a supreme grasp of truth and goodness. Certainty enabled them, indeed obliged them, to use all means, including coercion, to enforce their views and their policies. When the many had their chance to rule, one might have expected them in their diversity to back off from those claims. Often, alas, they have gone right on using the same cruel means to enforce the same archaic claims in the name of some absolute of God, Man, Nature, or History.

Happily their like were few among not only the Federalists but also their opponents. This did not mean that these men lacked commitment. Like the great mentor of the Revolution and the Constitution, Benjamin Franklin, they were ready to risk their necks for their beliefs. Like him, they could take satisfaction in the relative body count after the Battle of Bunker Hill. Yet they could not only speak but also to a great extent act in the spirit of his remarks when he opened the concluding session of the convention at Philadelphia saying, with modesty, not unmixed with policy:

> I confess that there are several parts of this constitution which I do not at present approve, but I am not sure I shall never approve them. For having lived long, I have experienced many instances of being obliged by better information, or fuller consideration, to change opinions even on important subjects, which I once thought right, but found to be otherwise.[6]

Notes

References

Index

Notes

Full bibliographical information for the works cited in short form in the Notes appears in the References.

Introduction: The National Idea in American Politics

1. Report of comment by R. Morris, *New York Times*, January 31, 1981; by H. S. Commager, *Christian Science Monitor*, February 19, 1981.
2. McDonald, *Hamilton*, p. 3.
3. Farrand, *Records*, p. 283 (June 18, 1787).
4. *Spirit of the Laws*, Book 8, ch. 16.
5. Commager, *Documents*, p. 171.
6. The phrase comes in Hamilton's *Report on the Public Credit* (January 14, 1790), which will be found in his *Papers*, vol. 6, pp. 51–168. This report was concerned not specifically with the national bank but with the funding of the domestic and foreign debt at par and the federal assumption of debts incurred by the states during the Revolution. Hamilton's nation-building aim, however, was served by all the reports, as Lodge emphasizes in his biography where he quotes the phrase (p. 89), and goes on to elaborate the broad outlines of Hamilton's fiscal and economic policy. Although Lodge's work has been outdated by later scholarship, his judgments are worth considering since they come from a man who was a leading Republican in the days before his party switched from the nationalist to the states' rights position (see below p. 18). Declaring that no single paper, except the Emancipation Proclamation, was of such importance in the history of the United States, Lodge called the report "the cornerstone of the Government of the United States and the foundation of the national movement" (p. 289).
7. *McCulloch v. Maryland* (1819) 4 Wheaton 316.
8. Ibid., at p. 421.

9. In a letter of May 22, 1779, to his intimate friend, Lt. Col. John Laurens. Quoted in Loss, "Alexander Hamilton and the Modern Presidency," p. 24, n. 53.

10. John C. Miller, noting that Hamilton sought to make the rich the pillars of the union, concludes that it was his nationalism that led to his elitism. *Growth of the New Nation,* p. 125. Also see Lodge, *Hamilton,* p. 89.

11. Miller, *Hamilton,* p. 289.

12. See especially *The Report on Manufactures* (December 1791), *Papers,* vol. 10, pp. 230–340.

13. Miller, *Hamilton,* p. 285.

14. Forrest McDonald points out that Hamilton used three institutions modeled on the British system—funding of the debt, a national bank, and a sinking fund—but for much broader ends. *Hamilton,* p. 161. Contrary to authoritative opinion, such as that of Adam Smith and David Hume, Hamilton believed that the public debt could be effectively used to enhance state power. See Park, *European Origins,* p. 161.

15. Report prepared for the South Carolina legislature's Committee on Federal Relations, November 1831. Calhoun, *Papers,* vol. 11, pp. 495–496.

16. Merriam, *American Political Theories,* p. 284.

17. Fuess, *Daniel Webster,* pp. 316–317.

18. Ibid., pp. 287–288, 290.

19. *Register* (1830), vol. 6, "First Session of the Twenty-first Congress." On January 18, Webster presented a petition in which the South Carolina Canal and Rail Road Co. requested a subsidy from the federal government. January 19 Senator Hayne objected. January 20 Webster replied. Hayne spoke again January 21 and 25. Webster made his famous speech January 26 and 27. Also on January 27 Hayne replied and Webster rebutted.

20. Bemis, *Adams and the Union,* ch. 4, "Liberty is Power," esp. on his public land policy, p. 78.

21. *Register,* pp. 44–45.

22. Ibid., pp. 45–46.

23. Scharf, *History of Delaware,* vol. 1, pp. 27, 28.

24. *Register,* p. 66.

25. *Register,* p. 38.

26. *Register,* p. 67.

27. "Reflections on the Revolution in France," Burke, *Writings and Speeches,* vol. 8, p. 147.

28. Speech of February 16, 1833 replying to Calhoun's Resolutions setting forth the compact theory of the Constitution.

29. Fuess, *Daniel Webster,* p. 31.

30. Webster, *Great Speeches,* pp. 123–135.

31. Lincoln, *Works,* vol. 4, pp. 434–435.

32. Lincoln, *Works*, vol. 4, p. 434. I have termed these two aspects of sovereignty "constituent" and "governmental."

33. Lincoln, *Works*, vol. 4, p. 438.

34. Lincoln's wartime messages were necessarily concerned mainly with the armed conflict. But he also showed his commitment to the Hamiltonian cause, or what Henry Cabot Lodge called "the national movement." In his second annual message of December 1, 1862, for instance, he dealt not only with "the fiery trial" but also with the consolidation of the union. Referring to "the vast extent" and "variety" of the United States, he observed that "steam, telegraphs, and intelligence have brought these to be an advantageous combination for one united people," and he went on to urge Congress to hasten the completion of "the Pacific Railroad" and to support the enlargement of "the great canals in New York and Illinois"; he also referred favorably to the activities of the newly created Department of Agriculture. Lincoln, *Works*, vol. 5, pp. 518–537.

35. Richardson, *Papers of Jefferson Davis*, vol. 1, p. 63.

36. Roosevelt, *Papers and Addresses*, vol. 2, p. 1.

37. Holcombe, *The New Party Politics*.

38. The National Recovery Act. U.S. Statutes at Large, vol. 48, p. 165.

39. Roosevelt, *Papers and Addresses*, vol. 5, pp. 230–236. See also Galbraith, *American Capitalism*.

40. Marshall, *Class, Citizenship, and Social Development*.

41. Alsop, *FDR*, pp. 10, 11.

42. Glazer, *Affirmative Discrimination*, pp. 177–178.

43. See President Johnson's speech to the graduating class of Howard University, June 4, 1965. Johnson, *Vantage Point*, p. 166.

44. Ibid., p. 165.

45. Schlesinger, *Disuniting of America*, p. 2.

46. So George C. Benson defines a federal government as "a government in which the written constitution, or an inviolable statutory precedent, specifies that certain fundamental authority adheres to a central government and that other governmental authority belongs to smaller areas." "Values of decentralized government." In Benson, ed., *Essays in Federalism*, p. 3.

47. Miller, *Hamilton*, p. 297.

48. See Walker, *Functioning Federalism*, pp. 7, 12, 173–180; and Beer, "Political Overload," pp. 6–7.

49. See Conlan, *New Federalism*, pp. 153–154.

Part One. From Hierarchy to Republicanism

1. Adams, *Works of John Adams*, vol. 3, p. 454.

2. Ibid., pp. 451, 455, 457, 462, 464.

1. The Rule of the Wise and the Holy: Thomas Aquinas

1. Lovejoy, *Great Chain of Being.*

2. For my analysis of Aquinas's thought I have relied chiefly, though not exclusively, on his *Summa Theologica, Summa Contra Gentiles,* and *De Regno, ad regem Cypri* (less correctly referred to as *De Regimine Principum*), using the Latin editions and English translations given in References. In the notes I cite these three works as *S.T., S.C.G.,* and *D.R.,* identifying the relevant passages by reference to the subdivisions of the Latin, which are also followed in the English translations.

3. In general I follow McIlwain, who wrote of St. Thomas: "he was the greatest of all contemporary exponents of pure monarchy . . . His specific political doctrine . . . is the normal political thought of the later middle ages, which might be illustrated without end from other contemporary sources from the thirteenth to the sixteenth century." McIlwain, *Growth of Political Thought,* p. 331.

For an indication of the different ways people have interpreted Saint Thomas's politics since the sixteenth century, see Thomas Gilby in the Blackfriars edition of *S.T.,* vol. 28 (1966), Appendix 5, pp. 175–176, esp. para. 3. It should be noted that neither of the two principal views, the "translation theory" and the "designation theory," makes Aquinas an advocate of popular government.

For contemporary works, see Bourke, *Thomistic Bibliography, 1920–1940,* sect. "Political and Legal Philosophy"; and Terry Miethe and Bourke, *Thomistic Bibliography (1940–1978),* sect. "Socio-Political-Legal Philosophy."

4. See "On Being and Essence" and Aristotle's *Metaphysics* in D'Arcy, *Thomas Aquinas,* pp. 157, 166.

5. For the classic discussion of this point, see Plato's *Republic,* 407b, 509d, and 510e.

6. D'Arcy, *Thomas Aquinas,* p. 157.

7. Lovejoy, *Great Chain of Being,* p. 67.

8. *S.T.,* 1, Q.96, a.3.

9. Lovejoy, *Great Chain of Being,* pp. 58–59, quoting from *De Anima,* 414a 29 and 415a.

10. Lovejoy, *Great Chain of Being,* p. 59.

11. *S.T.,* 1–2, Q.55, a.4.

12. *S.T.,* 1, Q.45, a.2.

13. Ibid.

14. *S.C.G.,* 3, 78 and 112.

15. *D.R.,* 1,1.

16. *S.T.,* 1–2, Q.63, a.1; and Bigongiari, p. ix.

17. *S.C.G.,* 3, 81.

18. *D.R.,* 1, 1.

19. *S.C.G.,* 3, 81.

20. Ibid., 3, 78.
21. Ibid.
22. S.C.G., 3, 79.
23. S.C.G., 3, 68.
24. See, for instance, the reproduction of an ancient picture of the parliament of Edward I in Wright and Smith, *Parliament*, p. 13.
25. *S.T.*, 1–2, Q.58, a.3; and Q.62, a.1.
26. *S.T.*, 1–2, Q.57, a.2; and Q.61, a.2, a.5, and a.3.
27. Ibid., Q.51, a.1.
28. Ibid., Q.95, a.1; and 1, Q.96, a.4.
29. *S.T.*, 1, Q.92, a.1.
30. Ibid., Q.103, a.1.
31. *S.T.*, 1–2, Q.91, a.3.
32. Ibid., Q.92., a.1.
33. Ibid., Q.96, a.5.
34. Ibid., Q.93, a.6. See also Q.109, a.2 and a.3.
35. Ibid., Q.95, a.1.
36. Ibid., Q.62, a.2.
37. Ibid., Q.62, a.1.
38. Ibid., Q.109, a.5.
39. Ibid., Q.111, a.1.
40. Ibid., Q.62, a.1.
41. Ibid., Q.112, a.2.
42. *S.T.*, 2–2, Q.2, a.6.
43. *S.T.*, 3, *Supplementum*, Q.36, a.2.
44. *S.T.*, 2–2, Q.1, a.10.
45. *S.T.*, 1–2, Q.105, a.1.
46. *S.T.*, 2–2, Q.11, a.3.
47. Milton, "Areopagitica," *Works*, vol. 2, p. 560.
48. *S.T.*, 1, Q.103, a.6.
49. Ibid., Q.103.
50. Ibid., Q.103, a.4.
51. Ibid., Q.103, a.6.
52. Ibid., Q.103, a.1.
53. *D.R.* 1, 1 and 2.
54. *S.T.*, 1–2, Q.95, a.2; and Q.96, a.6.
55. Ibid., Q.96, a.4.
56. For discussion of this question see Phelan-Eschmann translation of the *De Regno*, Introduction, by Eschmann, pp. xxii–xxvi and vol. 28 of the Blackfriars edition of *S.T.*, Introduction by Thomas Gilby, p. xxii, n. 8. Both accept *D.R.* as the work of Aquinas through *Lib. 2, cap. 4*.

57. *D.R.*, 1, 6.

58. Ibid.

59. *S.T.*, 1–2, Q.90, a.4; Q.97, a.4; Q.91, a.1; and Q.90, a.4.

60. *S.T.*, Q.95, a.4.

61. *S.T.*, 1–2, Q.105, a.1.

62. Ibid.

63. Ibid., and *S.C.G.*, 3, 81.

64. *S.C.G.*, 3, 81.

65. I wish to thank Michael Walzer for drawing my attention to this discrepancy.

66. *S.T.*, 1–2, Q.105, a.1, ad.2.

67. *S.T.*, 3, *Supplementum*, Q.40, a.6.

68. Ibid.

69. See *S.C.G.*, 3, 81.

70. Gerth and Mills, *From Max Weber*, p. 51. In his *Protestant Ethic*, Weber writes as if he had coined the term *Entzauberung dieser Welt* (there translated as "the elimination of magic from the world") and attributed it to Protestantism, p. 105.

71. Max Weber's discussion of charismatic authority helps clarify Aquinas's distinction between gratuitous grace and sacramental grace. On "personal charisma" and "charisma of office" see *Social and Economic Organization*, ch. 3, "Types of Authority." Weber emphasizes what I have called the deferential quality of the relationship. The charismatic leader must prove himself to his followers, who then recognize him. His authority, however, does not come from that recognition. On the contrary, the followers recognize his authority and, therefore, feel the duty to obey. As Parsons says in his introduction to his translation, "This is not . . . the ordinary case of 'consent' of the led in the usual democratic meaning. The authority of the leader does not express the 'will' of the followers, but rather their duty or obligation." Weber, *Social and Economic Organization*, p. 65.

72. *S.T.*, 1–2, Q.111, a.1.

73. Ibid., Q.111, a.5 and a.4.

74. Ibid., Q.99, a.3.

75. Ibid., Q.106, a.2.

76. Ibid., Q.101, a.2.

77. Ibid., Q.101 and 102.

78. Ibid., Q.102, a.2.

79. Quoted in Pelikan, *Development of Doctrine*, vol. 4, p. 125.

80. *S.T.*, 1–2, Q.102, a.4.

81. I have used the term "Old Tory Politics" to identify the political culture of Tudor and Stuart England in *Modern British Politics*, ch. 1.

82. Sigmund, *Cusa*, p. 11.

83. The quotations are from Otto Gierke and Harold Laski, quoted in Sigmund, *Cusa*, pp. 310, 308.

84. Ibid., *Cusa*, p. 140.

85. Ibid., *Cusa*, p. 143.

86. Ibid., *Cusa*, pp. 154, 138, 131, 225.

87. Morris, *Tyndale to Hooker*. Quentin Skinner also points out how Renaissance humanists such as Elyot accepted the traditional hierarchic picture of political life. Skinner, *Foundations*, vol. 1, pp. 214–242.

88. Elyot, *The Governor*, p. 9.

89. Tillyard, *Elizabethan World Picture*.

90. Hill, *Milton and the English Revolution*, p. 268.

91. Hooker, "The Laws of Ecclesiastical Polity," in *Works*, vol. 1, pp. 61, 66, 67, 73, 74.

92. Ibid., vol. 3, pp. 331, 332.

93. Ibid., vol. 1, p. 103.

94. Ibid., vol. 1, pp. 101, 102.

95. Faulkner, *Hooker*, p. 165.

96. McIlwain, *Works of James I*.

97. Ibid., p. 307.

98. Ibid., "Basilikon Doron" (1599), p. 38. On Aquinas see above pp. 37–38. Aristotle similarly held that a king must excel his subjects in "every quality"; otherwise, he would "only be a king by chance." Barker, *Aristotle's Politics*, p. 73; quoting the *Ethics* para. 1160b.

99. McIlwain, *Works of James I*, p. 315.

100. Ibid., "The Trew Law of Free Monarchies" (1598), p. 66.

101. Ibid., p. xc, Appendix C: "James and the Puritans." On James as an orthodox Calvinist, see Haller, *Rise of Puritanism*, p. 49.

102. McIlwain, *Works of James I*, pp. 118, 119; 169.

103. Neale, *Elizabeth I*, p. 189.

104. Ibid., p. 221.

105. Lockyer, *Tudor and Stuart England*, pp. 239–240.

106. Knachel, *Eikon Basilike*.

107. Hill, *Milton and the English Revolution*, p. 172.

108. Milton, "Eikonoklastes," *Works*, vol. 3, pp. 335–601.

2. The Idea of the National Republic: John Milton

1. The term "government by discussion" was coined by Walter Bagehot, appearing first in his *Physics and Politics* (1872), ch. 5, "The Age of Discussion." Bagehot contrasted this sort of interchange of information with the typical "parley" in a traditionalist society between a leader and followers which dealt with particular

"undertakings." In government by discussion the interchange took place on a higher plane of generality, dealing with "principles" under which many particulars could be classed whether as common means or common ends. In this process Bagehot saw the central expression of the rational spirit of modernity which, arising first in the political sphere, spread to the rest of society, giving rise to scientific research and capitalistic exchange. In his Darwinian scheme, government by discussion greatly added to the survival power of a society, enabling it to surpass and overcome other societies still stuck in "the cake of custom." I have sketched a very brief history of the theory and practice in "The Strengths of Liberal Democracy."

Current writing about "rational choice" and "rational deliberation" contribute to the theory of government by discussion, and at various places in this book I have used the ideas of these writers to clarify the thought of earlier authors.

2. *Abrams v. United States*, 250 U.S. 616 (1919).

3. Heclo, *Modern Social Politics*, p. 321.

4. Arber, *English Reprints*, "John Milton, Areopagitica: A Decree of Starre Chamber, concerning Printing (11 July 1637) and An Order of the Lords and Commons Assembled in Parliament for the Regulating of Printing (14 June 1643)."

5. Milton, "Areopagitica," *Works*, vol. 2, p. 527. In order to reduce distractions, I have modernized the spelling.

6. *Summa Theologica*, 1, Q.83, a.1.

7. See above, Chapter 1, pp. 43–44

8. Milton, "Areopagitica," *Works*, vol. 2, pp. 491, 492, 528, 514–517.

9. *Summa Theologica*, 1–2, Q.97, a.1.

10. See above, Chapter 1, p. 42.

11. Haskins, *Rise of the Universities*, pp. 70–72.

12. *Summa Theologica*, 2–2, Q.1, a.10.

13. Milton, "Areopagitica," *Works*, vol. 2, p. 543.

14. Ibid., pp. 548, 550.

15. Ibid., pp. 551, 543, 548.

16. Ibid., p. 550.

17. Ibid., pp. 557, 554.

18. Ibid., pp. 554, 561.

19. Ibid., p. 560.

20. Ibid., pp. 554, 550.

21. Ibid., p. 554.

22. Ibid., pp. 555, 556.

23. Calvin, *Institutes*, vol. 1, pp. 604, 608, 615, 614.

24. Hill, *Milton and the English Revolution*, p. 193.

25. Woodhouse, *Puritanism and Liberty*, pp. 236, 242, 390. Haller, *Rise of Puritanism*, p. 269.

26. Hill, *Milton and the English Revolution*, p. 254. Haller, *Rise of Puritanism*, p. 193.

27. Second Helvetic Confession, 1566, in Schaff, *Creeds of Christendom*, vol. 3, pp. 252, 274, 275.

28. First Scots Confession, 1560, in Schaff, *Creeds of Christendom*, vol. 3, p. 459.

29. Westminster Confession of Faith, 1647, in Schaff, *Creeds of Christendom*, vol. 3, pp. 638, 645, 653.

30. Hill, *Milton and the English Revolution*, ch. 21, "Radical Arminianism."

31. Milton, "Areopagitica," *Works*, vol. 2, p. 522.

32. Ibid., p. 565. See also Hill, *Milton and the English Revolution*, p. 256.

33. See below, Chapter 3, p. 126.

34. Hill, *Milton and the English Revolution*, pp. 160–161.

35. Ibid., p. 336.

36. Milton, "Areopagitica," *Works*, vol. 2, pp. 535, 557.

37. Ibid., pp. 566, 554, 566.

38. Ibid., p. 566.

39. Ibid., pp. 536, 551.

40. Ibid., pp. 553, 552, 553.

41. Ibid., pp. 557, 558.

3. A Constitution for the National Republic: James Harrington

1. *Oceana*, p. 182.

2. *The Commonwealth of Oceana* (London, 1656), cited in notes for this chapter as *Oceana*. I have followed the text printed in J. G. A. Pocock's edition of *The Political Works of James Harrington*, cited in this chapter as *Works*.

3. Montesquieu, *Spirit of the Laws*, vol. 1, p. 20.

4. *Oceana*, p. 179.

5. Ibid., p. 205.

6. Ibid., pp. 274, 257, 258.

7. Ibid., p. 272; and Machiavelli, *Discourses*, book 1, chs. 5 and 6.

8. *Oceana*, p. 273.

9. *Discourses*, Book 1, ch. 6.

10. *Discourses*, Book 1, chs. 5, 6.

11. Ibid., Book 1, ch. 6.

12. Dahl and Tufte, *Size and Democracy*, pp. 5–7.

13. *The Republic*, pp. 141–2 (462b-d).

14. *The Dialogues of Plato* (Jowett), *The Laws*, vol. 5, p. 120 (738). *The Politics of Aristotle* (Barker), p. 57 (1265a).

15. *The Republic*, p. 100 (432a).

16. *The Politics*, p. 46 (1262b).

17. Ibid., p. 291, 292 (1326a, b).

18. Aristotle systematically treated despotism as a form of government among the

barbarians of Asia who, being slaves by nature, submitted to an absolute hereditary ruler. Barker, p. 138 (1285a). See Melvin Richter, "Despotism," in *Dictionary of the History of Ideas,* vol. 2, pp. 1–18. Unlike Montesquieu, however, Aristotle did not explicitly link despotism with the very large polity. Montesquieu, *Spirit of the Laws,* vol. 1, pp. 121–122 (Book 8, chs. 17–19).

19. Mansfield, *New Modes and Orders,* p. 50. Harrington also understood Machiavelli's standard to be quantitative. See *Oceana,* p. 273.

20. Mansfield, *New Modes and Orders,* p. 50.

21. *Discourses,* Book 1, chs. 4–7.

22. Both Machiavelli and Milton agree that the rise of Marius from the democratic tumult of the Gracchi revealed the weakness that led to the fall of the Republic at the hands of Caesar. See *Discourses,* Book 1, ch. 5, and Milton, "Readie and Easie Way," *Works,* vol. 7, pp. 396–463.

23. See above, Chapter 1, p. 45.

24. See below, Chapter 7.

25. See below, Chapter 8.

26. Blackstone, *Commentaries* (1765), Book 1. ch. 2, sect. 3.

27. Quoted in Wood, *Creation,* p. 261.

28. *Oceana,* pp. 245, 165–166.

29. Ibid., p. 336.

30. Ibid., p. 227.

31. U.S. Constitution, Article VI, Section 3. In the House of Commons, the usual form of the oath is, "I swear by Almighty God that I will be faithful and bear true allegiance to Her Majesty Queen Elizabeth, her heirs and successors, according to law." May, *Law, Privileges and Proceedings,* p. 287.

32. "Speech to the Parliament . . . on Tuesday, the 12th of September, 1654," *Writings and Speeches,* vol. 3, p. 459.

33. Woodhouse, *Puritanism and Liberty,* pp. 356–367, 443–445.

34. Locke, *Second Treatise,* pars. 87, 96, 132.

35. *Oceana,* pp. 207, 209.

36. Ibid., p. 207, and on this citizen army see below, p. 122.

37. Ibid, pp. 339–340.

38. Ibid., pp. 165–166.

39. In *Oceana,* the shire ("tribe") has one governing body, the phylarch, which is also called the prerogative troop. In later writings Harrington uses these two terms to refer to two different governing bodies, one to administer the old pre-revolutionary law and the other the new enactments of the parliament in its effort to reform the legal system. The highly decentralized system of Oceana is slightly modified. Recognizing the need for occasional reapportionment, for instance, Harrington now gives the central parliament the power to alter boundaries. On these contrasts with *Oceana,* see *Brief Directions* (1658), *The Art of Lawgiving* (1659), and *Model of a*

Free State (1660), all in *Works*. On legal reform under the Commonwealth, see Veall, *Popular Movement*, which lumps Harrington's proposals with those of the Levellers, pp. 217–219.

40. Friedrich, *Constitutional Government*, ch. 7, "The Constitution as a Political Process."

41. *Oceana*, pp. 229–230.

42. *Oceana*, p. 300.

43. Blitzer, *Immortal Commonwealth*, p. ix.

44. *Oceana*, Foreword, p. 201.

45. Gunn, *Politics and the Public Interest*, p. xi.

46. Pocock, *Machiavellian Moment*, p. 52.

47. Holding that the interest of the public could be repesented in a legislature, "Harrington's novelty lay in his denial that the political system had previously secured the necessary identity of interest and his faith that his system could provide it." This makes "the chief locus of popular influences" the popular assembly which gives "considerable scope for the diversity of interests to be found on matters of public policy . . . Thus the problem of discovering the public interest was narrowed in scope to the operation of a legislature representing all interests and seeking occasional inspiration through various channels of communication with the public." Gunn, *Politics and the Public Interest*, pp. 139–140. Also see Gunn's Introduction on the transition from the medieval notions of "the common good" to modern notions of "the public interest."

48. "The Prerogative of Popular Government," *Works*, p. 467.

49. Ibid., p. 415.

50. *Oceana*, pp. 292–293.

51. Ibid., p. 169.

52. "The Prerogative of Popular Government," *Works*, p. 401.

53. Pocock, *Machiavellian Moment*, pp. 383–384.

54. Hooker, *Works*, vol. 1, p. 102.

55. Hume, "Perfect Commonwealth," pp. 500–501.

56. Pocock, "Introduction," *Works*, p. 87.

57. *Oceana*, p. 189.

58. Ibid., p. 231.

59. An "equal Agrarian" he defined as "a perpetual law establishing and preserving the balance of dominion, by such distribution that no one man or number of men within the compass of the Few or Aristocracy can overpower the whole people by their possession of lands." *Oceana*, p. 181.

60. Ibid., p. 212.

61. *Oceana*, p. 317. Blitzer, *Immortal Commonwealth*, p. 214.

62. *Oceana*, pp. 213, 334.

63. Ibid., pp. 215, 334.

64. Ibid., p. 163.

65. Pocock, "Introduction" to *Works*, p. 63, and "Machiavelli, Harrington, and English Political Ideologies," p. 553.

66. *Oceana*, pp. 197–198.

67. Ibid., p. 181.

68. Ibid., pp. 214, 215, 220, 224. See also "A System of Politics," ch. 5, sect. 6, *Works*, p. 840, and "The Rota," Part 1, sect. 1, *Works*, p. 809.

69. *Oceana*, pp. 218–220.

70. "An Agreement of the People . . ." in Wolfe, *Leveller Manifestoes*, pp. 295–297. Explaining the reasons for the table, the second section of the Agreement declared that since "the people of England" were "very unequally distributed by Counties, Cities, or Boroughs for the election of representatives," they should be "more indifferently proportioned." For the debate see Woodhouse, *Puritanism and Liberty*, pp. 52–83.

71. Morley, *The Commonwealth of Oceana*, "Introduction," p. 7. Morley was professor of English Language and Literature at Queen's College, London.

72. *Oceana*, p. 272.

73. Ibid., pp. 278, 280.

74. Ibid., p. 280.

75. Ibid., p. 252.

76. "Valerius and Publicola, Or the true Form of a Popular Commonwealth" (1659), *Works*, pp. 799–800.

77. *Oceana*, p. 281.

78. Ibid., pp. 278–280.

79. Hannah Pitkin observes that the Greeks had no concept of representation in the modern sense but did follow practices which we, like Harrington, might consider representative. Pitkin, *Representation*, p. 241.

80. See above Chapter 1, p. 61.

81. Sigmund, *Cusa*, pp. 308, 163–167.

82. Pitkin, *Representation*, p. 246.

83. De Grazia writes: "The King, like the Commons, had originally in England no theory of representing a corporate community. He was a personal sovereign, dealing with individual barons and subjects. Slowly, by a variety of means, he achieved a new role as head of a community with unified interests . . . An early example of the sort of thinking that would in time produce the idea of virtual representation is found in a homily which the Commons offered the King in 1401, comparing Parliment to a Trinity, the members of which were the person of the King, the Lords, and the Commons." *Public and Republic*, p. 17.

84. *Oceana*, p. 247.

85. Ibid., p. 245.

86. Ibid., p. 171.

87. "Debate" in the Senate includes not only speaking but also the business of voting by which a measure is moved through a committee and the whole house and becomes a decree. "Resolution" is the vote of the popular assembly, the act of decision which gives the proposal the force of law.

88. *Oceana*, p. 172.

89. Ibid., p. 172.

90. Rawls, *Theory of Justice*, p. 85.

91. "The Prerogative of Popular Government" (1658), *Works*, p. 417.

92. *Oceana*, p. 267 (Order no. 22).

93. Ibid., pp. 172–173.

94. Ibid., p. 173.

95. Ibid., p. 173.

96. Cited in Beer, *Modern British Politics*, pp. 12, 15–17.

97. *Oceana*, p. 183.

98. Ibid., pp. 257–259.

99. "The Prerogative of Popular Government," *Works*, p. 416.

100. "The Rota," *Works*, p. 810.

101. *Oceana*, p. 281.

102. Pocock, "Introduction," *Works*, p. 68.

103. *Oceana*, p. 272.

104. Ibid., p. 276.

105. "Thoughts on Government" (1776), Adams, *Works of John Adams*, vol. 4, p. 413.

106. Wood, *Creation*, pp. 214, 215.

107. Quoted in Wood, *Creation*, pp. 214, 215.

108. *Oceana*, p. 324.

109. *Oceana*, pp. 167, 169. In 1774 in a reply to "Massachusettensis" (Daniel Leonard) and amidst frequent quotations from Harrington, John Adams observed that this passage of *Oceana* was "written one hundred and twenty years ago" and that "the colonies are now nearer manhood than ever Harrington foresaw they would arrive in such a period of time." Letter 7, "Novanglus; or a History of the Dispute with America from its origin, in 1754, to the present time," in Adams, *Works of John Adams*, vol. 4, p. 104.

110. *Oceana*, pp. 218, 227.

111. Ibid., p. 267.

112. Ibid., pp. 295–298.

113. Ibid., p. 296.

114. "The Art of Law-Giving," *Works*, p. 667.

115. Weber, "Open and Closed Relationships," in *Theory of Social and Economic Organizations*, pp. 139–143. The relevance of the Weberian paradigm to central-local relations in seventeenth-century Britain is supported by a recent study of Bristol

during the years 1625–1641. Using the same contrasting metaphors of "a closed arena or an open gate" to frame the alternatives, David Sacks finds that "seventeenth century Bristol gives us an example of the second type of politics," in which the members of the municipal corporation regarded themselves as "simultaneously citizens and crown servants, city fathers and the legitimate agents of the state in their community, the one role reinforcing the other." "Bristolians," he writes, "were a politically integrated part of the realm." David Sacks, "The Corporate Town and the English State," pp. 105, 96.

116. *Oceana*, pp. 213, 317, 334; Blitzer, *Immortal Commonwealth*, p. 214.
117. *Federalist* 46, p. 320.
118. Blitzer, *Immortal Commonwealth*, p. 257.
119. *Oceana*, p. 226.
120. Ibid., p. 218.
121. Ibid., p. 225.
122. See above, note 39.
123. *Federalist* 10, p. 63.
124. *Oceana*, pp. 300, 301.
125. Milton, "The Readie and Easie Way" (2nd ed.), in *Works of Milton*, vol. 7, p. 423.
126. Ibid., p. 443.
127. Ibid., pp. 458–459.
128. Ibid., p. 461.
129. Ibid., p. 459.
130. "Letter to General Monk," *Works of Milton*, vol. 6, pp. 357–358.
131. *Oceana*, pp. 215–217.
132. Ibid., p. 217; "The Art of Lawgiving," *Works*, p. 681. Blitzer, *Immortal Commonwealth*, p. 167.
133. Ibid., p. 308.
134. Ibid., p. 204.
135. Ibid., pp. 310, 311.
136. Ibid., p. 299.
137. Ibid., pp. 332–333.
138. Ibid., pp. 323–324, 330.
139. Ibid., p. 318.
140. Ibid., p. 323.
141. Ibid., pp. 168, 196, 201; Gunn, *Politics and the Public Interest*, p. 126.
142. Ibid., pp. 201–213.

Part Two. The National and Republican Revolution

1. Schumpeter, *Capitalism, Socialism, and Democracy*, p. 267.

2. Cunliffe, *Washington*, p. 81; Morrison, *American People*, p. 220.

3. On the dissident movements generally in the colonies established by Britain "on the Western rim of the Atlantic," see Greene, *Peripheries and Center*, Book 2, "A Problem Defined, 1764–1775."

4. Schlesinger, Sr., *Colonial Merchants*, pp. 31–37, 50–55.

4. The Conflict of Ideas

1. As Thomas Pangle writes, "the classical historians and philosophers refuse to concede that popular consent is the sole or even the preeminent source of legitimate authority." "Idea of Virtue," . . . *this Constitution*, p. 22.

2. I have discussed this contrast in *Modern British Politics* and in the following pages use the terms Old Tory and Old Whig with the meaning given them in that book.

3. Burke, "Reflections on the Revolution in France," *Writings and Speeches*, vol. 4, pp. 263–265.

4. Burke, "A Letter to Sir Hercules Langrishe on the Subject of the Roman Catholics of Ireland" (January 3, 1792), *Writings and Speeches*, vol. 4, p. 301.

5. See *Modern British Politics*, p. 6, and above, Chapter 1, sect. "Toward Old Tory Politics."

6. John Toland, *The State Anatomy of Great Britain*, quoted in Kemp, *King and Commons*, p. 83.

7. Regarding the question of whether or not there was an American "aristocracy" in the European sense, Robert E. Brown concludes that "it is quite ridiculous to talk about an aristocracy in seventeenth or eighteenth century English terms in describing the eighteenth century American gentry." Quoted by Douglas Adair in *Fame and the Founding Fathers*, p. 297. See also Brown's *Reinterpretation*, p. 57, and the balanced account by H. J. Habakkuk writing on "England" in Goodwin, *European Nobility*.

8. Namier, *England in the Age*, p. 8.

9. Burke, *Writings and Speeches*, vol. 1, pp. 492, 477.

10. Burke, "An Appeal from the New to the Old Whigs" (1791), *Writings and Speeches*, vol. 4, pp. 173–176.

11. Burke, "A Letter to Sir Hercules Langrishe," *Writings and Speeches*, vol. 4, p. 293.

12. Ibid., pp. 293, 301, 302.

13. In 1760, out of 489 English MPs, 192 had been returned by patrons, along with 32 others returned by the Government influence. Namier, *Structure*, vol. 1, p. 182. See also Thorne, *History of Parliament*. In this period, Thorne reckons that 184 among the 203 English boroughs were controlled by a patron.

14. Quoted in Porritt and Porritt, *Unreformed House,* vol. 1, p. 311.

15. I have discussed this question in "Representation of Interests," pp. 613–650, and in *Modern British Politics,* p. 16. See also J. R. Pole, *Political Representation,* especially Part 4, ch. 4.

16. Burke, "Thoughts on the Cause of the Present Discontents" (1770), *Writings and Speeches,* vol. 1, p. 519.

17. Burke, "Speech to the Electors of Bristol" (November 3, 1774), *Writings and Speeches,* vol. 2, pp. 97, 96.

18. Pointing out that "the idea of virtual representation explained how it came about that the select few . . . might represent the totality of the country in the Commons," Alfred De Grazia wrote, "Political leadership was said to be a specialized thing, not mere sampling of the whims of the whole population . . . A more equal division of the constituencies, an extension of the suffrage, or a more immediate responsibility to constituents could only have a destructive effect on a constitution built upon an age-old representation of the true spirit of the nation." *Public and Republic,* p. 243.

19. Burke, "Speech on American Taxation" (April 19, 1774), *Works,* vol. 1, pp. 491–492, and "An Appeal from the New to the Old Whigs" (1791), *Works,* vol. 3, pp. 424–425.

20. Blackstone, *Commentaries* (1765), Book 1, pp. 160–161.

21. I must differ with the high authority of C. H. McIlwain when he says that the eighteenth-century Whig doctrine of sovereignty, of which Blackstone was an exponent, shares the view which McIlwain attributes to John Austin and Thomas Hobbes that "might makes right." McIlwain characterized that view in these words: "It is the mere physical fact of mastery, whether induced by consent, fear or force, which clothes those who obtain it, no matter how or why they obtain it, with the supreme authority in a state." *Constitutionalism,* p. 57. Blackstone did not say that parliament owed either its legal or its moral authority to physical mastery. I must also differ with Bernard Bailyn, who accepts McIlwain's view on this matter, when he says that the whig doctrine of sovereignty, as stated by Blackstone, "stripped the idea of sovereignty of its moral and legalistic qualities and laid bare the doctrine of naked force." *Ideological Origins,* pp. 199–201.

Blackstone would agree that the authority of parliament was "absolute" in the sense that no other person or body of persons could override its legal authority and that it was "arbitrary" in the sense that any and every parliamentary statute carried the legal obligation of obedience. He did not say that the authority of parliament was "arbitrary" in the sense that the mere say-so of parliament could make an immoral law moral.

22. Blackstone, *Commentaries,* Book 1, pp. 39, 41, 42.

23. Ibid., pp. 123, 55, 124.

24. Modern legal scholars draw this distinction quite sharply. H. L. A. Hart terms

the sovereignty of parliament a "rule of recognition" which identifies valid rules of law, especially for judges and officials. The term "principle" more adequately suggests the use of the body of theory from which the idea derived. As in the eighteenth century, this principle is taken to mean that since no statute established the principle that courts will obey acts of parliament, similarly no statute can repeal, alter, or abolish the principle; hence the sovereignty of parliament is "continuing."

Conceivably, judges and the community might accept and act on the different principle that sovereignty is "self-embracing" or self-limiting. In that case, parliament could by statute limit its future lawmaking powers. By such a "self-limiting" act, sovereignty could be divided, for example, with the European Community. This principle, however, is not accepted today, no more than in the eighteenth century, when the "continuing" sovereignty of parliament made impossible any federal division of power with the colonies. See H. W. Wade, "Basis for Legal Sovereignty," pp. 187–189. For a further discussion of these points, see Turpin, *British Government*, pp. 32–35.

25. Blackstone, *Commentaries*, Book 1, pp. 47, 48, 160, 48.

26. Ibid., p. 48.

27. Hence, my disagreement with McIlwain, above, note 21.

28. See above, Chapter 1, p. 46.

29. Blackstone, *Commentaries*, Book 1, pp. 48, 49.

30. Ibid., p. 200. The "indivisibility" of parliament's authority stood in the way of a federal arrangement with the colonies. This attribute, we should note, was an aspect of parliament's "continuing" sovereignty. That is, since parliament's authority was such that it could not limit itself, parliament could not conclusively empower colonial governments by delegating a portion of its authority to them.

31. Ibid., pp. 50–51.

32. Ibid., pp. 245, 213.

33. Ibid., p. 245.

34. Locke, *Second Treatise*, para. 149.

35. Barker, *Essays on Government*, p. 138, n.4. Blackstone referred to 1688 as a "revolution" but argued that since James did not subvert the constitution but only "endeavored" to do so, the government was not dissolved, society did not revert to the state of nature, and "the constitution was kept entire." *Commentaries*, Book 1, p. 213.

36. Blackstone, *Commentaries*, Book 1, pp. 160, 161. This assertion of Locke's is precisely the proposition with which James Otis wound up his introductory pages on "the origin of government" in his attack on parliamentary taxation of the colonies, "The Rights of the British Colonies Asserted and Proved" (July 1764), in Bailyn, *Pamphlets*, p. 434.

37. Blackstone, *Commentaries*, Book 1, p. 162. Richard Wooddeson, Blackstone's successor as Vinerian Professor, made the contrast explicit. Granting that govern-

ment acquires its authority from tacit consent, he denied that "such consent is subsequently revocable." *Elements of Jurisprudence*, p. 22.

38. Blackstone clearly thought that parliament could make and unmake "fundamental laws," as one can see from the examples he cites relating to the established religion, the succession of the crown, the union with Scotland, and the duration of parliaments. Republicans in Britain and America were not of one mind. Harrington thought the "orders" of Oceana would be "immortal." Sidney, on the other hand, emphasized that the people could both "institute" and "abrogate" forms of government and indeed welcomed frequent use of the latter power. In his circular letter Sam Adams claimed that the "fundamental rules of the constitution" were "unalterable." By the middle of the 1770s it was being said that constitutions could be amended by the people. Gordon Wood traces this confusing and complicated history in *Creation*, pp. 275–309.

39. Rossiter, *Seedtime*, p. 290.

40. Whitehead, *Aims*, p. 106.

41. Tilly, *Formation*, pp. 12–46.

42. Franklin, *Papers*, vol. 4, p. 233.

43. Ibid., p. 228.

44. Franklin to William Shirley (December 4, 1754), *Papers*, vol. 5, p. 444.

45. Ibid., p. 443.

46. Franklin to David Hume (September 27, 1760), *Papers*, vol. 9, p. 229.

47. Van Doren, *Benjamin Franklin*, p. 217.

48. Franklin to Lord Kames (February 25, 1767), *Papers*, vol. 14, p. 70.

49. Franklin, "Observations Concerning the Increase of Mankind," *Papers*, vol. 4, pp. 229, 331.

50. Franklin, "Reasons and Motives for the Albany Plan of Union," *Papers*, vol. 5, p. 399.

51. Ibid., p. 400.

52. Ibid., p. 402.

53. Franklin to William Shirley (December 22, 1754), *Papers*, vol. 5, pp. 449–500.

54. Franklin, "A Plan for Settling the Western Colonies," *Papers*, vol. 5, p. 457.

55. Merk, *Westward Movement*, pp. 79, 100.

56. See above, p. 129.

57. Merk, *Westward Movement*, pp. 80, 99, 101.

58. Franklin, "Reasons and Motives for the Albany Plan of Union," *Papers*, vol. 5, p. 390.

59. Ibid., p. 399.

60. Wright, *Franklin*, p. 189.

61. See Franklin, *Autobiography*, pp. 161–172.

62. Lawrence, *Studies*, p. 28.

63. Quoted in Wright, *Franklin*, p. 332.

64. Franklin, *Autobiography*, pp. 149, 150.

65. Franklin, *Writings*, vol. 1, p. 36.

66. Weber, *Protestant Ethic*, pp. 48–50, 71, 192, 195–198.

67. Franklin, *Autobiography*, pp. 166, 167.

68. Ibid., p. 147.

69. Franklin was born January 17, 1706; on January 1, 1748, having formed a partnership with David Hall, he retired from active participation in the printing business.

70. Fender, *American Literature*, p. 71.

71. Kelly, *Religious Consciousness*, pp. 76, 73.

72. JCC, vol. 1, September 17, 1774.

73. Paine, *Complete Writings*, vol. 1, p. 41.

74. The title of Herbert Croly's great statement of the theory and history of democratic nationalism in America, published in 1909.

75. Foner, *Tom Paine*, p. 74.

5. The Decade of Agitation

1. Blackstone, *Commentaries*, Book 1, p. 139.

2. Commager, *Documents*, p. 58.

3. Lockyer, *Tudor and Stuart Britain*, p. 94.

4. Robbins, *Commonwealthmen*, p. 46.

5. "Discourses Concerning Government," in Sidney, *Works*, ch. 3, pp. 497, 277, 495–500; ch. 2, pp. 144, 145; ch. 1, pp. 405, 496, 497, 500.

6. Sidney, *Works*, ch. 3, p. 500.

7. *Parliamentary History*, vol. 9, cols. 394–474.

8. Ibid., cols. 450–451.

9. Ibid., cols. 473–474.

10. Ibid., col. 435.

11. Franklin, *Papers*, vol. 1, pp. 27–32.

12. "Compared with England, the American colonies were all 'Radical'. They were radical in the sense that Cartwright and Jebb, Christopher Wyvill and the Yorkshire reformers were Radical." Pole, *Political Representation*, p. 342.

Pole dates the rise of instructions from 1740 (p. 72), and finds that the crisis in the relations with Britain at the time of the Stamp Act "aroused the towns to make it a regular practice to look beyond town interests and instruct representatives how to conduct themselves in defense of American Liberties" (pp. 72, 73). The earlier date of 1720 has been given for use of instructions on general questions by the town of Boston. See Dayton, *Representation and Consent*; Colegrove, *State Instructions*, ch. 1, pp. 14, 15; ch. 2, pp. 7–9; and "New England Town Mandates," in *Publications of the Colonial Society of Massachusetts*, xxi, 1919, pp. 411–449.

13. On this point I disagree with Gordon Wood and Bernard Bailyn, who hold

that the American experience was recreating the English medieval practice of attorneys or delegates specifically empowered by countries or towns to vote supplies and to present grievances from their constituencies. Wood, *Representation*, p. 16. Bailyn, *Ideological Origins*, pp. 162–164.

14. Wood, *Creation*, p. 89.

15. Bailyn, *Pamphlets*, pp. 471–474.

16. Rakove, *National Politics*, p. 31.

17. Ibid., p. 47.

18. Bailyn, *Pamphlets*.

19. Bailyn, Introduction to Otis, *Rights*, p. 409.

20. Otis, *Rights*, p. 415.

21. Ibid., pp. 446, 470.

22. Ibid., p. 445; *Vindication*, pp. 556, 564.

23. Otis, *Rights*, p. 424.

24. Otis, *Rights*, p. 424; Locke, *Second Treatise*, para. 132.

25. Quoted in Bancroft, *History*, vol. 3, p. 191.

26. Howard, *Letter from a Gentleman at Halifax* (February 1765), in Bailyn, *Pamphlets*.

27. Howard, *Letter*, pp. 526, 537.

28. For use of the term in parliament in 1765 and 1766, see Bancroft, *History*, vol. 3, chs. 8, 14, and 15. The concept, of course, was older, having medieval roots and figuring prominently, as we have seen, in the eighteenth-century debates on representation. The term also may have an earlier usage. Its history deserves to be written. The *OED* has no entry for it.

29. Whately, *Regulations*, p. 109.

30. Quoted in Bailyn, *Ideological Origins*, p. 169; Otis, *Considerations on Behalf of the Colonists*, London 1765, p. 9.

31. Burke, "Speech to the Electors of Bristol" (1774), *Works*, vol. 2, pp. 10–14.

32. McLaughlin similarly contrasts the two ideas of representation in his *Constitutional History*, p. 50. So also Francis W. Coker, writing on "Representation" in the *Encyclopedia of the Social Sciences* (1934), where he compares virtual representation to what the physician does when he represents the patient's real will although prescribing something the patient does not like.

33. On responsibility as duty, see Pennock, "The Problem of Responsibility," pp. 5–14.

34. See especially *Brief Remarks*, where Otis admits the colonies are virtually represented, yet also fiercely attacks Howard. Bailyn, *Pamphlets*, p. 737, n. 9.

35. Dulany, *Considerations*, in Bailyn, *Pamphlets*, pp. 598–658.

36. Ibid., p. 612.

37. Ibid., pp. 632, 627, 603, 604.

38. Franklin accepted Governor Shirley's suggestion of American MPs in a letter

of 1754. Franklin, *Papers*, vol. 5, pp. 449–500. On Governor Bernard's conversion, see Bailyn, *Thomas Hutchinson*, p. 88; Governor Pownall's in 1768 (Ibid., p. 89n). Text of the Report of the Carlisle Commission is in the *Annual Register* for 1778, p. 328.

39. In the seventh Novanglus letter (April 3, 1775), Adams said the greatest "inconvenience" would be parliamentary rule without American representation, the "next greatest" would be parliamentary rule with American representation, while the "least" would be to have parliament regulate trade and "our assemblies all other matters." Adams, *Works of John Adams*, vol. 4, p. 116. Smith, *Wealth of Nations*, pp. 587–590.

40. See *Dictionary of National Biography*, pp. 1292–1294. The title of his 1770 work is "Considerations of the Expediency of Admitting Representatives from the American Colonies to the House of Commons."

41. See the remarks of Thomas Carew during the debate on annual parliaments in 1745 in *Parliamentary History*, vol. 13, col. 1058, and the reply by Sir William Yonge, col. 1078.

42. See the resolutions drawn up by Sam Adams and passed by the Massachusetts Assembly in October 1765. McLaughlin, *Constitutional History*, p. 44.

43. "Massachusetts Circular Letter," Commager, *Documents*, p. 66.

44. See Martin Diamond, "What the Framers Meant by Federalism," pp. 24–41.

45. According to McIlwain (*American Revolution*, p. 153), the argument of *The Rights of the British Colonies* by James Otis, was based on "the central assumption that the Empire is *one* 'Commonwealth and Free State.'" In 1765 a spokesman for George Grenville asserted that the Empire in Europe and America is "the same people," "one Nation," not "an Alliance," but "a Union," "one State," not "a Confederacy of many." Three years later, in 1768, although the conflict had passed to a new and more acute stage, John Dickinson denied that "these provinces" are "states distinct from the British Empire . . . We are but parts of a *whole* and therefore, there must exist a power somewhere to preside, and preserve the connection in due order." In September 1774, when George Galloway presented to the Continental Congress his plan for a division of authority between the British parliament and the "grand council" of an American "confederacy," he declared that the colonists rejected with "abhorrence" the idea of being considered "independent communities on the British Government." Commager, *Documents*, p. 81, and Rakove, *National Politics*, pp. 55–61.

46. As asserted in the Massachusetts Circular Letter of 1768, in Commager, *Documents*, pp. 66, 67.

47. Although colonial protests were often based upon the rights granted by royal charters, the charters could not claim the status of a fundamental law beyond the reach of parliament. Even before the plenary sovereignty of parliament had been established by the conflicts of the seventeenth century, the statute of monopolies of

1624 had provided a precedent for parliamentary power to revoke rights given by royal charter. See McIlwain, *American Revolution,* pp. 152, 182.

48. While asserting the sovereignty of the prince over all intermediate bodies, Bodin thought of the state as an association of "families," each under the authority of a father and possessing rights which the prince must respect. According to Althusius, a series of social contracts joined together successively a pyramid of ever more inclusive associations rising from the family through the corporation, the local community, and the province, and culminating in the state. In this federal system the authority of each level of government was limited to what was necessary for its purposes.

See Bodin, *Six Books of a Commonweale,* Book 1, ch. 2, discussed by Allen, *History of Political Thought,* Part 3, ch. 8, esp. pp. 407–425. The standard authority on Althusius is the Introduction by Carl J. Friedrich to his edition of *Politica Methodice Digesta,* trans. Carney, *Politics of Althusius.*

49. Stephen Hopkins, *The Rights of Colonies Examined* (1765), in Bailyn, *Pamphlets,* pp. 507, 512, 504.

50. Franklin, "Examination before the Committee of the Whole of the House of Commons, 13 February 1766," in *Papers,* vol. 13, pp. 124–162, p. 127, and p. 139.

51. Ibid., pp. 144, 153.

52. Smith, *Wealth of Nations,* pp. 767, 680.

53. Musgrave, *Public Finance,* ch. 4, "The Benefit Approach," where Musgrave also notes that the concept dates back to Adam Smith. See also Samuelson, *Economics,* pp. 155–156.

54. Musgrave, *Public Finance,* pp. 179–180.

55. Oates, *Fiscal Federalism,* pp. 11–12.

56. Olson, "Strategic Theory," p. 482.

57. Ostrom, *Intellectual Crisis,* pp. 81–98, 122–130, finds the essential principles of a rational choice theory in the thinking of the Founders.

58. Objecting to the Townshend duties, for instance, Benjamin Franklin termed them "*Unnecessary* because in all the colonies (two or three new ones are excepted) Government and the Administration of Justice, were, and always had been, well supported without any charge to Britain." Franklin, "Letter to W. Strahan, 29 November 1769," *Writings,* vol. 5, p. 239.

59. See above, note 50.

60. Dickinson, *Political Writings,* vol. 1, pp. 312, 359.

61. Franklin, *Writings,* vol. 5, p. 114.

62. Dickinson, *Political Writings,* vol. 1, p. 366.

63. Ibid., p. 356.

64. Ibid., pp. 312, 313.

65. "Madison to Thomas Jefferson" (October 24, 1787), *Writings,* p. 275.

66. Rakove, *National Politics,* pp. 34–36; Adams, *Political Ideas,* pp. 55–64.

67. Rakove, *National Politics*, p. 36.

68. McCloskey, *Wilson*, p. 3, quoting Page Smith, *James Wilson*, p. 58, and McIlwain, *American Revolution*, p. 116.

69. Principally by the group of liberal imperialists who founded "The Round Table." The high point of their advocacy of federation was reached in 1917. See Conway, "The Round Table," p. 51. See also Mowat, *Britain Between the Wars*, pp. 109, 426.

70. Walker, *British Empire*, pp. 152, 153. Mowat, *Britain Between the Wars*, p. 426.

71. McIlwain, *American Revolution*, p. 3.

72. Williams, *Eighteenth Century Constitution*, p. 37.

73. Namier, *England in the Age*, p. 37. Echoing Namier's judgment, Esmond Wright also observes that the idea of imperial federalism ran against the whole trend of British constitutional history which was toward restriction of the crown by parliament. Both lords and commons, continues Wright, would have thought such divided sovereignty unconstitutional and heretical. Wright, *Franklin*, p. 211.

74. Such was the opinion of James Wilson. See Wilson, *Works*, pp. 10, 724.

75. So Massachusettensis (Daniel Leonard) pointed out in a reply to John Adams' inclination toward "imperial federalism." See Adams, *Works*, vol. 4, p. 114n.

76. Wilson, *Works*, p. 721.

77. Ibid., pp. 723–727.

78. Ibid., p. 732.

79. Ibid., pp. 740, 745n, 742, 746n. That the charters were compacts between monarch and settlers which parliament itself cannot override is asserted also in a speech of January 1775. Wilson, *Works*, p. 754 and note.

80. Ibid., p. 726.

81. Page Smith, *James Wilson*, p. 59; Wilson, *Works*, p. 758.

82. Wilson, *Works*, p. 746; Jefferson, "A Summary View," *Writings*, vol. 1, pp. 431, 439. John Adams on the need for "some superintending power," *Works*, vol. 4, p. 115, eighth Novanglus letter (April 17, 1775).

83. Bailyn, *Pamphlets*, pp. 512, 620; "Massachusetts Circular Letter of 1768," Commager, *Documents*, pp. 66, 67. John Dickinson, "Letters from a Pennsylvania Farmer," *Political Writings*, p. 313.

84. Commager, *Documents*, p. 83; Becker, *Declaration of Independence*, p. 120; Adams, *Works*, vol. 4, p. 115.

85. Madison, *Writings*, vol. 6, p. 373.

86. Burke, "Reflections on the Revolution in France," *Writings and Speeches*, vol. 8, pp. 67–70.

87. Rakove, *National Politics*, pp. 137, 141.

88. Rakove, *National Politics*, pp. 145, 146. In his letter of January 2, 1775, to Patrick Henry, proposing a confederation, Silas Deane made it quite clear that a

decision for independence had not yet been taken. See Rakove, *National Politics,* pp. 141–142. In a February 13, 1776, draft of an address to be delivered to the "inhabitants" of the thirteen colonies on behalf of the Continental Congress, James Wilson also stated that "we mean not to dissolve that Union" with "the Empire." Wilson, *Political Essays,* p. 116.

89. Rakove, *National Politics,* pp. 136, 137, 163, and Wood, *Creation,* pp. 354–357.

90. Burnett, ed., *Letters,* vol. 2, p. 556 (Letter of Thomas Burke to Governor Caswell of North Carolina, November 15, 1777).

91. *JCC,* vol. 7, p. 123. See also Burnett, *Letters,* vol. 2, pp. 345, 346 (Burke's letter to Governor Caswell of April 29, 1777). For an authoritative discussion of this episode and the issue it raised, see "Thomas Burke and the Problem of Sovereignty," in Rakove, *National Politics,* pp. 164–176.

92. Lutz, "Articles of Confederation," p. 65.

93. Richard Morris concludes that the external sovereignty of the United States was always attributed to the general government, never to the states, whether under the revolutionary government of the Continental Congress, the Articles of Confederation, or the Constitution. See Morris, *Forging of the Union,* p. 63.

6. The Discovery of the Nation

1. Rakove, *National Politics,* p. 184. See also Morris, "Forging of the Union Reconsidered," pp. 1068, 1074.

2. This account of how the delegates were chosen is based largely on Morris, "Forging of the Union Reconsidered," esp. pp. 1068, 1069, and Appendix.

3. Andrew McLaughlin pressed this comparison of "the method of organization and activity" of the Congress with "the present organization of a national political party." See his *Constitutional History,* p. 88, n.13.

4. For the eighteenth- and nineteenth-century history on the American side, see Ford, *Rise and Growth.* See also Holcombe, *Our More Perfect Union,* sect. "The Legislative Process under the Delegate Convention System," pp. 159–170. I have sketched the British view in *Modern British Politics,* especially the section entitled "Political Association and Party Development."

5. *JCC,* vol. 1, p. 66 (October 14, 1774).

6. See below, Chapter 9, pp. 328–329.

7. On the concept of "constituent power," see Friedrich, *Constitutional Government,* pp. 134–154.

8. Rakove, *National Politics,* p. 105.

9. Ibid., pp. 104, 106.

10. Rakove, *National Politics,* pp. 66, 63, 71, 65.

11. *JCC*, vol. 1, pp. 75–80. In the enforcement of the terms of the Association, according to Richard Morris, the Congress showed itself to be "superior" to the colonies. *Forging of the Union*, p. 55.

12. Commager, *Documents*, p. 304.

13. Morris, *Forging of the Union*, p. 58. "Authorize" is the correct word. Noting that "New Hampshire, the first state to make the transition to statehood," sought "the guidance of Congress in July 1775," he writes: "Acting on the prompting of John Adams and the New Hampshire delegates, the Continental Congress passed a resolution on 3 November 1775, authorizing New Hampshire to set up a civil government. The following day a similar authorization was extended to the inhabitants of South Carolina. Both took steps to carry out Congress's mandate." Gordon Wood also uses the term (*Creation*, p. 132). Pauline Maier uses the even stronger work "ordered" with reference to the resolution of May 10, 1776, *Resistance to Revolution*, p. 287.

14. *JCC*, vol. 1, pp. 59, 60.

15. *JCC*, vol. 2, p. 83; Rakove, *National Politics*, pp. 48, 76, 77.

16. *JCC*, vol. 3, pp. 319, 326, 327.

17. Morris, "Forging of the Union Reconsidered," p. 1070. *JCC*, vol. 3, pp. 319, 320.

18. *JCC*, vol. 4, p. 342; Rakove, *National Politics*, p. 96.

19. Adams, *Autobiography and Diary*, vol. 3, p. 335.

20. McLaughlin writes, "when the Continental Congress adopted resolutions recommending the establishment of governments in the various colonies, it was apparent that they were to be considered as no longer colonies, but states." McLaughlin, *Continental History*, p. 99. Richard Morris summarized the constitutional significance of this act: "The Declaration of Independence was by its own words a declaration by 'the representatives of the United States of America, in General Congress assembled.'" Since only four state governments, three of them provisional, had been formed prior to the Declaration, it was Congress—not a confederation of sovereign states—that proclaimed American independence from Great Britain. In essence, it was Congress which declared the colonies to be "states." Morris, "Forging of the Union Reconsidered," p. 1071.

21. Lincoln, "Message to Congress" (July 4, 1861), in Commager, *Documents*, p. 394.

22. As described by Jack Greene, *Peripheries and Center*, esp. Book 2, "A Problem Defined, 1764–1775."

23. Burke, *Works*, vol. 2, pp. 51, 46. The following account is based on Brebner, *Neutral Yankees*.

24. Brebner, *Neutral Yankees*, p. 314.

25. See above, pp. 12–13.

26. Burke, "Speech on Conciliation with the Colonies" (March 22, 1775), *Works*, vol. 2, p. 39.

27. I am taking issue with Jack P. Greene, who argues that "these new state governments were merely the creations and the newest political instruments of old corporate entities, each of which preserved its own well-defined territory and collective legal identity as it moved rapidly in 1775–76 through a series of statuses from colony to provincial revolutionary society to independent state." *Peripheries and Center,* p. 178.

28. Regarding the change in the colonies as a whole, Joseph H. Smith writes that the assertion of sovereignty of the people in the Declaration was "almost immediately apparent in such humdrum [sic] details as the titles of indictment and the forms of process, which no longer ran in the name of the King, but in the name of the People of a state or 'the Commonwealth'." *Cases and Materials,* p. 469.

29. In addition to Smith, sources for this paragraph are Davis, *Bench and Bar,* p. 67; Nelson, *Americanization of the Common Law,* p. 67; Cushing, *Notes of Cases; Acts and Laws* (Boston, 1776), ch. 12, pp. 49–50.

30. Paine, *Complete Writings,* vol. 1, pp. 3–46.

31. Fender, *American Literature,* p. 85.

32. Inglis, *The True Interest of America,* pp. 53, 54.

33. Montesquieu, *Spirit of the Laws,* Book 11, ch. 6; Book 29, ch. 19.

34. Foner, *Tom Paine,* pp. 9–11.

35. Veitch, *Genesis,* p. 44.

36. Foner, *Tom Paine,* p. 78. See also Conway, *Life of Paine,* p. 15; Foner, Introduction to Paine, *Complete Writings,* pp. ix–xlvi.

37. Foner, *Tom Paine,* p. 7. On his close relations with Benjamin Franklin, whom he called his "patron and introducer," see Paine, *Complete Writings,* vol. 2, p. 1251. See also Van Doren, *Benjamin Franklin,* p. 482.

38. E. P. Thompson, *Working Class,* pp. 36, 37; Fender, *American Literature,* p. 84.

39. Foner, *Tom Paine,* p. 74; Paine, "Liberty Tree" (September 1775), *Complete Writings,* vol. 2, pp. 1091, 1092; Maier, *Resistance to Revolution,* p. 291.

40. Paine, "Common Sense," *Complete Writings,* vol. 1, p. 10.

41. Fender, *American Literature,* p. 84.

42. Expressing his determination to go ahead with the trial of Charles I, Cromwell said, "I tell you, we will cut off his head with the crown upon it." Algernon Sidney to Robert Sidney, Earl of Leicester, October 12, 1660, in *Sidney Papers.* Ed. Robert W. Blencowe (London, 1825), p. 235.

43. Paine, "Common Sense," *Complete Writings,* vol. 1, p. 15.

44. A 1651 pamphlet by John Hall, referred to by Pocock in his Introduction to the *Works of Harrington,* p. xii.

45. Harrington, *Works,* pp. 380, 381, 642, 643, and Pocock's Introduction, p. 28n.

46. Paine, "Common Sense," *Complete Writings*, vol. 1, p. 9.

47. Paine, "Common Sense," *Complete Writings*, vol. 1, p. 6. Adams, *Diary and Autobiography*, vol. 3, p. 333.

48. Paine, "Common Sense," *Complete Writings*, vol. 1, pp. 27, 29, 43, 27, 44, 29, 30, 37.

49. Ibid., pp. 29, 26.

50. Maier, *Resistance to Revolution*, p. 295.

51. Paine, "Common Sense," *Complete Writings*, vol. 1, p. 28.

52. Ibid., pp. 28, 29.

53. Ibid., p. 29.

54. Ibid., pp. 31, 36, 46.

55. Ibid., pp. 41, 31–35, 41, 17.

56. Ibid., p. 45.

57. Paine, *Complete Writings*, pp. 302, 319, 332.

Part Three. The National and Republican Constitution

1. Edmund S. Morgan, *Inventing the People*, pp. 269, 245–246, 245, 254.

2. Ibid., pp. 246, 252–253, 275–276.

3. Paine, *Works*, p. 913. According to Philip Foner, Paine was the first person to call publicly for a national convention to remedy the weaknesses of the Articles and to create a stronger central government (*Complete Writings*, p. 302). When making this proposal in *The Crisis* for December 30, 1780, he claimed to be renewing a hint in *Common Sense* in favor of "a Continental convention for the purpose of forming a Continental constitution, defining the powers and authority of Congress" (*Complete Writings*, p. 332). Alexander Hamilton, needless to say, was no less exercised by the problem, which he analyzed at length in a letter of September 3, 1780, to James Duane of Philadelphia. He also suggested "a convention of all the states" with full authority to establish "a solid coercive union." See Syrett, *Hamilton Papers*, pp. 401–417, esp. 407. In *The Continentalist*, July 1781 to July 1782, Hamilton elaborated the points made in the letter to Duane. Paine continued to criticize the states and to call for a stronger central union. Some years after, when being vilified for his later writings, he replied, "I ought to stand first on the list of Federalists, for the proposition for establishing a central general government over the Union came originally from me in 1783," citing a letter (since lost) to Chancellor Livingston, Robert Morris and Governeur Morris. *To the Citizens of the United States*, November 19, 1802. *Complete Writings*, p. 913.

4. Wood, *Creation*, p. 499.

5. My references will be to this translation by Thomas Nugent. I have supplemented its use with Melvin Richter's greatly improved translation of selections from

The Spirit of the Laws and other works of Montesquieu in *The Political Theory of Montesquieu.* The Nugent translation is the text used by Americans, unless, of course, like Jefferson, they read the original French.

7. Montesquieu's Confederate Republic

1. "Men of Little Faith," p. 25; for specific mention of Montesquieu's influence, see pp. 6, 8, 23, 42.

2. Montesquieu, *Spirit of the Laws,* Book 9, ch. 1. The crucial French term "convention" is translated by Nugent as "convention," by Richter as "agreement," at Richter, p. 237.

3. Riley, "Origins of Federal Theory," p. 119, n. 97.

4. Montesquieu, *Spirit of the Laws,* Book 8, ch. 16.

5. Ibid., Book 8, chs. 17, 19.

6. For the variations on this theme, see Arthur O. Lovejoy's classic history of the Platonic conception of unity in diversity, *The Great Chain of Being.*

7. Kenyon, "Men of Little Faith," pp. 7–8, 38–39, and below n. 41.

8. Montesquieu, *Spirit of the Laws,* Book 8, chs. 17 and 16.

9. Ibid., Book 8, ch. 20.

10. Ibid., p. lxxi, and Book 5, ch. 2.

11. Ibid., Book 4, ch. 5.

12. Ibid., p. lxxi; for the contrast between the "general" and the "universal" in political theory at this time, see Patrick Riley, *The General Will before Rousseau,* pp. xii, 138–180, 202–213.

13. Ibid., Book 4, chs. 5 and 3.

14. Ibid., Book 5, chs. 4–6.

15. Ibid., Book 4, chs. 5 and 7.

16. See Davis, *The Federal Principle,* for a list.

17. Riley, "The Origins of Federal Theory," p. 88 and passim.

18. In *Federalist* 43 (p. 297) Madison wrote: "It is an established doctrine of the subject of treaties that all the articles are mutually conditions of the other; that a breach of any one article is a breach of the whole treaty; and that a breach, committed by either of the parties, absolves the others, and authorizes them, if they please, to pronounce the compact violated and void." All references to *The Federalist* are to Cooke's edition.

19. *Commentaries,* Book 1, ch. 2, sect. 3.

20. Riley, "Origins of Federal Theory," pp. 93–94.

21. Martin Diamond, "The Federalist's View of Federalism," p. 25 in Benson, ed., *Essays in Federalism.* See also "Federal" in *OED:* "pertaining to a covenant, compact, treaty" (A.D. 1660).

22. Riley, "Origins of Federal Theory," pp. 97–98.

23. Montesquieu, *Spirit of the Laws*, Book 9, ch. 1. See also Riley, *Historical Development*, ch. 6, p. 223.

24. On the contrast of such a process of bargaining or balancing with the process of rational deliberation, see James Q. Wilson, "The James Madison Lecture," p. 560.

25. Wood, *Creation*, p. 499.

26. Richter, *Political Theory of Montesquieu*, p. 16.

27. Montesquieu, *Spirit of the Laws*, Book 20, ch. 12 and *passim*.

28. See above, Chapter 3, p. 115.

29. Montesquieu, *Spirit of the Laws*, Book 11, ch. 8.

30. Nannerl O. Keohane, "Virtuous Republics and Glorious Monarchies," *passim*.

31. Montesquieu, *Spirit of the Laws*, Book 5, chs. 1, 14; Book 3, ch. 7; Book 11, ch. 4.

32. Ibid., Book 3, ch. 4; Book 9, ch. 6.

33. Ibid., Book 9, ch. 6. Contrast Madison's view, below, Chapter 9, pp. 280–283.

34. Ibid., Book 9, ch. 6.

35. Ibid., Book 2, ch. 4.

36. Contrary to what Franz Neumann asserts in his introduction to Montesquieu, *Spirit of the Laws*, p. xiv.

37. Montesquieu, *Spirit of the Laws*, Book 6, ch. 1.

38. Ibid., Book 11, ch. 6; Book 8, chs. 19, 20, 16; Book 20, ch. 21.

39. Richter, *Political Theory of Montesquieu*, p. 103.

40. According to Forrest McDonald, Madison's theory of the extended republic, set out in *Federalist* 10, "overcame two formidable theoretical stumbling blocks to republican nationhood, Montesquieu's dicta that republican forms were adaptable only to small territories, such as cities and towns, and that only monarchies could govern large areas." *Novus Ordo Seclorum*, p. 166.

41. Douglas Adair, "'That Politics May Be Reduced to a Science,'" in *Fame and the Founding Fathers*, p. 97.

42. Wood, *Creation*, p. 499.

43. Paul Spurlin has carefully traced the dissemination and popularization of Montesquieu's great work and its use in political controversies, and, after the revolution, in constitution-making in his *Montesquieu in America, 1760–1801*. Summarizing the evidence presented in that book, Spurlin goes on to argue for Montesquieu's influence, concluding in "Montesquieu and the American Constitution" that he was responsible for the tripartite separation of powers in the Constitution.

44. Martin Diamond calls it a "very old belief" that was popularized anew by a reading of Montesquieu, in "What the Framers Meant by Federalism," p. 35. When this idea was used against the centralizing proposals of the Federalists, Madison

brought some of them around—for instance, Oliver Ellsworth and Roger Sherman—by what Diamond regards as his new theory of national federalism. Diamond did not take into account that the theory of national federalism had strong roots in the republican tradition coming down from the Commonwealth. Marvin Meyers also says there was a "traditional teaching" that only a small state could be republican, but does not attribute this to Montesquieu or identify *Federalist* 10 as a reply. *The Mind of the Founder,* p. xxviii. Edmund S. Morgan speaks of the idea as "an accepted maxim." *Inventing the People,* p. 266.

45. One finds in the opposition ideology a fear of consolidated government and an advocacy of the mixed constitution as a means to avoid consolidated power by the "establishment of a perpetual struggle between the branches of government." Kramnick, *Bolingbroke,* p. 251. While the Anti-Federalists, following Montesquieu, supported small-scale government as a defense of liberty, they did not find a defense of local, or small-scale government, in the opposition ideology, which did not address the question of scale. No whig defense of small states is to be found, for instance, in Bailyn, *Faces of the Revolution.*

46. Lewis Namier, *England in the Age of the American Revolution,* p. 35. This local oligarchy continued into the nineteenth century and was reduced, although not by any means eliminated, by the newly enfranchised middle classes only through the agency of the central government. See J. S. Mill's apology to Tocqueville for this use of central power as the only way of liberalizing local politics. Mill, *Collected Works,* vol. 12, pp. 287–289.

47. Donald S. Lutz, ed., *Documents,* p. 207.

48. See above Chapter 5, p. 186.

49. See Elisha P. Douglass, "Thomas Burke: Disillusioned Democrat," and Jennings B. Sanders, "Thomas Burke in the Continential Congress."

50. David W. Carrithers, "Montesquieu, Jefferson and the Fundamentals of 18th Century Republican Theory." See also *The Commonplace Book of Thomas Jefferson,* pp. 268–269, 258.

51. Farrand, *Records,* vol. 2, p. 324 (June 19).

52. Rakove, *National Politics,* pp. 313–316, 327.

53. Kenyon, "Men of Little Faith," *passim.*

54. For example, in *Federalist* 47 (p. 324), where with regard to the separation of powers Madison terms Montesquieu "the oracle who is always consulted and cited on the subject."

55. In *Federalist* 10, when Madison disparages those "theoretic politicians" (that is, political theorists) who have patronized the ideal of the small republic, he may, however, very well be referring not to Montesquieu but to Rousseau, who followed Montesquieu's prescriptions for republican government in *The Government of Poland.* See Rousseau, "The Radical Vice," in *The Government of Poland,* ch. 5, p. 25–26; and Edward Millican, *One United People,* p. 117.

56. Luther Martin, "Genuine Information," as delivered to the Maryland legislature November 29, 1787, and subsequently published in the *Maryland Gazetter and Baltimore Advertiser* between December 28, 1787, and February 8, 1788; in Farrand, *Records*, vol. 3, pp. 183–184.

57. Storing, *Anti-Federalists*, pp. 73, 31.

58. Martin, "Genuine Information," in Farrand, *Records*, vol. 3, p. 182.

59. For instance, Forrest McDonald disagrees with Storing; see McDonald, *Novus Ordo*, p. 285, n. 42.

60. Storing, *Anti-Federalists*, pp. 45, 73.

61. Farrand, *Records*, vol. 1, p. 552 (July 7).

62. Ibid., p. 353 (June 20).

63. Ibid., p. 461 (June 29); p. 355 (June 21).

64. Lutz, "The Articles of Confederation as the Background to the Federal Republic," p. 62.

65. Martin, "Genuine Information," in Farrand, *Records*, vol. 3, p. 183; vol. 1, pp. 437–438 (June 27); and pp. 340–341 (June 20); vol. 3, pp. 192 and 184; *Federalist* 18 and 20.

66. Farrand, *Records*, vol. 1, p. 437 (June 27); vol. 3, pp. 186–187.

67. Storing, *Anti-Federalists*, p. 28.

68. Montesquieu, *Spirit of the Laws*, Book 9, ch. 1.

69. Farrand, *Records*, vol. 1, pp. 340–341 (June 20).

70. Ibid., p. 440 (June 27); pp. 486–487 (June 30).

71. Ibid., p. 502 (June 30).

72. Farrand, *Records*, vol. 3, p. 186.

73. Elliot, ed., *Debates*, vol. 3, pp. 22, 44; Storing, *Anti-Federalists*, pp. 12–13.

8. Madison's Compound Republic

1. Adair, *Fame and the Founding Fathers*, p. 134; see also Madison, *Papers*, ed. Rutland, at editor's introduction to "Notes on Ancient and Modern Confederacies," vol. 9, pp. 3–4; Meyers, *Mind of the Founder*, pp. 69–70.

2. Rakove, *National Politics*, pp. 342–348; "Vices of the Political System," in Madison, *Papers*, ed. Rutland, vol. 9, pp. 348–349; *Federalist* 22, p. 144.

3. Farrand, *Records*, 1, p. 19 (May 29).

4. "Vices," in Madison, *Papers*, ed. Rutland, vol. 9, p. 350.

5. *Federalist* 15, p. 93.

6. Ibid., p. 93.

7. Ibid., p. 93; *Federalist* 20, p. 128.

8. "Vices," in Madison, *Papers*, ed. Rutland, vol. 9, p. 352.

9. "James Madison: Preface to 'Debates in the Convention of 1787,'" in Farrand, *Records*, vol. 3, pp. 542–543.

10. "Vices," in Madison, *Papers*, ed. Rutland, vol. 9, p. 352.

11. Ibid., pp. 351–352.

12. Ibid., pp. 352–353.

13. Ibid., p. 352. Madison uses the term "extended republic" when he is concerned especially with the aspect of scale. The concept of the "compound republic" includes that aspect, but also the institutional aspect and therefore is more appropriate when one is referring to his fully elaborated theory, which included the "auxiliary precautions."

14. *Federalist* 37, p. 234.

15. *Federalist* 46, p. 315; John Locke, *The Second Treatise*, para. 153.

16. *Federalist* 21, pp. 129–130.

17. Tocqueville, *Democracy in America*, pp. 71–89.

18. *Federalist* 45 (Madison), p. 313. Hamilton shared Madison's expectation that state governments would be used by the federal government to enforce its laws. See *Federalist* 27. Early Congressional legislation contains many examples of such action. See Corwin, *The Constitution*, pp. 229–230. In his pioneering study (1962) of intergovernmental relations in the nineteenth century, Daniel J. Elazar brought out the nation-building role of the states. Summarizing this theme in a Foreword, Morton Grodzins wrote: "Aside from the Civil War, there is a continuous involvement of both the federal and state governments in all the great domestic tasks of building and maintaining a continent-wide nation." *The American Partnership*, p. viii.

19. *Federalist* 20, pp. 128–129.

20. Elliot, *Debates*, vol. 3, pp. 22, 44.

21. *Federalist* 22, pp. 145–146, 139.

22. Morgan, *Inventing the People*, p. 267.

23. The logic of the constitutional situation as well as parochial interests favored the antinational behavior of the states under the Articles. Bancroft, for example, notes that when Britain applied the Navigation Acts to American trade, the United States was unable to retaliate because it was not in the interest of any one state to exclude British vessels, unless all others did the same. Yet, this behavior was recognized as self-defeating. Hence, when the Annapolis convention called for the convention at Philadelphia, the Continental Congress promptly authorized the convention and nearly all states quickly appointed delegates. Bancroft, *History*, vol. 6, "Calling of the Convention," pp. 111 and 197–198.

24. *Federalist* 10, p. 63.

25. "To Thomas Jefferson," October 24, 1787, in Madison, *Papers*, ed. Rutland, vol. 10, pp. 212–213.

26. *Federalist* 10, pp. 63–64.

27. Ibid., pp. 57–59.

28. Ibid., pp. 59 and 57.

29. Ibid., pp. 58–59.

30. Edmund Burke, "Thoughts on the Present Discontents," in *Writings and Speeches,* vol. 1, p. 110.

31. Harvey C. Mansfield, Jr., *Statesmanship and Party Government,* p. 196. "Burke and Jefferson," writes Mansfield, "as founders of party government, were at first alone in their praise of party," p. 2.

32. See below, p. 275, where Madison terms freedom of expression "the only effectual guardian of every other right."

33. *Federalist* 10, p. 58.

34. Ibid., p. 61.

35. *Federalist* 45, p. 309.

36. *Federalist* 51, p. 351; *Federalist* 10, pp. 57 and 60.

37. Ibid., p. 57.

38. See discussion of justice and rights at *Federalist* 51, pp. 351–353.

39. *Federalist* 10, p. 65.

40. *Federalist* 30, p. 191.

41. *Federalist* 10, p. 64.

42. Burns, *Deadlock of Democracy,* pp. 6–7, and *passim.* See also Wills, *Explaining America,* pp. 117–125.

43. *Federalist* 27, pp. 172–173; *Federalist* 30, p. 191.

44. "Vices," in Madison, *Papers,* ed. Rutland, vol. 9, p. 350.

45. Also see below, Chapter 9, p. 353.

46. *Federalist* 51, pp. 352–353.

47. Wood, *Creation,* p. 203.

48. Rakove, *National Politics,* p. 389.

49. Adair, "That Politics May Be Reduced to a Science," in *Fame and the Founding Fathers,* pp. 93–106.

50. Hume, "Perfect Commonwealth," *Works,* vol. 3, p. 492.

51. Ibid., p. 481.

52. Ibid., pp. 487, 490.

53. Ibid., pp. 492, 487–488.

54. Ibid., pp. 481, 489, 483, 490.

55. Ibid., pp. 480–481.

56. Ibid., pp. 485, 490–491.

57. Ibid., pp. 482, 487–488.

58. *Federalist* 51, pp. 351–352. A longer passage making a similar point comes in the next to final paragraph of *Federalist* 10.

59. Meyers, *Mind of the Founder,* introduction to *Memorial and Remonstrance,* p. 8.

60. Quoted in Millican, *One United People,* pp. 121–122.

61. "Memorial and Remonstrance against Religious Assessments," in Madison, *Papers,* ed. Rutland, vol. 8, pp. 299–300, 304.

62. *Federalist* 10, pp. 58–59.

63. For a classic account, see R. H. Tawney, *Religion and the Rise of Capitalism,* ch. 3, part three, "The Growth of Individualism," pp. 175–193.

64. Locke, *Second Treatise,* ch. 5, "Of Property."

65. For instance, Thomas Jefferson, John Stuart Mill, and Oliver Wendell Holmes.

66. James Madison, "Report of 1800," January 7, 1800, *Papers,* ed. Mattern, vol. 17, p. 341.

67. McDonald, *Novus Ordo,* pp. 41–45.

68. Stephen Holmes, "Liberal Constraints on Private Power?," *Democracy and the Mass Media,* p. 30.

69. Stephen Holmes ("Liberal Constraints," p. 59, n. 36) summarizes the series of assertions of the essential proposition, starting with Milton's bold declaration, "Let [Truth] and Falsehood grapple; who ever knew Truth put to the worse in a free and open encounter?" (Milton, "Aereopagitica," *Works,* vol. 2, p. 561). Locke modestly echoes this claim, writing that, "the truth would do well if she were once left to shift for herself" ("A Letter Concerning Toleration," p. 45). Trenchard and Gordon continued this tradition: "Truth has so many advantages over Error, that she wants only to be shewn, to gain admiration and Esteem" ("Discourse upon Libels," *Cato's Letters,* vol. 3, pp. 298–299). Jefferson concurred more robustly: "Truth is great and will prevail if left to herself" ("A Bill Establishing Religious Freedom," 1777, *Writings,* p. 347). In *Federalist* 70 (p. 475), Hamilton succinctly and unpretentiously made the same point. Referring to the legislative process, he wrote, "The difference of opinion, and the jarring of parties in that department of government, though they may sometimes obstruct salutary plans, yet often promote deliberation and circumspection and serve to check excesses of the majority."

70. "Of Freedom of Speech; That the Same is inseparable from publick Liberty," in *Cato's Letters,* vol. 1, pp. 96–103.

71. *Four Letters,* p. 20.

72. James Madison, "Virginia Resolutions," in *Papers,* ed. Mattern, vol. 17, p. 190; and "Report of 1800," ibid., p. 339.

73. James Madison, "Report of 1800," pp. 346, 344, 341.

74. See above, Chapter 2, p. 67, quoting *Abrams v U.S.* 250 U.S. 616 (1919), Holmes, J., dissenting.

75. Hume emphasizes that governments must be supported by "general" or impartial laws in his essay, "On the Rise and Progress of the Arts and Sciences." It is "general laws" which protect liberty in republics and are "the source of all security and happiness." See Hume, *Works,* vol. 4, pp. 179, 185.

76. Hume, *Perfect Commonwealth,* in *Works,* vol. 3, p. 488; *Federalist* 49, p. 343.

77. See Madison's fear of "overbearing majorities," quoted by Bernard Bailyn in

an essay review of Julian Boyd's edition of Jefferson's *Papers* in *The New England Quarterly,* vol. 33 (1960), pp. 398–390.

78. *Federalist* 51, p. 353.

79. It is not number in itself that elevates deliberation but rather the diversity that number normally entails. So, as Madison says in a letter to Jefferson, an increase in the size of the majority alone does not necessarily mean that it will be more just. James Madison to Thomas Jefferson, October 24, 1787, in Madison, *Papers,* ed. Rutland, vol. 10, pp. 213–214.

80. See above, Chapter 3, p. 105.

81. Even in his later and less ardently nationalist years Madison remained faithful to the main thesis of *Federalist* 10. "Experience," writes McCoy of his opinions in the 1830s, "had vindicated the theory that under representative government, power was less likely to be abused by majorities in larger rather than smaller communities." McCoy, *Last of the Fathers,* p. 137.

82. *Federalist* 46, pp. 320, 322.

9. Auxiliary Precautions

1. *Federalist* 51, pp. 349, 351.

2. "Vices," in Madison, *Papers,* ed. Rutland, vol. 9, p. 357.

3. *Federalist* 14, p. 84.

4. *Federalist* 63, p. 428.

5. Madison's hostility to the rule of the few appears when, immediately after this statement, he addresses the charge that the senate will introduce "aristocracy" and goes on at length to show that that cannot happen without a long and unlikely train of corruption and certainly not in the face of "the immediate representatives of the people" in the lower house of Congress. *Federalist* 63, pp. 428–431.

6. *Federalist* 10, p. 62.

7. Ibid.

8. Ibid., p. 62.

9. Stephen Holmes, "Liberal Constraints," pp. 58–59, n. 33.

10. Comparing the delegate and trustee views of representation, Stephen Holmes writes that the trustee view gives the representative "more leeway" not because he is thought to be "better or wiser by nature" but because he is seen to be "more favorably placed for hearing all sides of an issue." See Holmes, "Liberal Constraints," pp. 58–59 n. 33.

11. *Federalist* 51, pp. 352–353. Hamilton's view of representation was clearly more elitist than Madison's. The choice of the voter, he thought, would naturally fall on men occupying coordinating roles in the economy and society. Mechanics and master craftsmen would choose merchants who would be more able and better

informed but would have the same interests at heart. Similarly, landlords would represent the interests of all landowners, large and small, and also of tenants. Accordingly, he expected that the representative body would be composed of landlords, merchants, and members of the "learned professions." *Federalist* 35, pp. 219–220.

12. This view of Sidney's is strongly emphasized by Alan Houston, *Algernon Sidney,* pp. 196–198.

13. Madison, "For the *National Gazette,*" February 4, 1792, in Madison, *Papers,* ed. Rutland, vol. 14, p. 217.

14. Wood, *Creation,* p. 152.

15. *Federalist* 48, p. 332.

16. *Federalist* 51, p. 349.

17. Meyers, *Mind of the Founder,* p. xxxvii; and James Madison to Thomas Jefferson, October 24, 1787, in Madison, *Papers,* vol. 10, p. 211.

18. Samuel H. Beer, *Modern British Politics,* pp. 13–14; Gwyn, *Separation of Powers,* p. 26.

19. Gwyn, ibid., p. 110.

20. Wood, *Creation,* p. 152; Montesquieu, *Spirit of the Laws,* Book 11, ch. 6.

21. On Montesquieu's contribution to the conception of controls by partial agency, see Gwyn, *Separation of Powers,* pp. 104, 110, 111.

22. Gwyn, *Separation of Powers,* p. 32.

23. See above, Chapter 3, "The Machinery of Rational Deliberation."

24. *Federalist* 70, p. 472; *Federalist* 78, pp. 524, 526, 528.

25. Almond and Powell, *Comparative Politics,* pp. 73–163.

26. Stephen Holmes, "Precommitment and the Paradox of Democracy," in *Constitutionalism and Democracy,* p. 228.

27. See above, Chapter 3, pp. 97–98.

28. *Federalist* 70, p. 472.

29. Wood, *Creation,* pp. 447–448.

30. *Federalist* 73, p. 497.

31. *Federalist* 77, p. 517; Meyers, *Mind of the Founder,* p. xxxvii.

32. *Federalist* 45, p. 313.

33. Madison to George Washington, April 16, 1787, in Madison, *Papers,* ed. Rutland, vol. 9, p. 383; Farrand, *Records,* 1, p. 164 (June 8).

34. Madison to Thomas Jefferson, October 24, 1787, in Madison, *Papers,* ed. Rutland, vol. 10, p. 212.

35. Farrand, *Records,* vol. 2, pp. 27–29 (July 17).

36. See *Federalist* 78, 80, 81 (Hamilton), and 44 (Madison).

37. The process began in the 1920s when the Court for the first time applied the guarantees of the First Amendment to the states through the due process clause of the Fourteenth Amendment. This opened the way to a vast expansion in the law of

civil liberties over the next fifty years. For a summary see Kelly and Harbison, *The American Constitution,* 5th ed., ch. 29, "The New Deal in Civil Liberties."

38. *Federalist* 51, pp. 351–353.

39. Farrand, *Records,* vol. 1, p. 21 (May 29).

40. *Federalist* 46, p. 316; *Federalist* 10, p. 63.

41. See above, Chapter 5, "The Federal Option."

42. Oates, *Fiscal Federalism,* pp. 11–12.

43. Hume, *Treatise on Human Nature,* Book 3, part 2, sect. vii, p. 538; Madison, "Vices," in Madison, *Papers,* ed. Rutland, vol. 9, p. 352; Adam Smith, *Wealth of Nations,* pp. 689, 767–768.

44. *Federalist* 51, pp. 351–353.

45. *Federalist* 28, p. 179.

46. Ibid., p. 179.

47. *Federalist* 46, p. 315. His second answer to these critics is that at the present time the people prefer the states, but this reassurance is qualified by Madison's ill-concealed hope that popular sentiment would shift toward the general government.

48. Ibid., pp. 315–316.

49. Ibid., pp. 320, 322.

50. *Federalist* 46, p. 320.

51. Bruce Ackerman takes note of these two papers, numbers 28 and 46, and the role they assign to the people-at-large as the "common superior" which uses the states for "mass mobilization." He regards such action as exceptional, however, taking place outside, though not contrary to, the limits set by the constitution. See his "Storrs Lectures," p. 1021n.

52. *Federalist* 51, pp. 315–316.

53. *Federalist* 51, p. 353; *Federalist* 46, pp. 320, 315.

54. Madison to Thomas Jefferson, October 24, 1787, in Madison, *Papers,* ed. Rutland, vol. 10, p. 212.

55. There are two different problems, oppression by factious majorities and oppression by government officials. Some scholars hold that according to the authors of *The Federalist,* the extended republic would deal with the former and the division of powers (checks and balances) with the latter. Martin Diamond read the *Federalist* to say that checks and balances were not intended to control faction among voters but only oppression by governments. See G. S. Benson, *Essays in Federalism.* David Epstein disagrees, finding that unjust majorities may act through unjust rulers. Yet he too seems to think that checks and balances were expected to work mechanically apart from popular control. See David F. Epstein, *The Political Theory of the Federalist,* pp. 51, 141–142.

I have argued that the authors of the *Federalist* did not expect the federal division of power alone to cope with either problem but rather to function as an institutional opportunity for intervention by the national will. Ambition alone might indeed lead government officials at either level to attempt to usurp the authority of the other. Such assaults on the constitutional equilibrium, however, were not expected to arise from or to enjoy the support of the broad, pluralistic constituency of the federal legislature.

In the case of a state, to be sure, since it is a small republic, the two problems could coincide when a local faction used its government to carry out oppressive designs. In *Federalist* 59, for instance, Hamilton, while examining how state legislatures may do injury to the Union, foresees the possibility of a coincidence of support by "a strong faction" with the "natural rivalship of power" on the part of "local rulers." *Federalist* 59, p. 402.

56. Farrand, *Records*, vol. 1, p. 447 (June 28).

57. Madison to Washington, April 16, 1787, in Madison, *Papers*, ed. Rutland, vol. 9, pp. 383–384.

58. *Federalist* 59, pp. 397, 402.

59. *Federalist* 78, 80, 81 (Hamilton), and 44 (Madison).

60. *Federalist* 78 (Hamilton).

61. *Federalist* 46, pp. 317–318.

62. *Federalist* 27, pp. 172–174.

63. *Federalist* 46, p. 318.

64. *Federalist* 31, p. 197.

65. Ibid., p. 198.

66. *Federalist* 46, pp. 315–316; *Federalist* 31, p. 198.

67. This is to apply to the federal structure Richard Neustadt's illuminating observation that the separation of powers actually created "separated institutions sharing powers." See Neustadt, *Presidential Power*, p. 101.

68. *Federalist* 52, pp. 358–359.

69. *Federalist* 46, pp. 320–322.

70. *Federalist* 26, p. 169.

71. *Federalist* 56, pp. 379–380.

72. Bryce, *American Commonwealth*, vol. 1, p. 353.

73. In a 1921 dissent Holmes objected to the use of the Fourteenth Amendment "to prevent the making of social experiments . . . in the insulated chambers afforded by the States." *Truax v. Corrigan*, 257 U.S. 312, 344. In a 1932 dissent Brandeis expressed a similar sentiment in a sentence that has often been quoted: "It is one of the happy incidents of the federal system that a single courageous state may, if its citizens choose, serve as a laboratory; and try novel social and economic experiments without risk to the rest of the country." *New State Ice Co. v. Liebmann* 285 U.S., 262, 311.

74. To Thomas Jefferson, October 24, 1787. Madison, *Papers*, ed. Rutland, vol. 10, p. 214.

10. Sovereignty and Ratification

1. Palmer, *Age of Democratic Revolution*, p. 214.

2. Hart, ed., *History of Massachusetts*, vol. 3, p. 191.

3. Ibid., vol. 3, p. 191.

4. Ibid., vol. 3, pp. 399–401.

5. Woodhouse, *Puritanism and Liberty*, pp. 356–367. Firth writes, "In January 1649 the Army presented the Agreement of the People to Parliament. They did not ask that it be imposed on the nation by law, but be tendered for acceptance. It was to be circulated somewhat as a petition, amongst the people for signatures. If most supporters of the cause approved it, steps were to be taken to give it effect." See Firth, *Oliver Cromwell*, p. 237.

6. *Oceana*, pp. 339–340.

7. See above, Chapter 3, p. 126; Chapter 8, p. 268.

8. See above, Chapter 3, p. 95.

9. *Federalist* 40, pp. 263–264. Some constitutional scholars have doubted that the Convention had the legal authority to recommend a new Constitution. Among them are Bruce Ackerman, see his "Storrs Lecture," p. 1017n; Gerald Gunther, "The Convention Method of Amending the U. S. Constitution," and Benjamin Fletcher Wright, ed., *The Federalist*, p. 2.

The reasons are, first, that the Continental Congress had explicitly limited the convention to the task of revising the Articles and, second, that several state legislatures had included restrictive language to that effect in the enabling acts authorizing their delegations. In reply, one can say that the Congress did recommend the Constitution to the states and that ultimately all thirteen ratified it, thereby giving it, as Madison wrote in *Federalist* 40 (pp. 265–266), the "approbation" of "the supreme authority" of the people.

In *Federalist* 43, Madison suggests another rejoinder. Defending the recommendation of the convention that ratification by nine would suffice to establish the Constitution, he argued that since the Articles were based on only the authority of "a league or treaty" under which a breach by one party absolves the others and frees them to pronounce the compact violated and void, and since various states had in fact committed "multiplied and important infractions," the other states were justified in "dispensing with the consent of particular States to a dissolution of the foederal pact" whereupon they were free to form a new frame of government based on the consent of nine (*Federalist* 43, pp. 297–298).

10. *Federalist* 40, pp. 265–266.

11. Article VII, Constitution of the United States of America.

12. *Federalist* 43, pp. 297–298.

13. Farrand, *Records*, vol. 2, pp. 89 (July 23), 93.

14. *Federalist* 22, p. 146.

15. Millican, *One United People*, pp. 23, 132–136.

16. *Federalist* 39, p. 254.

17. Ibid., p. 254.

18. *Register of Debates in Congress*, vol. 9, cols. 187–192 (January 22, 1833), and cols. 519–553 (February 15, 1833). The words are quoted from the Resolutions introduced by Calhoun, cols. 191–192.

19. Calhoun, *Papers*, vol. 11, pp. 495–496.

20. At the time of his great oratorical duel with Daniel Webster, Senator Hayne of South Carolina, the ally and mouthpiece of Vice President Calhoun, assumed on the basis of what Madison had said in 1798 that he would support the states' rights theory against the nationalist claims of Webster. See Drew McCoy, *Last of the Fathers*, p. 140.

21. Madison, "Notes on Nullification," in *Writings*, ed. Hunt, vol. 9, p. 607.

22. For sources of Madison's views at this time, see, ibid., pp. 573–607; also Madison to Edward Everett (also listed as 'to Robert G. Hayne', April 3rd or 4th), August 28, 1830, in Hunt, ed., *Writings*, vol. 9, pp. 383–403; and letters to various people cited and summarized in McCoy, *Last of the Fathers*, pp. 140–151.

23. "Notes on Nullification," in *Writings*, ed. Hunt, vol. 9, pp. 600, 555, 607, 604.

24. Ibid., p. 600.

25. McCoy, *Last of the Fathers*, p. 149.

26. Amar, "Of Sovereignty and Federalism," pp. 1452–1453, n. 113.

27. *Federalist* 39, p. 254.

28. Locke, *Second Treatise*, ch. 8, pp. 348–349, 355–356.

29. Farrand, *Records*, vol. 1, pp. 340–341 (June 20).

30. Amar, "Of Sovereignty and Federalism," p. 1460.

31. Ibid., p. 1460. Robert C. Vipond similarly reconciles Madison's inconsistencies by concluding that he followed the model of constitution-making presented in Locke's *Second Treatise*. First, the peoples of the several states agreed by compact to form "one people." Then this united people ordained the Constitution by the unanimous vote of the states. Vipond, *Federalism and the Problem of Sovereignty: Constitutional Politics and the Rise of the Provincial Rights Movement in Canada*, Ph.D. Dissertation, Harvard University, Cambridge, Mass., 1983, pp. 49–53.

32. Wood, *Creation*, p. 530.

33. Ibid., pp. 529–530.

34. John B. McMaster and Frederick D. Stone, *Pennsylvania and the Federal Constitution*, pp. 229, 389, 316, 302.

35. Ibid., pp. 385, 256.

36. Ibid., p. 302.

37. Farrand, *Records*, vol. 1, pp. 166–167 (June 8).

38. Ibid., vol. 1, p. 324 (June 19).

39. Ibid., p. 323 (June 19); p. 464 (June 29).

40. Morris, "The Forging of the Union Reconsidered," p. 1073.

41. Termed the "classic" exposition by Professor Jeff Powell in "A Belated Review," 94 *Yale Law Journal* 1285 (1985).

42. Story, *Commentaries,* vol. 1, para. 201.

43. Ibid., para. 214.

44. Ibid., para. 214, 211.

45. Ibid., vol. 1, paras. 214, 211, 208, 215, 210, 214.

46. Ibid., vol. 1, pp. 248 and 281, n. 2; para. 349; p. 327, n. 3; para. 291.

47. Millican, *One United People,* p. 38.

48. See the discussion of the concept of "a people" in Karl Deutsch, *Nationalism and Social Communication,* ch. 4, "Peoples, Nations, and Communication," esp. pp. 96–104.

49. *Federalist* 39, p. 254.

50. Farrand, *Records,* vol. 2, pp. 468–469 (August 30).

51. Ibid., p. 469 (August 30).

52. Ibid., pp. 475, 477 (August 31).

53. Millican, *One United People,* p. 25.

54. Farrand, *Records,* vol. 1, p. 123 (June 5).

55. King at ibid., vol. 2, p. 92 (July 23); Mason at ibid., vol. 2, p. 88 (July 23).

56. Ibid., vol. 1, p. 22 (May 29); vol. 2, pp. 92–93 (July 23).

57. Ibid., p. 479 (August 31).

58. I have used the apportionment given in Article I as the index of representation, since that is the standard used by Madison during the debate at the Convention. See Farrand, *Records,* vol. 2, p. 475 (August 31). Hamilton made a calculation with a different result. In *Federalist* 22 (December 14, 1787), referring to the representation under the Articles, he asserted that it was possible to "enumerate nine states which contain less than a majority of the people." When measured by Madison's standard, however, the population of the nine states named by Hamilton do make a majority. See *Federalist* 22, pp. 139–140.

59. Farrand, *Records,* vol. 2, p. 475 (August 31).

60. Bernard Bailyn, *Ideological Origins,* p. 221.

61. My distinction between "constituent" and "governmental" sovereignty is much the same as Story's distinction between "absolute" and "subordinate" sovereignty.

62. See above, Chapter 4, pp. 147–148.

63. Wood, *Creation,* p. 599.

64. Ibid., p. 599.

65. McMaster and Stone, eds., *Pennsylvania and the Federal Constitution,* p. 229.

66. Corwin, *The Constitution,* p. 222.

67. Thomas McKean in Elliot, *Debates,* vol. 2, p. 529; quoted in Merrill Jensen,

Documentary History of the Ratification, vol. 2, p. 387. Referring to "the people . . . in whom the sovereign power resides," James Wilson wrote: "From their authority the constitution originates: for their safety and felicity it is established: in their hands it is as clay in the hands of the potter: they have the right to mould, to preserve, to improve, to refine, and to finish it as they please." McCloskey, *Wilson,* vol. 1, p. 304.

11. *James Wilson's Social Union*

1. Corwin, *The Constitution,* p. 1. Justice Story indicated how the Preamble affects the way the powers granted by the Constitution are to be construed: "Its true office is to expound the nature, and extent, and application of the powers actually conferred by the constitution, and not substantively to create them." Story, *Commentaries,* 1, para. 462.

2. *Federalist* 14, p. 84.

3. Martin Diamond, "The Ends of Federalism," p. 129.

4. The summary of Thomistic constitutionalism in the following comparison is based on Chapter 1, above, "The Rule of the Wise and the Holy." I have occasionally called attention to specific passages in that part of the book.

5. For "Constitution," the *OED,* having given the medieval meaning of "law or decree," as for example in a 1393 reference to the Constitutions of Clarendon of 1164, dates the meaning of "the mode in which a state is organized, especially as to the location of sovereign power" from 1610. "Constitutionalism" dates from 1832, but "constitutionalist" is found in 1766.

6. In *Federalist* 38, Madison, while discussing the role of the founders of ancient republics, asked "how far they might be clothed with the legitimate authority of the people" (*Federalist* 38, p. 240). During the discussion of ratification at the Constitutional convention, Rufus King argued for ratification by state conventions rather than legislatures as "the most certain means of obviating all disputes & doubts concerning the legitimacy of the new Constitution," in Farrand, *Records,* vol. 2, p. 92 (July 23). This is surely a very early use of the term "legitimate" to describe a property of a principle of government rather than a person claiming authority in a government. When hereditary monarchy was the typical form of government, the term "legitimate" referred to a ruler whose title to rightful power depended upon his or her being lawfully begotten. The *OED* finds this meaning in a reference to the "legitimacy of the Prince of Wales" in 1691. The challenge of nonmonarchical forms of government led to the more general usage, as in the statement dating from 1812, "I never hear an American citizen speak of the legitimacy of princes without indignation or pity."

7. The term "rule of law" owes its present wide currency to A. V. Dicey's use of

the term in his influential *Law and the Constitution* (1885). The idea itself, however, goes far back in the history of political thought. We have seen the prominence given it by Harrington in his advocacy of a "government of laws, not men." Hume likewise argued for "general laws" as a restraint on "arbitrary power" in his defense of "free government" (see his essay on "The Rise and Progress of the Arts and Sciences," in *Works,* vol. 4, pp. 174–197, esp. pp. 178–180). Blackstone defined as "the first property of civil law" that "it is a *rule,* not a transient sudden order from a superior to or concerning a particular person; but something permanent, uniform, and universal" (*Commentaries,* para. 44). Benjamin Jowett translated Aristotle's formulation of the idea in the *Politics* as "the rule of law is preferable to that of any individual" (*Aristotle's Politics,* Book 3, p. 139; also *The Politics of Aristotle,* trans. Ernest Barker, Book 3, ch. 16, p. 146).

8. See above, Chapter 1, p. 46.

9. See above, Chapter 2, pp. 71–72; Chapter 1, pp. 42–43.

10. Wright, *American Interpretations of Natural Law,* ch. 4; see also Edwin S. Corwin, *The Higher Law Background of American Constitutional Law.*

11. See above, Chapter 8, p. 274.

12. Compare the authority structure of the Mosaic regime set forth in Chapter 1, p. 49, with the definition of federalism in the Introduction, p. 36. That regime, we may say, had a constitution which had been ordained by the divinely appointed prophet and which therefore was positive law, legally superior to law made by any authority established by it.

13. See above, Chapter 1, pp. 46.

14. The amending power, as Corwin writes, is not unlimited, being "like all other powers in the Constitution . . . in form a delegated power." Thus the Constitution limits the amending power when it says that no state, not even by constitutional amendment, can be deprived without its consent of its "equal suffrage in the Senate." "The one power known to the Constitution," he continues, "which clearly is not limited by it is that which ordains it—in other words, the original, inalienable power of the people of the United States to determine their own political institutions." See *The Constitution,* p. 222. James Wilson expressed the same idea in a notable metaphor when he said in his Lectures on Law that in the hands of the people the Constitution "is as clay in the hands of the potter; they have the right to mould, to preserve, to improve, to refine and to finish it as they please." *Works,* ed. Robert G. McCloskey, vol. 1, p. 304.

15. For the parallel with the constitutionalism of Harrington, see above, Chapter 3, p. 97. Harrington, however, made no provision for amendment of the fundamental law of Oceana, terming it "unalterable." For discussion of the so-called paradox of a democracy limiting itself by a constitution, see Stephen Holmes, "Precommitment and the Paradox of Democracy," pp. 195–240.

16. Friedrich's definition is discussed above, Chapter 3, pp. 97–98. Taking a

similar view of constitutionalism, Gottfried Dietze, in *The Federalist,* holds that the purpose of the Constitution as stated in *The Federalist* was confined to the protection of individual rights of person and property. Edward Millican severely criticizes this view (*One United People,* pp. 64, 67, 227). David Epstein in *The Political Theory of the Federalist* also plays down the concern with the "public good," for which he is taken to task by Millican at p. 228.

17. Millican, *One United People,* pp. 64, 67, 78–79. Hamilton gives the reasons for thinking that a bill of rights would not only be "unnecessary" but also "dangerous" in *Federalist* 84, p. 579. The reason for the first assertion was that since Congress only had specific powers, there was no need to say what it could not do. Developing the latter point, James Wilson argued that since all of our natural rights cannot be definitively enumerated, to set down a list in a bill of rights would necessarily be restrictive. For "who will be bold enough to undertake to enumerate all the rights of the people?" Wilson asked at the Pennsylvania ratifying convention. Wilson's conception of popular sovereignty made him view a bill of rights as "superfluous and absurd," for where supreme sovereignty resides in the people, they reserve "every right and authority" which they did not explicitly delegate by "the positive grant expressed in the instrument of the union" (see McMaster & Stone, *Pennsylvania,* pp. 253–254, 143–144). At the federal convention, Colonel Mason's proposal for a bill of rights was dismissed with no discussion. See Farrand, *Records,* vol. 2, p. 588 (September 12).

18. Adam Smith argues that an active state is needed to support a robust capitalist economy, for the economy depends at least on the regular administration of justice and the protection of private property. See Smith, *Wealth of Nations,* pp. 669–681, 859–864.

19. See 'Trespasses of the States on the Rights of Each Other,' in Madison, "Vices," *Papers,* ed. Rutland, vol. 9, pp. 249–250.

20. *Federalist* 11, p. 71.

21. Madison, "Vices," *Papers,* ed. Rutland, vol. 9, p. 350.

22. *Federalist* 31, p. 198; *Federalist* 30, p. 191.

23. *Federalist* 11, p. 71.

24. For example, in *Federalist* 9, where Hamilton disingenuously tried to fob off onto Montesquieu the theory of the extended republic as a control on faction; and *Federalist* 27, where, as we have seen, he summarizes the Madisonian theory in his demonstration that the federal government will be "better administered" than the states. See *Federalist* 9, pp. 52–54, and *Federalist* 27, pp. 172–173.

25. Hamilton, *Federalist* 30, p. 191; Madison, *Federalist* 46, p. 319.

26. Hamilton on a standing army, *Federalist* 23–30, and on revenue for defense, *Federalist* 31–35.

27. *Federalist* 10, 14, 18–20, 41–46.

28. *Federalist* 11, p. 73.

29. *Federalist* 38, pp. 248–249.

30. Douglass C. North, *Growth and Welfare in the American Past*, p. 68.

31. Farrand, *Records*, vol. 1, p. 541 (July 6). King was arguing that the number of representatives in the House from each state should be based not only on population, but also on property.

32. Joyce Appleby, "The Social Origins of the American Revolutionary Ideology," p. 958.

33. As James Wilson in a memorandum for his Lectures on Law and entitled "On the History of Property" wrote: "Property is the right or lawful power, which a person has in a thing," and which includes the three "degrees" of right, to possess, to use, and to dispose of a thing. He then traced historically the various opinions regarding "the origin and true foundation of property," leading to a summary of the reasons why "the establishment of exclusive property may justly be considered an essential to the interests of civilized society." Wilson, *Works*, pp. 711–720.

34. Farrand, *Records*, vol. 2, p. 248 (August 10).

35. Ibid., vol. 1, pp. 605–606 (July 13), and vol. 2, p. 249 (August 10). The vote came after Wilson's celebrated declaration that "the cultivation & improvement of the human mind," not property, was the "primary object of Government and Society." See ibid., vol. 1, p. 605 (July 13).

36. *Federalist* 10, p. 58; *Federalist* 51, p. 352.

37. *Federalist* 1, p. 3.

38. The widespread fear for the fragility of the republican regime is richly documented in Wood, *Creation*, chs. 2, 3, esp. pp. 65–70, 91–97, 107–114. The concern of both Federalists and Anti-Federalists with this question is a main theme of Storing's *Anti-Federalists*.

39. "Reflections on the Revolution in France," Burke, *Writings and Speeches*, vol. 4, p. 147.

40. Storing, *Anti-Federalists*, p. 74.

41. Jefferson's proposal dealt with Virginia, but Madison treated the idea as a proposal for the government of the United States.

42. *Federalist* 49, p. 340.

43. *Federalist* 46, pp. 316, 318.

44. *Federalist* 17, p. 107.

45. *Federalist* 46, p. 317; *Federalist* 27, pp. 172–174.

46. Long, *Memoirs of Robert E. Lee*, pp. 93, 88, 92, 95.

47. Farrand, *Records*, vol. 1, p. 65 (June 1). See also Frank Bourgin, *The Great Challenge*, p. 55.

48. Wilson, *Works*, p. 2. McCloskey also cites tributes from "historians of high authority," James Bryce, A. F. Pollard, Andrew McLaughlin, and Max Farrand. Farrand rated Wilson "second to Madison and almost on par with him." *Works*, p. 6.

49. Ibid., p. 4.

50. Farrand, *Records,* vol. 1, p. 49 (May 31).

51. Wilson, *Works,* p. 1, n. 1; p. 264. And Stephen A. Conrad, "Metaphor and Imagination in James Wilson's Theory of Federal Union," p. 42.

52. Wilson, *Works,* pp. 4, 2.

53. Ibid., p. 37.

54. Ibid., pp. 401–406. Some parts of this discussion were amplified in a speech at the state constitution in 1789, in ibid., pp. 786–787.

55. Ibid., pp. 266–268.

56. Rush in a letter to David Ramsay, the historian. Cited in Conrad, "Metaphor and Imagination," p. 57.

57. Wilson, *Works,* pp. 403–404.

58. Ibid., pp. 788–789.

59. *Federalist* 49, p. 340 (Madison); *Federalist* 27, p. 172 (Hamilton).

60. The argument is distinctly Humean. Persons, according to Hume, have a lively sense of their own interest and through sympathy can take pleasure in those practices and institutions which work to the benefit of humankind. Although our original motive in supporting institutions like the rules of justice and promise keeping, or practices like allegiance to the government, is self-interest, the repeated observation of advantageous effects, over time, gives rise to a separate source of moral approbation founded in sympathy. Hume says, "Thus self-interest is the original motive to the establishment of justice: but a sympathy with the public interest is the source of the moral approbation which attends that virtue." Hume, *Treatise,* Book 3, Part 2, sect. 2, pp. 499–500. Also see *Treatise,* sect. 5, p. 523; sect. 6, p. 533; sect. 10, p. 553. I wish to thank Russ Muirhead for this comment.

61. Farrand, *Records,* vol. 1, p. 133 (June 6).

62. "Rational choice models of political behavior," writes James Q. Wilson, "cannot explain why anyone votes. It is irrational, in that casting a vote entails costs for which there are no compensating political benefits except in the absurdly rare case in which one vote can make or break a tie." "The James Madison Lecture," p. 560.

63. Wilson, *Works,* p. 778.

64. Ibid., p. 786.

65. Ibid., pp. 267, 132, 232, 234.

66. Ibid., pp. 237, 228, 241, 227.

67. Ibid., pp. 240, 234–235.

68. Wilson, *Works,* pp. 126–127, 130, 232–233.

69. As McCloskey brings out, Wilson offered a "comprehensive solution" to what E. S. Corwin termed "the great theoretical problem of the time," that is, the reconciliation of "the venerable Western idea of a binding higher law with the relatively new idea of the will of the people." "For," continues McCloskey, "given the premise of an innately moral and essentially social human nature, it follows that

popular consent will tend to reflect God's natural law." Wilson, *Works,* introduction, p. 38, citing Corwin, *The Higher Law Background,* p. 89.

70. Wilson, *Works,* p. 132.

71. In making the will unitary, Reid and Wilson subtly but importantly depart from Hume. Though in Hume's account, passions and not reason determine the will, Hume makes a crucial distinction between the more social "calm passions," which though often "confounded with reason" are in fact "real passions," and more selfish "violent" passions. While Hume does not describe a Madisonian confrontation between reason and passion as such, the calm and violent passions often stand in "opposition" (Hume, *Treatise,* Book 2, part 3, sect. 3, pp. 417–418). By diminishing the confrontation of selfish and social passions, and giving short shrift to the possibility of conflict between passions of varying vitality or beween reason and passion, Reid and Wilson make the will unitary.

72. Conrad, "Metaphor and Imagination," p. 25, citing Norman S. Fiering, "Irresistible Compassion," p. 195.

73. Wilson, *Works,* pp. 234, 230.

74. Ibid., pp. 233–234.

75. "Government is indeed highly necessary," writes Wilson, "but it is highly necessary to a fallen state. Had man continued innocent, society, without the aid of government, would have shed its benign influence even over the bowers of Paradise." Wilson, *Works,* p. 87.

76. Wilson, *Works,* p. 236.

77. Ibid., pp. 266–268.

78. Ibid., pp. 266–268.

79. Ibid., p. 146; p. 235.

80. Farrand, *Records,* vol. 1, p. 605 (July 13).

81. Wilson, *Works,* pp. 146–147, 776.

82. On Franklin's view of virtue, see above, Chapter 4, pp. 158–160. On the American founders' view of character formation and politics, Martin Diamond wrote: "In place of the utopian end postulated by the ancients, the forced elevation of human character, the moderns substituted a lowered political end, namely, human comfort and security." He termed this the "removal of the tasks of character formation from its previously preeminent place on the agenda of politics." "Ethics and Politics," pp. 75, 83.

83. Wilson, *Works,* p. 159.

84. Stephen A. Conrad, "Polite Foundation," p. 362.

85. Wilson, *Works,* pp. 162–164.

86. "Nationalism—our identification with the life and aspirations of uncounted millions whom we shall never know, with a territory we shall never visit in its entirety—is qualitatively different from the love of family or of home surroundings." See Hans Kohn, *The Idea of Nationalism,* p. 9.

87. Wilson, *Works,* p. 163.

88. Ibid., p. 163. Wilson is quoting Thomas Rutherford, *Institutes of Natural Law*, pp. 463–464.

89. *Federalist* 51, p. 353.

90. Wilson, *Works*, pp. 238–239, 284–285, 574–575.

91. Ibid., pp. 174, 285.

92. John Adams, *Thoughts on Government* (1776), vol. 4, p. 413.

93. Wilson, *Works*, pp. 414–417.

94. Wilson, *Works*, pp. 242–243, 304.

95. On "the dry light of reason" in Bacon's 'New Logic' see my "Two Models of Public Opinion," pp. 165–166.

96. Wilson, *Works*, pp. 136–138.

97. *Federalist* 46, p. 316.

98. Wilson, *Works*, p. 237.

99. Ibid., pp. 266–267.

100. The states, said Hamilton at the convention, "have evidently in a high degree, the esprit de corps," by which he meant: "they constantly pursue internal interests adverse to those of the whole." Farrand, *Records*, vol. 1, p. 284 (June 18).

101. Wilson, *Works*, pp. 266, 268.

102. Wilson, *Works*, pp. 787 and 403.

103. Wilson, *Works*, p. 402.

104. Floyd Stovall, ed., *Walt Whitman*, vol. 1, p. 25.

Conclusion: Liberty and Union

1. Morgan, *Inventing the People*, p. 267.

2. John Dickinson, for example, told the convention that "limited monarchy" despite its merits was out of the question since such institutions were "the growth of ages, and could arise only under a complication of circumstances none of which existed in this Country." Farrand, *Debates*, vol. 1, p. 87 (June 2).

3. *Federalist* 10, pp. 58–59.

4. I have discussed these changes in *Modern British Politics*, chs. 1 and 2.

5. I wish to thank Dr. Eileen McDonagh for the term "well-springs for reform," which she has used to characterize the role of the states in the Progressive Era. The states, she writes, diffused "policy innovation in a federal structure by transferring it from the periphery contributing to the emergence of the new American state at this time." "Representative Democracy and State-Building."

6. Farrand, *Records*, pp. 641–642 (Sept. 17).

References

Ackerman, Bruce A. "The Storrs Lectures: Discovering the Constitution." *Yale Law Journal,* vol. 93, no. 6 (May 1984), pp. 1013–1072.

Acts and Laws, Passed by the Great and General Court or Assembly of the Colony of Massachusetts-Bay in New England (Boston, 1776).

Adair, Douglas. *Fame and the Founding Fathers: Essays by Douglas Adair.* Ed. Trevor Colburn. New York: W. W. Norton & Company, 1974.

Adams, John. *The Works of John Adams.* Ed. Charles Francis Adams. 10 vols. Boston: Little Brown, 1850–1856.

——— *Diary and Autobiography of John Adams.* Ed. L. H. Butterfield. 4 vols. Cambridge, MA: Harvard University Press, 1961.

Adams, Randolph G. *The Political Ideas of the American Revolution: Britannic-American Contributions to the Problem of Imperial Organization, 1765–1775.* 3rd ed. New York: Barnes & Noble, 1958.

Allen, J. W. *A History of Political Thought in the Sixteenth Century.* London: Methuen, 1928.

Almond, Gabriel, and G. Bingham Powell. *Comparative Politics: A Developmental Approach.* Boston: Little Brown, 1966.

Alsop, Joseph. *FDR: A Centenary Remembrance.* London: Thames and Hudson, 1982.

Althusius, Johannes. *Politica Methodice Digesta.* Intro. Carl J. Friedrich. Cambridge, MA: Harvard University Press, 1932.

Amar, Akhil Reed. "Of Sovereignty and Federalism." *Yale Law Journal,* vol. 96, no. 7 (June 1987), pp. 1425–1520.

Appleby, Joyce. "The Social Origins of the American Revolutionary Ideology." *Journal of American History,* vol. 64 (March 1978), pp. 935–958.

Aquinas, Thomas. *Opera Omnia.* Parma: P. Fiaccadori, 1852–1873. 25 vols. Reimpression: New York: Matsurgia, 1948–1950. Intro. Vernon J. Bourke. *Summa Theologica,* vols. 1–4; *Summa Contra Gentiles,* vol. 5; *De Regimine Principum,* vol. 16, pp. 225–291.

———— *Summa Theologiae*. Rome: Leonine edition, 1888–1906. 61 vols. Cambridge: Blackfriars, 1963–1976.

———— *Summa Theologica*. Trans. Fathers of the English Dominican Province. 19 vols. New York: Benzinger, 1911–1925.

———— *The Basic Writings of Saint Thomas Aquinas*. Ed. and Intro. Anton C. Pegis. 2 vols. New York: Random House, 1945.

———— *On Kingship, to the King of Cyprus*. Trans. Gerald B. Phelan and Ignatius Eschmann. Toronto: Ponitifical Institute of Medieval Studies, 1949.

———— *The Political Ideas of Saint Thomas Aquinas*. Ed. and Intro. Dino Bigongiari. New York: Hafner, 1953.

———— "On Being and Essence." *Thomas Aquinas: Selected Writings*. Ed. M. C. D'Arcy. London: Everyman Library, 1939.

———— "Aristotle's *Metaphysics*." *Thomas Aquinas: Selected Writings*. Ed. M. C. D'Arcy. London: Everyman, 1939.

Arber, Edward, ed. *English Reprints*. New York: AMS Press, 1869, 1966.

Aristotle. *The Politics*. Trans. Benjamin Jowett. Oxford: Clarendon Press, 1905.

———— *The Politics*. Trans. Ernest Barker. Oxford: Oxford University Press, 1958.

Ayres, Linda. *Harvard Divided*. Cambridge, MA: Fogg Art Museum, 1976.

Bagehot, Walter. *Physics and Politics* in *The Collected Works of Walter Bagehot*. Ed. Norman S. John-Stevas. 8 vols. Cambridge, MA: Harvard University Press, 1965–1974.

Bailyn, Bernard. *Faces of Revolution: Personalities and Themes in the Struggle for American Independence*. New York: Knopf, 1990.

———— *The Ordeal of Thomas Hutchinson*. Cambridge, MA: Harvard University Press, 1974.

———— *The Ideological Origins of the American Revolution*. Cambridge, MA: Harvard University Press, 1967.

Bailyn, Bernard, ed. *Pamphlets of the American Revolution, 1750–1776*. Cambridge, MA: Harvard University Press, 1965.

Bancroft, George. *History of the United States*. 6 vols. New York: D. Appleton & Company, 1882–1886.

Barker, Sir Ernest. *Essays on Government*. Oxford: Clarendon Press, 1945.

Beer, Samuel H. *Modern British Politics: Parties and Pressure Groups in the Collectivist Age*. 3rd ed. New York: W. W. Norton & Company, 1982.

———— "Political Overload and Federalism." *Polity*, vol. 10 (Fall 1977), pp. 5–17.

———— "The Strengths of Liberal Democracy." In *A Prospect of Liberal Democracy*. Ed. William S. Livingston. Austin: University of Texas Press, 1979.

———— "Two Models of Public Opinion: Bacon's 'New Logic' and Diotima's 'Tale of Love.'" *Transactions of the Royal Historical Society*, 5th ser., vol. 24 (1974), pp. 79–96.

———— "The Representation of Interests in British Government: Historical Background." *American Political Science Review,* vol. 51, no. 3 (September 1957), pp. 613–650.

Bemis, Samuel Flagg. *John Quincy Adams and the Union.* New York: Knopf, 1956.

Becker, Carl. *The Declaration of Independence: A Study in the History of Political Ideas.* New York: Vintage Books, 1942, 1958.

Benson, George C., ed. *Essays in Federalism.* Claremont, CA: Institute for Studies in Federalism, 1961.

Blackstone, Sir William. *Commentaries on the Laws of England.* Original Edition. 1765–1769.

Blitzer, Charles. *An Immortal Commonwealth: The Political Thought of James Harrington.* New Haven: Yale University Press, 1960.

Bodin, Jean. *The Six Books of a Commonweale.* Trans. R. Knolles. Ed. K. D. McRae. Cambridge, MA: Harvard University Press, 1963.

Bourgin, Frank. *The Great Challenge: The Myth of Laissez-Faire in the Early Republic.* New York: Harper & Row, 1989.

Bourke, Vernon. *Thomistic Bibliography, 1920–1940.* St. Louis: Modern Schoolman, 1945.

Bourke, Vernon, and Terry Miethe. *Thomistic Bibliography, 1940–1978.* Westport, CT: Greenwood Press, 1980.

Brebner, John Barlett. *The Neutral Yankees of Nova Scotia: A Marginal Colony during the Revolutionary Years.* New York: Columbia University Press, 1937.

Brown, Robert E. *Reinterpretation of the Formation of the American Constitution.* Boston: Boston University Press, 1963.

Bryce, James. *The American Commonwealth.* New York: Macmillan Company, 1888, 1924.

Burke, Edmund. *The Writings and Speeches of Edmund Burke.* Gen. Ed. Paul Langford. Oxford: Clarendon Press, 1981–.

————— *The Works of Edmund Burke.* 9 vols. Boston: Little, Brown & Co., 1839.

Burnett, Edmund C., ed. *Letters of the Members of the Continental Congress.* Washington: The Carnegie Institution of Washington, 1921–1936.

Burns, James MacGregor. *The Deadlock of Democracy: Four Party Politics in America.* New York: Prentice Hall, 1963.

Calhoun, John C. *The Papers of John C. Calhoun.* Ed. Robert L. Meriwether et. al. 19 vols. Columbia: University of South Carolina Press, 1959–.

Calvin, John. *Institutes of the Christian Religion.* 7th ed. Trans. John Allen. 2 vols. Philadelphia: Presbyterian Board of Christian Education, 1936.

Carney, Frederick S. *The Politics of Johannes Althusius.* London: Eyre and Spottiswood, 1964.

Carrithers, David W. "Montesquieu, Jefferson, and the Fundamentals of Eighteenth

Century Republican Theory." *French American Review,* vol. 6 (Fall 1982), pp. 179–182.

Colegrove, Kenneth. *The Early History of State Instructions to Members of Congress, 1774–1812.* Ph.D. Dissertation, Harvard University, 1915.

Commager, Henry Steele, ed. *Documents of American History.* 7th ed. New York: Appleton-Century-Crofts, 1963.

Conlan, Timothy. *New Federalism: Intergovernmental Reform from Nixon to Reagan.* Washington: Brookings, 1988.

Conrad, Stephen A. "Metaphor and Imagination in James Wilson's Theory of Federal Union." *Law and Social Inquiry,* vol. 13 (1988), pp. 619–636.

——— "Polite Foundation: Citizenship and Commonsense in James Wilson's Republican Theory." *Supreme Court Review,* 1984, pp. 359–388.

Conway, John. *The Round Table: A Study in Liberal Imperialism.* Ph.D. Dissertation, Harvard University, 1951.

Conway, Moncure D. *The Life of Thomas Paine.* London: Watts, 1909.

Corwin, Edward S. *The Constitution and What It Means Today.* 13th ed. Princeton: Princeton University Press, 1973.

Corwin, Edward S. *The Higher Law Background of American Constitutional Law.* Ithaca: Cornell University Press, 1955.

Croly, Herbert. *The Promise of American Life.* New York: Macmillan, 1909.

Cromwell, Oliver. *Writings and Speeches.* Ed. W. C. Abbott. 4 vols. Cambridge, MA: Harvard University Press, 1937–1947.

Cunliffe, Marcus. *George Washington: Man and Monument.* Boston: Little, Brown and Co., 1958.

Cushing, William. *Notes of Cases Decided in the Superior and Supreme Judicial Courts, 1772–1789.* Harvard Law School. Treasure Room. MS

Dahl, Robert, and Edward A. Tufte. *Size and Democracy.* Stanford: Stanford University Press, 1973.

Davis, J. Rufus. *The Federal Principle: A Journey through Time in Quest of Meaning.* Berkeley: University of California Press, 1978.

Davis, Jefferson. *The Messages and Papers of Jefferson Davis and the Confederacy, including Diplomatic Correspondence, 1861–1865.* Ed. James D. Richardson. New York: Chelsea House, 1966.

Davis, William T. *Bench and Bar of the Commonwealth of Massachusetts.* 2 vols. Boston, 1895.

Dayton, Cornelia. "Representation and Consent in the American Republic: The Theory and Practice of Constituent Instructions." B.A. Thesis, Harvard University, 1979.

De Grazia, Alfred. *Public and Republic: Political Representation in America.* New York: Knopf, 1951.

Deutsch, Karl W. *Nationalism and Social Communication: An Inquiry into the Foundations of Nationality.* 2nd ed. Cambridge, MA: MIT Press, 1966.

Diamond, Martin. "Ethics and Politics: The American Way." In *The Moral Foundations of the American Republic*. 3rd ed. Ed. Robert H. Horowitz. Charlottesville: University Press of Virginia, 1986.

———— "The Ends of Federalism: The Federal Polity." *Publius,* vol. 3, no. 2 (Fall 1973), pp. 129–152.

———— "What the Framers Meant by Federalism." In *A Nation of States: Essays on the American Federal System*. Ed. Robert A. Goldwin. Chicago: Rand McNally & Company, 1961, 1963.

Dicey, A. V. *The Law and the Constitution*. London, 1885.

Dickinson, John. *The Political Writings of John Dickinson*. 2 vols. Ed. Paul Leicester Ford. Philadelphia, 1895.

Dietze, Gottfried. *The Federalist: A Classic on Federalism and Free Government*. Baltimore: Johns Hopkins University Press, 1960.

Douglas, Elisha P. "Thomas Burke: Disillusioned Democrat." *North Carolina Historical Review,* vol. 26 (1949), pp. 150–186.

Elazar, Daniel J. *The American Partnership: Intergovernmental Cooperation in the Nineteenth Century*. Chicago: University of Chicago Press, 1962.

Elliot, Jonathan, ed. *The Debates in the Several State Conventions on the Adoption of the Federal Constitution*. Philadelphia, 1863.

Elyot, Sir Thomas. *The Boke Named the Governour*. London: J. M. Dent & Co, 1531, 1907.

Epstein, David. *The Political Theory of The Federalist*. Chicago: University of Chicago Press, 1984.

Farrand, Max, ed. *The Records of the Federal Convention of 1787*. 4 vols. New Haven: Yale University Press, 1911–1937, 1966.

Faulkner, Robert. *Richard Hooker and the Politics of a Christian England*. Berkeley: University of California Press, 1981.

Fender, Stephen. *American Literature in Context, I: 1620–1830*. London: Methuen & Co., 1987.

Fiering, Norman S. "Irresistible Compassion: An Aspect of Eighteenth Century Sympathy and Humanitarianism." *Journal of the History of Ideas,* vol. 37, no. 2 (1976), pp. 195–218.

Fink, Zera. *The Classical Republicans: An Essay in the Recovery of a Pattern of Thought in Seventeenth Century England*. Evanston, IL: Northwestern University Press, 1945.

Firth, C. H. *Oliver Cromwell and the Rule of the Puritans in England* (London, 1929).

Foner, Eric. *Tom Paine and Revolutionary America*. New York: Oxford University Press, 1976.

Ford, Henry Jones. *The Rise and Growth of American Politics*. New York, 1898.

Ford, Worthington C., et al., eds. *Journals of the Continental Congress*. 34 vols. Washington: U.S. Government Printing Office, 1904–1937.

Four Letters on Interesting Subjects. Philadelphia: Styner & Cist, 1776.

Franklin, Benjamin. *The Papers of Benjamin Franklin.* Ed. Leonard Labaree. 28 vols. New Haven: Yale University Press, 1959–.

———— *The Autobiography of Benjamin Franklin.* Eds. Leonard Labaree et al. New Haven: Yale University Press, 1964.

———— *The Writings of Benjamin Franklin.* Ed. Albert Henry Smyth. 10 vols. New York: Macmillan, 1905–1907.

Friedrich, Carl J. *Constitutional Government and Democracy: Theory and Practice in Europe and America.* 4th ed. Waltham, MA: Blaisdell Publishing Co., 1968.

Fuess, Claude. *Daniel Webster.* Boston: Little, Brown & Co., 1930.

Galbraith, John Kenneth. *American Capitalism: The Concept of Countervailing Power.* Boston: Houghton Mifflin, 1952.

Gerth, H. H., and C. Wright Mills. *From Max Weber.* New York: Oxford University Press, 1946.

Glazer, Nathan. *Affirmative Discrimination: Ethnic Inequality and Public Policy.* New York: Basic Books, 1975.

Greene, Jack P. *Peripheries and Center: Constitutional Development in the Extended Polities of the British Empire and the United States, 1607–1788.* Athens, GA: University of Georgia Press, 1986.

Gunn, J. A. W. *Politics and the Public Interest in the Seventeenth Century.* London: Routledge & Kegan Paul, 1969.

Gunther, Gerald. "The Convention Method of Amending the United States Constitution." *Georgia Law Review,* vol. 14, no. 1 (Fall 1979), pp. 1–25.

Gwyn, William B. *The Meaning of the Separation of Powers.* New Orleans: Tulane University Press, 1965.

Habakkuk, H. J. "England" in *The European Nobility in the Eighteenth Century.* 2nd ed. Ed. A. Goodwin. London: Adam and Charles Black, 1967.

Haller, William. *The Rise of Puritanism.* New York: Harper, 1957.

Hamilton, Alexander. *The Papers of Alexander Hamilton.* Ed. Harold C. Syrett. New York: Columbia University Press, 1961–1979.

Hamilton, Alexander, James Madison, and John Jay. *The Federalist.* Ed. Benjamin F. Wright. Cambridge, MA: The Belknap Press of Harvard University Press, 1961.

———— *The Federalist.* Ed. Jacob E. Cooke. Middletown, Conn.: Wesleyan University Press, 1961.

Harrington, James. *The Political Works of James Harrington.* Ed. J. G. A. Pocock. Cambridge: Cambridge University Press, 1975.

———— *The Commonwealth of Oceana.* Ed. Henry Morley. London, 1883.

Hart, Albert Bushnell, ed. *Commonwealth History of Massachusetts.* 5 vols. New York: The States History Company, 1929.

Haskins, Charles Homer. *The Rise of the Universities*. Ithaca: Cornell University Press, 1957.

Heclo, Hugh. *Modern Social Politics in Britain and Sweden*. New Haven: Yale University Press, 1974.

Hill, Christopher. *Milton and the English Revolution*. London: Oxford University Press, 1977.

———— *The Experience of Defeat: Milton and Some Contemporaries*. London: Faber & Faber, 1984.

Holcombe, Arthur H. *Our More Perfect Union: From Eighteenth Century Principles to Twentieth Century Practice*. Cambridge, MA: Harvard University Press, 1950.

———— *The New Party Politics*. New York: Norton, 1933.

Holmes, Stephen. "Liberal Constraints on Private Power? Reflections on the Origins and Rationale of Access Regulation." In *Democracy and the Mass Media*. Ed. J. Lichtenberg. Cambridge: Cambridge University Press, 1990.

———— "Precommitment and the Paradox of Democracy." In *Constitutionalism and Democracy*. Ed. Jon Elster and Rune Slagstad. New York: Cambridge University Press, 1988.

Hooker, Richard. *The Folger Library Edition of the Works of Richard Hooker*. Ed. W. Speed Hill. Cambridge, MA: The Belknap Press of Harvard University Press, 1977.

Houston, Alan C. *Algernon Sidney and the Republican Heritage in England and America*. Princeton: Princeton University Press, 1991.

Hume, David. *Philosophical Works*. Eds. T. H. Green and T. H. Grose. Darmstadt, Germany, 1882.

———— *Treatise on Human Nature*. Ed. L. A. Selby-Bigge. 2nd ed. Oxford: Clarendon Press, 1978.

Inglis, Charles. *The True Interest of America . . . Strictures on a Pamphlet Intitled Common Sense*. Philadelphia, 1776.

Jefferson, Thomas. *Writings*. Ed. Merrill Peterson. New York: Library of America, 1984.

———— *The Papers of Thomas Jefferson*. Eds. Julian P. Boyd et al. 24 vols. Princeton: Princeton University Press, 1950–.

———— *The Commonplace Book of Thomas Jefferson: A Repertory of his Ideas on Government*. Ed. Gilbert Chinard. Baltimore: The Johns Hopkins Press, 1926.

Jensen, Merrill. *Documentary History of the Ratification*. 16 vols. Madison: University of Wisconsin Press, 1976.

Johnson, Lyndon Baines. *The Vantage Point: Perspectives on the Presidency, 1963–1969*. New York: Holt, Rinehart and Winston, 1971.

Kelly, Alfred H., and Winifred A. Harbison. *The American Constitution: Its Origin and Development*. 5th ed. New York: Norton, 1976.

Kelly, George Armstrong. *Politics and Religious Consciousness in America*. New Brunswick, NJ: Transaction Books, 1984.

Kemp, Betty. *King and Commons, 1660–1832*. London: Macmillan, 1957.

Kenyon, Cecilia. "Men of Little Faith: The Anti-Federalists on the Nature of Representative Government." *William and Mary Quarterly*, 3rd ser., vol. 12 (1955), pp. 3–45.

Keohane, Nannerl O. "Virtuous Republics and Glorious Monarchies: Two Models in Montesquieu's Political Thought." *Political Studies*, vol. 20 (1972), pp. 383–396.

Knachel, Philip A., ed. *Eikon Basilike: The Portraiture of His Sacred Majesty in His Solitudes and Sufferings*. Ithaca: Cornell University Press, 1966.

Kohn, Hans. *The Idea of Nationalism: A Study of its Origins and Background*. Toronto: Macmillan, 1967.

Kramnick, Issac. *Bolingbroke and His Circle: The Politics of Nostalgia in the Age of Walpole*. Cambridge, MA: Harvard University Press, 1968.

Lanyi, George. *Oliver Cromwell and His Age: A Study of Nationalism*. Ph.D. Dissertation, Harvard University, 1939.

Lawrence, D. H. *Studies in Classical American Literature*. Garden City, NY: Doubleday, 1951.

Lincoln, Abraham. *The Collected Works of Abraham Lincoln*. 8 vols. Ed. Roy P. Basler. New Brunswick: Rutgers University Press, 1953.

Locke, John. *Two Treatises of Government*. Ed. Peter Laslett. Cambridge: Cambridge University Press, 1967.

———— *A Letter Concerning Toleration*. Ed. James H. Tully. Indianapolis: Hackett Publishing Company, 1689, 1983.

Lockyer, Roger. *Tudor and Stuart Britain, 1471–1714*. New York: St. Martin's Press, 1964.

Lodge, Henry Cabot. *Alexander Hamilton*. New York: Greenwood Press, 1898, 1969.

Long, A. L. *Memoirs of Robert E. Lee: His Military and Personal History*. New York, 1887.

Loss, Richard. "Alexander Hamilton and the Modern Presidency, Continuity or Discontinuity?" *Presidental Studies Quarterly*, vol. 12, no. 1 (Winter 1982), pp. 6–25.

Lovejoy, Arthur O. *The Great Chain of Being: A Study of the History of an Idea*. Cambridge, MA: Harvard University Press, 1936.

Lutz, Donald S., ed. *Documents of Political Foundation Written by Colonial Americans: From Covenant to Constitution*. Philadelphia: Institute for the Study of Human Issues, 1986.

———— "The Articles of Confederation as the Background of the Federal Republic." *Publius*, vol. 20, no. 1 (Winter 1990), pp. 55–70.

Machiavelli, Niccolò. *The Discourses of Machiavelli*. Trans. Leslie J. Walker. 2 vols. New Haven: Yale University Press, 1950.

Madison, James. *The Writings of James Madison*. Ed. Gaillard Hunt. New York: G. P. Putnam's Sons, 1910.

—— *The Papers of James Madison*. 17 vols. Eds. David B. Mattern et al. Charlottesville: University Press of Virginia, 1991.

—— *The Papers of James Madison*. Eds. Robert A. Rutland et al. Chicago: University of Chicago Press, 1975.

Madison, James, Alexander Hamilton, and John Jay. *The Federalist*. Ed. Benjamin Fletcher Wright. Cambridge, MA: Harvard University Press, 1961.

—— *The Federalist*. Ed. Jacob E. Cooke. Middletown, CT: Wesleyan University Press, 1961.

Maier, Pauline. *From Resistance to Revolution: Colonial Radicals and the Development of American Opposition to Britain, 1765–1776*. New York: Knopf, 1972.

Mansfield, Harvey C., Jr. *Machiavelli's New Modes and Orders: A Study of the Discourses on Livy*. Ithaca: Cornell University Press, 1979.

—— *Statesmanship and Party Government: A Study of Burke and Bolingbroke*. Chicago: University of Chicago Press, 1965.

Marshall, T. H. *Class, Citizenship, and Social Development*. Garden City, NY: Anchor Books, 1965.

Masseres, Francis. *Considerations on the Expediency of Admitting Representatives from the American Colonies into the British House of Commons*. London, 1770. 23 pages.

May, Eskine. *Treatise on the Law, Privileges and Proceedings of Parliament*. 17th ed. Ed. Sir Barnett Cocks. London: Butterworth, 1964.

McCoy, Drew. *The Last of the Fathers: James Madison and the Republican Legacy*. Cambridge: Cambridge University Press, 1989.

McDonagh, Eileen. "Representative Democracy and State-Building in the Progressive Era." *American Political Science Review*, Dec. 1992.

McDonald, Forrest. *Novus Ordo Seclorum: The Intellectual Origins of the Constitution*. Lawrence: The University Press of Kansas, 1985.

—— *Alexander Hamilton: A Biography*. New York: W. W. Norton, 1979.

McIlwain, Charles H. *Constitutionalism and the Changing World*. Cambridge: Cambridge University Press, 1939.

—— *The Growth of Political Thought in the West*. London: Macmillan, 1932.

—— *The American Revolution: A Constitutional Interpretation*. New York: Macmillan, 1923.

McIlwain, Charles H., ed. *The Political Works of James I*. Cambridge, MA: Harvard University Press, 1918.

McLaughlin, Andrew. *Constitutional History of the United States*. New York: Appleton Century, 1936.

McMaster, John B., and Frederick D. Stone. *Pennsylvania and the Federal Constitution.* Philadelphia: Historical Society of Pennsylvania, 1888.

Merk, Frederick. *History of the Westward Movement.* New York: Alfred A. Knopf, 1978.

Merriam, Charles E. *A History of American Political Theories.* New York: Macmillan, 1920.

Meyers, Marvin, ed. *The Mind of the Founder.* New York: The Bobbs-Merrill Company, 1973.

Mill, John Stuart. *Collected Works.* Toronto: University of Toronto Press, in progress.

Miller, John C. *Alexander Hamilton and the Growth of the New Nation.* New York: Harper & Row, 1959.

Millican, Edward. *One United People: The Federalist Papers and the National Idea.* Lexington: The University Press of Kentucky, 1990.

Milton, John. *Complete Prose Works of John Milton.* Ed. Don. M. Wolfe. New Haven: Yale University Press, 1959.

Montesquieu, Baron de. *The Political Theory of Montesquieu.* Ed. Melvin Richter. Cambridge: Cambridge University Press, 1977.

———— *The Spirit of the Laws.* Trans. Thomas Nugent. Introduction by Franz Neumann. New York: Collier-Macmillan, 1949.

Morgan, Edmund S. *Inventing the People: The Rise of Popular Sovereignty in England and America.* New York: W. W. Norton & Company, 1988.

Morris, Christopher. *Political Thought in England: Tyndale to Hooker.* London: Oxford University Press, 1953.

Morris, Richard. *The Forging of the Union, 1781–1789.* New York: Harper and Row, 1987.

———— "The Forging of the Union Reconsidered: A Historical Refutation of State Sovereignty over Seabeds." *Columbia Law Review,* vol. 74, no. 6 (October 1974), pp. 1056–1093.

Morrison, Samuel Eliot. *The Oxford History of the American People.* New York: Oxford University Press, 1965.

Mowat, Charles Loch. *Britain between the Wars, 1918–1940.* Chicago: University of Chicago Press, 1955.

Musgrave, Richard. *The Theory of Public Finance: A Study in Political Economy.* New York: McGraw-Hill, 1959.

Namier, Lewis B. *England in the Age of the American Revolution.* 2nd ed. London: Macmillan, 1961.

———— *The Structure of Politics at the Accession of George III.* London: Macmillan, 1957.

Neale, J. E. *Elizabeth I and Her Parliaments, 1584–1601.* 2 vols. London: Cape, 1953.

Nelson, William E. *Americanization of the Common Law: The Impact of Legal Change on Massachusetts Society, 1760–1830.* Cambridge, MA: Harvard University Press, 1975.

Neustadt, Richard. *Presidential Power: The Politics of Leadership.* New York: John Wiley & Sons, 1960, 1976.

North, Douglass C. *Growth and Welfare in the American Past: A New Economic History.* 2nd ed. Englewood Cliffs, NJ: Prentice Hall, 1974.

Oates, Wallace E. *Fiscal Federalism.* New York: Harcourt Brace Jovanovich, 1972.

Olson, Mancur, Jr. *The Logic of Collective Action.* Cambridge, MA: Harvard University Press, 1965.

———— "Strategic Theory and its Applications: The Principle of 'Fiscal Equivalence': The Division of Responsibility among different Levels of Government." *American Economic Review,* vol. 59, no. 2 (May 1969), pp. 479–532.

Ostrom, Vincent. *The Intellectual Crisis in Public Administration.* Tuscaloosa: University of Alabama Press, 1989.

Otis, James, Jr. *Brief Remarks on the Defence of the Halifax Libel on the British-American Colonies.* Boston, 1765. Repub. in *University of Missouri Studies,* vol. 4, no. 4 (October 1, 1929).

———— *Considerations on Behalf of the Colonists in a Letter to a Noble Lord.* Boston, 1765. Repub. in *University of Missouri Studies,* vol. 4, no. 4 (October 1, 1929).

———— *The Rights of the British Colonies Asserted and Proved.* Boston, 1764. Repub. in Bailyn, *Pamphlets.*

———— *A Vindication of the British Colonies, against the Aspersions of the Halifax Gentleman.* Boston, 1765. Repub. in Bailyn, *Pamphlets.*

Paine, Thomas. *The Complete Writings.* Ed. Philip S. Foner. New York: The Citadel Press, 1945.

Palmer, R. R. *Age of Democratic Revolution: History of Europe and America, 1760–1800.* Princeton: Princeton University Press, 1959, 1964.

Pangle, Thomas. "The Federalists and the Idea of 'Virtue.'" *This Constitution,* no. 5 (Winter 1984), pp. 19–25.

Park, James. *The European Origins of the Economic Ideas of Alexander Hamilton.* New York: Arno Press, 1977.

Parliamentary History of England from the Earliest Period to the Year 1803. 36 vols. Ed. William Cobbett. London: T. C. Hansard, 1806–1820.

Parrington, Vernon. *Main Currents in American Thought.* New York: Harcourt, Brace, 1954.

Pelikan, Jaroslav. *A History of the Development of Doctrine: Reformation of Church and Dogma (1300–1700).* Chicago: University of Chicago Press, 1984.

Pennock, J. Roland. "The Problem of Responsibility." In *Responsibility, Nomos IV.* Ed. Carl Friedrich. New York: New York University Press, 1960.

Pitkin, Hannah. *The Concept of Representation.* Berkeley: University of California Press, 1967.

Plato. *The Republic of Plato.* Trans. with Intro. by Allan Bloom. New York: Basic Books, 1968.

—— *The Dialogues of Plato.* 3rd ed. Trans. Benjamin Jowett. 5 vols. Oxford, 1892.

Pocock, J. G. A. *The Machiavellian Moment: Florentine Political Thought and the Atlantic Republican Tradition.* Princeton: Princeton University Press, 1975.

—— "Machiavelli, Harrington, and English Political Ideologies in the Eighteenth Century." *William and Mary Quarterly,* vol. 22, no. 4 (October 1965), pp. 549–583.

Pole, J. R. *Political Representation in England and the Origins of the American Republic.* New York: Macmillan, 1966.

Porritt, Edward, and Annie Porritt. *The Unreformed House of Commons: Parliamentary Representation before 1832.* Cambridge: Cambridge University Press, 1903.

Rakove, Jack N. *The Beginnings of National Politics: An Interpretative History of the Continental Congress.* New York: Knopf, 1979.

Rawls, John. *A Theory of Justice.* Cambridge, MA: Harvard University Press, 1971.

Register of Debates in Congress. 14 vols. Washington: Gales and Seaton, 1825–1837.

Riley, Patrick. *The General Will before Rousseau.* Princeton: Princeton University Press, 1986.

—— *Historical Developments of the Theory of Federalism from the Sixteenth to the Nineteenth Century.* Ph.D. Dissertation, Harvard University, 1968.

—— "The Origins of Federal Theory in International Relations Ideas." *Polity,* vol. 6, no. 1 (Fall 1973), pp. 87–121.

Robbins, Caroline. *The Eighteenth-Century Commonwealthmen.* Cambridge, MA: Harvard University Press, 1959.

Roosevelt, Franklin D. *The Public Papers and Addresses of Franklin D. Roosevelt.* Ed. Samuel I. Rosenman. 13 vols. New York: Random House, 1938–1950.

Rossiter, Clinton. *Seedtime of the Republic.* New York: Harcourt, Brace, 1956.

Rousseau, Jean-Jacques. *The Government of Poland.* Trans. Willmoore Kendall. New York: Bobbs-Merrill, 1972.

Russell-Smith, Hugh Francis. *Harrington and His Oceana: A Study of a Seventeenth Century Utopia and Its Influence in America.* Cambridge: Cambridge University Press, 1914.

Rutherford, Thomas. *Institutes of Natural Law.* 2 vols. Cambridge, 1754–1756.

Sacks, David. "The Corporate Town and the English State: Bristol's 'Little Businesses,' 1625–1641." *Past and Present,* no. 110, February 1986.

Samuelson, Paul. *Economics.* 11th ed. New York: McGraw-Hill, 1980.

Sanders, Jennings B. "Thomas Burke in the Continental Congress." *North Carolina Historical Review,* vol. 9 (1932), pp. 22–37.

Schaff, Philip. *The Creeds of Christendom, with a History and Critical Notes.* New York: Harper & Brothers, 1877.

Scharf, John Thomas. *History of Delaware, 1608–1888.* Philadelphia, 1888.

Schlesinger, Arthur M., Jr. *The Disuniting of America: Reflections on a Multicultural Society.* New York: Whittle Books, 1991.

Schlesinger, Arthur M., Sr. *The Colonial Merchants and the American Revolution, 1773–1776.* New York: Frederick Ungar Publishing Co., 1957.

Schumpeter, Joseph. *Capitalism, Socialism, and Democracy.* New York: Harpers, 1947.

Shaw, William. *A History of the English Church, 1640–1660.* New York: Longmans Green, 1900.

Sidney, Algernon. *The Works of Algernon Sidney.* Ed. J Robertson. London, 1772.

Sigmund, Paul E. *Nicholas of Cusa and Medieval Political Thought.* Cambridge, MA: Harvard University Press, 1963.

Skinner, Quentin. *The Foundations of Modern Political Thought.* 2 vols. Cambridge: Cambridge University Press, 1978.

Smith, Adam. *The Wealth of Nations.* Ed. Edwin Cannan. New York: The Modern Library, 1937.

Smith, Charles Page. *James Wilson: Founding Father.* Chapel Hill: University of North Carolina Press, 1956.

Smith, Joseph H. *Cases and Materials on the Development of Legal Institutions.* St. Paul, MN: West Publishing, 1965.

Spurlin, Paul. *Montesquieu in America, 1760–1801.* Baton Rouge: Louisiana State University Press, 1940.

——— "Montesquieu and the American Constitution." In *The French Enlightenment in America.* Athens, GA: The University of Georgia Press, 1984.

Storing, Herbert J. *The Complete Anti-Federalist.* 7 vols. Chicago: University of Chicago Press, 1981.

——— *What the Anti-Federalists Were For: The Political Thought of the Opponents of the Constitution.* Chicago: University of Chicago Press, 1981.

Story, Joseph. *Commentaries on the Constitution of the United States.* Boston, 1833.

... *this Constitution: A Bicentennial Chronicle.* Washington, D.C.: Project '87, 1983–1988. Nos. 1–18.

Thompson, E. P. *The Making of the English Working Class.* New York: Vintage Books, 1963, 1966.

Thorne, R. G., ed. *The History of Parliament.* 5 vols. London: Secker and Warburg, 1986.

Tilly, Charles, ed. *The Formation of National States in Western Europe.* Princeton: Princeton University Press, 1975.

Tillyard, E. M. W. *The Elizabethan World Picture.* New York: Macmillan, 1944.

Tocqueville, Alexis de. *Democracy in America.* Ed. J. P. Mayer. Trans. George Lawrence. New York: Anchor Books, 1969.

Trenchard, John, and Thomas Gordon. *Cato's Letters.* New York: Da Capo Press, 1971.

Turpin, Colin. *British Government and the Constitution.* London: Weidenfeld and Nicolson, 1985.

Van Doren, Carl. *Benjamin Franklin.* New York: The Viking Press, 1938, 1956.

Veall, Donald. *The Popular Movement for Law Reform, 1640–1660.* Oxford: Oxford University Press, 1970.

Veitch, George S. *The Genesis of Parliamentary Reform.* Hamden, CT: Archon Books, 1913, 1965.

Wade, H. W. "The Basis of Legal Sovereignty." *Cambridge Law Journal,* vol. 172 (1955), pp. 172–197.

Walker, David B. *Toward a Functioning Federalism.* Cambridge, MA: Winthrop Publishers, 1981.

Walker, Eric A. *The British Empire: Its Structure and Spirit, 1497–1953.* Cambridge, MA: Harvard University Press, 1956.

Weber, Max. *The Theory of Social and Economic Organization.* Trans. A. M. Henderson and Talcott Parsons. Intro. Talcott Parsons. New York: Oxford University Press, 1947.

——— *The Protestant Ethic and the Spirit of Capitalism.* Trans. by Talcott Parsons. New York: Scribner's, 1958.

Webster, Daniel. *The Papers of Daniel Webster.* Ed. Charles M. Wiltse et al. 13 vols. Hanover, NH: University Press of New England, 1975–1988.

——— *The Great Speeches and Orations of Daniel Webster.* Ed. Edwin P. Whipple. Boston: Little, Brown, & Co., 1879.

Whately, Thomas. *The Regulations Lately Made Concerning the Colonies, and the Taxes Imposed upon Them, Considered.* London, 1765.

Whitehead, Alfred North. *Aims of Education.* New York: Free Press, 1967.

Whitman, Walt. *Walt Whitman: Prose Works 1892.* Ed. Floyd Stovall. 2 vols. New York: New York University Press, 1964.

Williams, Neville. *The Eighteenth Century Constitution, 1688–1715.* Cambridge: Cambridge University Press, 1965.

Wills, Garry. *Explaining America: The Federalist.* Garden City, NY: Doubleday & Company, 1981.

Wilson, James. *The Works of James Wilson.* Ed. Robert G. McCloskey. 2 vols. Cambridge, MA: Harvard University Press, 1967.

——— *Selected Political Essays of James Wilson.* Ed. Randolph G. Adams. New York: Knopf, 1930.

Wilson, James Q. "The James Madison Lecture: Interests and Deliberation in the

American Republic." *PS, Political Science and Politics,* vol. 23 (December 1990), pp. 558–562.

Wolfe, Don M. *Leveller Manifestoes of the Puritan Revolution.* New York: Humanities Press, 1967.

Wood, Gordon S. *The Creation of the American Republic, 1776–1787.* New York: W. W. Norton & Company, 1972.

—— *Representation in the American Revolution.* Charlottesville: University Press of Virginia, 1969.

Wooddeson, Richard. *Elements of Jurisprudence.* London, 1783.

Woodhouse, A. S. P. *Puritanism and Liberty.* London: Dent & Sons, 1938.

Wright, Arnold, and Philip Smith. *Parliament: Past and Present.* London: Hutchinson, 1902.

Wright, Benjamin Fletcher. *American Interpretations of Natural Law.* Cambridge, MA: Harvard University Press, 1931.

Wright, Esmond. *Franklin of Philadelphia.* Cambridge, MA: Harvard University Press, 1986.

Index

Abrams case, 66–67, 70

Absolutism, 61–62, 83, 225

Accountability of elected officials, 167, 173–174, 288–289

Adams, John, 64, 116, 120, 286, 305; attack on canon and feudal law, 27–28; on legislature, 116, 117, 285, 371; on common good, 142; imperial federalism and, 176, 186, 191, 211; on creation of state governments, 201, 204, 265; attack on Stamp Act, 274

Adams, John Quincy, 9

Adams, Sam, 176

Administration, direct vs. indirect, 253–254

Advice to a Young Tradesman (Franklin), 159

Agreement of the People, The, 94, 104, 310–311

Agriculture, 7, 272

Albany conference, 153

Albany Plan, 156–158, 162, 175, 234

Alien Act, 275

Althusius, 180

Amendments to the U.S. Constitution, 110–111, 333, 334; Fourteenth, 291

American colonies, 133, 134, 135, 213; voting rights in, 174, 328; "interior police," 180, 183; British naval protection of, 183; power of legislation, 191; mode and unit of government, 195, 204; transition to statehood, 200–206, 327; joined by Articles of Confederation, 202–203; charter, 211–212; military power, 213; intergovernmental relations,

216, 234. *See also* Articles of Confederation; War of independence

American Commonwealth (Bryce), 306

American Revolution. *See* War of independence

Amphictyonic confederation, 240

Analogy, use of, 50–52

Anti-Federalists, 130, 216, 219, 292; oppose ratification of Constitution, 216, 233, 236, 237–243, 254, 322, 323, 325, 329, 332–333, 335–336, 386; support Montesquieu's confederate republic model, 221, 225, 232–233; legitimacy of authority and, 250; states' rights and, 320, 324, 384

Areopagitica (Milton), 66, 68–69, 77, 78, 80, 274

Aristocracy, 59, 113, 140, 233, 285, 380–381; natural, 111, 112, 146; and democracy in Hume's model, 267. *See also* Elitism and elites

Aristotle, 31, 34–35, 36, 40, 113, 160, 225; unilinear gradation principle, 35, 64; on the law, 41, 48; on authority, 50, 60, 61, 107; dilemma of scale and, 88–89

Arminianism, 79, 161

Articles of Confederation, 137, 193, 194, 196, 312; ratification and adoption, 197, 200, 308, 326, 329; federalism in, 214; scale of government and, 215, 235; weaknesses and failure of, 244–249, 294, 342, 380, 381, 382; authority of federal and state governments, 246–247, 250–254; enforcement of, 314

Augustine, Saint, 31, 56

Authoritarianism, 22

Authority (general discussion), 1, 64, 75, 133, 379; national theory of, 9; hierarchic tradition and, 32, 39, 62–63; intellectual vs. operative, 37–38; of rulers, 38, 40–41, 49, 53–56, 61; secular, 41, 42, 347, 348; of popes, 50–53, 57, 60; elitism and, 77–78, 345; vertical distribution and separation of powers, 85, 96, 120, 136–137, 178; American vs. British theory of, 135; legitimacy of, 343; limited government and, 349–350. *See also* Centralization of power; Decentralization of power; Government; Law; Separation of powers; Sovereignty

Authority in the United States, 135, 216; under Articles of Confederation, 246–247, 250–254; federal vs. state, 246–249, 250–255; legitimacy of, 249–255, 277, 341; failure of, 256. *See also* Constitution of the United States

Bacon, Francis, 65, 374

Bagehot, Walter, 67

Balance of power. *See* Decentralization of power; Executive branch/power; Judicial branch/power; Legislative branch/power; Separation of powers

Banking and currency, 5, 6, 14

Bentham, Jeremy, 67

Bicameralism, 114, 116, 121, 268, 285, 296, 300, 371, 373, 383

Big republic theory, 279–280, 281, 282, 317, 363. *See also* Compound republic; Scale in government

Bill of Rights, 97, 193, 291, 302, 339

Blackstone, William, 92, 135, 145, 146, 189; sovereignty and, 146–153, 170, 204, 223, 323, 337, 338; on taxation, 163; on authority of government, 256

Bodin, Jean, 180

Bonifacius (Mather), 161

Book Named the Governor, The (Elyot), 57

Borough system, 233

Boston, 12, 204; Tea Party, 186, 203; massacre, 206

Brandeis, Louis, 306

Britain, 22; conflict with colonies, 27–29, 134–135, 152, 158, 163; colonial and imperialistic policies, 135, 136, 153, 203;

taxation in, 175; commerce, 180; coercion tactics, 186. *See also* Stamp Act

Brutus (Anti-Federalist writer), 315

Bryce, James, 306

Burgh, James, 208

Burke, Edmund, 112, 113, 135, 146, 185, 358; Old Whig politics and, 139–141, 142, 281; on hierarchy, 143; on representation, 144–145, 164, 173; on sovereignty, 148, 149, 150, 151, 204; prerevolutionary agitation and, 203; on creation of American nation-state, 204–205, 206, 329; on authority of government, 256; on political parties, 259

Burke, Thomas, 194, 235

Calhoun, John C., 224, 316, 321

Calvin, John/Calvinism, 59, 65, 77–79, 161

Capitalism, 355

Capitalism, Socialism and Democracy (Schumpeter), 133

Carlisle Commission, 175

Catholic Church, 56, 59, 128; popes and papacy, 50–53, 57, 60, 62, 71

Cato's Letters, 167, 238, 274

Censorship, 68, 70, 72–73, 79, 141, 225. *See also* Press, freedom of

Centralization of power, 91, 183; common good and, 11, 24; national theory and, 21; of representation, 122, 124; Constitutional, 253, 342; democracy and, 361

Chain of being/great chain of being, 57–59, 74

Charles I, 63, 68

Chatham, William Pitt, 185

Checks and balances. *See* Constitution of the United States: limiting power of; Government: limited; Separation of powers

Christian doctrine, 31, 39–40, 42, 128

Church of England, 28

Church of Scotland, 79

Civil rights, 18–19, 273, 275. *See also* Individual, rights of

Civil War, 377

Class conflict, 90

Clay, Henry, 162

"Closed rule" voting, 110

Coercion, 41–42, 46, 68–69, 391; as power

of government, 148, 149, 251, 271, 295–296; British acts of, 186
Colonies. See American colonies
Commentaries (Blackstone), 92, 147, 223
Commentaries on the Constitution of the United States (Story), 326
Commerce and trade, 273; as basis for Stamp Act, 180–181, 183; regulation of, 183, 184, 191; protection of, through coercion, 186; liberty vs. union issue and, 191; creation of states and, 203; interstate, 352, 353; in confederate republic model, 225; states' rights and, 245, 246; expansion of, 353. See also Commonwealth: for increase
Common good doctrine, 10–11, 24, 28, 113, 389; vs. individual rights, 37, 51, 160, 230, 262; separation of powers and, 38–39, 40–41, 46, 50–51; authority and, 53–54, 81, 345; Tudor debates over, 63, 141, 164; public debate/free choice and, 69, 73; public vs. private interest and, 98–99, 113, 181–182; representation and, 173, 280; vs. factions, 262, 269, 277, 345. See also Community
Commonplace Book (Jefferson), 235
Common Sense (Paine), 162, 206–207, 208, 210, 211, 216
Common sense philosophy, 361
Commonwealth, 65, 66, 387; republicanism, 22, 328; failure of, 84; for increase, 87, 91, 106, 116, 120, 128–131, 155, 158, 231, 243, 350, 355; for preservation, 87, 224, 231, 243; nationalism, 128; representation, 167; national federalism and, 212, 216; ratification issue and, 322; reputation of, 352
Commonwealth of Nations, 187
Community, 131, 179–180, 181–182, 242–243, 292, 386; small state theory of, 89; compact federalism and, 348–349; justice and, 374. See also Common good doctrine
Compact federalism, 2, 4–6, 120; sectionalism and, 8, 14–15; separation of powers and, 20–21; Constitutional debate and, 23, 216, 316; representation issue and, 171, 177, 178, 250;

sovereignty issue and, 186, 253; Declaration of Independence and, 193; radical, 194; creation of United States by Articles of Confederation, 202, 292; vs. national federalism, 216, 224–225, 232–233, 236–237; Anti-Federalist case for, 219, 237–243; dilemma of scale and, 220, 239; criticism and weaknesses of, 244–249, 292, 316; free rider problem of, 293; ratification process and, 313, 316; community and, 348–349
Compact theory, 14, 349, 379
Compound republic (Madison), 381, 389; critique of compact federalism, 244–249, 308; legitimacy of authority in, 249–255, 349; critique of small republic theory, 255–261, 308; justice and the public interest in, 261–264, 280; government by discussion, 264–270, 275; diversity in, 270–275, 317; power and justice in, 275–278; auxiliary precautions in, 279–280, 282, 283, 288, 295, 383, 385; representation of the elite, 280–283; separation of powers in, 283–289; justification for the existence of states, 289–295; control of factions in, 301–307
Condorcet, Marie Jean, 67
Confederacy. See Articles of Confederation
Confederate model, 122, 126, 129–130, 224, 308–309. See also Compact federalism
Confederate republic (Montesquieu), 122, 129–130, 216, 219, 231–237; structure, 220–224; right of secession in, 223–224; mechanics and political process, 224–231, 296; in America, 231–237; compact solution and, 233, 242, 245; small republic theory and, 233–235, 236, 245; Anti-Federalists and, 237–243; decentralization and, 387
Confederation, 292, 327. See also Articles of Confederation
Congress of the United States, 202, 246–247. See also Continental Congress; House of Representatives; Senate; Stamp Act: Congress
Connecticut, 202, 234, 335; Compromise, 238–239
Conscience, liberty of, 44, 66, 75, 79, 82, 141, 274; dissent and, 84; protection of,

Conscience (*cont.*)
97; religion and, 128, 271; natural rights
theory and, 271–272, 348
Consent of the governed, 53–56, 57, 59,
60, 64, 195, 254, 343, 344; in
monarchies, 61–62; common good and,
81
*Considerations on the Nature and Extent
of the Legislative Authority of the British
Parliament* (Wilson), 188
Constant, Benjamin, 67
Constitution (general discussion), 2, 4, 9,
23–24, 67, 94, 98, 152
Constitution of Britain, 285; vs.
Constitution of the United States, 92–93,
94
Constitution of the United States, 98, 133,
137, 380, 384; "necessary and proper"
clause, 5–6, 24, 240, 292; vs.
Constitution of Britain, 92–93, 94;
framed without public discussion, 95;
limiting power of, 96–97; national
federalism in, 178, 214, 317–325;
Anti-Federalist opposition to, 216, 233,
236, 237–243, 254, 322, 323, 325, 329,
332–333, 335–336, 386; authority in,
216–217, 246–248, 249, 323, 341, 342,
343, 381; purpose in, 217; Federalist
case for, 219, 232, 236, 304, 313, 329,
332, 352, 380; states' rights
interpretation of, 219, 313, 316, 317,
330; supremacy clause, 240, 320;
national sovereignty in, 253–254,
323–324, 341; auxiliary precautions in,
279–280, 282, 283, 288, 295, 383, 385,
389; adoption by states, 327–328; Article
VII, 330–336; Article I, 333–334, 335,
351; Article V, 334; Preamble, 350;
allocation of power, 350–351, 352. *See
also* Ratification
Constitutional Convention, 216, 217, 289,
312, 382; veto issue, 301–302; drafting
process, 310, 312; purpose of, 312;
delegate system, 333–334. *See also*
Ratification; Virginia, Plan
Constitutional convention model: origins
of, 309–313; Madison's view of
ratification and, 313–317, 318, 319, 320,
330, 335; nationalist theory in, 317–325
Constitutionalism, 161; separation of

powers and, 46, 47, 96–97, 98, 149,
229; American vs. British theory of, 92;
public interest and, 92–101; restrictive,
114–115, 287; democracy and, 130, 339;
American, 211, 340, 348; negative, 263,
270; incentive, 287; medieval and
modern, 343–349; defined, 350;
self-government and, 383–386. *See also*
Government by discussion
Continental Association, 199
Continental Congress, 326
Continental Congress, First, 137, 168, 190,
195, 209; colonial legislation and, 191;
compact federalism and, 193–194;
delegate system, 196–199; boycott
against Britain, 199–200; governing
authority, 199–200; creation of states,
200–206
Continental Congress, Second, 197, 199
Contract obligation/law, 262, 291, 314
Contract theory, 320, 321–322
Convention. *See* Constitutional
Convention; Constitutional convention
model; Ratification
Copernicus, 65
Corporatism, 22, 32, 226
Cosmos, 31–32, 35, 39, 52; hierarchal
tradition and, 31–32, 35, 39, 52; world
order and, 57–59, 74; divine, 179,
346–347
Crisis, The (Paine), 212–213
Cromwell, Oliver, 84, 94, 210
Cunliffe, Marcus, 134
Cusanus (Nicholas of Cusa), 56–57, 107
Custom duties, 15, 24. *See also* Taxation

Davis, Jefferson, 14–15, 24
Deane, Silas, 193
De Anima (Aristotle), 34
Decentralization of power, 23, 94, 311; in
national republic and federalism, 85,
120, 127–128; constitutional, 96, 126;
popular government and, 120–121; in
democracies, 121, 127; economic theory
and, 181–182, 293, 352–353
Declaration of Independence, 133,
192–193, 196, 235, 324–325; compact
federalism in, 193; right to create new
governments and, 205–206, 236
Declaratory Act, 183

Defense, 246, 264, 351. *See also* Military power and administration
Delaware, 335
Democracy, 149, 171, 380–382; republicanism and, 29, 31, 32, 53–54, 86; common good and, 53–54; British, 85; small state theory of, 88, 89, 90, 368; defined, 133–134; nationalism and, 133–134, 368; American, 134, 340; Hume's theory of, 267–270; direct, 280, 344; centralization and, 361
Democratic party, 18
Dickinson, John, 184–185, 188, 191, 361
Dionysius, 43, 55
Discourses, The (Machiavelli), 86–87, 89
Discourses Concerning Government (Sidney), 165
Dissent, 78, 84, 198
Dissertation on the Canon and Feudal Law, A (Adams), 27
Diversity, 383; in Madison's theory, 5, 260, 270–275, 277, 317, 356, 381, 385; nationalism and, 391. *See also* Pluralism
Division of labor, 36–38, 259, 369
Division of power. *See* Separation of powers
Dominion status, 186, 187
Dulaney, Daniel, 174–175, 179, 191

East India Company, 140
Economy and economic theory, 351–352, 379, 387; free, 7, 351, 355, 356; centralization of power and, 11; industrialization and, 15–18; Franklin on, 159, 160–161; decentralization of power and, 181–182, 293, 352–353; fiscal federalism, 181, 183; security and, 354; market, 385. *See also* Commerce and trade
Education, 82–83, 125, 126–127, 128–129; federal aid to, 14; in confederate republic model, 222, 230
Edwards, Jonathan, 161
Eikon Basilike (The Royal Image) (Charles I), 63
Eikonoklastes (The Image Breaker) (Milton), 63–64
Elections. *See* Voting and elections
Electoral college, 120
Electoral process, dual, 304
Elitism and elites, 6; rule and authority of,

77–81, 345, 380; political, 102, 104; senatorial, 112–114, 115, 267; intellectual, 116; republicanism and, 118, 345; voters and, 118; in American colonies, 142; defined, 142; British, 164; representation and, 280–283
Elizabeth, Queen, 63, 68, 108
Ellsworth, Oliver, 332
Elyot, Thomas, 57
Enlightened despotism, 155, 225
Episcopacy, 62
Essentialism, 33–34, 35, 51
Euclid, 33
Executive branch/power, 284–285, 286–287, 288, 289, 360; in confederate republic model, 228–229; in state government, 265; efficiency of, 286. *See also* Separation of powers
Expansionism, 129, 354–355; commonwealth for increase, 87, 91, 106, 116, 120, 128–131, 155, 158, 231, 243, 350, 355; Franklin and, 156–158, 162, 213, 354–355; Paine and, 213; Federalist support of, 342, 354
Expression, freedom of. *See* Speech, freedom of
Extended republic, 91, 108, 116, 130, 240, 242; government by discussion in, 96, 276; political virtue and, 222; scale in government and, 222, 229, 266; expansionism and, 231; political process in, 231, 268; national sovereignty in, 251, 256–257; individual rights vs. majority in, 262–264; pluralism of, 277, 329; representation and factions in, 279–281, 368; rational deliberation in, 290, 366; ratification issue and, 321, 335; constitutionalism and, 351; majority coalitions in, 372; nationality in, 385. *See also* Harrington, James; Madison, James

Factions, 258–259, 353; vs. common good and public interest, 262, 269, 277; defined, 275; extended republic and, 280–281, 368; control of, 301–307; within states, 301; market economy and, 385. *See also* Political parties; Public interest
Federalism, 2, 4–6, 85, 124, 161;

Federalism (*cont.*)
  sectionalism and, 8–15; industrialism
  and, 15–18; political theory and, 20–25,
  179, 343; juristic, 23–25; Christian
  doctrine and, 45–50; commonwealth for
  increase and, 120; war of independence
  and, 136; constitutional, 175, 183, 343,
  383; imperial, 176, 185–190; defined,
  177–178; fiscal, 181, 183, 293;
  horizontal, 251–252, 253; separation of
  powers and, 268, 279, 290, 387;
  argument for existence of states and,
  292; public affections theory and,
  372–377; liberty and, 386–388. *See also*
  Centralization of power; Compact
  federalism; National federalism; National
  republic; Representation: federal option;
  Republicanism
Federalist, The, 237, 244, 254, 282, 285,
  291, 342, 350, 352, 355; *Federalist 1,*
  103; *Federalist 10,* 5, 118, 231–232,
  241, 262, 263, 272, 273, 297, 300, 356,
  390; *Federalist 11,* 352–353; *Federalist
  14,* 353; *Federalist 15,* 246, 248;
  Federalist 20, 253; *Federalist 22,*
  314–315, 323; *Federalist 27,* 303, 359;
  Federalist 28, 295; *Federalist 30,* 303,
  304; *Federalist 31,* 303, 304; *Federalist
  33,* 320; *Federalist 37,* 250; *Federalist
  39,* 315, 316–317, 318, 320, 322, 328,
  331; *Federalist 45,* 252; *Federalist 46,*
  250, 264, 299, 302–303, 304, 305, 314,
  316–317, 318, 320, 358, 359, 388, 390;
  Federalist 48, 284; *Federalist 51,* 264,
  270, 279, 282, 295, 300, 356, 373, 390;
  Federalist 56, 306; *Federalist 70,* 286
Federalist party, 18
Federalists, 216, 306, 382, 383, 391;
  support of Constitution in ratification
  debates, 219, 232, 236, 304, 313, 329,
  332, 352, 380; and confederate republic,
  232; failure of the Confederation and,
  246, 248; Virginia Plan and, 290; on
  centralization of power, 342, 380;
  expansionist policy, 342, 354, 355, 369;
  on property rights, 355–356
Feudalism, 142, 226, 233
Fifth Monarchy, 78
Finance, 180, 182, 246–247
Fox, Charles James, 144

France, 168, 309, 357
Franklin, Benjamin, 67, 136, 167, 214,
  274, 293, 391–392; national purpose
  issue and, 153–162; expansionist policy,
  156–158, 162, 213, 354–355; on virtue,
  158–160, 161, 355, 356, 370; economic
  theory, 159, 160–161; on representation,
  175; Stamp Act and, 180–181, 234; on
  taxation, 184; on trade regulation, 184;
  whig politics, 208. *See also* Albany Plan
Free choice, 68–74, 75, 79
Freedom. *See* Conscience, liberty of;
  Individual, rights of; Liberty; *specified
  Constitutional freedoms*
French Revolution, 309
Friedrich, Carl, 97, 98

Galileo, 65
George III, 192, 206, 209, 235
Georgia, 335
Gerry, Eldridge, 325
Glorious Revolution, 193
Gothic Constitution, 103, 115
Gothic government, 226, 227
Government (general discussion):
  institutions of, 77, 84, 85, 87, 101, 102,
  103, 106–107, 108, 195, 204, 296–297,
  349, 371, 384; incentive system of, 100,
  383; bicameral, 114, 116, 121, 268, 285,
  296, 300, 371, 373, 383; units,
  133–134, 195, 204; limited, 170, 171,
  263, 270, 283, 287, 349–350; origin of,
  170, 171; consolidated, 233–234;
  unicameral, 274; mixed, 285, 372;
  functions of, 286–287; purpose of, 347,
  349–357. *See also* Centralization of
  power; Decentralization of power;
  Intergovernmental relations;
  Representation; Scale in government
Government, ecclesiastical, 39–40, 42,
  43–44, 347, 348; federalism and, 45–50;
  authority of, 50–53, 55, 60; consent of
  ruled and, 54
Government, federal (central), 1–2; veto
  power of, 269; bias of people toward,
  303; restraint of, by states, 304–306,
  387–388. *See also* Executive
  branch/power; Judicial branch/power;
  Legislative branch/power; Separation of
  powers

Government, local: federal aid to, 24, 252; authority of, 94, 252, 293, 387; in Oceana, 95–96, 120, 122; representation and, 179

Government, popular, 22, 85, 86, 216, 277; dilemma of scale and, 86–92, 121; separation of powers and, 96, 97, 98, 390–391; decentralization of power and, 120–121, 178–179; federalism and, 220; threat to, 259; representation in, 279–280

Government, state, 1–2; federal aid to, 24, 252; separation of powers and, 96, 265; localism and, 215–216; authority to form, 236; authority of, 245–249, 251; authority to tax, 246, 252, 303, 304; conflict with federal government, 295; legislation by, 301–302, 315; bias of people toward, 303; national will and, 304–305

Government by discussion, 145, 385; Milton's theory of, 66, 74–77; Harrington's theory of, 85, 96, 100, 114; in extended republic, 96, 276; Old Whig politics and, 141, 167; Franklin's theory of, 154; political activism and, 198; Hume's theory of, 267–270; Madison's theory of, 275; republicanism of, 345. See also Constitutionalism; Rational deliberation

Great Chain of Being, The (Lovejoy), 31

Great Society, 19, 24

Grenville, Charles, 185

Hamilton, Alexander, 4, 23, 103; support of nationalism, 5–6, 7–8, 9, 11, 24, 353, 361, 379; elitism of, 6; fiscal and economic policy, 6–7, 24, 246–247, 352, 353; growth policy, 162, 214, 263; on authority, 246–247, 248, 255, 295, 314–315; on separation of powers, 286, 295–296; on administration of federal government, 303; on taxation, 303–304, 352; on control of federal government by the states, 304, 306; on security, 353–354; on state government, 359. See also Federalist, The

Harrington, James, 67, 83, 214, 274, 387, 389; national republic theory, 22, 84, 85–86, 88, 98, 130–131, 161, 178–179, 229–230, 243, 345, 383; on institutions

of government, 87, 101, 102, 103, 106–107, 108, 225; constitutional government and, 92, 93, 94, 98, 101, 108; on sovereignty, 93–94, 95, 97–98, 109; on public debate, 95, 230, 286; on common good, 98, 99–101, 230; interest and virtue, 98–101, 108, 109, 110; economic theory, 103, 155; rational deliberation concept, 108–119, 121; on elites, 112–114, 118; federalism and, 119–128, 178, 216, 229, 233, 245; on education, 125, 127, 128–129, 230; benevolent imperialism and, 129, 155, 157, 158; on political parties, 259; on state government, 265–266; Hume on, 266–270; separation of powers and, 286, 287; on ratification, 311–312. See also Oceana

Hastings, Warren, 140

Hegel, Georg, 113

Helvétius, 67, 226

Henry, Patrick, 242, 254

Henry VII, 103

Henry VIII, 108

Hierarchy, 63–64, 139, 226; vs. republicanism, 29, 31, 32, 53–54, 210; cosmic, 31–32, 35, 39, 52; authority and, 32, 39, 62–63, 151; inequality in, 32–35; intellectual vs. operative, 37–38; in ecclesiastical government, 43; world order and, 57–58; consent of the governed in, 60; common good and, 164–165; monarchy and, 210; rule of law and, 228

Hobbes, Thomas, 51, 83, 93

Holmes, Oliver Wendell, 66–67, 70, 76, 275, 306

Homogeneity, 7, 91, 237, 238–239, 257, 259–261, 263; tyranny of the majority and, 277; of small assemblies, 311. See also Diversity

Hooker, Richard, 58–60, 100–101

Hopkins, Stephen, 180, 183, 191

House of Representatives, 110, 113–114, 116, 302, 306, 333

Howard, Martin, Jr., 172, 173

Howell, David, 236

Humanism, 57

Hume, David, 101, 113, 154–155, 293, 361, 383; dilemma of scale and, 121; on

Hume, David (*cont.*)
  political parties and factions, 259, 275;
  revision of Harrington's national republic
  model, 266–270, 311; on government by
  discussion, 267–270; on rational
  deliberation, 268, 276
Hutchinson, Thomas, 336

Idea of the Perfect Commonwealth
  (Hume), 266
Imperial Conference of 1926, 187
Imperialism. *See* Commonwealth: for
  increase; Expansionism
Individual, rights of, 342, 350; vs. common
  good, 37, 51, 160, 230, 262; protection
  of, 97; justice and, 350–351
Industrialism, 7, 8, 15–18
Inequality, 32–35, 36; natural, 40, 41; of
  ruler and ruled, 38; political, 64, 115,
  116; economic, 115, 116; of leagues,
  119; of virtue, 365
Inglis, Charles, 207–208, 235
Instrument of the Government, The
  (Cromwell), 94
Interest. *See* Harrington, James: interest
  and virtue; Madison, James: on interests
  and interest groups; Public interest
Intergovernmental relations: Madison's
  theory of, 237, 241, 300, 305; of states,
  237, 241, 295–297; military conflict,
  295–297; separation of powers and, 305
International relations theory, 223, 224
Iredell, James, 186
Ireton, Henry, 104
Iron Act, 154
Isolation strategy, 264, 270; separation of
  powers and, 228–229, 239, 390

James I, 60–63, 107, 141, 149
James II, 193
Jay, John, 286
Jealousy of Commerce (Hume), 154–155
Jefferson, Thomas, 7, 191, 202, 286;
  compact federalism and, 5–6, 186, 244;
  on free speech, 67, 274; imperial
  federalism and, 211, 235; on democracy,
  361
Johnson, Lyndon, 3, 18–20, 24–25
Johnson, Samuel, 239
Judicial branch/power, 123, 284–285,

286–287, 288; in confederate republic
  model, 228–229; in state government,
  265; judicial review, 291–292, 302, 305,
  313, 337; separation of powers and, 291.
  See also Law; Separation of powers
Justice, 376, 385; distributive, 109;
  individual rights and, 350–351, 356;
  community and, 374
Judicial process, 206

Kelly, George Armstrong, 161
Kennedy, John F., 18–19
Kentucky Resolutions, 192
King, Martin Luther, 19
King, Rufus, 325, 331–332, 333, 355
Knox, John, 62, 65, 79

Laissez faire doctrine, 154, 225
Land distribution and ownership, 101–102,
  103. *See also* Property
Law: federalism as, 23–25, 49, 92, 179;
  human, 41–42, 46, 71, 147, 165;
  natural, 41, 46, 71, 147, 148, 150, 337,
  346, 347, 348, 351, 366; divine, 46, 47,
  49, 55, 147, 337, 346, 347, 348;
  universal, 52, 54; moral, 68, 337; of
  political number, 88–89, 90, 91, 120,
  121, 129, 220, 221, 233, 265;
  constitutional, 93–94, 163, 287, 372;
  -making power, 93, 124, 147–148, 152,
  227, 231, 246, 285, 287, 346; orders
  and, 93–94, 96; statutory, 93–94, 287;
  rational deliberation and, 108–109;
  reformation, 124; veto power and, 127;
  parliamentary, 148, 150; fundamental,
  152, 177, 308, 309, 310, 346, 350; rule
  of, 228, 288, 343, 345–346, 386;
  enforcement, 246, 252; states' rights and,
  247–248; international, 253; contract,
  262, 291, 314; governing office-holders,
  284; judicial review of, 291–292, 302,
  305, 313, 337; regulatory, 306; of
  agency, 314; eternal, 346, 347
Laws, The (Plato), 88
Laws of the Ecclesiastical Polity (Hooker),
  58
Lee, Robert E., 360
Legislative branch/power, 284–285,
  286–287, 288, 289; in confederate
  republic model, 228–229; initiative to

propose bills, 267. *See also* Separation of powers

Legitimacy of power, 249–255, 277, 333, 341, 343

Letters from a Pennsylvania Farmer (Dickinson), 184–185

Levellers, 80, 94, 102, 130, 387

Leviathan (Hobbes), 93

Liberty, 178–179, 295, 347, 353, 359; vs. union in American colonies, 190–194, 195; vs. absolutism, 225; preservation of, through separation of powers, 228–229, 287, 350–351; republican, 341–342; federalism and, 386–388. *See also* Conscience, liberty of; Individual, rights of

Lincoln, Abraham, 8, 13–14, 15, 162, 200, 202, 322

Localism, 294, 358–360, 373

Locke, John, 67, 95, 274, 331; on sovereignty, 150, 151; on common good, 171; on authority of the people, 170, 204, 250, 256; on property rights, 273; on origin of government, 320

Lovejoy, Arthur, 31, 34, 35

Loyalists, 198, 199

Luther, Martin, 65, 159

Machiavelli, Niccolò, 65, 86–91, 106, 127, 207, 389; law of political number, 88–89, 120, 121, 129, 220, 221, 233, 265; extended republic and, 116, 256

Madison, James, 23, 379, 382; on diversity, 5, 260, 270–275, 277, 356, 381, 385, 390; on rights of the individual, 67, 262, 271, 274–275, 348; republicanism and extended republic theory, 91, 118, 216, 231–232, 237, 244, 245, 251, 256, 257, 263, 266, 268, 277–278, 282, 300, 348, 365–366, 371, 381, 383, 390; on interests and interest groups, 113, 257–264, 273, 287, 293–294, 307, 385; on dilemma of scale, 121, 216, 221; on military administration, 122, 297–299; on states' rights, 124, 247, 248, 289–295, 302–303, 305, 325, 358–359, 373, 375, 387–388; on representation, 179, 279–280, 281, 344, 384–385; on taxation, 186; on intergovernmental relations, 237, 241, 300, 305; on

separation of powers, 237, 279, 283–289, 292, 390; critique of compact federalism, 244–245, 247–249, 256, 259, 277, 292; reform of Articles of Confederation/constitutionalism, 244–245, 253, 256, 312–313, 343; on works of utility, 245, 262, 264, 352, 353; on legitimacy of authority and sovereignty, 249–250, 252, 277, 343, 346, 354, 372, 383; critique of small republic theory, 256–257, 263, 276–277; on majority rule and factions, 257–258, 259, 263, 264, 265, 276, 277, 372; on Hume, 266, 269–270; on liberty, 271–272, 273–274, 275, 353; on property rights, 272–273, 356; on rational deliberation, 276; on common good, 277, 342, 344; on federalism, 279, 289; on elites, 282; on judicial power, 302; on ratification, 313–317, 318, 319, 320, 330, 335; on security, 353–354. *See also* Compound republic

Maine, 203

Majority rule, 257–258, 263, 300, 331, 386; tyranny of, 15, 258, 259, 277, 290, 301, 304, 31; single-interest, 259; multi-interest or civic, 264, 265, 276, 282; rational deliberation and, 276; in ratification debates, 333–334; in extended republic, 372–373; state, 388

Mansfield, Harvey, Jr., 89, 90, 185

Markets: free, 3, 272; foreign, 7

Martin, Luther, 237, 239–240, 241, 242, 320; Anti-Federalist opinions, 325, 332

Maryland, 335

Mason, George, 333, 334

Massachusetts, 12, 167, 168, 203, 241, 335; representation issue in, 169, 176–177; Stamp Act crisis and, 175; delegates to Continental Congress, 197; granted authorization for self-government, 200–201; statehood, 201; prerevolutionary agitation, 205; in New England Confederation, 234; local law enforcement in, 252; separation of powers based on Oceana model, 265; ratification process, 309–310, 333. *See also* Boston

Masseres, Francis, 176

Mather, Cotton, 161

Mayhew, Jonathan, 28

McCloskey, Robert G., 360–361

McKean, Thomas, 339

Memorial and Remonstrance (Madison), 271

Military power and administration, 122, 296, 306; of small states, 220; for law enforcement, 246–247; of Confederacy, 251; intergovermental conflict and, 295–296, 298; paradigm, 297–299, 304, 305. *See also* Security

Military service, 122–123, 129

Mill, John Stuart, 67

Milton, John, 44, 63–64, 125, 387, 389; on free choice and debate, 68, 69, 70, 71, 74–77, 79, 80; on censorship, 72–73, 79; on religion, 73, 271; elitism and, 80–81; on private interests, 113; decentralization plan, 125–126, 178–179; education plan, 125, 126–127, 128–129; on separation of powers, 127; compact federalism and, 245. *See also* National republic (Milton)

Monarchy, 45–47, 48, 59, 84, 381; authority of ruler, 61, 62; as divine sanction, 61, 63, 140; American republicanism and, 209–210, 227; political balance in, 226–227, 229. *See also* Federalism: imperial

Monism, 33, 35

Monroe doctrine, 354

Montaigne, Michel, 65

Montesquieu, Charles, 4–5, 23, 84–85, 119, 216, 386, 389, 390; law of political number, 90, 91; criticism of republican government and extended republic, 207–208, 256, 263; dilemma of scale and, 220–221, 233–235, 236, 264–265; on virtue, 221–222, 230–231, 238; on education, 222; on monarchy, 226–228, 229; on separation of powers, 226, 228–229, 230–231, 232, 237, 285, 295–296. *See also* Confederate republic

Morris, Christopher, 57

Morris, Gouverneur, 238, 333, 334

Mosaic regime, 48, 49, 77, 348, 349

National federalism, 1–8, 20–25, 92, 93, 96, 120, 122, 129; sectionalism and,

8–15, 18; industrialism and, 15–18; racism and, 18–20; republicanism and, 64–65; purpose and, 81–83, 349; vs. compact federalism, 178; Commonwealth models of, 212, 216; separation of powers in, 268, 307

National federalism, American, 134, 177, 214; early conflict of theories, 134–135, 136–137; Old Whig politics and, 140–146; sovereignty and, 152, 170–171, 323; colonial union, 155, 156, 157–158, 328; expansionism and, 156–157; economy and, 159, 160–161; vertical distribution of authority, 178; concept of liberty in, 179; Paine and prerevolutionary agitation, 206–214; vs. compact federalism, 216, 224–225, 232–233; concept of reason in, 358. *See also* Representation: federal option; Republicanism, American

Nationalism, 296, 357, 371, 379–380, 382, 383, 389–390; democracy and, 133–134; independence and, 236; existence of states and, 289–290; ratification issue and, 313–314, 317–325; sovereignty and, 337–338, 339; protection of liberty and, 387–388; diversity and, 391. *See also* National republic *entries*

Nationality, bonds of, 20, 21, 381, 382

National republic, 349, 380

National republic (Harrington). *See* Oceana

National republic (Milton), 66–68, 71, 72, 76, 126, 130; elites and, 77–81; purpose and, 81–83; institutions, 84

National theory. *See* Authority in the United States; Purpose

National will, 290, 304, 366–367, 373–374, 381, 388

Natural rights theory, 271

Neo-Platonists, 31

New England Confederation, 193, 196, 234

New federalism, 2–4, 19–20, 24

New Hampshire, 201, 335

New Jersey, 335; Plan, 239

New York, 197, 332, 335

Nicholas of Cusa. *See* Cusanus

Nominalism, 34

Nova Scotia, 203–204

Nullification, 13, 249, 313, 316, 317, 318

Observations Concerning the Increase of Mankind (Franklin), 153

Oceana (Harrington), 84, 85–86, 116, 118, 126, 208, 266

Oceana (national republic of Harrington), 92; constitution, 22, 92, 93, 94, 97, 98, 101, 119, 231, 281, 311–312, 334; federal government, 22; government by discussion in, 84, 85, 108–119, 121; laws (orders), 93–95; council of legislators, 95, 111–112; local government, 95–96, 120, 122; public interest in, 98–101; representation and elections, 101–108, 118, 120, 121–122, 123, 281, 311, 334; rational deliberation in, 108–109; property qualification, 111; federalism in, 119–128, 231; law-making process, 121, 231; military service, 122, 129; judicial administration, 123, 252; education, 125, 127; as commonwealth for increase, 128–131, 155, 158; sovereignty and, 231; separation of powers in, 265; Hume on, 266–270, 311

Office, public. *See* Representation; Voting and elections

Old Tory politics, 140, 141, 142, 143, 176, 188

Old Whig politics, 145, 199, 281; American national federalism and, 135, 136; constitutional, 135, 137, 140–146; vs. Old Tory politics, 140, 141, 142, 143, 176, 188; government by discussion and, 141, 167; parliamentary sovereignty and, 147; representation issue and, 166–167, 173–174; creation of colonial nation-state and, 204

Olson, Mancur, 182

One man, one vote philosophy, 361

Order: social, 42, 52, 62, 83, 115, 147–150, 152, 204, 347, 348; world, 57–59, 74; political, 83; law and, 89. *See also* Hierarchy

Otis, James, Jr., 168–171, 172–173, 174, 176

Overton, Richard, 94

Paine, Thomas, 162, 206–214, 216, 235

Parker, Henry, 210

Parliament, 60, 63, 92–93, 179; sovereign power of, 93–94, 137, 145, 147, 148, 149–150, 152, 156, 165; law-making procedure, 110–111, 113; reform proposals, 174–175, 208; imperial federalism and, 186–190; self-limiting aspect of, 337, 339–340. *See also* Representation: parliamentary option

Patriotism, 357, 364, 369, 371

Pennsylvania, 197, 241, 335, 361, 362, 365, 376

Philadelphia Convention. *See* Constitutional Convention

Physiocrats, 225, 226

Pinckney, Charles Coatesworth, 332, 355

Plato, 31, 33, 34, 40, 79, 84, 88, 89

Pluralism, 5, 35, 381, 391; ethnic, 18; hierarchy of virtue and, 40; social, 83, 263; class conflict and, 90; authority and, 150, 349; dilemma of scale and, 220; vs. self-government, 256; in constitutional structure, 261; economic, 263; balanced, 271; of extended republic, 277, 329. *See also* Diversity

Political Discourses (Hume), 266

Political institutions. *See* Government (general discussion): institutions of

Political parties, 198, 258–259, 266, 274–275

Political process: in confederate republic model, 230–231; in extended republic, 231, 268; balancing model of, 271; discussion model of, 271, 391

Political rights and freedoms, 262, 274, 287, 292

Political science, 225, 226, 265, 284, 390; separation of powers and, 286, 288

Political theory, 242; federalism and, 20–25, 179, 343; authoritarianism, 22; corporatism, 22, 32, 226; hierarchic tradition in, 29, 31; colonial, 170–171, 209, 232–233

Poor Richard's Almanac, 159, 355

Popes and papacy, 50–53, 57, 60, 62, 71

Power. *See* Authority; Separation of powers

Predestination, 78–79

Presbyterianism, 28

Press, freedom of, 141, 167, 274, 275, 348

Price, Richard, 208

Priesthood (priests and bishops), 42–44, 69

Priestly, Joseph, 208
Property, 131, 367; rights, 28, 97, 262,
    355; as qualification for voting, 116,
    167, 170, 228, 310; representation and,
    116, 167, 170, 228, 257–258, 267, 310;
    Madison on, 272–273, 356; as
    qualification for office-holding, 355
Prosperity, 350, 351, 352, 353, 359
Protestantism, 159, 272
Pseudo-Dionysius, 31
Public affections theory, 363–364
Public choice theory, 109–110, 287. See
    also Rational choice theory
Public debate: free speech and, 67–68,
    74–75; individualism and, 76;
    republicanism and, 77, 80–81, 82; elites
    and, 80; formation of government and,
    92–101. See also Rational deliberation
Public finance theory, 181–182
Public good. See Common good doctrine
Public interest, 98–101, 108, 109–110,
    112, 124, 276; vs. private interest,
    98–100, 109–110, 113, 229, 230, 356;
    senatorial elite and, 114; vs. individual
    interest, 118–119; justice and, 261–264;
    political factions and, 262, 269; in big
    republics, 277; government
    determination of, 280; separation of
    powers and, 287. See also Common
    good doctrine; Madison, James: on
    interests and interest groups
Public opinion, 289
Public policy, 3, 4, 356–357, 373, 379
Puritan(s), 78, 207; Party, 63;
    Commonwealth, 79–80; religion, 128,
    131
Purpose: in national federalism, 81–83,
    349; American theory of, 153–162, 217,
    245; of governments, 347, 349–357

Racism, 8, 18–20, 379
Radicalism, 167, 174, 198, 209, 233,
    389–392
Ramsay, David, 117
Randolph, Edmund, 245, 334
Ratification, 291: debates, 232, 236,
    237–243, 253, 329–330; Constitutional
    Convention model of, 309–317, 382;
    drafting and, 310, 312; Madison on,

313–317, 318, 319, 320, 330, 335;
    states' rights view of, 313, 316, 317,
    324, 330; national solution to, 317–325;
    process of, 330–336; unanimous, 335
Rational choice theory, 124, 224, 248, 332,
    364. See also Public choice theory
Rational deliberation, 108–119, 130, 269,
    276, 381, 386; representation and,
    283–284; separation of powers and, 286,
    290, 390, 391; in extended republic,
    290, 366
Rationalism, 357–360
Readie and Easie Way to Establish a Free
    Commonwealth, The (Milton), 126
Reagan, Ronald, 2–4, 24–25, 379
Reason, 71, 72, 74, 100, 357–360, 374,
    385
Reform, 308, 312
Reform act of 1832, 143
Reformation, 73, 78, 207, 272
Reid, Thomas, 361, 367
Religion, 39–44; colonial, 28, 207;
    discipline of wrongdoers, 44; freedom of,
    66, 68, 102, 271–272, 273–274, 275,
    348; elites and, 78–79; freedom of
    conscience and, 128, 271; national, 128.
    See also Christian doctrine; Government,
    ecclesiastical; Law: divine; Rulers: divine
Representation, 142–143, 279; corporate,
    104, 384–385; actual, 106, 107, 136,
    164–168, 170, 174, 175, 176, 178, 208,
    267, 282; vitual, 107, 108, 136,
    144–145, 164–168, 172, 173, 174, 175,
    199, 282, 337, 339, 344; by suffrage,
    108, 227; property qualification for, 116,
    167, 170, 228, 257–258, 267, 310;
    American vs. British theory of, 135–136,
    163–164, 168–169, 173; taxation and,
    136, 154, 156, 163, 169; parliamentary
    option, 163–164, 167, 168–177, 185,
    195–196, 216, 234; federal option, 164,
    167, 175, 177–185, 191, 195–196, 216,
    234, 293, 386; instruction and
    supervision of representatives by voters,
    167, 168, 171, 173–174, 227, 282,
    288–289, 344; by population, 167, 170,
    241–242, 281; common good and, 173,
    280, 344; defined, 173; proportionate,
    241, 242, 290, 384; in popular

government, 279–280; elites and, 280–283; direct, 290; arithmetical, 311; constitutionalism and, 343

Republic, The (Plato), 34, 88

Republicanism (general discussion), 22–23, 67, 75, 161, 283, 328–329, 348, 357, 381; vs. hierarchic tradition, 29, 31, 32; conscience and, 44; common good and, 53–54, 64; barriers to opposition to, 56–64; national concept in, 64–65; elites and, 77–81; institutionalized opposition and, 104. *See also* Big republic theory; Compound republic; Extended republic; National federalism, American; National republic; Small state theory

Republicanism, American, 164, 265, 350; Paine and, 206–214; representation and, 209; popular sovereignty and, 227; public vs. private interests in, 229–230. *See also* Compound republic

Republicanism, British, 208, 268, 350

Republican party, 18

Restoration, 234

Revenue, 181, 246–247. *See also* Taxation

Revere, Paul, 168

Rhode Island, 197, 202, 236, 251, 335

Rights of the British Colonies Asserted and Proved, The (Otis), 169

Rome, republic of, 86–87, 89, 90, 95, 98, 106, 115, 116, 127

Roosevelt, Franklin, 16, 17, 291

Rota (Harrington), 208

Rule of wise and holy. *See* Thomas of Aquinas: on authority

Rulers: authority of, 38, 40–41, 43, 49, 56, 61, 64; ecclesiastical, 39–40, 42, 43–44, 48–49, 54–56; medieval, 42, 44, 51; deviation of, from law, 46–47, 62; defined, 47; divine, 48–49, 62, 345–346; common good and, 53–54, 81; consent of the ruled and, 53–56, 57, 59, 60, 139. *See also* Authority; Government

Rush, Benjamin, 209, 362

Salvation, 42–43, 79

Scale in government, 86–92, 106, 121, 219–220, 266; compact federalism and, 220; extended republic and, 222, 229; ratification debates and, 238–239. *See also* Big republic theory; Small state theory

Schlesinger, Arthur, Jr., 20

Schumpeter, Joseph, 133, 134, 135, 136, 341

Scots Confession, 79

Secession, 13–15, 24, 223–224, 249, 313, 314, 316–318; Lincoln and, 322

Second Helvetic Confession, 78

Second Treatise (Locke), 273

Sectionalism, 8–15, 18, 379

Security, 350, 351, 352, 353, 359; in separation of powers, 389, 390. *See also* Defense; Military power and administration

Sedition Act, 275

Self-love concept, 257, 259–261, 267, 367, 368, 383

Senate: elite, 112–114, 115, 267; election of, 116–117; representation in, 241, 242; in Hume's democracy, 265, 267, 268–269; state representation in, 290, 305

Separation of powers, 20–21, 23, 24–25, 38–39, 40–41, 119, 307, 386–387; constitutional, 46, 47, 96–97, 98, 149, 229, 383; liberty as criterion for, 126, 127; colonial, 136, 178, 212, 232; territorial, 137, 268; British, 170, 285; in confederate republic model, 226, 228–229, 230–231, 232; isolation strategy of, 228–229, 239, 390; federalism and, 268, 279, 290; in compound republic model, 283–301; in national theory, 300–301; bicameral competition, 371–372; security in, 389, 390

Septennial Act, 166, 176

Shakespeare, William, 57–58

Sherman, Roger, 238–239, 332

Sidney, Algernon, 130, 165, 166, 167, 174, 272, 282

Sigmund, Paul, 57, 107

Slavery, 241

Small state theory, 88–89, 129, 131, 335, 368, 386; of community, 89; in Machiavelli, 220, 221, 233; in confederate republic model, 220–221, 233–235, 236, 368–369; isolation theory

Small state theory (*cont.*)
and, 228–229, 239; criticism of, 255–261, 263, 266, 276–277; factions in, 368

Smith, Adam, 176, 181, 293, 387

Social contract theory, 320

Social order, 42, 52, 62, 83, 115, 147–150, 152; government and, 204, 347; change in, 348

Social union theory (Wilson), 360, 385; participation and public affection, 360–365; social passion, 364, 365–372, 373; public affection and federalism, 372–377

Sons of Liberty, 197

South Carolina, 201, 316, 335

Sovereignty, 95, 97–98, 101, 194, 336–340; parliamentary, 43–44, 137, 145, 147, 148, 149–150, 152, 156, 165, 169, 337; American vs. British theory of, 135–136, 146–153; popular, 137, 146, 151–152, 170–171, 178, 185, 189, 210, 216, 227, 254, 312, 340, 366; international relations theory and, 223; governmental, 245, 256, 314, 338; national, 248, 250, 251, 253–255, 256–257, 277, 323; constituent, 312, 314–315, 316, 318, 319, 320–321, 323, 324, 338, 339, 358; unitary nationalist theory of, 325–330

Speech, freedom of, 66–67, 274, 385; public debate and, 67–68, 74–75; republicanism and, 77; Madison on, 262, 271, 274–275, 348; political, 274–275

Spirit of the Laws, The (Montesquieu), 216, 225, 232, 235, 238, 266

Stamp Act, 27, 28, 164, 167–169, 172, 175, 183; Congress, 163, 176–177, 197; British commerce as basis for, 180–181; federal vs. parliamentary option debate and, 180; protests, 203, 234

States: federal aid to 24, 252–253; authority/ sovereignty of, 124, 245–249, 250–251, 253, 255, 256–257, 327; intergovernmental relations of, 237, 241, 295–297; collection of federal taxes by, 252, 253; justification for the existence of, 289–295, 305, 386; boundaries of, 294; usurpation by, 295, 296–297; factions within, 301; restraint of federal government by, 304–306, 387–388; in confederate model, 308; interstate commerce, 352, 353; localism and, 358–359; in social union theory, 373–376; equal representation in Senate, 384; federalism and, 388. *See also* American colonies; Government, state; Ratification, states' rights view of

Story, Joseph, 325–330

Stuart monarchy, 63, 68, 102, 120, 142, 233

Suffolk Resolves, 161–162, 168

Summa contra Gentiles (Aquinas), 37

Summa Theologica (Aquinas), 39, 45–46

Supreme Court, 291, 302, 316

Symbolism, 55, 71

Tariff, 14, 15, 24. *See also* Taxation

Tax: stamp, 163, 164, 167–168, 169, 175, 203; sugar, 163

Taxation, 123, 184; /representation issue in American colonies, 136, 154, 156, 163, 175, 179, 185; in Britain, 175; colonial authority for, 175; "benefit," 181, 183, 184; for regulation vs. revenue, 184, 185–186; by states, 246, 252, 303, 304; federal, collected by states, 252, 253, 316; federal power of, 303–304, 306, 352. *See also* Stamp Act

Thomas of Aquinas/Thomistic system, 22, 78, 113, 179; hierarchic principle of, 31, 33, 35, 48–49, 56, 344; essentialism and, 33–34, 36; monism and, 33; division of labor and, 36–38; common good in, 38–39, 46, 50, 91, 148, 277, 344, 349; on virtue and grace in hierarchy, 39–44, 53, 61, 344; on order, 42, 52, 148; on government, law, and constitutionalism, 45–50, 54, 59, 71, 74, 343, 346, 347–348, 349; monarchy and, 45–46, 48, 59, 81, 149; on authority (rule of the wise and holy), 50–53, 60, 62, 343–344, 345–346, 349; consent of the ruled in, 53–56, 344; on symbolism, 55, 344; on free choice, 69, 71; scholastic inquiry and, 70–71

Thoughts on Government (Adams), 265

Thoughts on the Present Discontents (Burke), 143

Tocqueville, Alexis de, 252

Tory party, American, 19, 207, 328, 329
Tory politics, 176, 177, 207. *See also* Old
    Tory politics
Townsend duties, 177, 181, 183, 184
Trade. *See* Commerce and trade
Transportation, 10–11, 14
Treaty alliances, 223, 240
Treaty of Paris, 245
Truth, 71–72, 73; free choice/debate and,
    68–74, 75, 76
Tudor monarchy, 59, 62, 63, 141, 164
Tyranny, 97, 108, 229; of majority rule,
    15, 258, 259, 277, 290, 301, 304, 381;
    big state theory of, 88, 90, 91;
    ministerial, 190; within small states, 245,
    258, 259, 270

Unequal leagues concept, 119
Unilinear gradation principle, 35, 64
Union and unity, 381; liberty in American
    colonies and, 190–194, 195, 210, 213;
    Lincoln on, 200, 202; perpetual, 249; in
    small state theory, 255, 256; Madison
    on, 277. *See also* Social union theory
Unitary nationalist theory, 325–330
Usury, 273
Utility, 32, 179, 180, 182, 191, 196, 234,
    293, 376, 386–388; works of, 245, 262,
    264, 352, 353, 365; public affections
    theory and, 363–364

Value, 32, 36, 39
Veto, power of, 127, 251, 268, 284;
    federal, 269; executive, 284, 288–289;
    congressional, 291, 292, 301–302, 305;
    state, 331, 332, 335
Virginia, 241, 271, 275, 335; Resolutions,
    192, 318; Plan, 239, 245, 290–292, 333,
    334, 360
Virtue: Franklin on, 158–160, 161, 355,
    356; in confederate republic model,
    221–222, 230; political, 222, 230–231,
    238, 356; individual, 355, 356, 357;
    inequality of, 365–366; patriotism as, 369
Virtue and grace in hierarchies, 39–44, 53,
    59, 89, 139, 143; gratuitous vs.
    sacramental, 54–55; authority and, 60,
    61, 64–65, 107; constitutionalism and,
    96, 370; public interest and, 100;

suffrage and, 106–107; representation
    and, 108
Voltaire, François, 67, 226, 271
Voting and elections; senate, 116–117;
    electoral college, 120; qualifications of
    voters, 144, 145, 228, 267, 310;
    competence of voters, 166, 267, 363;
    qualifications of candidates, 210–211;
    apportionment of voters to legislators,
    269; dual electoral process, 304; restraint
    of government by, 304; direct, 361; voter
    turnout, 364–365. *See also* Ratification;
    Representation
Voting rights, 66, 80, 97, 167, 238,
    282–283, 299; in Harrington's national
    republic, 102, 103–104, 105; colonial,
    174, 328; of legislators, in confederate
    republic theory, 227; scale of choice and,
    362, 363

Walpole, Robert, 166, 167, 199, 233
War, 66–67, 245, 246
War of independence, 22, 133, 205, 245;
    representation issue and, 134, 136,
    167–168; sovereignty issue and, 151;
    national purpose issue and, 153;
    prerevolutionary agitation, 167–168,
    183, 192, 195, 203, 234
Washington, George, 134, 255
Wealth of Nations, The (Smith), 181
Weber, Max, 122, 159, 160
Webster, Daniel, 162, 204, 205, 319, 387
Welfare programs, 3
Westminster Assembly, 79
Whately, Thomas, 172, 174
Whig politics, 18, 102, 143; representation
    issue and, 106, 117, 173–174, 176;
    radical, 167, 174, 233; Opposition, 233,
    234. *See also* Old Whig politics
Whig politics, American, 328–329, 368,
    381; sovereignty issue and, 152–153,
    185, 205, 337; representation issue and,
    162, 163, 167, 172, 176, 179, 249–250,
    364; separation of powers and, 167;
    agitation at First Continental Congress,
    198; conservative, 198; radical, 198,
    209; Stamp Act Congress and, 199;
    prerevolutionary agitation, 203; support
    of confederate republic model, 232;

Whig politics (*cont.*)
  support of imperial federalism, 235;
  individual rights and, 355
Whitehead, Alfred North, 153
Wilkes, John, 208
William III, 193
Wilson, James, 23, 67, 186, 188–190, 191,
  192, 286, 326; imperial federalism and,
  211; Declaration of Independence and,
  236; defense of Constitution, 323, 328;
  on sovereignty, 323–325, 329, 360; on
  ratification, 330; biography, 361; public

affections theory, 363–365, 367,
  370–371, 373, 374, 377; on virtue,
  369–370; moral abstraction theory,
  370–371; bicameral model, 371–372,
  373, 376. *See also* Social union theory
Witherspoon, John, 239
World order, 57–59, 74

Yates, Robert, 315
Yonge, William, 166
Yorkshire Association, 197–198